Leadership Coaching
for Results

Marc

you are an inspiration!

Good luck with your

Book —

Sunny

xx

Leadership Coaching for Results

Cutting-edge practices for coach and client

by

Sunny Stout-Rostron

with contributing author

Nick Wilkins

PUBLISHING

2014

First published in 2014

ISBN: 978-1-86922-470-7

Published by Knowres Publishing (Pty) Ltd
P O Box 3954
Randburg
2125
Republic of South Africa

Tel: (011) 706-6009
Fax: (011) 706 1127
E-mail: orders@knowres.co.za
Website: www.kr.co.za

Printed and bound: Shumani Printers (Pty) Ltd, Parow Industria, Cape Town
Typesetting, layout and design: Cia Joubert, cia@knowres.co.za
Cover design: Nadia du Plessis, Design Figment, nadia@designfigment.co.za
Editing and proofreading: Nick Wilkins
Project management: Cia Joubert, cia@knowres.co.za
Index created with: TExtract, www.Texyz.com

ENDORSEMENTS

"Very occasionally a book comes along that makes it truly worthwhile – despite all the frenzy of deadlines, rush, ever-on communications – to stop, turn aside from all that, sit quietly, and read. If you are a business executive or leadership coach, or you work with top coaches, this is such a book. With it, leadership coaching has arrived. ... In this game-changer of a book, Sunny gives leadership coaching a mighty kick into the twenty-first century. It starts with a broad-ranging and authoritative one-stop survey of the academic literature on leadership; that alone would make it indispensable. But it then sweeps on to a global description of leadership coaching right now which in its depth, comprehensiveness and practicality is entirely new. And concludes by offering several challenging scenarios of what the next ten years may hold. This may well be the coaching book of the year for 2014 – and for many years to come."

– Anne Scoular, Managing Director, Meyler Campbell;
author of *The Financial Times Guide to Business Coaching*

"Once again Sunny has lifted us up and set us right at the developing edge of the coaching profession. She has done it accessibly and with a lilt so that we can absorb and use what she knows. And given that she knows more than I can imagine ever knowing about anything, this is a stunning achievement. I hope everyone in every coaching capacity will read this – because I want coaching to change the world."

– Nancy Kline, Time To Think, Inc.; author of *Time to Think* and *More Time to Think*

"Here is an amazing opportunity to learn from a master coach, brilliant teacher and leader in the field of leadership coaching. Read what matters when it comes to achieving success in results-driven coaching. What defines leadership in moving forward isn't what we considered leadership in the past. Increasingly diverse, decentralised teams and constant economic turmoil demand a different style of coaching. This book will give you a myriad of perspectives, insights and pearls of wisdom to use and strengthen your practice and your leadership. A skilful and world-renowned coach, Sunny Stout-Rostron has captured what you need to pay attention to with regards to cutting-edge practices of coaching. This is a must read!"

– Donna Karlin, international leadership coach, speaker and author of *Leaders:
Their stories, their words: Conversations with Human-Based Leaders*™

"Sunny has provided an amazing resource for coaches, which highlights the best of contemporary thinking and leading-edge work in our field side-by-side with the historical context. Impressively, she conveys all this information in a writing style that is clear and engaging. Packed with useful insights, this book is an indispensable addition to a coach's toolkit."

– David B. Peterson PhD, Director: Executive Coaching and Leadership, Google, Inc.

"During the past decade Sunny Stout-Rostron has moved to the forefront of thinkers, practitioners, teachers and contributors in the field of coaching. This book is set to become a primary source of reference for coaching, but more particularly for shaping how we think about leadership development in general. Sunny has managed to merge the practice of coaching with the core quest of improving the efficacy of leadership development. It is a must-read for leaders, coaches, academics and anyone involved in unleashing the great capacity of the leader within."

– Christo Nel, Nyenrode Business Universiteit, Netherlands; Programme Director of International and Executive MBA programmes and Visiting Lecturer Extraordinaire, University of Stellenbosch School of Business; programme head of the Leadership Development Programme, Riga Business University, Latvia; author of *The Leadership (R)evolution and The Age of Participation*.

"Hundreds of books have been published about leadership coaching, but few as comprehensive, readable, and immediately applicable to coaches, their clients and students in the field. This book ensures understanding and practicality by defining each key element of leadership coaching, and describing with examples how it can be applied for maximum impact. The author draws on diverse perspectives, models, and resources to bring a full picture of how to think about leadership coaching; how to utilise it as a coach, leader, and organisation; and what we need to further explore and build for a truly evidence-based, useful, and socially responsible discipline in the decade ahead."

– Lew Stern PhD, President: Stern Consulting; Senior Advisor, Institute of Coaching McLean/ Harvard Medical School; Co-Founder and Leader of The Executive Coaching Forum; author of *Executive Coaching: Building and managing your professional practice.*

"Sunny Stout-Rostron always impresses with her well-referenced, highly readable and inspirational books. An incisive review of leadership theory contextualises a global perspective of the complexities that leaders face now and in the future. Motivating leaders to excel in this environment is achieved through guidance on applying an extensive range of coaching models and frameworks from diverse disciplines. In an unregulated industry the future of coaching will depend on professional services and practices, making this an essential resource for all those involved in leadership development and business coaching."

– Lise Lewis, President, European Mentoring and Coaching Council (EMCC)

"Dr Sunny Stout-Rostron has given the coaching community a generous gift. In one volume, here is a clear and essential road map for any business coach who seeks to improve his or her professional effectiveness, as well as for clients keen to improve how they might select and engage productively with a suitable coach. One of the significant challenges for business coaches, particularly in the early years of practice, is to understand and utilise the strengths of the often bewildering and seemingly contradictory myriad of models and frameworks in leadership development, business coaching, and psychology. And if summaries of significant models across all of these fields was not a feat in itself, the book adds chapters on key professional issues as well as emergent trends in coaching for new leadership. I highly recommend this book. It truly is a sanity-saving, generous resource and reference from a generous and sanity-saving colleague."

– Nic Eddy, Organisational Psychologist, private practice, Melbourne; National Convener of the Australian Psychological Society's Interest Group on Coaching Psychology (IGCP).

"Sunny Stout-Rostron brings her wealth of experience as a practitioner and researcher to this highly valuable book. It is immensely practical and will more than repay the time invested in reading and re-reading it. I thoroughly recommend it."

– Professor David A. Lane, Professional Development Foundation, UK

"Sunny Stout-Rostron is a powerful voice in the world of coaching. She brings to the table a unique blend of expert knowledge, business acumen, and clear communication. This book presents theories and practical tools that will be vital to anyone in coaching or HR who wants to be more effective in developing leaders."

– Dr Robert Biswas-Diener, Managing Director, Positive Acorn LLC; author of *The Courage Quotient*

"This book is a must-read for all leaders and coaches who want to take their coaching to the next level, but are not sure how. While Sunny Stout-Rostron's thought-provoking book provides a framework for leaders and coaches to understand the complexities, it is above all a practical book. Sunny is the ultimate coach, clarifying the goals, anticipating the barriers and future challenges, identifying the skills and encouraging new behaviours."

– Jo Larbie MSc, Human Resource Management, HRD Director and Management Consultant, Executive Coach; Director, Redstone Consultants.

"Breadth and depth, context and content, Sunny Stout-Rostron and contributing author Nick Wilkins paint an extraordinarily rich panorama of the field of business coaching and within it, leadership coaching. This volume brings theory and application together to inform coach and client alike about the transformational journey that coaching can be. It offers the reader accessible perspectives, workable models, and provocations for reflection and exploration. A valuable resource on any coach's bookshelf. Well done!"

– John B. Lazar MA, MCC, executive coach; Executive Editor, *The International Journal of Coaching in Organisations*® (IJCO)

"Comprehensive, well researched, with a wide range of topics and perspectives. A modern compendium of coaching for our field!"

– Mary Wayne Bush EdD, Colorado Technical University; co-author, *Coaching for Change*

"Sunny Stout-Rostron has filled a critical gap in this clear and thorough overview of leadership and business coaching. Her realistic assessment of a range of coaching modalities in adding value to business performance is essential reading for students, coaches, human resource practitioners and business leaders at every level. Dynamic snapshots of coaching models with practical advice offer business leaders insight into making the right choice when it comes to choosing a coach."

– Dorrian Aiken DProf Executive Coaching

"This book is highly relevant for those who like to see where all the pieces fit. History, current context and future direction of business and leadership coaching are overarching themes. Embedded within, Sunny addresses the vast array of contemporary topics that require consideration if one is to consistently reach for excellence in coaching, inviting coaches and purchasing clients to dip into the chapters that are relevant for them. Woven throughout are case studies and selected practical instructions to demonstrate and entice. This is both theoretical and applied – Sunny achieves an enormous amount!"

– Vicki Crabb, Coaching Psychologist; Victorian Coordinator and National Treasurer, Coaching Psychology Interest Group, Australian Psychological Society

"The book is a veritable treasure chest of wisdom, enabling readers to master their craft. It will prove most valuable to coaches, managers and nurturers of talent who want to help their clients develop enabling platforms within complex environments. The book covers the full spectrum of the theory and casework necessary to tip leadership coaching practices already at the cutting edge, for greater authenticity, attentiveness and impact."

– Dr Salome van Coller-Peter, Head of MPhil in Management Coaching, University of Stellenbosch School of Business

"Sunny Stout-Rostron is far ahead of the crowd in understanding the uniquely powerful impact coaching can have on leaders of large, family-controlled companies. She knows that coaching, when informed by a deep understanding of family systems, has the capacity to transform leaders of these powerful engines of economic growth in many nations and across many cultures. This book can raise the level of coaching for leaders and managers of these firms, and thereby generate profound public policy impacts. This is a much-needed text for anyone who works to open family shareholder control groups to management effectiveness."

– Richard L. Narva, Esq., Founder, Narva & Company LLC

DEDICATION

To Susan and Theo, with thanks for support and wisdom.

TABLE OF CONTENTS

List of tables

List of figures

FOREWORD BY MICHAEL CAVANAGH

Coaching, as a discipline, is still young. It is emerging into a world where previously accepted orthodoxies of leadership and change management are being questioned. Governments, businesses and communities are grappling with the implications of accelerating rates of discontinuous change created by a mix of technological innovation, hyper-connectivity and systemic and environmental challenges.

It is easy to think of these challenges as a Goliath menacingly set against the puny David of leadership, desperately reaching for the stone of coaching to somehow save the day. However, I think this is the wrong metaphor. It is wrong because it still seeks to hang on to the notion of the heroic leader who saves the day in the face of overwhelming odds. By extension, the role of the coach is to help the leader rise to meet this challenge.

Rather, I stand with experts such as Manfred Kets de Vries (2011) who point to the demise of the heroic leader as a salve for the complexity we are facing. I would argue that these complex challenges are not the antagonists of coaching, but its progenitors. In other words, coaching has emerged as a response that is capable of matching the complexity of the world in which we live and do business. So, rather than emerging into a hostile world, the discipline of coaching is emerging into a world that is full of possibility and promise, in equal measure with its challenge and confusion.

How, then, is coaching to capitalise on this promise and possibility? How is it to sift through the confusion and meet its challenge? This is no small task, and the stakes are high. They reach to peoples' livelihoods, the viability of organisations and industries, and ultimately, the sustainability of human wellbeing on our planet. Einstein is reputed to have said, "If I had an hour to solve a problem and my life depended on the solution, I would spend the first 55 minutes determining the proper question to ask, for once I know the proper question, I could solve the problem in less than five minutes" (Einstein, 2014:1).

In this book, Sunny Stout-Rostron asks many of the right questions. She begins by asking us to critically reflect on what we mean by leadership, as she canvasses a wide range of theories and approaches to leadership. What is the role of the leader in the modern organisation? Our answer to this question is crucial to our understanding of the role of the coach in business.

Beyond leadership, Sunny asks us to reflect on the purpose of business coaching. What ends are coaching interventions designed to achieve, and how would one measure success? What practices are being used? Which models shape one's practice, and how do these fit the range of coaching contexts in the real world of business? Rather than give unitary answers to these questions, Sunny has sought to provide a range of current coaching responses to guide the client in thinking about coaching, and to guide the coach in examining their practice in the light of a range of potential practices.

It is the diversity of perspective that I most like about this book. It is a book that reflects its subject, coaching, as a discipline still experimenting with multiple ways of being in the world. Listening and being open to a diverse range of voices is an important part of coaching's capacity to be of use to the world. The issues that face business, and the contexts that give rise to them, are new. They require the sort of novel and creative solutions that only engagement with diverse voices can generate. Sunny's book provides a very useful compendium of approaches, ideas and models, at a time when listening to diverse voices is crucially important.

Elsewhere I have argued that we need to harness the creative power of diversity in order to respond to the challenges facing business and the world (Cavanagh, 2013b). However, engaging diversity means engaging with tension. By tension I mean the apparent conflict between values, assumptions, understandings, worldviews and approaches, and the differences in the relationships, commitments and purposes that drive us. Rather than these tensions being a problem (as uncomfortable things are often thought to be), they are a rich blessing if we have the capacity to engage with them. They require us to see the issue at hand (and the world) in bigger, more expansive ways. These bigger perspectives open up new possibilities and new pathways toward the future. Nelson Mandela (discussed later in this book), among all recent leaders, seemed most fully to understand this.

I believe dialogue is the bridge that links the diversity of perspectives needed to fashion synergetic and novel responses to the challenges facing us. Listening to and understanding of another's perspective is at the heart of dialogue, and as Sunny points out, it is at the heart of the coaching enterprise.

It has become a cliché to begin books and articles with a statement of how complex and challenging the world has become, and to ponder what this means for business and organisations. Some may say that in this foreword I am guilty of reinforcing that cliché. The danger with clichés is not that they cease to point to something important, but that we cease, through repetition and familiarity, to look to where they are pointing. While the confusion and challenges are real, so too are the possibilities and promise.

For this reason, I commend Sunny's book to the reader, as one that contains a diverse range of voices and approaches. I ask that you read it thoughtfully, and bring to bear your capacity to listen and turn toward the tensions to which it points. In this way you may be able to build on the fine work begun here. For in the world facing us, our task is to use what is to build what can be, so that together we may create a surprising, delightful and sustainable future.

Michael Cavanagh
Sydney, Australia
February 2014

Michael Cavanagh PhD MClinPsych is both a Coaching Psychologist and a Clinical Psychologist, and is Deputy Director of the Coaching Psychology Unit at the University of Sydney. He was twice elected National Convenor of the Australian Psychological Society Interest Group in Coaching Psychology, and is Co-ordinating Editor of the International Coaching Psychology Review, *a journal published jointly by the Australian and British Psychological Societies. Dr Cavanagh has published widely in the academic press, and is principle author of Standards Australia's (2011) handbook on* Coaching in Organisations.

ABOUT THE AUTHOR

Sunny Stout-Rostron, DProf MA

Professional practice

Sunny coaches at senior executive and board level, and has a wide range of experience in leadership development and business strategy. She works with executive leaders and their teams to help them achieve individual, team and organisational goals. With over 25 years' international experience as an executive coach, Sunny believes there is a strong link between emotional intelligence and business results.

Sunny has played a leading role in building the emerging profession of coaching, and her passion is to develop the knowledge base for coaching through research and the critical reflective practice of dedicated practitioners. She has developed a range of international programmes for leaders and business coaches in the corporate, legal and education fields.

She is Executive Director of Sunny Stout-Rostron Associates, a Founding Fellow and Research Advisor at the Institute of Coaching at Harvard / McLean Medical School, a director of Professional Development Foundation UK (PDF), and was founding President of COMENSA (Coaches and Mentors of South Africa) during 2006–2007. She completed her Doctoral research in executive coaching with Middlesex University in London, and continues to lecture and supervise coaching research at several graduate schools of business to contribute to the development of executive coaches.

Sunny was Chair of the Working Group on a Research Agenda for Development of the Field for the Global Convention on Coaching (GCC), which provided input into the GCC's *Dublin Declaration on Coaching* in 2008. She has also taken part in several international research projects of the Worldwide Association of Business Coaches (WABC) to develop standards and competences for business coaches worldwide. During 2013, she worked with Origo Consultants and Knowledge Resources to conduct a leadership development survey of 160 companies and other organisations in South Africa.

Coaching philosophy

Sunny's philosophy is that coaching is about helping clients to "learn from and create wisdom from their own experience". Looking at "mastery of practice" rather than simply "being the expert" to promote our own and our clients' personal and professional growth, Sunny encourages coaches and clients to create the space for conversations that get to the heart of issues and concerns, and create change at an individual, team and systemic level. Her coaching looks at deepening the level of conversation to move from *performance* (what needs to be done differently), to *learning* (what learning is needed cognitively and emotionally for change to happen in terms of thinking, feeling and behaviour), and *being and becoming* (who you are, how you "do you", and who you want to become).

Publications

As an author, Sunny's books include: *Business Coaching International: Transforming individuals and organisations* (Karnac, 2009/2014), *Business Coaching Wisdom and Practice: Unlocking the secrets of business coaching* (Knowres, 2009/2012), *Accelerating Performance: Powerful new techniques to develop people* (Kogan Page, 2002), and *Managing Training* (Kogan Page, 1993). She is also a contributing author of the *UK Handbook on the Psychology of Coaching and Mentoring* (Wiley-Blackwell, 2013); *Positive Psychology as Social Change* (Springer, 2010); *Human Capital Trends: Building a sustainable organisation* (Knowres, 2011); *The Complete Handbook of Coaching* (Sage, 2014); and *Sharing the Passion: Conversations with coaches* (Advanced Human Technologies, 2006). Her earlier books are *Doing Business in France* (BBC Books, 1990); *Doing Business in Germany* (BBC Books, 1990); *Doing Business in Italy* (BBC Books, 1990); *An Insider's Guide to the European Communities* (BBC Books, 1991); and *Eastern Europe: Open for business?* (editor) (BBC Books, 1991).

CONTRIBUTING AUTHOR – NICK WILKINS

Nick is an economist and management consultant, with extensive experience in applied research, training, consulting, coaching and management. After completing a diploma in practitioner coaching, he was instrumental in helping establish Coaches and Mentors of South Africa (COMENSA), as Administrator of the founding Steering Committee and member of the Constitutional Committee during 2005–2006, and as Secretary of COMENSA's first Executive Committee during 2006–2007. Nick's active support for the professionalisation of coaching has also included editorial and administrative input into the Global Convention on Coaching (GCC) during 2008–2010, editing several doctoral dissertations and books and many other publications on coaching, and co-authoring several articles on coaching practice. He currently focuses on consulting, research and writing in a range of fields.

ACKNOWLEDGEMENTS

The beginning of wisdom for a coach and a leader is to realise that they don't have all the answers. So for this book, I am deeply indebted to all those wise colleagues and clients whom I interviewed in order to glean from their unparalleled knowledge and deep, collective experience.

Permission is also gratefully acknowledged for the republication of excerpts from the following articles.

From the CEO / President of the Worldwide Association of Business Coaches (WABC):

- Stout-Rostron, S. (2008). Coaching models for business success: Can coaching produce sustainable behaviour change? WABC *Business Coaching Worldwide eZine*, 4(1):23–25.

- Stout-Rostron, S. (2008). Coaching models for business success: How can coaching produce sustainable behaviour change? WABC *Business Coaching Worldwide eZine*, 4(2):12–14.

- Stout-Rostron, S. (2008). Coaching models for business success: How can coaching create sustainable behaviour change? WABC *Business Coaching Worldwide eZine*, 4(3):23–25.

- Stout-Rostron, S. (2009). Working with coaching models. WABC *Business Coaching Worldwide eZine*, 5(1), February.

- Stout-Rostron, S. (2009). Working with coaching models: The Nested-Levels Model. WABC *Business Coaching Worldwide eZine*, 5(2), June.

- Stout-Rostron, S. (2010). Contracting the relationship and setting boundaries. WABC *Business Coaching Worldwide eZine*, 6(3), October.

From the editor of COMENSA*news*:

- Stout-Rostron, S. (2009). Research: Developing your practice. COMENSA*news*, January.

- Stout-Rostron, S. (2009). To be or not to be a profession? COMENSA*news*, February.

- Stout-Rostron, S. (2009). The question of supervision. COMENSA*news*, March.

- Stout-Rostron, S. (2009). Contracting the relationship. COMENSA*news*, April.

- Stout-Rostron, S. (2009). The practice of ethics and the ethics of practice. COMENSA*news*, May.

- Stout-Rostron, S. (2009). Diversity, equality and power. COMENSA*news*, July.

- Stout-Rostron, S. (2009). Innovation: Working with coaching models. COMENSA*news*, August.

- Stout-Rostron, S. (2009). Contracting service for success. COMENSA*news*, September.

- Stout-Rostron, S. (2009). Team coaching is crucial for organisational transformation. COMENSA*news*, October.

- Stout-Rostron, S. (2009). The coaching conversation: An experiential road map to knowledge and personal mastery. COMENSA*news*, November.

- Stout-Rostron, S. (2009). Gifts to practitioners: Research, conferences and grants. *COMENSAnews*, December.

- Stout-Rostron, S. (2010). Achieving your desired outcomes! *COMENSAnews*, February.

- Stout-Rostron, S. (2010). The reconstruction of meaning. *COMENSAnews*, March.

- Stout-Rostron, S. (2010). Contracting boundaries. *COMENSAnews*, April.

- Stout-Rostron, S. (2010). Ethics and integrity. *COMENSAnews*, May.

- Stout-Rostron, S. (2010). Rules of the game: Living organisational values with integrity. *COMENSAnews*, June.

- Stout-Rostron, S. (2011). Key questions on coaching supervision. *COMENSAnews*, June.

- Stout-Rostron, S. (2012). The scientist practitioner model. *COMENSAnews*, February.

- Stout-Rostron, S., and Wilkins, N. (2010). Celebrate work on international standards. *COMENSAnews*, December.

- Stout-Rostron, S., and Wilkins, N. (2011). Be upfront about ethics. *COMENSAnews*, February.

- Stout-Rostron, S., and Wilkins, N. (2011). Will COMENSA be an ostrich or an eagle? *COMENSAnews*, April.

- Stout-Rostron, S., and Wilkins, N. (2011). Gender issues in business coaching. *COMENSAnews*, May.

- Wilkins, N., and Stout-Rostron, S. (2010). Business coaching – going beyond the balls. *COMENSAnews*, July.

- Wilkins, N., and Stout-Rostron, S. (2010). Balancing interests in business coaching. *COMENSAnews*, August.

- Wilkins, N., and Stout-Rostron, S. (2010). Behavioural boundaries in business coaching. *COMENSAnews*, September.

- Wilkins, N., and Stout-Rostron, S. (2010). Practise safe coaching – always use protection. *COMENSAnews*, October.

- Wilkins, N., and Stout-Rostron, S. (2010). ROI warning – your mileage may vary! *COMENSAnews*, November.

- Wilkins, N., and Stout-Rostron, S. (2011). The development of corporate management. *COMENSAnews*, March.

From Knowledge Resources, publishers of *Human Capital Review*:

- Stout-Rostron, S. (2009). So what do business coaches do? *Human Capital Review*, March.
- Stout-Rostron, S. (2011). Developing leaders through coaching. *Human Capital Review*, January.
- Stout-Rostron, S. (2011). Coaching for leadership transformation. *Human Capital Review*, September.

- Stout-Rostron, S. (2011). Emerging trends in coaching for transformational leadership. In Boninelli, I., and Meyer, T. (eds), *Human Capital Trends: Building a sustainable organisation* (pp. 304–326). Randburg: Knowres.
- Stout-Rostron, S., Cunningham, N., and Crous, W. (2013). *Leadership Development Survey Report 2013*. Randburg: Knowres.

From the editors of *Finweek*:

- Stout-Rostron, S. (2008). Integrity and values-based actions. *Finweek*, February.

From the editors of *Coaching: An International Journal of Theory, Research and Practice*:

- Stern, L.R., and Stout-Rostron, S. (2013). What progress has been made in coaching research in relation to 16 ICRF focus areas from 2008 to 2012? *Coaching: An International Journal of Theory, Research and Practice*, 6(1):72–96.

From the editors of the *International Journal of Coaching in Organisations*:

- Stout-Rostron, S. (2011). How is coaching impacting systemic and cultural change within organisations? *International Journal of Coaching in Organisations*, 8(4):5–27.

From Springer Science and Business Media BV, publishers of *Positive Psychology as Social Change*:

- Stout-Rostron, S. (2011). How does coaching positively impact organisational and societal change? In Biswas-Diener, R. (ed.), *Positive Psychology as Social Change* (pp. 237–266). Dordrecht: Springer.

Sunny Stout-Rostron, DProf MA

PREFACE

Drawing from multiple disciplines including psychology, industrial and organisational psychology, neuroscience and anthropology, coaching is developing into a discipline and profession in its own right. An evidence-based body of knowledge and codes of professional conduct are in the making.

Executive coaching is now a very important methodology and intervention to accelerate and develop leaders. Results from the recent *Leadership Development Survey* of private and public sector organisations in South Africa (Stout-Rostron, Cunningham and Crous, 2013) indicated executive coaching as the second most important approach to leadership development. The survey indicated that team coaching is also growing in importance.

In addition, organisations are realising that leaders and managers require sound coaching skills to unlock the potential of their teams and direct reports. This is confirmed in an article in a recent issue of the *Harvard Business Review* (Garvin, 2013) which showed that being a good coach is considered the most important behaviour demonstrated by the best managers in Google, Inc.

In building and developing a profession it is important that new knowledge, ongoing research and the principles of best practice be disseminated among the members of the fraternity as quickly and widely as possible. In this regard, Knowledge Resources has played a role since 2002 in publishing books, articles and offering events in the field of best-practice coaching. For example, *Business Coaching Wisdom and Practice: Unlocking the secrets of business coaching* by Sunny Stout-Rostron, the first edition of which was published in 2009, was regarded as the go-to handbook in the field. In publishing Sunny's *Leadership Coaching for Results: Cutting-edge practices for coach and client*, with contributing author Nick Wilkins, the journey continues.

With leadership and leadership development being increasingly challenged worldwide, this book goes a long way to equip the reader, and specifically the coach, with the necessary knowledge and expertise to substantially improve their leadership coaching expertise.

In the words of Christo Nel:

> In her latest book, *Leadership Coaching for Results: Cutting-edge practices for coach and client*, Sunny comes as close as possible to offering the definitive guide for coaching people in a business environment. Coaching is gaining rapid prominence and respect in the business community, and her book is an invaluable source of rigorous and liberating guidelines on the role of coaching in business in general, and for growing leadership talent in particular.

The development of professions lies in the hands of the leaders in the field who are prepared to research, plough back, and lead from the front. In this regard, Sunny Stout-Rostron unselfishly invests tremendous personal resources and expertise to develop and lead the coaching profession internationally. Knowledge Resources is proud to partner with her in publishing *Leadership Coaching for Results: Cutting-edge practices for coach and client*.

Wilhelm Crous
Managing Director, Knowledge Resources

1

Introduction

COACHING FOR NEW LEADERSHIP

Collectively, tipping points for change reveal the need to develop coaching practice at the highest level, embracing a new perspective on real change in leadership coaching for transformation. There is an emerging consciousness of global issues; there is a need to effectively manage change and complexity in organisational environments; and there is a desire of people to ensure that their work makes a positive contribution to their communities (Stout-Rostron, 2011b:304).

As people look to their leaders worldwide for more accountability, integrity and authenticity, coaching seems to be one of the ways in which corporations are charting their way forward, pioneering a new way of working. But it requires a shift in how leaders "be" leaders, and how coaches coach leaders, and how both inspire leadership in others.

Thinking about thinking, i.e. the coaching conversation, involves reflecting on and changing the reasoning behind our actions, and allowing for seeing problems and solutions in new ways – that is where *new leadership* has a role to play.

THE CONTEXT OF COACHING

The idea for this book came from reflection on the many articles I have written, and lectures and talks I have given at conferences alone or in collaboration with others, over the past few years. I thought long and hard about these articles and conference papers on the emerging discipline of business coaching. My focus is on a wide range of topics that impact both coaches and clients at every stage of the coaching intervention, from beginning to end. However, it occurred to me that the target audiences for each of these journal articles, university lectures, conference presentations and a few *ad hoc* book chapters, would have been only a small number of people at a time. Hence this book – to ensure that a wider audience is able to do some deeper thinking on "hot topics" in business and executive coaching – and in particular the need for coaches to help develop new leadership at every level within business and society.

There is a broad range of matters that coaches – and their clients – need to think about in business coaching – including the discovery process that takes place inside the coaching conversation between executive and coach; core questions about the ethics and boundaries of the coaching intervention; how-to's in terms of contracting; and the controversial topic of coach supervision. Many coaches are not yet aware of the critical need for coach supervision, including the need for coach and client to have several conversations with the client's immediate line manager. This is to ensure that coaching is not something taking place within a "silo" of coach and client, but that it also takes into consideration emergent themes within the organisation that impact on success.

Business coaching takes place within a particular *context* that must be taken into account if coaching is to be effective. Sometimes coaches fall into the trap of thinking that their "client" is always right, and that the organisation or line manager is not aware of the gifts, talents and expertise that the client brings to the table. Alternatively, if the coach is not brought into supervision with other coaches, they might literally become part of the problem, having an impact on the client in a way that may overlook the blind spots of both coach and client – what a thought! And yet it happens every day around the world inside many coaching conversations.

Coaching is at a stage of emerging maturity worldwide, and coaches within their own geographical surroundings are sometimes unaware of what influences them in terms of ethics, standards, continuing professional education, and legislation in their own corner of the world, if not worldwide. My suggestion is to read through the outline of each of the chapters in this book to pick and choose those topics most relevant to you. However, if you do have a growing coaching practice, you will find that all the chapters are relevant to you at some point in your coaching career.

A debate has been raging within South Africa during the past few years about how to "professionalise" coaching practice. South Africa, like Australia, is in the southern hemisphere – and yet the Australians are striding ahead to collaborate and work in conjunction with other coaching bodies in the northern hemisphere. Their own handbook on *Coaching in Organisations* (Standards Australia, 2011), developed through the collaboration of 26 professional bodies in Australia, is a benchmark for continuing professional development. And the Global Coaching and Mentoring Alliance (GCMA) recently established in the northern hemisphere is now looking at the southern hemisphere to see how we can all work together to align coach education curricula, ethics, standards and supervision practice. What will coaching bodies in South Africa do to match these developments?

It is important for all coaches to maintain their own professional practice – and not just hang out a sign that says "I am a coach". Who says you're a coach? And what are you doing to grow and develop yourself and your practice? This takes continual growth through rigorous training and development, including being coached and in supervision yourself so that you know what your clients are experiencing – and particularly understanding the discomfort that clients experience as they learn how to develop new skills and competences. As a practitioner, you will have your own blind spots to which you tend to remain blind, unless you are in supervision. The work on yourself never stops.

If you can work and collaborate with those fellow practitioners in your own regional area – and also with practitioners in other professional bodies around the world – you will stretch, learn, grow and never look back. It has been said many times that what you sow you will reap. So your contribution to your own professional practice is part and parcel of your willingness to develop yourself and grow your discipline. I wish you enjoyment of the topics within this book!

WHO SHOULD READ THIS BOOK?

This book is for you if you are engaged in any way within the field of coaching, especially business coaching, and particularly if you are working with leadership development. You may be a practising coach; a coaching psychologist; an organisational psychologist who is training to be a coach; a leader or manager wishing to adopt a coaching approach; head of the leadership development programme within your institute or organisation and wishing to understand more about the why's and wherefore's of coaching; a consultant wishing to understand how coaching may impact your clients; a member of a coaching professional body wishing to contribute more to the development of its members; or simply in business and looking to understand if coaching can help you and your organisation to grow. If you wish to understand what more is needed in terms of continuing professional development for you as a leader, manager, practitioner or consultant involved in the field of coaching – then this book is for you.

OVERVIEW OF CHAPTERS

This book covers the depth and breadth of issues that will help you to transform your leadership coaching practice – whether you are an advanced coach practitioner, a practitioner continuing your professional development, a coaching psychologist with many years' experience, an HR or OD practitioner, an internal organisational coach, an external business or executive coach, a leader with a coaching approach in the organisation, or a manager stepping into an executive leadership position. You will not only refresh your learning at a deeper level to become a more transformational coach, it will help you to delve deeper into the gaps in your own competence, and help you to understand client issues at a more complex level.

The following chapters look with a fresh eye at what is really needed to be an effective business coach. They explore the major differences between coaching and other helping professions, explain the history of leadership development and key leadership styles, and position the coaching conversation within structural, learning, psychological and existential frameworks. The book identifies key issues when contracting with clients or direct reports, or supervising a suite of business coaches working within the complexity of an organisation. It delves into key areas of consideration when coaching men and when coaching women, and reviews what the author considers to be the most useful coaching models to enhance your coaching practice.

Based on original research through interviews with leading coach practitioners and coaching psychologists, and with leaders who are using coaching within their organisations to transform organisational culture and the development of people, this book will also deepen your understanding of some of the complexities of the environment in which we coach leaders today.

Chapter 2: Seven decades of leadership development

If we are to coach leaders we need to identify what is leadership, what we are looking for from leaders today, and what is the difference between leadership and management. This chapter takes a journey through the last seven decades of leadership and management theory, and a wide range of leadership styles. The chapter goes on to share key results of a survey conducted in South Africa in 2013 of 160 private sector companies and public sector entities, who were asked to define leadership, what a leader is, and how they are currently developing leaders.

Studies of leadership have produced a variety of theories. The chapter reviews trait theory, behavioural theories, contingency theories, functional leadership theories, situational theories, attitude pattern approach, transactional and transformation theories, relationship theories, distributed leadership, and ethical and values-based theories. A new definition of leadership is beginning to emerge globally, as are key leadership attributes such as determination and drive, self-confidence, integrity and sociability, core self-evaluation, and emotional intelligence.

Gender differences in leadership styles are a contemporary hot topic. The issues of diversity, culture and gender help us to understand the developmental needs of leaders due to individual perspectives, culture, gender, ethnicity and experiences of isolation. Research also reveals that *mindfulness* is beneficial to the best leaders; mindfulness helps to improve personal and professional effectiveness and overall organisational productivity.

Chapter 3: What is business coaching?

This chapter takes a deeper dive into what is business coaching, and why business leaders and managers find it useful. Executives and senior managers are often so busy dealing with a never-ending series of urgent and challenging issues that they have little room for reflection. This is problematic, because an executive who does not reflect on their experience, nor think about how to improve their practice, is unlikely to deliver excellent performance. And since executive performance leads the company's results, the same applies to the firm as a whole – an organisation's performance is shaped by the quality of thinking by its management.

This chapter looks at when and where coaching, training, counselling and therapy are most useful. Managers are likely to reap greater benefit from coaching, as opposed to training and mentoring, once they are experienced enough to identify and prioritise the issues they need to focus on. However, although the unique contribution and potential value of business coaching are increasingly recognised, the discipline has not yet been clearly defined – hence the need to clarify the confusion that remains in the marketplace as to the differences between coaching and other helping professions, and the core benefits of coaching.

Chapter 4: How to get the best from your coaching

This chapter looks at why you might need a coach, what you need to bring to the coaching session, what form of support you really need, and what value you can expect from the coaching intervention.

Working with a coach means going on a journey of self-discovery. It is a journey into who you are and how you be who you are, building an understanding of how people experience you in your day-to-day professional and personal life. It is a chance to reflect, to develop a more mindful approach to your work, and to ask yourself the hard questions that you avoid in the busyness of your working day. The space with your coach is where you can bring your authentic self – letting go of the need to play a role and to have all the answers.

The chapter outlines how to find the right coach and identify the coach criteria that will suit your needs, and also looks at what to do if the coaching experience doesn't work out for you. The value you take out of your coaching sessions depends entirely on the energy that you put into them, knowing that both your coach and you, as the client, are constantly moving towards "mastery of practice".

Chapter 5: The business coaching conversation

This chapter teases out the intricacies of the business coaching process, examining how the coaching conversation provides a "thinking environment" where business professionals are able to develop self-awareness and a depth of understanding of themselves and others. It is in this process of reflection, where coach and client reflect on the client's experience, that potential for learning and action emerges.

The chapter examines the psychology of goals and motivation, and explores new thinking about setting goals and motivation using *Self-Determination Theory*. It assess the importance of working with metaphor and analogy, examining assumptions and existential issues, and what is needed to develop the tacit dimension. The tacit dimension focuses on how to *be* in the relationship rather than referring to the skills and competences of the coach, or what the coach *does* to facilitate the conversation.

Are you so intent on being the brilliant coach that you are actually in the way of liberating the stories from those that you coach? Because coaching is a relationship-based process, the coach must be as aware of their own potential assumptions as well as those of the client. Ideally coaches must divest themselves of their own limiting paradigms, so that they can more effectively question and probe the client's articulated reality and assumptions. *Listening, asking questions* and *silence* are core skills for the business coach – as they help to create a safe thinking environment for their client.

Chapter 6: The power of coaching models

Coaching models help us to understand the coaching intervention from a systems perspective and to appreciate the need for "structure" in the interaction between coach and client. They offer flexibility and a structure for both the coaching conversation and the overall coaching journey. Models are useful to us in managing and dealing with complexity, particularly when working in environments where adaptability and systemic thinking are needed, and where there is continual change.

The Scientist-Practitioner Model, adapted from the world of clinical psychology, has proven to be extremely valuable to the business coach. The Nested-Levels Model works first at the horizontal level of "doing", eventually moving into deeper "learning" one level down; reflecting about self, others, and experience at a third "ontological" level where new knowledge emerges about oneself and the world.

Kolb's Experiential Learning Model helps both coach and client to bring their concrete experiences into the coaching conversation. Coach and client reflect and observe, think and theorise based on the client's observations, and agree what new thinking, feeling and behaviour needs to be applied back in the working environment. The chapter also reviews the Cynefin decision-making framework, which is a potentially useful tool for working in the complex environments of large corporations today.

Chapter 7: Facilitating the coaching conversation

As Chapter 6 explains, models offer structure and an outline for both the coaching conversation and the overall coaching journey. However, we also need to understand the *structure, process* and *underpinning philosophy* or *rationale* behind each model. This chapter describes how to facilitate the coaching conversation using Daniel Goleman's Emotional Intelligence (EQ) Model, the Domains of Competence Model of Jürgen Habermas and James Flaherty, Ken Wilber's Integral Model, Ernesto Spinelli's Existential Model, and the six-stage coaching process of the Nancy Kline Thinking Partnership®.

The coach can use the EQ Model to help the client learn how to manage themselves and relationships, but the coaching journey begins with developing the self. The Domains of Competence Model is a pre-cursor to understanding Wilber's four-quadrant Integral Model. The chapter moves on to discuss working with Wilber's four quadrants in the coaching conversation, a useful way of examining the subjective and objective realities within each of us.

Existential philosophy emphasises freedom of choice and taking responsibility for one's acts. This concern with choice, change and the client's journey through life is a core component of the coaching process, hence the usefulness of Ernesto Spinelli's Existential Model in helping to address existential dilemmas. The underlying premise of Nancy Kline's Thinking Partnership® is that the individual is best able to do their own thinking, and it provides a rigorous approach coaches can use to help to liberate their clients' thinking.

Chapter 8: Bring neuroscience to leadership coaching practice

Learning is the focus of coaching, and it is through learning that the brain enables us to adapt to our ever-changing environment. This chapter looks at the brain as a social system, mindfulness practice to develop awareness, and how to use the brain's working memory – particularly to change habits, to work with attention, and to sustain positive emotions. This is crucial for coach practitioners, as insights into the mind, brain and experience can help us to understand human development.

In order to be present for our clients, we need to practise focused attention and mindfulness as a regular practice. At the heart of this process is an "internal tuning-in" to oneself that enables you to become cognisant of your own behaviour, understanding how others may experience you in the workplace. Working with sustained attention on another, as in coaching, helps to develop the potential of those engaged in it – developing self-awareness and transforming thoughts and feelings into new behaviours.

Chapter 9: Gender diversity – coaching men and women to lead

Practitioners need to understand the socio-political dynamics of all their clients, including their gender, educational, cultural and ethnic backgrounds. Each practitioner has a responsibility to integrate cultural knowledge and sensitivity into their own education and practice – and to culturally evaluate themselves to understand their own worldview. It is only in this way that practitioners can increase their competence and empower their clients.

This chapter focuses on gender diversity in coaching across six contemporary areas:

- understanding gender diversity, power and culture;
- contemporary psychological research;
- gender management and organisational culture;
- diversity and identity within a Thinking Environment®;
- cultural contexts on gender issues in business; and
- academic research in coaching women leaders and managers.

This is a critically important topic for everyone connected with coaching, from practitioners and psychologists to academics, researchers and organisational leaders. Today, more than ever, it is vital that the business coach is able to raise the leader's awareness of crucial diversity issues within themselves, their teams, and their organisational culture.

Chapter 10: Coaching in organisations

Chapter 10 examines the complexities of contracting, how to use team learning to enhance performance in the workplace, and the difficulties in determining return on investment (ROI) for coaching interventions.

The process of *contracting* with clients is probably the most neglected area of coaching practice. The coaching contract sets out ground rules for the coaching relationship between the parties involved. This helps prevent future misunderstandings, and provides a firm basis to deal with disagreements. The purpose of the contract is to open up the potential for trust between coach and client. As the agreement lays the foundation for the relationship, it must be adhered to for trust to develop. Business coaching typically aims to improve an organisation's results through enhancing performance, whether working with individuals or teams. The chapter therefore discusses how to approach coaching a team or group rather than an individual.

Coaching ROI is a "hot topic" in the business world, but figures for return on investment (ROI) should be treated with a great deal of caution. The chapter analyses the conceptual difficulties involved in estimating ROI for business coaching, and considers different ways of evaluating the benefits from coaching.

Chapter 11: Safe and ethical practice

In coaching, there are five key fundamentals of safe practice: *competence, supervision, ethics, contracting,* and *credentialing.* This chapter explains how protecting oneself against professional risk involves some effort and foresight. Developing *competence* in coaching means undergoing effective education and training at a suitable coach training institution, then carrying out the necessary level of continuing professional development (CPD) every year after qualifying. The key roles of *coach supervision* are to ensure that the coach understands what the client goes through, to support the coach in working through their own issues so that they do not become entangled with client concerns, to support the development of the coach practitioner, and to assess the practitioner's competence.

The chapter reviews how COMENSA's *Revised Code of Ethics* serves to set the ethical standards for South Africa in the field of coaching with its four core values (autonomy, beneficence, non-maleficence and justice), and its seven guiding principles (inclusivity, dignity, competence, context, boundary management, integrity and professionalism). Finally, *credentialing* is very important to coaches, because if it is done properly, with effective implementation of standards of competence and a code of ethics (including meaningful sanctions for unethical conduct), prospective clients will feel confident that accredited coaches will know what they're doing.

Chapter 12: Coach supervision

This chapter explores the dynamics of coach supervision: why do we need it, what is the role of the supervisor, and what are the benefits of individual and group supervision? What happens when supervision doesn't work, and what types of supervision are available? The key role of the supervisor is to support the development of the coach practitioner, and to assess the practitioner's competence.

The chapter also looks at the *shadow* in coaching, as the coach and the client can influence each other in hidden and unexpected ways. Working with shadow in supervisory relationships, the coach works on understanding their own shadow first – noticing their own physical, mental and emotional reactions in the coach–client relationship.

Chapter 13: The future of business coaching

This chapter covers five areas key to the future of business coaching as we move rapidly into the 2020s: *professionalisation; mastery of practice; education and development of coaches; coaching research;* and *coaching and society.*

For the foreseeable future, it looks as if coaching will continue to "professionalise". While the need for evidence-based practice is largely accepted, as is the need for coaching to be a reflective practice, a crucial question emerges: "Is it incumbent on all practitioners to contribute to the emerging profession through research from their practice?" The role of research is to determine the competences necessary to educate and develop coaches, and most importantly to create a definition of coaching that the global coaching community will accept.

The new and innovative context worldwide is not just for academic researchers to contribute to relevant evidence-based practice, but also for coach practitioners and leaders within organisations who have adopted a coaching approach to contribute to the development of self-reflective practice and practitioner research. In this way we may begin to move forward to being "professional".

Chapter 14: Epilogue – coaching for new leadership

This chapter includes a wide range of "stories" and "self-reflexive" inquiry from emerging global corporate thinkers, business school leaders, coach practitioners and academics who are using coaching to manage people in new ways, to develop innovative leaders in their business schools, or to introduce systemic coaching interventions within their client organisations.

The chapter outlines the challenges facing leadership coaching globally, identifying tipping points for change. We acknowledge how coaching is making a difference in organisations and in society, and what is emerging in terms of transformational leadership. We also look at leaders who are working from a values-based platform, or working with family narrative and entrepreneurship, or opening up emotional intelligence in their organisations to build trusting relationships and sustainable policies which can impact change systemically, within their organisation, in society or in government.

The purpose of these interviews has been to hear the voices of those who are working at the cutting edge of coaching for systemic and cultural change in organisations and institutions within a business context. Common themes have emerged from this study that help us understand what coaching has achieved in developing people, improving performance, managing organisational change, developing leaders, and making a positive impact on local communities – and what stands out from these themes that we need to carry forward and continue to address proactively.

FURTHER READING

The "further reading" section at the end of each chapter contains an abbreviated list of useful resources on related topics to include in your library. A full bibliography is included at the end of the book.

Stout-Rostron, S. (2012b). *Business Coaching Wisdom and Practice: Unlocking the secrets of business coaching.* Second edition. Randburg: Knowres.

Stout-Rostron, S. (2014). *Business Coaching International: Transforming individuals and organisations.* Second edition. London: Karnac.

2

Seven decades of leadership development

WHAT IS LEADERSHIP?

In order to talk about coaching leaders, it is important to first identify what is leadership, and what we might be looking for from our leaders today. We need to prepare future generations to take on leadership roles, training supervisors and managers to move up the corporate and institutional ladder – helping executives to do more with less resources, time and skills, engaging their employees to create a trusting and transparent workplace culture. And more particularly, developing mindful leadership. The workplace has changed tremendously in the past 70 years, but the need to develop strong, capable leaders to succeed in an increasingly fast-paced working environment has remained constant. And this is where leadership coaching has a critical role to play in strategic alignment with talent development.

There's no one-size-fits-all leadership development programme. We need to create programmes that help high-potential executives and managers to gain the soft skills needed to motivate employees and to communicate effectively, and to help them establish an innovative culture that celebrates risk and reward. If leadership is about providing direction, what do organisations need to do to equip new leaders with the ability to inspire followers, and to contribute to a shared vision and direction? It would be helpful to look at the development of leadership over recent decades, understanding different theories and styles of leadership – and finally identifying what we are looking for today from our "new leaders".

We have had seven decades of leadership development. Bennis and Nanus (2003:4) complained that:

> Decades of academic development have given us over 500 definitions of leadership. Literally thousands of empirical investigations in leadership have been conducted in the last 75 years alone, but no clear and unequivocal understanding exists as to what distinguishes leaders from non-leaders, and perhaps more important what distinguishes effective from ineffective leaders, and effective organisations from non-effective organisations.

By the end of the 1990s it had been concluded that scholars and practitioners do not know with any certainty what leadership is, with Rost (1993) criticising writers on leadership for not defining or even attempting to define the concept in many of their works. However, when people talk about leaders today, words like "transparency" and "trust" come up often, as do concepts such as creating an innovative environment, engaging employees, and building a succession plan that includes knowledge sharing and organisational development (Ketter, 2013:10).

Renowned commentators who have examined many facets of leadership include:

- Ken Blanchard and Spencer Johnson, authors of *The One Minute Manager* (1982), who insisted that the key to successful leadership is influence, not authority.
- Warren Bennis, author of *On Becoming a Leader* (2009), concluded that although managers do things right, leaders do the right thing.
- Rosabeth Moss Kanter, author of *Men and Women of the Corporation* (1993), said that the new workforce wants to feel that its work is meaningful.
- Ed Cohen, author of *Leadership Without Borders: Successful strategies from world-class leaders* (2007), wrote that there are two types of leaders – those who use the best talent and those who develop the best talent.
- Edward Betof, author of *Leaders as Teachers* (2009), who examined how leaders learn from other leaders, advocating using an organisation's leaders as the keystone of a successful learning strategy.

The search for the characteristics or traits of leaders has been going on for centuries. As far back as Plato's *Republic* and Plutarch's *Lives*, philosophers have explored the question, "What qualities distinguish an individual as a leader?" Plato classified leaders as either timocratic (ruling on principles of honour and military glory), plutocratic (ruling by wealth), democratic (ruling by popular consent on the basis of equality), or tyrannical (ruling by coercion) (Bass and Bass, 2008:32).

Plutarch provides a "picture of the ideal leadership, in which the power of the king is united with the insight of the philosopher: such a ruler is an example of virtue, and the people submit to him without compulsion" (Duff, 1999:90). Underlying these principles was the early recognition of the importance of leadership and the assumption that leadership is rooted in the characteristics that certain individuals possess. This idea that leadership is based on individual attributes has become known as the trait theory of leadership.

However, trait theory – which details the "Big Five" personality traits of openness, conscientiousness, extraversion, agreeableness and neuroticism – neglects cognitive abilities, motives, values, social skills, expertise, and problem-solving skills (Zaccaro, 2007). Over the decades, studies of leadership have produced a variety of other theories, some of which we will discuss in this chapter, including:

- trait theory;
- behavioural theories;
- contingency theories;
- functional leadership theories;
- situational theories;
- attitude pattern approach;
- transactional and transformational theories;
- relationship theories;
- distributed leadership; and
- ethical and values-based theories.

What is the difference between leadership and management?

A manager may have excellent skills in organising work, creating policies and procedures, following disciplines and delivering services. But if others don't willingly follow their lead, they are not a leader. Key differences between leadership and management include the following:

- Leaders are not always managers or supervisors, formally appointed by others. Managers are invariably appointed from above, while leaders are often appointed from below by their followers.
- Leaders don't need to have responsibility for a team.
- Sometimes people are recognised as having leadership characteristics or qualities by others, who then simply choose to follow what the person says or does.
- Being a manager does not make you a leader.

Different to leadership, management is a profession. Management is about purpose, structure, disciplines, processes, delivery and the mechanics of an organisation. Managers get their authority and power from being appointed to a position by more senior managers. Leaders, in contrast, must offer their followers a cause, a direction or objective that is interesting, attractive or satisfying enough for others to wish to follow. Is a leader created, or is leadership defined by giving someone a job title? In most instances, in fact, we find that leaders are defined by what their qualities are, by the skills they have learned and the actions they take. Others recognise these attributes and choose willingly to follow.

So far we can assume that:

- A leader is someone who influences others to follow a given direction, and someone whose direction and approach other people are willing to follow. Leaders get their authority and power from being able to influence and persuade others to follow them.
- Leadership has been described as a "process of social influence in which one person can enlist the aid and support of others in the accomplishment of a common goal" (Chemers, 2001:376). Therefore, leadership is about vision, direction, influence, communication and the aspirations of people.

Good leaders today are striving to be highly productive, visionary, creative and innovative, authentic and balanced. Leadership development programmes can help to develop many skills – such as public speaking, strategic thinking, problem solving, giving feedback, leading change and building teams – but cannot tell leaders when to use those skills. And there are some qualities of terrific leaders that cannot be developed by merely learning about their value or the right times to develop them. Authentic leadership is something that others recognise and acknowledge.

What is a leader?

If we look at contemporary popular definitions, a leader is defined as:

- A person that guides, conducts, is at the head of, or leads.
- A person who rules or guides or inspires others.
- Someone that can direct others in a positive direction, setting good examples for the company and the people they lead.
- Peter Drucker, in his foreword to *The Leader of the Future*, says: "*The only definition of a leader is someone who has followers*" (Drucker, 1996:xii).
- Peter Maxwell, author of *The 21 Irrefutable Laws of Leadership* (1998), was renowned for repeatedly pointing out that "*Leadership is influence – nothing more, nothing less*".
- Someone whose direction and approach other people are willing to follow, and therefore we can assume that leadership is *influencing others to follow a given direction*.
- A person who influences a group of people towards a specific result and is not dependent on title or formal authority (Lubar and Halpern, 2003).

What are the characteristics of a good leader?

Several characteristics that seem to be crucial are:

- self-awareness;
- self-direction;
- vision;
- ability to motivate;
- ethical integrity; and
- social awareness.

The popular definitions of a leader listed above reflect an aspect about purpose and empowerment:

- focusing on the greater good of the people;
- engaging authentically, energising and empowering; and
- dealing in possibility, engaging all in a transformative journey.

Debate has gone on for years about the difference between transactional and transformational leadership. Burns (1979) talked about transactional leadership, characterised by an emphasis on procedures, contingent reward and management by exception. Transformational leadership (Bass and Riggio, 2006:2–5), on the other hand, is characterised by charisma, personal relationships, creativity, and transforming followers into leaders themselves.

Emergence of a new definition of leadership

New definitions of leaders and leadership are continuing to emerge globally:

- Human-Based Leaders™ embrace people, recognise their talents, fundamentally desire to see others succeed in their own right, and earn the loyalty and respect of those working with them. People pay attention to what they say, trust in the safe environment they create to share their thoughts and critiques, and choose to engage more fully. They know these leaders have their backs (Karlin, 2011:x).
- Visionary leaders articulate a purpose that rings true for themselves and attune it to values shared by the people they lead. And because they genuinely believe in that vision, they can guide people toward it with a firm hand. When it comes time to change direction, self-confidence and being a change catalyst smooth the transition (Goleman, Boyatzis and McKee, 2002:54–59).
- Effective leadership involves simple governing principles such as guiding visions, sincere values, and organisational beliefs – the few self-referential ideas individuals can use to shape their own behaviour. The leader's task is first to embody these principles, and then to help the organisation attain the standard it has declared for itself (Wheatley, 2006:130).
- True leadership stems from individuality that is honestly and sometimes imperfectly expressed (Buckingham, 2012).
- Leaders should strive for authenticity over perfection (George, Sims and McLean, 2007).
- Leaders who work with a panoramic view of success do not operate with total selflessness, but they do define their own success within the context of the bigger picture. If "we" don't succeed, "I" won't succeed (Lipkin, 2013:135).
- Successful leadership is a lifelong task of constant self-examination. When you are in touch with your own vision, values, perspectives, and roles, you will find a rewarding leadership path (King, Altman and Lee, 2011).
- Resonant leaders help blend financial, human, intellectual, environmental, and social capital into a potent recipe for effective performance in organisations. In addition to being great to work with, they get results. To be great, a leader needs to understand the market, the technology, the people, and a multitude of other factors affecting the organisation (Boyatzis and McKee, 2005:4–5).
- Great leadership works through the emotions, whether it's creating strategy or mobilising teams to action, and the success of leaders depends on how they do this. If leaders fail in this primary task of driving emotions in the right direction, nothing they do will work as well as it should. The leader acts as the group's emotional guide (Goleman, 1998:3–5).
- Leadership is a process of social influence in which one person can enlist the aid and support of others in the accomplishment of a common goal (Chemers, 2001).

Leadership development survey (South Africa, 2013)

In a survey of 160 companies employing 2 million people in South Africa, conducted in 2013 by Natalie Cunningham of Origo Consultants, Wilhelm Crous of Knowledge Resources and myself, respondents defined "leadership" in various ways. They said leadership is defined in hierarchal ways that are similar among private and public companies, and among government departments, government agencies, or parastatal institutions. However, their definitions of leadership tended to focus on executive and senior management levels within organisations (Table 1), with leadership being defined as "anyone at director / executive level" by:

- 60 per cent of public company respondents;
- 48 per cent of private companies;
- 68 per cent of parastatals; and
- 50 per cent of government departments and agencies (Stout-Rostron, Cunningham and Crous, 2013:9).

Table 1: Definition of leadership, by type of organisation (% of total)

Definition of leadership	Type of organisation:						
	Private co.	Public co.	Non-profit	Govt	Para-statal	Other	All
Anyone at Director / Executive level	48	60	44	50	68	100	55
Anyone at Senior Manager or Manager level	49	54	22	50	68	67	52
Anyone supervising a group, team or function	51	49	44	42	52	33	48
Anyone whose role enables them to influence a group	48	54	67	42	32	33	47
Anyone described as critical to success of the business	32	30		13	12		23
Anyone who is a top performer yet not managing others	29	19	22	17	12		21
Other	5	8		4	8		6
Category totals	100	100	100	100	100	100	100

Source: Stout-Rostron, Cunningham and Crous (2013:9)

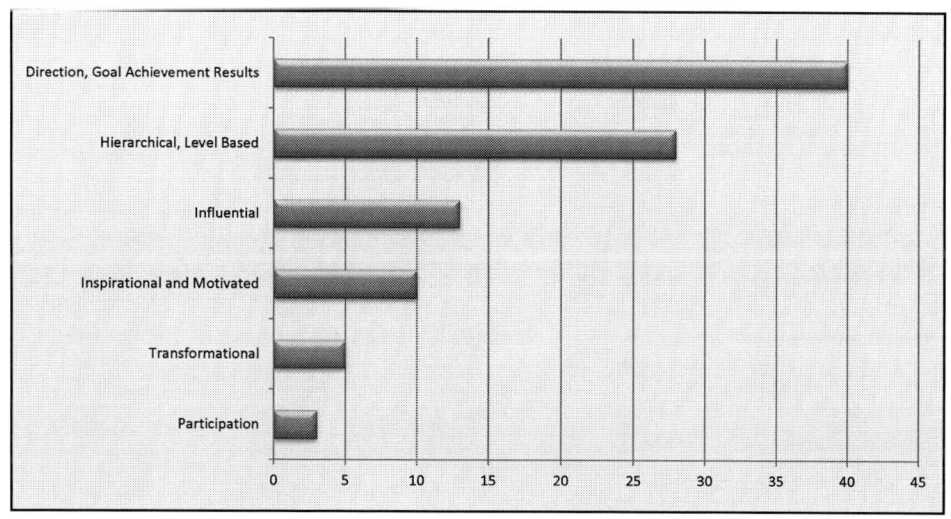

Figure 1: Qualitative description of current leadership in organisations

Source: Stout-Rostron, Cunningham and Crous (2013:6)

When asked what is leadership in their organisations, the most frequent responses were that leadership is linked to providing strategic direction, achieving common goals and getting results (Figure 1). The second dominant theme was that leadership is still defined by the hierarchical positions of people in the organisation and linked to graded levels of work. The ability of leaders to inspire and motivate teams was a theme supported by the ability of the leader to be influential. These findings indicated a strong focus on leadership being trait- or characteristic-based. Few responses looked at leadership in a transformational way, focusing on the "way of being" or the process of leading (Stout-Rostron, Cunningham and Crous, 2013:6–7).

Table 2 illustrates the employee groups targeted for leadership development programmes by the various types of organisation who responded to the survey. Private and public companies, together with government and parastatal organisations, target not only "C-suite" executives (i.e. CEO, CFO, COO, etc.), but also managers identified as potential successors to the C-suite, and individuals generally identified as "high-potential" employees. The latter employee group received the highest overall weighting across all organisation types (45 per cent of total responses) (Stout-Rostron, Cunningham and Crous, 2013:10–11).

Table 2: Employee groups targeted for leadership development programmes, by type of organisation (% of total)

Group of employees targeted	Type of organisation:						
	Private co.	Public co.	Non-profit	Govt	Para-statal	Other	All
C-suite-level executives - e.g. CEO, CFO, COO	35	41	11	29	40	50	35
Managers identified as potential successors to the C-suite	38	43	22	42	48	50	41
All employees identified as "high-potentials"	41	54	22	33	52	75	45
All employees with job / management duties overseas	16	24		17	16	25	17
All employees with likely duties / management overseas	14	11		4	16	25	12
Any manager expressing interest in global / advanced LD	16	22		13	24	50	18
Any employee expressing interest in global / advanced LD	19	11		29	28	25	19
Any employee nominated by one in their line of supervision	19	22	11	17	24	25	20
All managers are required to participate in LD programme	35	24	11	42	52	50	35
Any other		3			8	25	3
Category totals	100	100	100	100	100	100	100

Source: Stout-Rostron, Cunningham and Crous (2013:11)

LEADERSHIP AND MANAGEMENT THEORIES

A range of formal leadership theories have emerged in the last 70 years as interest in leadership has taken on a greater role in contemporary society. The early leadership theories focused on what core attributes distinguished leaders from followers, while subsequent theories looked at other variables such as situational factors, behaviour, social skill and emotional intelligence.

Naturalistic theories

The first theories of leadership to develop were naturalistic, built on the assumption that leaders are born, not made. In most societies, it was assumed that the great leader was a man, and that greatness was inherent rather than learned. We have often heard the phrase that someone is born to lead. According to this theory, great leaders are born with the necessary internal characteristics to lead such as charisma, confidence, intelligence, and the social skills that make them natural-born leaders. These leaders are portrayed as heroic or mythic and destined to rise to leadership when needed. The term "Great Man" was used due to the thinking that leadership is primarily a male quality, which emerged from the development of leadership strategy in the military (Cherry, 2013a:2).

As scientific psychological studies began to be applied to human behaviour, the trait theory emerged, although still assuming that leaders are born, not made. Eventually, more advanced theories of leadership have appeared through research. Some of the early studies on leadership include the Ohio Leadership Studies, the Michigan Leader Studies, and motivational and behavioural studies.

Ohio Leadership Studies

The Ohio Leadership Studies began in the 1940s and sought to identify and catalogue the traits affecting individual leadership ability. The researchers used factor analysis of data from surveys of individual leaders to identify two dimensions or "factors" said to account for variations across leadership style and group performance. One factor, termed "initiation of structure", emphasised the formal roles and organisation of tasks of the leader and subordinates; a leader who scored high on this factor would focus on the goals of the group and on planning how to achieve them. The other factor, termed "consideration", emphasised the "socio-emotional" aspects of leadership; a leader who scored high on this factor would focus on reducing interpersonal tensions and promoting co-operation and trust within the group (Khurana, 2007:354).

Michigan Leadership Studies

The Michigan Leadership Studies (Boje, 2000) began in the 1950s and indicated that leaders could be classified as either employee-centred or job-centred. The objective was to identify the principles and types of leadership styles that led to greater productivity and enhanced job satisfaction among workers. These studies identified three critical characteristics of effective leaders: task-oriented behaviour, relationship-oriented behaviour, and participative leadership.

McGregor's Theories X and Y

Theories X and Y were developed by Douglas McGregor in the 1960s at the MIT Sloan School of Management to describe employee motivation at work. McGregor's book, *The Human Side of Enterprise* (1960), had a profound influence on the field of management. His two theories described opposing models of motivation, and how management viewed human behaviour at work. Based upon Maslow's Hierarchy of Needs, McGregor grouped the hierarchy into lower-order needs (Theory X) and higher-order needs (Theory Y), suggesting that management could use either set of needs to motivate employees, although better results would be gained through the use of Theory Y (McGregor, 1960:43–82).

Theory X is an authoritarian management style which assumes that workers inherently dislike work and will avoid it if they can. The Theory X manager believes that workers need to be closely supervised with comprehensive systems of control put in place. This includes a hierarchical structure with control at each and every level. According to this theory, employees will not show ambition without an incentive programme, and will try to avoid responsibility if they can. Because the Theory X manager may rely on threat and coercion, this can lead to mistrust, highly restrictive supervision, and a retributive atmosphere (McGregor, 1960:43–58).

Theory Y is a participative management style and assumes that workers are ambitious, self-motivated, enjoy their work, and can exercise self-control. A Theory Y manager believes that, given the right conditions, most people will want to do well at work, and that the satisfaction of doing a good job is strongly motivational. Many people interpret Theory Y as a positive set of beliefs about workers. McGregor thought that Theory Y managers are more likely than Theory X managers to develop a climate of trust with employees, which is required if employees are to grow and develop (McGregor, 1960:59–82).

In addition to these studies, academics have gone on to examine leadership through a variety of other lenses.

Trait theories

Trait theories assume that people inherit certain qualities and traits that make them better suited to leadership. Trait theories often identify particular personality or behavioural characteristics shared by leaders. For example, traits like extraversion, self-confidence, and courage are all traits that could potentially be linked to great leaders (Cherry, 2013a:2). The question is, if particular traits are key features of leadership, then how is it that some people possess those qualities yet do not aspire to be leaders?

Although studies of leadership have produced theories involving traits, situational interaction, function, behaviour, power, vision and values, charisma and intelligence, among others, there does not seem to be a single attribute that accounts for leadership effectiveness. LaPort (2012) argues for seven types of leadership attribute: cognitive ability, cognitive complexity, motivation to lead, achievement motivation, social intelligence, extraversion, and emotional stability.

Along with intelligence, personality has also been thoroughly studied as an attribute of leaders. The "Big Five" personality traits specified five categories of personality traits: conscientiousness, agreeableness, neuroticism (or emotional stability), openness and extraversion. All five have been significantly associated with leadership effectiveness (Rumsey, 2013:26).

However, Zaccaro noted that trait theories fail to "consider patterns or integrations of multiple attributes; they do not distinguish between those leader attributes that are generally not malleable over time and those that are shaped by, and bound to, situational influences; and they do not consider how stable leader attributes account for the behavioural diversity necessary for effective leadership" (Zaccaro, 2007:16).

Behavioural theories

In response to the early criticisms of the trait approach, academics began to research leadership as a set of behaviours, evaluating the behaviour of successful leaders, and identifying broad leadership styles. McClelland (1961) held that leadership needs a strong personality with a well-developed and positive ego, and that to lead, self-confidence and high self-esteem are also useful if not essential. McClelland's (1961) Needs-Based Model suggests that a manager's motivational style and behaviour is a combination of the need for achievement, the need for authority and power, and the need for affiliation (McClelland, 1987:303;318;348;355).

According to Derue et al. (2011:8), the "influence of the leader behaviour paradigm can be seen across leadership theories, including Fiedler's (1967) contingency model, Blake and Mouton's (1964) managerial grid, and the work on transformational and transactional leadership". One consistent theme in the literature is that leadership behaviours "can be fit into four categories: task-oriented behaviours, relational-oriented behaviours, change-oriented behaviours, and what we refer to as passive leadership" (Derue et al., 2011:15).

Blake and Mouton's Managerial Grid

The managerial grid model is also based on behavioural theory. This model was developed by Robert Blake and Jane Mouton (1964) and suggests five different leadership styles, based on a leader's concern for people and concern for goal achievement – i.e. people-orientation versus task-orientation. The grid focuses on concern for results on one axis, and concern for people on the other axis. Each concern is measured on a Grid Diagram on a continuous scale of 1 to 9 to denote an uninterrupted sequence. As Miner (2002:713) points out, "task-oriented leadership is job-centred, with goal emphasis. People-oriented leadership is relationship-oriented and supportive". The two concerns interact on the Managerial Grid to create five styles of management:

- 1/1 impoverished management (neither committed to mastering the work environment nor to be appreciated by the people);
- 1/9 social management (placing high value on personal relationships);
- 5/5 organisational management (aiming for security through compromise and being a member of the team);
- 9/1 authoritative management (having maximum concern for getting the job done, motivated by achievement through control of people); and
- 9/9 team management (involved, participative and placing high value on creativity and new ideas) (Miner, 2002).

Contingency theories

In 1967, Fiedler published A *Theory of Leadership Effectiveness* in which he presented a theoretical approach called the Contingency Model. This model proposed that leaders approach group task situations strongly oriented either to maximising interpersonal success or to task achievement. Fiedler's Contingency Model explored the interaction of the motivations and personal characteristics of the leader with the current situation the group faces. Relationship-oriented leaders were more attuned to interpersonal and morale-related issues, and most likely to employ participative decision making and considerate behaviour (Chemers, 2001:387). Thus, the Contingency Model shifted the focus of leadership effectiveness from attributes to personality (Forsyth, 2010).

Contingency leadership theories focus on variables within the organisational environment that help determine which particular style of leadership is best suited for the situation. Success depends upon a number of variables, including the leadership style, the abilities of the followers and various characteristics of the situation. "Leadership was no longer primarily associated with traits of the individual; rather, it was driven by the situation. This approach dominated the zeitgeist in leadership until the 1970s" (LaPort, 2012:91).

Functional leadership theory

Functional leadership theories are based on what leaders do – i.e. on their functions and actions. In the Functional Leadership Model, leadership is seen as a set of behaviours that helps a group to perform a task or achieve a goal. In this model, the leadership function meets needs in three specific areas: task, team and individual.

During the 1960s and 1970s, John Adair, a British leadership theorist, developed the Action-Centred Leadership Model, which suggested that effective leader-managers should be equally able to achieve the task, manage the team or group, and manage individuals. Leadership resides in the functions rather than in the person. This approach sees leadership functions as touching upon three areas (task / team / individual), either directly or indirectly (Adair, 1988:43–45;51).

While functional leadership theory has most often been applied to team leadership (Zaccaro, Rittman and Marks, 2001), it has also been effectively applied to broader organisational leadership (Zaccaro, 2001).

Situational theories

Another major approach to understanding leadership focuses upon the situation. The situational leadership theory was developed by Paul Hersey, author of *The Situational Leader* (1984), and Ken Blanchard and Spencer Johnson, authors of *The One Minute Manager* (1982). The premise is that it is "always the situation which determines who emerges as the leader and what style of leadership" the leader is to adopt (Adair, 1988:15). First introduced as the Life Cycle Theory of Leadership (Hersey and Blanchard, 1969), it was later renamed Situational Leadership Theory (Hersey and Blanchard, 1988).

Underpinning this theory is that there is no single best style of leadership. In other words, effective leadership is task-relevant, and most successful leaders are those who adapt their leadership style to the maturity of the individual or the group. Effective leadership varies, not only with the person or group that is being influenced, but it also depends on the task, job or function (Hersey and Blanchard, 1988).

The Situational Leadership Model has two axes for the leader: supportive relationship behaviour and directive task behaviour. The behaviours tend to be either:

- high task / low relationship (S1 telling);
- high task / high relationship (S2 selling);
- high relationship / low task (S3 participating); or
- low relationship / low task (S4 delegating) (Hersey and Blanchard, 1988).

Follower readiness is identified as:

- R4: able and willing or confident (high);
- R3: able but unwilling or insecure (moderate);
- R2: unable but willing or confident (moderate);
- R1: unable and unwilling or insecure (low) (Hersey and Blanchard, 1988).

Situational theories propose that leaders choose the best course of action based upon the situational context; thus the type of decision to be made influences which style of leadership is appropriate. For example, in a situation where the leader is the most knowledgeable and experienced member of a group, a more directive style might be appropriate. In other instances where group members are skilled experts, a more democratic or participative style would be more effective (Hersey and Blanchard, 1988).

Attribute pattern theories

The attribute pattern approach emerged due to criticism of the trait theory. The premise of the pattern approach is that in order to understand human functioning, researchers need to focus on subgroups of persons over time, and recognise that a person is more than the sum of his or her parts (Foti and Hauenstein, 2007:347–348).

This approach is based on the argument that the impact of individual characteristics on outcomes is understood by considering the person as an integrated totality rather than a summation of individual variables (Mumford *et al.*, 2000). The attribute pattern approach argues that integrated combinations of individual differences may explain substantial variance in leader emergence and leader effectiveness.

Transactional and transformational theories of leadership

James MacGregor Burns (1979) conceptualised leadership as either transactional (i.e. leadership takes place through social exchange between leaders and followers) or transformational (i.e. leaders inspire followers to achieve extraordinary outcomes). Transformational leaders inspire followers "to commit to a shared vision for an organisation or unit, challenging them to be innovative problem solvers, and developing followers' leadership capacity via coaching, mentoring, challenge and support" (Bass and Riggio, 2006:3–5).

Transactional leadership

Eric Berne (1975) analysed the relationship between a group and its leader in terms of transactional analysis. He claimed that there are three types of leader – the responsible, effective and psychological leader – and that we can understand group process through transactional analysis (Berne, 1975:65;155). Transactional leadership, also known as managerial leadership, focuses on the role of supervision and group performance. This theory is based on a system of reward and punishment. Transactional leaders lead through social exchange, and offer financial rewards for productivity or deny rewards for lack of productivity (Burns, 2003:3).

Transactional leadership is often used in business: when employees are successful, they are rewarded; when they fail, they are reprimanded or punished. Rules, standards and procedures are considered to be essential in transactional leadership, and followers are not encouraged to be creative or to seek out solutions. Although transactional leadership can serve a purpose and be effective, transformational leadership creates greater performance and follower satisfaction (Bass and Riggio, 2006:10).

Transformational leadership

Through the strength of their vision and personality, transformational leaders are able to inspire followers to change expectations and to motivate them to work towards common goals. Transformational leadership addresses the "follower's sense of self-worth to engage the follower in true commitment and involvement in the effort at hand" (Burns, 2003:3). It emphasises

> intrinsic motivation and the positive development of followers, and provides a better fit for leading today's complex work groups and organisations, where followers not only seek an inspirational leader to help guide them through an uncertain environment, but where followers also want to be challenged and to feel empowered if they are to be loyal, high performers (Burns, 2003:xi-xii).

Researcher Bernard Bass expanded upon Burns's original ideas to develop what is today known as Transformational Leadership Theory. According to Bass, transformational leadership can be defined based on the impact that it has on followers. Transformational leaders, he suggests, create trust, respect, and admiration (Cherry, 2013b:1). Bass and Riggio suggested four components of transformational leadership that help leaders to achieve superior results:

- Intellectual stimulation: challenging the *status quo* and encouraging creativity and learning.
- Individualised consideration: encouraging and supporting individual followers, keeping the lines of communication open so that followers can share ideas, and the leader can recognise each individual's contribution.
- Inspirational motivation: transformational leaders articulate a clear vision, enable followers to experience their passion, and motivate them to fulfil their goals.
- Idealised influence: the transformational leader is a role model, and is respected and trusted as a leader. Followers emulate the leader, or internalise their ideals (Bass and Riggio, 2008:6–7).

In *Transformational Leadership*, Bass and Riggio (2008:3) explain that

> Transformational leaders ... are those who stimulate and inspire followers to both achieve extraordinary outcomes and, in the process, develop their own leadership capacity. Transformational leaders help followers grow and develop into leaders by responding to individual followers' needs by empowering them, and by aligning the objectives and goals of the individual followers, the leader, the group, and the larger organisation.

Relationship theories

Relationship theories, also known as transformational theories, focus upon the connections formed between leaders and followers. Transformational leaders motivate and inspire people by "helping group members see the importance and higher good of the task. These leaders are focused on the performance of group members, but also want each person to fulfil his or her potential. Leaders with this style often have high ethical and moral standards" (Cherry, 2013a:2).

There are many levels in which leadership operates, including the different types of relationship between follower and leader. Grint (2005) stresses the relational component of leadership, emphasising that it is a function of the relationship between leader and follower – whereas "leader-focused" is a focus on the character of an individual. Graen and Uhl-Bien (1995) identify three categories of leadership: leader-based, relationship-based and follower-based:

- leader-based: establishing and communicating vision, inspiring and instilling pride;
- relationship-based: building strong relationships with followers, with mutual learning, trust and accommodation; and
- follower-based: empowering, coaching, facilitating, and giving up singular control.

Other categories of leadership continue to emerge with ongoing research.

Distributed leadership – the learning organisation

Peter Senge's definition of a learning organisation is "where people continually expand their capacity to create the results they truly desire, where new and expansive patterns of thinking are nurtured, where collective aspiration is set free, and where people are continually learning how to learn together" (Senge, 1990:3).

According to Senge, leadership can be shared by many. This means that leadership is distributed throughout all levels of the organisation, and is concerned with the interactions amongst many leaders, rather than being individually focused on the actions of one leader (Senge, 1996). In Senge's definition of leadership we see that it is not exclusive to one individual. "Leadership is the capacity of a human community – people living and working together – to bring forth new realities. This simple notion of human communities creating new realities unifies the extraordinarily diverse individuals whom we see as exemplary leaders" (Senge, 1999).

This is in alignment with a premise underpinning executive coaching, which is to develop the leadership potential within each individual.

Ethical and values-based theories

Servant Leadership Theory

In the 1970s we were exposed to Robert Greenleaf's Servant Leadership Theory, which specified a "caring and ethical approach, with a strong element of supportive leadership behaviour" (Howell, 2013:22). Servant leadership describes a situation where the leader puts a greater priority on serving others. This type of leadership is meant to be beneficial for the followers.

Authentic Leadership Theory

The Authentic Leadership Theory "borrows heavily from positive psychology", stressing the identification and nurturing of people's strengths: "the psychological capacities of authentic leaders include self-confidence, optimism, hope, happiness, resilience, emotional intelligence, and high moral character" (Howell, 2013:22). Authentic leaders realise that their role includes a "responsibility to act morally and in the best interest of others. These leaders strive to do what is right and fair for followers and associates and openly discuss their own weaknesses while emphasising their own and followers' growth and development" (Howell, 2013:23).

Bass and Riggio explain that authentic, transformational leaders

> transcend their own self-interests for one of two reasons, utilitarian or moral. If utilitarian, their objective is to benefit their group or its individual members, their organisation or society, as well as themselves and to meet the challenges of the task or mission. If a matter of moral principles, the objective is to do the right thing, to do what fits principles of morality, responsibility, sense of discipline, and respect for authority, customs, rules and traditions of a society. There is belief in the social responsibility of the leader and the organisation (Bass and Riggio, 2006:14).

Principle-centred leadership

Developed by Stephen Covey, principle-centred leadership emphasises the leader's character and competence as "essential for effective leadership. For Covey, character is comprised of integrity, maturity, and an abundance mentality " (Howell, 2013:24).

In *Principle-Centred Leadership* Covey outlines ten dilemmas for professional managers, four levels of natural law, and how to turn a company mission statement into a constitution. According to Covey, "the only thing that survives over time is the law of the farm: I must prepare the ground, put in the seed, cultivate it, weed it, water it, then gradually nurture growth and development to full maturity" (Covey, 1991:17). He emphasises the importance of:

- personal and organisational values;
- the principles of trust and trustworthiness;
- follower empowerment;
- service orientation;
- continuous learning;
- radiating positive energy;
- believing in others;
- seeing life as an adventure;
- showing humility;
- listening and obeying one's conscience;
- refraining from speaking unkindly;

- keeping all promises and commitments;
- involving followers in creating a mission; and
- vision and purpose for the organisation (Howell, 2013:24–25).

"Principle-centred leadership introduces a new paradigm – that we centre our lives and leadership of our organisations and people on certain true north principles" (Covey, 1991:18). He advocates that leaders work with these principles, treating people how you wish to be treated by them. According to Covey, only then will an organisation experience genuine cultural transformation (Covey, 1991:23).

LEADERSHIP STYLES

Autocratic, democratic and *laissez-faire* leadership

A "leadership style" is the way in which a leader mobilises and motivates people, provides them with direction and guidance, and implements strategies and plans. Individual leadership styles are the products of the personal characteristics, philosophy and experience of the leader. Invariably, however, different situations call for different leadership styles.

In 1939, Kurt Lewin led Ronald Lippitt and Ralph White in a research study which identified three different climates of leadership: authoritarian (autocratic); participative (democratic), and delegative (*laissez-faire*) (Lewin, Lippitt and White, 1939). Although later research identified more specific types of leadership, this early study was very influential.

The autocratic leader dictates how the task will be done, and tends to stay aloof from those performing the work (Miner, 2002:40). All decision-making power resides with the leader, and although the autocratic leader is not necessarily hostile, they are remote or detached from the workers. The major difference between autocratic and democratic leaders is that productivity drops off when the autocratic leader leaves, but tends not to drop off when the democratic leader departs (Miner, 2002:40).

Democratic leaders offer guidance to group members, but they also participate in the group process, and input is allowed from everyone. Technical advice may be provided by the leader, and the group decides on the division of labour (Miner, 2002:40). Democratic leaders are thus more participative and work with the collective in a more encouraging way, even if they have the final say over the decision-making process. Group members feel engaged in the process, and are more motivated and creative.

Delegative (or *laissez-faire*) leaders offer little structure or guidance to group members, and leave decision making up to group members. The leader may not take part in the division of work, and rarely offers praise or criticism – in fact, the delegative leader tends to supply information only when asked (Miner, 2002:40). Although this style can be effective in situations where group members are highly qualified in an area of expertise, it can also lead to poorly defined roles and a lack of motivation.

Emotional intelligence leadership styles

Daniel Goleman's (2000) emotional intelligence (EQ) research claims that leaders today use six styles of leadership. Each is the result of different components of emotional intelligence. Below is a summary of the styles, their related competence, the organisational climate within which they work, and the type of phrase or question a leader is likely to use when working with each individual style.

- *Coercive* – Demands immediate compliance. (EQ competence: drive to achieve, initiative, self-control. Says "Do what I tell you." Used in a negative climate, crisis, or to kick-start a turnaround.)
- *Authoritative* – Mobilises people towards a vision. (EQ competence: self-confidence, empathy, change catalyst. Says, "Come with me." Used when changes require a new vision, or when a clear direction is needed. Works when the climate is mostly positive.)
- *Affiliative* – Creates harmony and builds emotional bonds. (EQ competence: empathy, building relationships, communication. Says "People come first." Used in a positive climate and heals rifts in a team or motivates people during stressful circumstances.)
- *Democratic* – Forges consensus through participation. (EQ competence: collaboration, team leadership, communication. Asks "What do you think?" Used in a positive climate, and builds buy-in or consensus, or gets input from valuable employees.)
- *Pace-setting* – Sets high standards for performance. (EQ competence: conscientiousness, drive to achieve, initiative. Says "Do as I do now." Used in a negative climate, and gets quick results from a highly motivated and competent team.)
- *Coaching* – Develops people for the future. (EQ competence: developing others, empathy, self-awareness. Suggests "Try this." Used in a positive climate, and helps an employee improve performance or develops long-term strengths) (Goleman, 2000:81–86).

Other styles of leadership worth understanding for the business coach are those that are engaging, narcissistic and toxic.

Engaging leadership style

An engaging style of leadership is when a leader reaches out to their staff and is involved in their achievements and disappointments. Cohen (2009) recommends the following "four key leadership practices for leading in tough times":

- make more informed personnel decisions;
- define roles and expectations;
- ensure continual skill development; and
- engage employees (Cohen, 2009:3–5).

Engagement is seen here as the fourth key leadership practice, and Cohen addresses the need for leaders to involve followers, particularly in difficult economic times:

What all of these initiatives do for the organisation is engage both leaders and employees in understanding the existing conditions and how they can collectively assist in addressing them. Reaching out to employees during difficult times to better understand their concerns and interests by openly and honestly conveying the impact of the downturn on them and their organisations can provide a solid foundation for not only engaging them but retaining them when things do turn around (Cohen, 2009:5).

Narcissistic leadership style

Narcissistic leadership is a leadership style in which the leader is interested only in themselves. The narcissistic leader's priority is themselves at the expense of their people or followers. They exhibit the characteristics of a narcissist, i.e. arrogance, dominance and hostility. Considered to be a common leadership style, narcissism may range from healthy to destructive behaviour. To critics, "destructive narcissistic leadership is driven by unyielding arrogance, self-absorption, and a personal egotistic need for power and admiration" (Neider and Schriesheim, 2010:29).

Narcissistic leadership occurs when a leader's actions are principally motivated by their own egomaniacal needs and beliefs, superseding the needs and interests of the constituents and institutions they lead (Rosenthal and Pittinsky, 2006:629). Egomaniacal needs and beliefs include many of the patterns pervasive in a narcissistic personality, i.e. a grandiose sense of self-importance, preoccupation with fantasies of unlimited success and power, excessive need for admiration, entitlement, lack of empathy, envy, inferiority, and hypersensitivity. However, narcissists also possess the charisma and grand vision that are vital to effective leadership (Rosenthal and Pittinsky, 2006:617).

Toxic leadership style

It is important to understand the damage and destruction to people and the organisation that can be caused by a toxic style of leadership. Toxic leadership is related to an autocratic leadership style. Toxic leaders do not trust their followers, and need to feel that they are in control of others. This can have a destructive effect on the morale and self-confidence of individuals and teams within the organisation. "Toxic leadership is brought about by lack of self-awareness, lack of self-control and confidence, all of which are sown by self-interest. Toxic leaders care only about themselves, thinking only of their own feelings and disregarding those of others" (Lacida, 2012).

Toxic leadership prevents creativity, innovation, and the individual and independent expression of ideas:

> In a toxic leadership environment, people are rewarded for agreeing with the boss and punished for thinking differently. In a toxic leadership environment, 'yes' people are rewarded and promoted to leadership roles, while people who more fully engage their critical thinking and questioning skills are shut out from decision making and positions of influence (Wilson-Starks, 2003).

The characteristics of a toxic leader are those of being self-destructive, irritable, arrogant, incompetent, maladjusted and lacking in confidence (Wilson-Starks, 2003). They are capable of not just setting unrealistic objectives, but leading purely by power and control.

OTHER KEY LEADERSHIP ATTRIBUTES

Determination and drive

Leadership is complex and cannot be reduced to a few key traits of an individual. However, each trait may be applied to situations differently, depending on the circumstances. Howell (2013:4) characterises determination and drive as follows:

> Determination and drive include traits such as initiative, energy, assertiveness, perseverance, masculinity, and sometimes dominance. People with these traits often tend to wholeheartedly pursue their goals, work long hours, are ambitious, and often are very competitive with others (Howell, 2013:4).

Self-confidence, integrity and sociability

Self-confidence seems to be a core attribute for leaders throughout the recent decades of research:

> Unless an individual has a considerable degree of self-confidence or faith in his own ability and the 'worthwhileness' of his own ideas he probably will never attempt leadership in any really significant capacity. The leader's ability to carry his programme to completion seems to depend very largely upon the maintenance of self-confidence (Rumsey, 2013:27).

> Self-confidence encompasses the traits of high self-esteem, assertiveness, emotional stability, and self-assurance. Individuals that are self-confident do not doubt themselves or their abilities and decisions; they also have the ability to project this self-confidence onto others, building their trust and commitment (Howell, 2013:4).

Core self-evaluation

Although emotional intelligence has become a very popular concept among consultants and coaches in the business world, it is not clear that intelligence applies to emotions but more to the "willingness and ability to introspect" (Rumsey, 2013:68). Some researchers see emotional intelligence as a fad to avoid. Recent research has begun to focus on a trait pattern called core self-evaluation "which combines four personality and motivational attributes – self-esteem, locus of control, generalised self-efficacy, (e.g. self-confidence) and emotional stability" (Rumsey, 2013:27).

Another view is that emotional intelligence "helps leaders understand and identify with followers, which also assists in evoking self-confidence, optimism and other positive emotions and beliefs in followers" (Howell, 2013:23).

Emotional intelligence

In the last decade emotional intelligence has become one of the most researched attributes of effective leaders, and researchers have offered evidence indicating that emotional intelligence contributes to leadership outcomes beyond the effects of cognitive abilities or personality. However, other researchers have questioned the validity of this, having observed that emotional intelligence overlaps with general mental ability and personality (Rumsey, 2013:26).

Although current psychological research is seriously questioning the construct of emotional intelligence, the term has entered the common vernacular when discussing leadership characteristics and traits. Leadership can be perceived as a very emotion-laden process, with emotions entangled within the process of social influence, and the emotions of a leader can greatly influence their group.

A pioneering model of emotional intelligence was proposed in the 1980s by Reuven Bar-On, although the early definitions of social intelligence influenced the way emotional intelligence was later conceptualised (Bar-On, 2006:13). "The EQ-I was originally constructed as an experimental instrument designed to examine the conceptual model of emotional and social functioning" that Bar-On began developing in the early 1980s (Bar-On, 2006:5).

Salovey and Mayer (1990) originally viewed emotional intelligence as part of social intelligence. They later defined emotional intelligence in terms of "being able to monitor and regulate one's own and others' feelings and to use feelings to guide thought and action" (Goleman, 1998:317).

Goleman defines emotional intelligence as the capacity for recognising our own feelings and those of others, for motivating ourselves, and for managing emotions in ourselves and in our relationships, and includes five basic emotional and social competences: self-awareness, self-regulation, motivation, empathy and social skills (Goleman, 1998:318). Emotional intelligence traits associated with leaders with high EQ are that they:

- are intrinsically more self-aware;
- understand their mental processes;
- know how to direct themselves;
- are more in touch with what they are deeply passionate about;
- naturally care more for others and receive more compassion in return;
- are more socially in tune (e.g. engage with social media);
- know leadership is more about soft skills; and
- understand that what drives the bottom line is valuable, yet the leader who gets others to perform at their best ultimately creates winning organisations (Goleman, 1998).

Nelson Mandela – a leader with strong emotional intelligence

The one leader who stands out in recent history as embodying the strongest qualities of emotional intelligence is Nelson Mandela. In his autobiography, *Long Walk to Freedom* (1994),

Mandela recalls attending the Councils of the Thembu King, the Regent of his rural area in the Eastern Cape of South Africa, as a very young man. This experience, in many ways, formulated Mandela's understanding of leadership and achieving consensus. Rather than give his views, the Regent would instead listen attentively to all his Councillors. Each person was allowed to speak fully and freely. In this way, the Regent could be sure that he was not hearing the advice his Councillors thought that he might like to hear, but instead was able to gain a clear idea of the whole variety of opinions on any matter. He saw his job as summing up the emerging consensus of the meeting (Mandela, 1994:19–20). But there was also a more subtle approach behind the leader not stating his views right from the start. It was the idea that the leader is like a shepherd. Mandela wrote, "I always remember the Regent's axiom: a leader, he said, is like a shepherd, who stays behind the flock, letting the most nimble go on ahead, whereupon the others follow, not realising that all along they are being directed from behind" (Mandela, 1994:20–21).

One of the most common evaluations of Mandela is that he lacked bitterness. Even before his lengthy imprisonment, his own father was removed from a chieftainship by a white magistrate. His father had stood firm on a point of principle which the white magistrate thought "impertinent" (Mandela, 1994:6–7). So, from a very early age Mandela had cause for anger and resentment. Indeed, as a young man, he admits that he was often angry and intemperate. But as his leadership qualities grew, he understood that such emotions were detrimental to his own wellbeing and clouded his judgement. Perhaps one of the most extraordinary signs of his emotional intelligence, and far-sighted vision, is that during his 27 years of imprisonment, Mandela not only studied Afrikaans, but also read Afrikaans novels and poetry. The point was not simply to be able to speak the language of the people who had imprisoned him – he knew that one day he would have to negotiate with them. He wanted to read their literature to understand their culture and their way of thinking – in order to comprehend the people with whom he would be conducting the toughest possible negotiations.

In this sense, he gained an immeasurable advantage. He later often dealt with people whose emotions and fears he understood, while they – the ostensibly all-powerful – had very little understanding of his real feelings or way of thinking. The irony is that, in this case, the prisoner was streets ahead of his jailers. It took a rare form of emotional intelligence to put himself in a position of having the stronger hand when he was face-to-face with his opponents – although they may not have realised it.

The fact that Mandela had a very consensus-oriented style of leadership should not be confused with the fact that when he felt strongly about something, he was prepared to go out on a limb – even risking the distrust of his own colleagues. For example, during his last years in prison, he began to negotiate with the National Party, his jailers (Mandela, 1994:522–524). This was, at first, unknown to his own closest companions in jail. He knew this was risky, and that some of them would fear he had "sold out". Some of them did indeed feel he had given in when they first discovered he had been conducting negotiations. However, Mandela felt that not only was this important, but that it was the right time for him to go out in front as a leader, presenting his followers with a *fait accompli*. His success lay in his judgement of knowing when to consult, and when to go out ahead alone. This is a supreme test of emotional intelligence in leadership.

Shortly after his release from prison, he attended an event where one of those present was Wilhelm Verwoerd, grandson of the supreme apartheid ideologue and former Prime Minister, Hendrik Verwoerd. Embarrassed, young Wilhelm tried to avoid Mandela, but the ex-prisoner soon tracked him down. Whereupon Wilhelm began to apologise for the system of racial tyranny that had imprisoned Mandela and the part that his own grandfather had played. Mandela interrupted him to say that, with his surname, he had a voice which people would listen to. "So you have to think carefully", counselled Mandela, "what you do with that power" (*Sunday Times*, 2013). This is a good example of intuitive leadership – putting someone at their ease and potentially winning over an unlikely ally to his own cause and vision.

When someone asked Mandela what it was like to be free after 27 years, Mandela said, "We are now free to become free" (*Sunday Times*, 2013). There was no triumphalism, always moving towards the bigger goal, and no resting on his laurels. But it was a goal that had to include everyone – something that he achieved triumphantly.

CURRENT THINKING ON LEADERS AND MOTIVATION

Leaders help people to flourish – and flourishing is at the heart of coaching. Good leaders fuel people – motivating them with valuable and interesting work. If work fuels people it produces wellness and wellbeing. To flourish is to develop, to become more differentiated and integrated as a human being – and to be fully functioning. But it needs nourishing. This is why people make choices about where they work, and why they will move to an environment where they feel motivated, happy and nourished.

Self-determination theory

Richard Ryan is co-developer, with Edward Deci, of Self-Determination Theory (Ryan and Deci, 1985), an internationally researched theory of human motivation, personality development, and wellbeing. Self-Determination Theory is a theory of motivation concerned with supporting our natural or intrinsic tendencies to behave in effective and healthy ways. "To be self-determined is to endorse one's actions at the highest level of reflection. Self-determined people experience a sense of freedom to do what is interesting, personally important and vitalising" (Ryan, 2013). Deci and Ryan (1990) expanded on their earlier work, differentiating intrinsic from extrinsic motivation, and proposing three main intrinsic needs involved in self-determination: autonomy, competence and relatedness.

Volitional motivation and wellbeing as basic needs

Ryan (2013) talks about the basic psychological needs which underpin volitional motivation and wellbeing. He says that our most basic list of nutrients includes autonomy, competence and relatedness, and that these three things lead to volitional motivation and wellbeing. If deprived of any one of these conditions, people will go probably downhill. But when people experience all three of these basic needs they will be optimally motivated at work. In other words, when people are satisfied at work – and these three basic needs are activated – they will thrive. If this is critical, then leaders need to have the relational skills to motivate followers using autonomy, competence and relatedness (Ryan, 2013).

Autonomy

Autonomy supports volition. According to Ryan, autonomy is when behaviour is in alignment with the individual's values and interests, and that individual's actions at work are self-endorsed, and are congruent with implicit and explicit motives. If you have autonomy, you want to do your work, and you believe in what you are doing. Autonomy is not about independence, individualism or self-interest, but is instead an endorsement of them. Autonomy means that your actions and behaviour are self-endorsed, and in alignment with your values and interests (Ryan, 2013).

Competence

Competence is about controlling the outcome and experiencing mastery. Competence supports structure and positive feedback, and means that you have a sense of effectiveness and competence within your working context (Ryan, 2013).

Relatedness

Relatedness is the collective wish to interact with others, to be connected to others, and to experience caring for others. Relatedness supports inclusion, empathy and care. It also means feeling cared for, connected to, and having a sense of belonging with others.
    Ryan talks about how these conditions facilitate intrinsic motivation:

- Autonomy means there is an absence of pressure, and there is individual goal choice, choice of strategy, involvement and interest in the task.
- Competence means there is optimal challenge, with positive feedback and rewards.
- Relatedness means there is empathy and warmth which acknowledges the individual's emotions (Ryan, 2013).

However, certain aspects of these conditions can also undermine intrinsic motivation:

- Autonomy is undermined by pressure toward outcomes, punishment contingencies, goal imposition, deadlines, controlling rewards, ego involvement, and surveillance.
- Competence is undermined by non-optimal challenges and negative feedback.
- Relatedness is undermined by lack of collective interaction and positive involvement, and even watching somebody closely (Ryan, 2013).

Ryan (2013) explains that autonomy supports minimal external pressure and provides maximum choice, and the internal frame of reference is shared; competence supports optimal challenge, and the development of appropriate demands with relevant feedback; and relatedness supports warmth and involvement which conveys belongingness. The more aware a leader is, the more likely they will create these three conditions for people. Ryan discusses the following behaviours that are useful to leaders to support these three conditions of motivation:

- Autonomy-supportive environments (to motivate someone to do something):
  – understand the other's perspective;
  – encourage self-initiation and self-reflection;
  – offer meaningful choices;
  – provide a rationale for requested behaviour; and
  – minimise use of controlling language or rewards.

- Competence-supportive environments:
  – design activities so that mastery is the dominant experience;
  – provide structure scaffolding for active development;
  – give informational feedback rather than controlling feedback; and
  – focus praise on effort and specific accomplishments – not on ability or comparisons.

- Relatedness-supportive environments:
  – convey respect for the individual;
  – ensure the individual feels valued and significant;
  – offer care and concern when facing challenges;
  – radiate warmth; and
  – let the individual know that their coach / boss / teacher likes them (Ryan, 2013).

How are you impacting the workplace?

As a coach or leader, what are some of the main ways that you see your leadership skills impacting your own workplace performance and the performance of those you lead, manage or coach? In what way do you embody these three conditions of autonomy, competence and relatedness?

GENDER DIFFERENCES IN LEADERSHIP STYLE

Issues of diversity, culture and gender may have a major impact on the individual coaching client, the context within which they work, and the developmental needs of certain leaders due to their individual perspectives, culture, gender, ethnicity and experience of isolation. This is relevant to coaching both men and women (Stout-Rostron, Janse van Rensburg and Marques Sampaio, 2014:174–180).

In many societies, "characteristics such as assertiveness, initiative and leadership are seen as masculine, whereas obedience and a concern for the domestic sphere are seen as feminine qualities" (Stout-Rostron, Janse van Rensburg and Marques Sampaio, 2014:198). Gatrell and Swan (2008) examine the gendered binary of organising the world, identifying how traditional stereotypes of masculinity and femininity have created the gendered division of labour at work, with particular emphasis on the discrimination of women with and without children (Gatrell and Swan, 2008:36–37). Gender discrimination is so deeply embedded in organisational life as to be often virtually indiscernible, and although it is generally agreed that women add enormous value, organisational definitions of competence and leadership are still predicated on traits stereotypically associated with men: tough and aggressive (Meyerson and Fletcher, 1999:129–131).

A report by the Committee on Equal Opportunities for Women and Men of the Council of Europe's Parliamentary Assembly noted that "Many employers wrongly fear the cost and hassle motherhood may entail. In fact, according to recent ILO research, the additional cost of hiring a woman is less than 1 per cent of the monthly gross earnings of women employees. But women are not only discriminated against for economic reasons – they are mainly discriminated against because of stereotyping and misguided preconceptions of women's roles and abilities, commitment and leadership style" (Čurdová, 2005:1).

In Chapter 9 we examine coaching men and women in today's organisational environments with their multicultural, power and diversity complexities. This is a critically important topic for everyone connected with coaching, from practitioners and psychologists to academics and researchers, as well as organisational and institutional leaders. For the growing discipline of business coaching, organisational research into gender diversity is relatively new – yet it is critical for coach education and leadership development, and for practitioners and academics working with leaders.

STATES OF BEING AND MINDFULNESS

Research reveals that "the best leaders have some method to manage the constant onslaught of inputs and stimuli to maintain their presence of mind and good health. Mindfulness is being taught and practised in a growing number of organisations worldwide in an effort to improve personal and professional effectiveness and overall organisational productivity" (Garms, 2013:32).

Some of these qualities are referred to as states of being, such as being relaxed, alert, curious, close-minded, open-minded, negative, positive or self-confident. These states of being are attained by having experiences, and discussing the experience of others who have attained them. This is all about learning from experience, which is an underlying premise of business coaching.

Jon Kabat-Zinn (1994:4) says that mindfulness is "paying attention in a particular way: on purpose, in the present moment and non-judgmentally". Mindfulness is achieved by regulating one's attention – focusing attention on one's thoughts and emotions. Daniel Siegel says that mindfulness is "good brain hygiene, as important to health as brushing one's teeth" (Siegel, 2009:146).

The benefits of mindfulness are that it:

- improves mental focus and reduces mind wandering;
- extends our attention span;
- discourages "black-and-white" thinking;
- assists in staying organised, managing time and setting priorities;
- lifts us from a constant, low level of panic and guilt;
- lowers wear and tear on our bodies;
- toughens immunity;
- improves mood and emotional stability;
- builds self-monitoring capacity; and
- offers neuro-protective effects and reduces cognitive decline associated with ageing (Garms, 2013:34).

Being mindful requires working with attention, i.e. mastery of attention; clarity of attention; optimisation of attitude and emotional intelligence and integration into every domain of daily life, work and relationships (Garms 2013:34–35). Throughout this book, I will refer to the work of the Thinking Environment® for coaches and leaders to develop mindful practice and leadership.

Developing others mindfully

- How are you helping your direct reports to think for themselves – individually and independently?
- In what way do you interfere or intervene or direct their thinking processes?
- What needs to shift in you in order to facilitate change or facilitate a shift in them?

Bridging the canyon

In every Road Runner cartoon, "Wile E. Coyote speeds after his adversary full of confidence and vigour. However, in more than 60 years of re-runs, he has never made it across the canyon. For a few seconds, he stands suspended in mid-air staring at the camera in disbelief. Then gravity kicks in, sending him hurtling to the ground in absolute failure" (Lang and Thomas, 2013:37;39). The message is that organisations need to do a better job of supporting new leaders. This starts with improving new leaders' skills and competence, in part through aligned talent development and providing more support such as coaching and mentoring for ongoing learning and growth.

Coaches need an understanding of leadership theories and styles, but it is also useful to understand that deep self-awareness and interpersonal skills are integral to success in a leadership role. Leaders face challenging situations that require them to identify and respond to the interpersonal and skill needs of their teams. With the right training, learning development and managerial support, new managers will be able to make the leap – stepping from managerial responsibilities to those of a leader who is task- and relationship-oriented, with high emotional maturity, and who can also provide the conditions for autonomy, competence and relatedness.

COMPLEXITY IN LEADERSHIP DEVELOPMENT

As previously discussed in this chapter, thousands of conceptual and empirical studies have emerged in the last 70 to 80 years. Contemporary leadership studies have looked at leadership from relational and systemic perspectives that have an impact on how we develop leaders. "The term complexity captures the greater levels of uncertainty, ambiguity, interdependences and interrelatedness that now characterise the environments in which organisations operate" (Clarke, 2013:135).

If leaders are to continue to use their interpersonal influence to motivate the workforce to achieve organisational goals, we may have to think differently about how we define leadership. Underpinning most approaches is the assumption that "leadership is essentially a process of interpersonal influence, whereby leaders exert influence to achieve desired goals" (Clarke, 2013:136). However, most definitions of leadership:

> have yet to expand sufficiently to accommodate a much wider systemic perspective on the nature of leadership. This recognises leadership as an emergent possibility within the social system where the interaction of individuals becomes the central focus. The increasing complexity facing organisations requires us to consider leadership as embedded not merely in sets of interpersonal relationships, but more widely as constituting an array of interacting organisational processes that facilitate intelligent and innovative organisational adaptation (Clarke, 2013:136).

Conceptual complexity theories "describe the articulation of organisational purpose within increasingly greater time spans". And behavioural complexity theories "emphasise the need for senior leaders to co-ordinate the demands and requirements of multiple constituencies in accordance with organisational purpose" (Zaccaro, 2001:13).

Zaccaro defines executive leadership as:

that set of activities directed toward the development and management of the organisation as a whole, including all of its subcomponents, to reflect long-range policies and purposes that have emerged from the senior leader's interactions within the organisation and his or her interpretations of the organisation's external environment (Zaccaro, 2001:13).

He goes on to ask four essential questions for leadership development:

- How do the requirements for executive leadership performance differ from those requirements at lower organisational levels?
- At what organisational level do performance requirements shift in quality?
- How are leader effectiveness and influence defined and operationalised at different organisational levels?
- What is the relationship between the accomplishment of executive leadership performance requirements and organisational effectiveness? (Zaccaro, 2001:14).

Two further questions that Zaccaro addresses that are particularly useful for executive coaches and for leaders themselves are:

- What individual characteristics distinguish executive leaders from lower-level leaders?
- What individual characteristics distinguish successful executive leaders from unsuccessful executive leaders? (Zaccaro, 2001:15).

At an individual level, complexity leadership development tends to move away from focusing on the structures and processes within the organisation, to the behaviours required of leaders individually within their social system. Both informal and formal leaders are seen as critical "to harnessing the creative effects" of intelligence within the organisation (Clarke, 2013:141).

However, what is important in this conversation is the need to focus on the "dynamic systems comprising leadership" (Clarke, 2013:142) in conjunction with a focus on the leaders.

CONCLUSION

This chapter has summarised evidence that there is no one-size-fits-all leadership development programme. And despite seven decades of research, we have yet to find an unequivocal definition of "leadership" itself. Renowned academics, researchers, and innovators on leadership have examined many facets of this very complex topic to try to reach a common understanding of what leadership is.

This vast range of study shows that while some traits and characteristics of successful leaders can be identified, analysed and even emulated, "leadership" is not a formula that can be bottled. There are elements of intuition, courage and the ability to react to the unexpected which are impossible to pin down or quantify. Leaders who lead merely by emulation or following others' examples are probably not good leaders. The fact is that the abilities and qualities that define good leadership may also vary according to circumstance and change over time.

Because the inherent nature of leadership in the workplace has changed, we need altogether different expressions of leadership. We need to break from current mental models that limit our thinking, learning from past forms of leadership, and defining new ways of leading in our own organisations. We need to create a realistic future, inspiring new possibilities for leaders and followers today – with a focus on greater self-awareness, emotional maturity and leadership competence working in multicultural diversity. Leaders not only have an impact on transforming individuals in the workplace, but also one of transforming their organisations and the communities in which they operate (Stout-Rostron, 2011a).

People at work today are driven by sustainable values such as trust, integrity, bringing heart into relationships, health, and work–life balance. People want to have a reason, a purpose and a mission in their working lives (Stout-Rostron, 2011a). Recent research has highlighted the importance of the following issues, which I will discuss in Chapter 14:

- innovative and authentic leadership;
- specifically working with personal narrative, for deep growth and learning;
- values-driven leadership;
- allowing for independent and individual thinking;
- personal, professional and spiritual alignment;
- an acceleration of "deep-dive" work for personal transformation;
- inter-disciplinary teams and action research projects; and
- personal commitment on the part of the leader to change (Stout-Rostron, 2011a).

With this in mind, we will move through the next chapters to explore the logistics of the business coaching conversation, understanding how to thrive through coaching, and bringing neuroscience to coaching. Chapter 14 discusses the challenges facing leadership coaching globally.

FURTHER READING

Bar-On, R. (2006). The Bar-On model of emotional-social intelligence (ESI). *Psicothema*, 18(S1):13–25.

Bass, B.M., and Bass, R. (2008). *The Bass Handbook of Leadership: Theory, research and managerial application.* Fourth edition. New York, NY: Free Press.

Bass, B.M., and Riggio, R. (2006). *Transformational Leadership.* Second edition. Mahwah, NJ: Erlbaum.

Bennis, W.G. (2009). *On Becoming a Leader.* Twentieth anniversary edition. Philadelphia, PA: Basic.

Bennis, W.G., and Nanus, B. (2003). *Leaders: Strategies for taking charge.* Third edition. New York, NY: HarperCollins.

Betof, E. (2009). *Leaders as Teachers: Unlock the teaching potential of your company's best and brightest.* San Francisco, CA: Berrett-Koehler and Alexandria, VA: ASTD.

Boyatzis, R.E., and McKee, A. (2005). *Resonant Leadership: Renewing yourself and connecting with others through mindfulness, hope and compassion.* Boston, MA: Harvard Business School.

Buckingham, M. (2012). Leadership development in the age of the algorithm. *Harvard Business Review*, 90(6):86–94.

Burns, J.M. (2003). *Transforming Leadership*. New York, NY: Grove.

Chemers, M.M. (2001). Leadership effectiveness: An integrative review. In Hogg, M.A., and Tindale, R.S. (eds), *Blackwell Handbook of Social Psychology: Group processes* (pp. 376–399). Oxford: Blackwell.

Clarke, N. (2013). Model of complexity leadership development. *Human Resource Development International*, 16(2):135–150.

Cohen, E. (2007). *Leadership Without Borders: Successful strategies from world-class leaders*. Singapore: Wiley.

Forsyth, D.R. (2010). Leadership. In *Group Dynamics (Fifth Edition)* (pp. 245–280). Belmont, CA: Wadsworth.

George, B., Sims, P., and McLean, A. (2007). Discovering your authentic leadership. *Harvard Business Review*, 85(2):129–138.

Goleman, D. (1998). *Working with Emotional Intelligence*. New York, NY: Bantam Dell.

Goleman, D. (2000). Leadership that gets results. *Harvard Business Review*, 78(2):78–90.

Goleman, D., Boyatzis, R., and McKee, A. (2002). *Primal Leadership: Learning to lead with emotional intelligence*. Boston, MA: Harvard Business School.

Grint, K. (2005). *Leadership: Limits and possibilities*. Basingstoke: Palgrave Macmillan.

Howell, J.P. (2013). *Snapshots of Great Leadership*. Hove: Routledge.

Karlin, D. (2011). *Leaders: Their stories, their words: Conversations with Human-Based Leaders®*. Ottawa, ON: A Better Perspective.

Ketter, P. (2013). The seven decades of leadership development. *T+D*, 8 March.

King, S.N., Altman, D.G., and Lee, R.J. (2011). *Discovering the Leader in You: How to realise your leadership potential*. San Francisco, CA: Jossey-Bass.

Lipkin, N. (2013). *What Keeps Leaders Up At Night? Recognising and resolving your most troubling management issues*. New York, NY: American Management Association.

Lubar, K., and Halpern, B.L. (2003). *Leadership Presence*. New York, NY: Gotham.

Mandela, N.R. (1994). *Long Walk to Freedom*. Edinburgh: Little, Brown.

Maxwell, P. (1998). *The 21 Irrefutable Laws of Leadership: Follow them and people will follow you*. Nashville, TN: Thomas Nelson.

Miner, J.B. (2002). *Organisational Behaviour: Foundations, theories and analyses*. Oxford: Oxford University.

Neider, L.L., and Schriesheim, C.A. (eds) (2010). *The "Dark" Side of Management. Research in Management Series*. Miami, FL: University of Miami.

Rosenthal, S.A., and Pittinsky, T.L. (2006). Narcissistic leadership. *The Leadership Quarterly*, 17(6):617–633.

Rumsey, M.G. (ed.) (2013). *The Oxford Handbook of Leadership*. Oxford: Oxford University.

Siegel, D.J. (2009). Mindful awareness, mindsight, and neural integration. *The Humanistic Psychologist*, 37(2):137–158.

Stout-Rostron, S., Cunningham, N., and Crous, W. (2013). *Leadership Development Survey Report 2013*. Randburg: Knowres.

Wheatley, M.J. (2006). *Leadership and the New Science: Discovering order in a chaotic world*. Third edition. San Francisco, CA: Berrett-Koehler.

Zaccaro, S.J. (2001). *The Nature of Executive Leadership: A conceptual and empirical analysis of success*. Washington, DC: American Psychological Association.

Zaccaro, S.J. (2007). Trait-based perspectives of leadership. *American Psychologist*, 62(1):6–16.

Zaccaro, S.J., Rittman, A.L., and Marks, M.A. (2001). Team leadership. *Leadership Quarterly*, 12(4):451–483.

3

What is business coaching?

BUSINESS COACHING DEFINED

by Nick Wilkins and Dr Sunny Stout-Rostron

An executive scenario

What is business coaching? And why would business leaders and managers find it useful? To answer these questions, imagine the following scenario.

You're a 40-year-old executive heading an operational division of a large company. You get to work at 07:30, scan the business news, then respond to 57 priority email messages that you can't delegate to your line managers or PA. A message from the CEO reminds you to forward him a key strategy proposal with headline budget by noon Friday, for discussion by the Board next week. You <u>must</u> get to grips with this today, or you won't have a fully worked-out proposal ready in time; and there are some tricky issues to consider.

But HR calls: one of your line managers has objected to an unfavourable performance review and non-promotion, and is threatening a CCMA action; you quickly draft a brief for HR and the Legal Department, and schedule a meeting with the manager. You field a call from a journalist wanting comment on an allegation that company officials rigged an environmental impact assessment. Then your husband calls; your son's teachers want to meet with both of you to discuss his "behaviour issues", which you suspect are due to bullying, of which the school denies all knowledge.

You rush to chair two scheduled meetings with prospective clients, and one with a project management team. You planned to snatch 40 minutes during lunch to work on your strategy proposal, but are asked to advise Procurement on an unresolved dispute with a supplier about faulty equipment. You quickly read through your last round of direct report performance reviews and have a tough meeting with the disgruntled line manager and the Deputy Director of HR. Then it's a two-hour round trip through heavy traffic for a site visit to a major project; while driving you conduct seven cellphone calls with HR, a client, the Finance Director, a project manager, a project accountant, and two engineers.

You get back to the office in time only to rush off for your school meeting, and a difficult evening trying to communicate with your son. And this was just an average day. As you get into bed, exhausted, you realise you still haven't thought through your strategy proposal.

Executives and senior managers have to keep many balls in the air. They're often so busy dealing with a never-ending series of urgent or challenging issues that they have little room for reflection on their work experiences, or for clear-headed thinking about future strategy. This is problematic: as Kolb (1984:68–69) pointed out, reflecting on one's concrete experience is a crucial part of the experiential learning cycle (concrete experience, reflective observation, abstract conceptualisation, active experimentation). An executive who does not reflect on their experience, nor think about how to improve their practice, is unlikely to deliver excellent performance. And since executive performance leads the company's results, the same applies to the firm as a whole – an organisation's performance is shaped by the quality of thought of its management. In effect, if executives are not reflecting on and learning from operational experience, and thinking carefully about the future, the company is strategically brain-dead.

Going beyond keeping the balls in the air

So how can busy and highly-stressed executives, having to field and shoot a myriad of different balls every day, make the time and space for high-quality thinking? Business coaching can help, in two fundamental ways.

The coaching intervention provides a formal and acceptable way of taking executives out of their frenetic daily rush, and giving them time and space for discussion and thought. As Kline (2009:cover) says, "The greatest gift we can offer each other is the framework in which to think for ourselves". An executive demanding an hour alone "just to think" risks being considered hopelessly self-indulgent by their colleagues. But a formal, structured and disciplined business coaching intervention, seen to improve executive performance and company results, is a different matter.

More importantly, within that quiet time and space, a good business coach will be a "thought partner" for the executive, helping them to think clearly about the issues they need to address. The coaching conversation is a thinking partnership, where coach and client reflect on the client's experience, transforming it into potential for learning and action. The coach's job is to help the client to think clearly about the core issues which challenge them – in their job, career and daily working life. The client is encouraged to think for themselves and to develop an awareness of their own conscious and unconscious behaviours, which may influence performance and systemic change.

By asking the right questions, in the right way, at the right time, the coach helps the client find their own solutions. The coaching conversation literally provides a "thinking environment" where business professionals are able to develop self-awareness and a depth of understanding of themselves and others. The coach's job is not to provide answers or solve the client's problems for them. The greatest gift the coach can offer is to help the client to consider experiences, approaches, ideas, strategies, behaviours, and actions they have not previously considered.

For the harassed executive in the example above, the most important issues a business coach could help her reflect on, and develop clear strategies for, would probably include:

- developing her strategic leadership competences;
- sustaining complex but rapid decision-making processes;

- effectively motivating, developing and managing the performance of her direct reports;
- managing complexity within her teams, the division and the firm;
- effectively addressing diversity issues (particularly around gender, race, and age) in a sector historically dominated by middle-aged white males;
- effectively dealing with workplace conflict, and managing difficult people and situations;
- transitioning into a new position and role(s);
- gaining insight into her own intrinsic personal and professional drivers;
- dealing with corporate stress levels; and
- balancing business and personal life demands.

And for any busy executive, under pressure to deliver big results in a competitive industry under difficult economic, financial and systemic circumstances, real help in getting to grips with these issues can be absolutely priceless.

The essence of best-practice business coaching

Coaches help someone think clearly about something. That might sound naively simple, but it's both the real core and the real value of best-practice coaching. Because business leaders the world over are finding it more and more difficult to think clearly about anything – for a variety of reasons. That is why executives are turning to business coaches – not because they need therapy, or mentoring, or consulting input, or moral support, or even to develop new skills – but because they need help to think clearly about the big issues currently challenging them, and to work out better ways of addressing them.

Coaching is unique. It involves helping people to systematise their conscious thoughts about the immediate actions needed to address specific practical issues, and to understand the mental and systemic processes that may be sabotaging their success. What other discipline does this? And it's difficult to do that simple-sounding task well – to be an effective thought partner – which is why coaches need to be properly educated, trained and professionalised.

If this description of the core process of business coaching makes sense, and if the potential value of business coaching to clients is intuitively obvious, why does business coaching still struggle to articulate exactly what it is and what real value it can contribute? There is as yet no single clear and authoritative definition of "coaching", and coaches have not yet reached agreement among themselves on what coaching is, what processes it does and doesn't involve, and what it can really do for their clients. So, it is not surprising that prospective clients also remain confused, which has been noted by various external observers.

This situation stems partly from the fact that most coaches come into the industry from other disciplines, and continue to apply the methodologies of their earlier vocations within coaching. It is also partly due to a fundamental insecurity that coaches in general seem to have about the industry: many are tempted to hype what they're doing to their clients in order to sell it, because they're not actually sure of, or confident in, what they're doing. This is manifested as a continuing urge to be all things to all people, to be the hottest thing in town, the next big thing.

If the discipline is to make progress it might help to go back to first principles, and underline the very real and inherent value at the core of best-practice coaching. Only when coaches engage with this simple fact, and abandon the need to sell coaching by smothering the basic process with gimmicks, is coaching likely to receive the recognition and respect it deserves as an emerging profession. One that can give its clients real value – beyond merely helping them keep the balls in the air.

BUSINESS COACHING VERSUS EXECUTIVE COACHING

There is a lot of misunderstanding about the difference between business coaching and executive coaching. In fact, executive coaching is simply a subset of business coaching. The definition of business coaching used by the Worldwide Association of Business Coaches (WABC) is:

> Business coaching is the process of engaging in regular, structured conversation with a 'client': an individual or team who is within a business, profit or non-profit organisation, institution or government and who is the recipient of business coaching. The goal is to enhance the client's awareness and behaviour so as to achieve business objectives for both the client and their organisation. Business coaching enables the client to understand their role in achieving business success, and to enhance that role in ways that are measurable and sustainable ... This dual focus is what distinguishes business coaching from other types of coaching. The business coach helps the client discover how changing or accommodating personal characteristics and perspectives can affect both personal and business processes. Successful coaching helps the client achieve agreed-upon business outcomes as an individual or team within the context of an organisation ...
>
> 'Business coaching' is an inclusive term that refers to all types of business and organisational coaching. It is practised by internal and external coaches who may identify as corporate coaches, executive coaches, leadership coaches, organisational development coaches or other types of business coaches. Regardless of the practitioner's title, business coaching is defined by its dual focus on the client and the client's organisation (WABC, 2011:1).

In my view, it is important to note further that:

> Business coaches encourage their clients to think for themselves and to develop an awareness of their own conscious and unconscious behaviours, which may influence performance in the workplace. Business coaching is essentially about the results experienced through the dynamic relationship between coach and client, and how those results impact on individual, team and organisational performance (Stout-Rostron, 2012b:13).

Hence, executive coaching fits within the context of business coaching:

> One of the reasons why business coaching has become increasingly popular is because organisations understand the importance of getting the best out of talented people. It is now widely accepted that the best way to do this is by investing in people's professional development and encouraging them to participate in decision-making processes. It follows, therefore, that a key component of business coaching is a focus on executive coaching – on the development of senior managers and executives to improve their individual performance, and by doing so to optimise organisational results (Stout-Rostron, 2012b:15).

The next section highlights how business coaching ensures that executives not only think through their current experience with a coach, but learn new ways of thinking, feeling and behaving by continually *reconstructing* their experience in the workplace. In building a relationship with their business coach, leaders and managers can develop new ways of understanding the complexities of their business, strategically managing all stake holders, customers, employees' performance and financial success. This in turn enables them to critically define where their own thinking and behaviour need to change, and the importance of managing their own emotions in the workplace. The way the brain is hardwired (with the verbal, higher-thinking cortex connecting with the non-verbal limbic brain) means that we cannot think without feeling, nor feel without thinking. Research shows that all decisions at the end of the day are emotional – despite the myth that decision making in the workplace is a purely rational act.

BUSINESS COACHING VERSUS OTHER DISCIPLINES

How do corporate leaders develop the competences they need? And how should they be supported in their development?

These are important questions, because the answers determine the precise forms of support executives and managers will need at particular stages in their professional development. This section briefly reviews the various forms of developmental support available to corporate management, outlining their appropriate applications, and highlighting key issues concerning the most suitable roles for coaching. All forms of support are useful at different times in the career of a manager or executive; what is most important is understanding how they each differ one from the other, in order to select the appropriate continuing professional development path for the coaching client, or for your direct reports.

Training: can leaders be trained?

Training methodology has evolved considerably over the past century. In essence, however, training can be defined as the communication of information to someone in a systematic way to achieve the knowledge and understanding required for the development of a specific competence. Training is necessary for young people entering the job market to attain the necessary technical and professional skills they will need in their vocations. It is also useful throughout the career of any corporate executive as they climb their professional ladder. In training, the trainer or facilitator sets the agenda and is essentially a teacher or facilitator of new learning.

The real question, however, is whether corporate leaders can be trained. Management is a profession, and the core definition of management is "achieving results through the efforts of others". Leadership is not a profession, yet similar to management, it requires sets of competences which are defined differently dependent on the leadership model with which an organisation selects to work. For our purposes, the eight leadership competences defined by the Jungian Insights® Discovery instrument are a useful benchmark which speaks to four types of leadership: *results, visionary, relationship and centred* leadership (Lothian, 2006):

- leading from within;
- agile thinking;
- delivering results;
- leading change;
- creating a compelling vision;
- communicating with impact;
- fostering teamwork; and
- facilitating development.

People come to their leaders for their knowledge-based expertise, which can be organisational, strategic, financial, technical, legal or transactional. But there is a less obvious expertise they want from their leaders and managers – it is the ability to create an environment in which the best thinking, decision making and problem solving can happen between them. In coaching terms this allows for more than one expert in the room, with the leader helping others to want to discover and figure things out for themselves. But more importantly, people at work want to be listened to, to be heard and to work with a manager who can liberate the expert in them. A core competence for leaders today is to facilitate coaching conversations with individual direct reports as well as with their teams.

One of the hallmarks of a good leader is the wisdom to always know exactly what to do next. And managerial wisdom is difficult to teach – it develops through the use of all four phases of Kolb's (1984:68–69) experiential learning cycle (*concrete experience, reflective observation, abstract conceptualisation, active experimentation*). In one key respect, leading and managing is similar to driving a car or flying an aircraft – the only really effective way of learning is by doing.

Mentoring: domain-specific expertise

Mentoring and coaching are often confused, although they involve very different approaches. The roles of a mentor are to directly share their experience, expertise, advice and wisdom with the "mentee"; to support the "mentee's" learning and development; and to introduce the "mentee" to their network. In keeping with the broad definition of best-practice coaching that is steadily gaining ground, it is arguable that being "directive" by giving advice is the function of a mentor, rather than a coach (Stout-Rostron, 2012b:16). One of the key differences between mentoring and coaching is that in mentoring it is acceptable for the mentor to share advice and expertise regarding their previous handling of a situation – while this is not commonly accepted in best-practice coaching. Also, coaches work with a coaching process that has adult learning and experiential learning as its foundation, and most coach education programmes worldwide support the view that the coach's job is to help the client think through situations in terms of the client's own thinking, feeling and behaviour – not the coach's.

When combined with appropriate training programmes or qualifications in specialised competences, mentoring can be a particularly useful form of support for younger managers learning the ropes. Mentoring is often domain-specific, the mentor working either within the organisation and introducing the mentee to the politics and machinations of that organisation; or the mentor, working within the same field as the mentee, introduces the mentee to their network and professional bodies.

Until recently, with the explosion of technological media, it was accepted that the role of mentor needed to be fulfilled by an older person with greater experience in the same industry and job type as the younger mentee. Today, some mentors are a generation younger than those they are mentoring due to their specific technical expertise. Domain-specific expertise and experience therefore need to be carefully matched between the two parties if mentoring is to work – in addition to compatibility or "chemistry", mutual respect and trust on a personal level. Because today some of the elder, wiser professionals in the business community are being mentored by the younger, technically smarter and more adept newcomers into the workplace, this brings a new challenge to mentoring across every industry.

Counselling and therapy: psychological literacy needed

When things go awry in life, managers invariably benefit from competent counselling, whether professional or non-professional. Counselling is a form of help and support for people troubled by emotional trauma or other personal challenges, involving sympathetic listening and a modicum of advice, usually on a short-term basis, typically in response to a particular event or concern. Some organisations offer counselling support through their system for people, or the coach may recommend the client speak to their medical doctor for a referral.

Counselling generally deals with the personal side of a corporate leader's life, including such issues as bereavement, divorce, substance abuse by themselves or a family member, or dependence issues. Counselling is the "solution of troubling problems through the resolution of dilemmas and the improvement of strategic coping from frustrating, impaired (inadequate) adaptation to competent or normal adaptation" (Rock and Page, 2009:12–13).

Mentoring, in contrast, focuses on the leader's working life. Counsellors (and mentors) need to be able to refer the person involved to an appropriate professional (such as a psychotherapist) for help with more intractable challenges, such as clinical or personality disorders. I consistently advocate, when teaching or supervising coaches, that all coaches need to develop a degree of psychological literacy. This is so they can recommend counselling for immediate issues where healing is required, or therapy to clients who may be suffering from a past wound, or who keep referring back to the past or to events that have yet to be resolved.

What is distinctly different, is that the therapist will interpret and diagnose a client's behaviour. "Psychotherapy is the healing of distressing disorders through relief of suffering and the correction of maladaptive habits, conflicts, attitudes from painful, symptomatic (abnormal) dysfunction to asymptomatic or adequate functionality" (Rock and Page, 2009:12). The coach plays a different role, observing and challenging the client's behaviour to help them to learn, developing an awareness of self, others and the complex system within which they work, at multiple levels.

Where coaching is about learning, therapy is about healing. Although this is an important difference, often confusion arises because coaching can be therapeutic, and in counselling or therapy learning also happens. Coaching is clearly about learning from one's own experience of self and others, developing self-awareness when engaging with and interacting with others. This is particularly important for the leader who needs to improve performance of their team, and to inspire and motivate them in the toughest of times. Rock and Page (2009:12) define coaching as "the optimisation of unrealised potential through the development of talent and the refinement of effective skills from unsatisfying, limited (average) performance to enhanced or outstanding effectiveness".

Coaching: executive, performance, team and peer coaching

A coach often acts as a sounding board, using question frameworks and coaching models to help the corporate leader work out solutions to specific issues (Stout-Rostron, 2012b:16). In Kolb's experiential learning cycle, the role of coaching is to help leaders and managers to reflect on their current corporate experience, so that they work out how to address critical issues facing them. In this way, both "coach and client reflect on the client's experience and behaviours, devising new thinking, feeling, behaviours and actions" to take (Stout-Rostron, 2012b:118).

The issues identified by managers as important topics for coaching sessions could include:

- developing their leadership competences;
- developing, motivating and managing the performance of their teams;
- addressing issues around diversity and corporate culture;
- dealing with workplace conflict and managing difficult people and situations;
- gaining insight into their own personal and professional motivators or drivers;
- coping with high stress levels; and
- balancing business and personal life demands.

There are many different types of business coaching, including:

- executive coaching, developing senior managers and executives to improve their individual performance, and by doing so to optimise organisational results;
- performance coaching, particularly useful for enhancing the competence of line managers and other mid-level corporate leaders;
- team coaching, helpful in boosting the cohesion and effectiveness of functional teams within companies; and
- peer coaching, usually between people at similar levels and in similar jobs within the organisation.

And there are many different coaching models and frameworks to apply within each of the various types of coaching. These models need to be carefully chosen to fit the specific corporate context, and the particular needs of the corporate leaders being coached. I explore a range of models to be used in coaching in Chapters 6 and 7.

For example, the Thinking Partnership® model developed by Nancy Kline (1999) is arguably the purest and most high-level form of coaching, because it is completely and absolutely non-directive. In most forms of best-practice coaching, the coach will directly intervene in the coaching conversation to help catalyse the manager's thinking, by asking a carefully considered and appropriate question that will "unlock" any confusion or blockages. In contrast, a Thinking Partner does not intervene directly in the coaching conversation at all – in fact, they ask only a limited and carefully-defined range of absolutely neutral and non-directive questions. This is because the key principle underpinning the Thinking Environment® model is that the thinker is fully capable of thinking through the issue and working out the solution themselves. The critical role of the Thinking Partner is simply to provide a supportive "thinking environment" within which the thinker is entirely free to think for themselves, without interruption, or prompting, or "help". The only "help" offered is a series of questions to unlock limiting assumptions that may be blocking the thinker's thinking.

Managers are likely to reap greater benefit from coaching (as opposed to training and mentoring) once they are experienced enough to identify and prioritise the issues they need to be coached on. Similarly, corporate leaders are likely to reap the greatest benefit from the Thinking Partnership® once they have achieved the further experience necessary to develop their self-confidence to be free and unfettered thinkers and visionaries.

Corporate leaders and managers need different forms of support at different stages in their career development, and different forms of support to meet particular challenges within each stage. This means that business coaches need to be careful not to oversell the usefulness of their craft – coaching is not a corporate panacea. As Maslow (1966:15) famously remarked, "I suppose it is tempting, if the only tool you have is a hammer, to treat everything as if it were a nail." Good business coaches should know better than that.

CONCLUSION

In this chapter we have defined both business coaching and executive coaching, and looked at the fundamental ways that coaching can help stressed, and over-stretched leaders and managers. Although the potential value of business coaching is unique and increasingly recognised, the industry has not yet clearly defined business coaching, and much confusion remains in the marketplace as to the differences between coaching and the other helping professions. Most of the professional bodies for coaching advocate continued research, and are forming collaborative alliances to develop best-practice coaching services to corporate executives and their teams.

However, until there is more clarity from the professional bodies and the graduate schools of business where the research is taking place, coaches themselves will continue to struggle to sell their services and to develop their own competences at the same level of continuing professional development as the executives with whom they work. Chapter 13 considers options for the future of business coaching.

FURTHER READING

Kline, N. (1999). *Time to Think: A way of being in the world.* London: Ward Lock.

Kline, N. (2009). *More Time to Think: A way of being in the world.* Pool-in-Wharfedale: Fisher King.

Kolb, D.A. (1984). *Experiential Learning: Experience as the source of learning and development.* Upper Saddle River, NJ: Prentice Hall.

Stout-Rostron, S. (2012b). *Business Coaching Wisdom and Practice: Unlocking the Secrets of Business Coaching.* Second edition. Randburg: Knowres.

Stout-Rostron, S. (2014). *Business Coaching International: Transforming individuals and organisations.* Second edition. London: Karnac.

4

How to get the best from your coaching

WHY MIGHT YOU NEED A COACH?

There are many different reasons why you might decide to hire a coach. You might hire a coach exclusively for yourself due to professional difficulties that you are experiencing in the workplace, or because you feel you have become stale in your job and need to move on. Or, through a variety of assessments and executive decisions, the business may have decided to invest in a leadership development programme for the executive team and senior managers to help facilitate succession and performance improvements. Or, it could be that your organisation has embarked on an extensive management development programme across the board, working with supervisors, line managers and executives to complement a change management process, or to develop a new culture, within the organisation. Or, you might be a coach practitioner, or coaching psychologist, who wants to ensure that you are dealing adequately with your professional concerns, and ensuring that you are not being triggered by client issues.

The list is as long as there are organisations who wish to improve performance, enhance communication, break down silos, manage complexity, transition into a new culture based on re-visioned values ... any number of reasons. What is crucially important, is that you, as an individual, take an active part in understanding what the organisation requires in terms of performance and behaviour, what your individual needs are, and how the two can be dovetailed to match.

I would strongly recommend reading a few articles or books on coaching to understand how it will help you, or speaking to any of the members of your team or organisation who might be adopting a coaching approach in their management style. One of the best books to begin with is John Whitmore's (2002) *Coaching for Performance*.

What would a coach do for you?

As Chapter 3 explains, one of the best ways to think of a coach is that they operate as a thinking partner for you. Their job isn't to fix you, or to give you answers that you and your team need to find for yourselves, or even to condone what actions or decisions you think should be taken to improve the business. Their job is to challenge your thinking, to make observations on your behaviour and the way you engage with the world, and to observe how they experience you and how they notice others experiencing you.

Your coach may ask you to complete a 360° feedback survey as you begin your journey together. I highly recommend this is done manually through face-to-face interviews whenever possible – as a way to create a picture of how others at every level experience working alongside you. The face-to-face interviews give the coach an idea of the systemic issues operating within the system as well. The role of the coach is also to help you identify your blind spots, and to understand how others experience those blind spots, and to assist you in dealing with them constructively.

How can you assess whether business coaching is for you?

What is your reason for working with a business coach? As a manager or executive, you do not leave your personal life behind when you walk into work. You are simply stepping into another role or function that frames who you are. So it follows that business coaches cannot be effective without looking at clients holistically. A business coach primarily helps you to identify your core purpose, strategies, developmental objectives, strengths, weaknesses and obstacles to overcome. Business coaching takes in all aspects of your life, from the meaning and purpose of the work that you are doing, to managing the people, processes and systems for which you are responsible, helping you to create some balance between work and personal life. But don't be fooled. We spend two-thirds of our day at work, and one-third at home – there is already an imbalance between work and personal life which needs to be managed well.

A business coach encourages you to think for yourself and to develop an awareness of your own conscious and unconscious behaviours, which may be influencing your performance in the workplace. Business coaching is essentially about the results experienced through the dynamic relationship that develops between you and your coach, and how those results impact on your own individual performance.

The coach may chat to you about the importance of adult and experiential learning which takes place in the business coaching process. The coach will help you to probe the essence of an experience to understand its significance, and the learning to be gained from it. However, ultimately, business coaching needs to be aligned with all the leadership, management and talent development initiatives within the organisation.

WHAT DO YOU NEED TO BRING TO THE COACHING SESSION?

You need to bring yourself – all of you – authentically. You need to take responsibility and accountability for what you bring to the coaching conversation: what you want to think about, talk about and work on. Working with a coach is not a superficial exercise. You need your cognitive, emotional, and spiritual intelligences all to be operating as you delve into developing greater self-awareness, greater awareness of how you manage interactions with others, what your understanding is of your contribution to, and influence on, the culture and the system within which you work, and also what are the systemic issues and your engagement with them.

How will the coaching process unfold?

Traditionally, coaching has been one-on-one and face-to-face. However, today, due to the growth and popularity of the internet and social media, many coaches work with clients on the telephone, Skype or Google, telephone bridge lines through their organisation, or WebEx if they need to show slides or presentations. Email coaching is also growing in popularity, although I have my concerns about it – with email it is harder to access the dimension of emotional intelligence, and the physical dimension of face-to-face engagement is missing. This physical dimension is an important aspect in developing rapport. However, one of the positives in working with a system such as Skype or Google is that you can see your coach face-to-face on the screen. It adds to the physical dimension of being together.

Group coaching, face-to-face, is also becoming an economical choice for organisations who want their managers to engage in coaching, but who don't have the budget for one-on-one coaching. You, your organisation and your coach will choose the type of coaching most relevant to your budget, your needs and the organisation's requirements.

How you structure your sessions will also best serve you and the organisation's needs. Typically you might work every other week, or on a monthly basis with your coach. I prefer to work every two or three weeks with my clients, and gradually stretch it out to a monthly or six-weekly basis. That ensures there is time to process and work on goals set in the early stages of the coaching process, and also most executives have very full schedules. Contracts tend to stretch from six to 12 months with a request for a Leadership Development Plan to be created in association with your line manager. You would be wise to engage during the entire coaching intervention at least once or twice with your line manager to ensure your professional goal setting is in line with organisational vision and strategy. You will certainly have your own personal and professional goals, but you will want to ensure that you include the goals the organisation expects from you.

When you meet with your coach and line manager, you only need share over-arching goals, achievements to date, and the process with which you are working. You never need share the conversation itself – that is a confidential conversation between you and your coach. However, it is useful to have a three-way conversation with your line manager to understand expectations for the entire coaching intervention. What is critically important is to identify your own values and where they are in alignment or misalignment with the company.

When you set goals, you will only achieve them if they are in alignment with your intrinsic drivers – values, beliefs and feelings that motivate you and help you to stretch yourself to learn, grow and reach your potential. Internal motivators are the drive within each of us; at their roots are your core values and beliefs. Key motivators at work include achievement, life balance, peace of mind, recognition, a higher purpose, and affiliation. Extrinsic motivators are when someone else tries to hook our internal drivers, to encourage us or to make us want to do something. Examples of extrinsic motivators are environment, feedback, recognition and titles, salaries and benefits, titles, education and training.

We need to link our goals to our intrinsic drivers. To understand those intrinsic drivers ask yourself these questions. Remember that we are looking for the intangibles that are qualitative and that we cannot measure:

- What's important to you personally and professionally?
- What is important about that?
- What else if anything is important to you?

These intrinsic drivers tend to be subjective and qualitative, such as achieving my potential, making a difference, honesty and integrity, family, and friendship. They are not goals which are measurable and quantitative, such as attaining the highest position in the company, or an increase in salary, or a promotion.

Your coach may suggest that you keep a learning journal. One of my clients used his notebook from front to back for notes taken during the coaching session; he also included the topics he wanted to work on with me for each new session. From back to front, he jotted down his reflections, thoughts, concerns, achievements and anxieties in between sessions.

What could be the final results?

Working with a coach means going on a journey of self-discovery. It is a journey into who you are, how you be who you are, building an understanding of how people experience you in your day-to-day professional and personal lives. It is a chance to reflect, develop a more mindful approach to your work, and to ask yourself the hard questions that you avoid in the busyness of your working day. The space with your coach is where you can bring your authentic self – letting go of the need to play a role and to have all the answers. It is the place to explore your own personal and professional concerns, shout about your achievements and identify and work constructively on your blind spots. I look at the time with my coach, and my coach supervisor, as a gift. A gift of time to reflect, to sit back and take stock of where I am now, where I am going – what is in my way, and to ask how I am creating the path forward or blocking my own way.

WHAT FORM OF SUPPORT DO YOU REALLY NEED?

As you continue on your journey with your coach, you will begin to understand the depth and importance of relationships, and how those relationships contribute to your own success. You will begin to consider who else you need to support you, and what other forms of support you need. Your coach's aim is to work themselves out of their job from the first day they begin working with you. They will walk alongside you, attend meetings with you, even shadow you to events and observe your presentations – but one day the contract will end. Your aim is to become a self-organised learner, able to create your own learning ground, and to eventually mentor and coach those you manage. You may want to bring in other forms of support, letting your family, boss and colleagues know that you are working with a coach – asking them at various times to comment on any changes they notice (for the better!).

Finding the right coach and knowing what to look for

So how do you go about finding the right coach? There are a number of ways. You can have your HR or OD department find a few coaches for you to interview. Or, if you have an internal suite of coaches available in your organisation, ask your HR or OD manager to recommend who might be most relevant for you. If unsure, you can always identify the coaching bodies in your region, looking at their website for coaches with the experience and expertise you require. One of the best ways to find a coach is to listen to other colleagues' experiences and find out who they recommend. There are a number of different qualities that you might look for in a business coach.

Coach competences

As you begin to research to find yourself a coach, it is useful to understand the competences that the various coaching bodies advocate for their professional coaches. The European Mentoring and Coaching Council (EMCC) competency framework recommends the following competences:

- *Understanding self.* Demonstrate awareness of own values, beliefs and behaviours, recognise how these affect their practice and use this self-awareness to manage their effectiveness in meeting the client's, and where relevant, the sponsor's objectives.
- *Commitment to self-development.* Explore and improve the standard of their practice and maintain the reputation of the profession.
- *Managing the contract.* Establish and maintains the expectations and boundaries of the coaching contract with the client and, where appropriate, with sponsors.
- *Building the relationship.* Skilfully build and maintain an effective relationship with the client, and where appropriate, with the sponsor.
- *Enabling insight and learning.* Work with the client and sponsor to bring about insight and learning.
- *Outcome and action orientation.* Demonstrate approach, and use the skills, in supporting the client to make desired changes.
- *Use of models and techniques.* Apply models and tools, techniques and ideas beyond the core communication skills in order to bring about insight and learning.
- *Evaluation.* Gather information on the effectiveness of their practice and contribute to establishing a culture of evaluation of outcomes (EMCC, 2010).

The Worldwide Association of Business Coaches WABC *Professional Standards for Business Coaches* recommend that the business coach–client interaction embraces:

- professionalism and ethics;
- client focus;
- business and organisational context;

- business coaching process and contracting factors affecting the coaching intervention, i.e. boundaries, confidentiality, diversity, responsibility and respect; and
- developing the profession: professional development, and promotion of the profession (WABC, 2013).

The International Coach Federation (ICF) recommends the following core professional competences:

- *Setting the foundation*:
  - meeting ethical guidelines and professional standards; and
  - establishing the coaching agreement.

- *Co-creating the relationship*:
  - establishing trust and intimacy with the client; and
  - coaching presence.

- *Communicating effectively*:
  - active listening;
  - powerful questioning; and
  - direct communication.

- *Facilitating learning and results*:
  - creating awareness;
  - designing actions;
  - planning and goal setting; and
  - managing progress and accountability (ICF, 2008a).

You will have a range of experiences as you begin to work with your coach. It is always useful to start with a series of professional management assessment profiles which identify your working preferences, personality traits, communication and management strengths and weaknesses, blind spots and areas for development. This is the beginning stage to develop greater self-awareness, and to understand how you engage with others, for better or worse! For some it is the beginning of a roller coaster ride as they begin to get in touch with how they think and feel, and begin to understand how their direct reports, colleagues and customers experience them.

There are many books on leadership and management, and this isn't the place for me to elucidate some of the ways that you may develop. However, it is important to recognise that the coaching conversation is the space where you can explore, in great depth with your coach, why people react to you in the way they do, and why you may not be achieving the performance you desire for yourself and others. The more you can understand how you think, feel, act and make decisions, the more in tune with yourself you are, the greater will be your understanding of how to motivate and inspire others who work with and for you.

WHAT VALUE CAN YOU EXPECT FROM THE COACHING INTERVENTION?

The value you take out of your coaching sessions depends entirely on the energy that you put into it. I have clients who arrive at the coaching session with one particular issue to work on, or with a variety of concerns or events that are troubling them. Sometimes you will simply reflect on what is changing in the way you chair team meetings or customer meetings, manage conflict situations or engage with staff in your management by walk-about. Other times you may be perplexed by the lack of decision-making processes within your team, or even be unsure what decision-making processes are useful for different contexts.

The complexity and stresses that exist in current working environments with corporate matrix structures, deeply engrained silo mentalities, communication difficulties, competition and jealousy, even corruption and fraud, alongside your own management and leadership competence gaps, ensure that there is never a shortage of issues for you to engage in. Use your journal and your last session with your coach as a guide, always bringing your own experience into the coaching session from which to gain your best learning.

Spend a few minutes prior to each coaching session thinking about what has taken place recently that has gone well unexpectedly, or an event or individual you found difficult to manage – and bring other questions to the session that you are constantly asking yourself. Be sure to share with your coach your stream of consciousness thinking, and the voice in your head that talks to you from morning till night. The coaching conversation helps you to reframe your own experience and gain wisdom from it.

Understanding the importance of EQ

One of the things I have noticed in my coaching sessions with clients is that they are not aware of what may be useful to bring to a coaching session. There are four areas to consider which relate to the Emotional Intelligence (EQ) Model discussed in Chapter 7. The EQ Model developed by Daniel Goleman (1996) usually starts with addressing questions about self-awareness and self-management, moving to develop relationship awareness and relationship management at a systemic level (i.e. teams working with teams, or the organisation working with the wider community).

All of the following qualities are worth talking about and bringing into your conversations with your coach. It is your responsibility to bring issues, concerns, achievements, successes, failures, developmental progress, interpersonal challenges such as giving feedback or public speaking, lack of confidence in specific areas, and progress towards achieving your overarching goals.

Self-awareness

The first is *self-awareness*. *Self-awareness is about knowing yourself, understanding your own resistance to situations, and having a deep understanding of your purpose.* How aware are you of your own blind spots in terms of how you think, what you feel and how you behave? What have you begun to notice about yourself in relation to your own thinking and feeling in easy or difficult situations. What behaviour do you default to when you are not thinking? And how aware are you of what you say and do, as you engage with others? In other words, how aware are you of what you say and do, what you sound like, and the way you engage with others?

Self-management

The second area is *self-management*. *Self-management is how you engage with others, your interpersonal behaviour, communication and management skills.* How are people experiencing you as you engage with them? How are you engaging with others in talking, managing, negotiating, dealing with conflict and giving feedback – and how are you engaging with others on a good day, as well as on a bad day? What behaviours bring success, and which behaviours sabotage your success? This will apply to every interaction you have on a daily basis. Who do you show favouritism to, who do you exclude from conversations or meetings, and who do you never engage with? And who are you not engaging with that is of critical importance to you and your organisation's success – such as networking and creating visibility through public speaking or the attendance of professional social or business events?

Relationship awareness

The third area is *relationship awareness*. *Relationship awareness is understanding the organisational culture (values, beliefs, feelings), the environment, and being aware of the politics operating within your organisation.* What is the culture and what are the values and beliefs which underpin how the organisation operates, and what are the diverse relationships which operate concurrently within the organisation? What are the unspokens in the working environment? They relate to values, culture and diversity issues that lie below the surface, and which might not be openly spoken about. How are you contributing to the values and culture in the way you speak, behave and engage with superiors, direct reports, customers and the wider community within which you live? How are you actually living the values of the organisation? And what issues exist within your team that need to be addressed, and spoken about openly to ensure a more transparent and collaborative culture? What is needed from you to make this happen?

Relationship management

The fourth area is *relationship management*. *Relationship management is about team behaviour and client management, conflict management and the integration of the systems within the organisation or those linking you to the wider community.* These relate to the interaction of all the systems within the organisation. What is your responsibility in ensuring that different divisions engage positively with each other, and what influence do you have on the organisation to make a positive contribution to your community at large? How does your behaviour influence the team, and how does the team influence the organisation? What is working and what needs to change? This might be something as core to the success of the business as the way you facilitate meetings across all units or divisions, or how your customer call centres manage their interactions with customers. What influence do you have – and how aware are you of it?

Why do you need to shop for a best-practice business coach?

"Best practice" is a set of guidelines, ethics or ideas that represent the most effective, efficient or prudent course of action. It can be a technique or methodology that, through experience and research, has proven to reliably lead to a desired result. Hence our need as coaches and leaders for standards, ethics, competences – and levels of practice.

However, in coaching there are no universally accepted set of operational standards or best-practice guidelines. The coaching bodies and providers of coaching set the standard of practice, and the client organisations make the choice of coach and type of service provided. You, as the user of the service, determine the quality of service required, and as a result there is an increased need for regulation and standardisation across the market. For this reason, coaching bodies are working together through national, regional and worldwide representation to find common ground (Stout-Rostron, 2009).

Both your coach and you, as the client, are constantly moving towards "mastery of practice". Mastery is comprehensive knowledge or skill in a subject or practice; it is the action or process of mastering a subject of accomplishment. For you it might be mastery of leadership. Coaching practice is moving towards a craftsperson's view of professional practice – blending science and art in pursuit of conscious mastery to become a scientist-practitioner (Lane, Stelter and Stout-Rostron, 2009:341). However, something I have learned from my mentor, Nancy Kline, is that when you as the client and the coach both enter the coaching space – there are *two* experts in the room. We need to give up the idea that the coach, as the "professional", is the one with the answers. Rather look at the coach as the "expert" who brings out the "expert" in the client.

Working with assumptions helps us to develop mastery at different levels in our working life. To do so, we need to understand the general levels of thought that we engage in on a daily basis. Your ongoing narrative is organised by three general levels of thought:

- *Automatic thoughts*: These are on the surface, and are like short tapes that flash through your mind; they are a form of "self-talk" which you use throughout the day.

- *Assumptions*: Are positioned midway between automatic thoughts and your core beliefs; they act as a translation between the two.
- *Core beliefs*: Develop over time, usually from childhood and through the experience of significant life events or particular life circumstances. They are the very essence of how we see ourselves, other people, the world and the future (Nathan, Lim and Correia, 2004).

Developing mastery: working with assumptions

The following exercises help us to understand our deeper levels of assumptions that can limit or liberate us and help us to develop mastery of practice.

A challenge

- What has gone well for you in your life, and what is a challenge you have successfully faced, and how have you faced it?
- What were you positively assuming about yourself as you faced that challenge?
- What is a decision you have made at a turning point in your life or career, and what were you positively assuming about yourself and how life works before making that decision?

Working with liberating assumptions

- What are you assuming about yourself as a leader that motivates and inspires you?
- What are you assuming that gets in your way?
- And what would be a more credible, liberating alternative that would take you the next step?

Your next challenging step

This exercise designed by Nancy Kline helps us to step powerfully into our next challenge.

> What challenging step do you want to take in your life or work right now?
>
> What might you be assuming that is stopping you from taking that step?
>
> I am assuming that ...
>
> What else might you be assuming that is stopping you from taking that step?
>
> I am assuming that ...
>
> What are you assuming that is most stopping you from taking that step?
>
> I am assuming that ...
>
> What would you credibly have to assume instead in order to take that step?
>
> If you knew that [new assumption] how would you take that step? (Kline, 2012).

WHAT CAN YOU DO IF IT DOESN'T WORK OUT FOR YOU?

Lipkin (2013:236–237) reflects at length on areas in which she had resisted change as a leader, noting three simple rules:

- seek self-awareness;
- help others to gain self-awareness; and
- remember we're only human after all.

She talks about her formula to get back on track, which is to:

- admit the problem;
- recognise that my thoughts and actions contribute to the problem;
- identify the cause of those thoughts and actions;
- detect the cognitive biases involved;
- think up new ways to manage the causes and biases;
- adjust my leadership approach accordingly;
- make amends with the people I hurt;
- and expect to make more mistakes but strive to deal with them differently (Lipkin, 2013:236–237).

So, there are a number of things that help us to consider how you can approach your coaching sessions:

- Are you bringing the right or the most important issues about people, goals, strategy and process to your coaching sessions?
- Have you been able to develop rapport and a good working relationship with your coach?
- Are you having sessions with enough frequency to make the best of your own development?
- Have you created a leadership development plan which reflects your strengths and areas for development?
- Are you bringing your authentic self to the coaching conversation, or are you treating the conversation as a nice-to-have without commitment to your own ongoing development?

These are important questions to consider. If you are unhappy with your coach, then you might like to let your HR or OD division or your sponsor know that you would prefer another practitioner, and ask them to recommend a few people for you to interview.

Are you willing to break out from your current mental models and create a realistic and visionary future for yourself? If so, what are the skills and competences you need to develop? How are you helping your direct reports, peers and stakeholders to think individually and independently for themselves – in order to inspire new ideas and innovation within the workplace?

My research has shown that a diversified workplace today needs to be driven by sustainable values, such as trust, integrity, bringing heart into relationships, health and work–life balance. And people want to have a reason, a purpose and mission in their working lives today. Not only do they want an interesting job, they want to know they are contributing to something bigger than themselves – and often something that will make a difference to their community or society. Are you working on your meaning and purpose with your coach – what is important to you about your job, and your personal life?

Values exercise

- Of all the values that most matter to you, which are most important in your professional practice?
- Which values do you leave at home that you could use at work? And which values do you leave at work that you could use at home?

How are you using your coaching sessions to think about and build sustainable policies which will impact positive change in your own organisation? What impact is your coaching, and that of your direct reports and peers, having on systemic change within your organisation? How is your coaching helping you to *rethink*, *renew* and *inspire new possibilities* for yourself? What do you need to shift in yourself to help make this happen? In other words, what is your personal commitment to yourself?

CONCLUSION

We've looked at the many reasons that you might want to find a business coach, and there are a number of different qualities that you might look for. As you begin your research to find a coach, it is useful to understand the competences that the various coaching bodies advocate for their professional coaches. Know that both you and your coach will constantly move towards "mastery of practice".

We've also talked about what is your responsibility in the coaching conversation – bringing issues, concerns, achievements, successes, failures, developmental progress, and interpersonal challenges to the conversation. The time with your coach is a gift. It is a time to reflect, to sit back and take stock of where you are now, where you are going – and how you can consistently create a path forward. Remember the importance of using your journal from your sessions with your coach as a guide, always bringing your own experience into the coaching session from which to gain your best learning. The value you take out of your coaching sessions depends entirely on the thought and the energy that you put into it.

FURTHER READING

Goleman, D. (1996). *Emotional Intelligence: Why it can matter more than IQ*. London: Bloomsbury.

Goleman, D., Boyatzis, R., and McKee, A. (2002). *Primal Leadership: Learning to lead with emotional intelligence*. Boston, MA: Harvard Business School.

Kline, N. (1999). *Time to Think: Listening to ignite the human mind*. London: Ward Lock.

Kline, N. (2009). *More Time to Think: A way of being in the world*. Pool-in-Wharfedale: Fisher King.

Lipkin, N. (2013). *What Keeps Leaders Up At Night? Recognising and resolving your most troubling management issues*. New York, NY: American Management Association.

Stout-Rostron, S. (2009). The global initiatives in the coaching field. *Coaching: An International Journal of Theory, Research and Practice*, 2(1):76–85.

Stout-Rostron, S. (2011a). How is coaching impacting systemic and cultural change within organisations? *International Journal of Coaching in Organisations*, 8(4):5–27.

Whitmore, J. (2002). *Coaching for Performance: Growing people, performance and purpose*. London: Nicholas Brealey.

5

The business coaching conversation

THE BUSINESS COACHING PROCESS

The business coaching process is one that helps business executives and leaders to develop a clear understanding of their roles and responsibilities. Another aspect is about developing a greater depth of self-awareness, emotional intelligence and a deeper understanding of how to tap into the intrinsic drivers of direct reports – to motivate and inspire their thinking and performance. Business coaching is about high performance, and ultimately about sustained behavioural change and breakthrough results.

Some practitioners have had a difficult time differentiating coaching from other areas of practice or approaches, because coaches themselves have tended to define it very loosely in terms of a wide range of practices currently applied under the name "coaching". A further reason is that some coaching providers see themselves more as business consultants, with their consulting services structured around the coaching process (Stout-Rostron, 2012b:40).

An alliance between coach, client and organisation

The coaching conversation provides a "thinking environment" where business professionals are able to develop self-awareness and a depth of understanding of themselves and others – embedding newly-acquired skills, competences and attitudes which subsequently impact the actions they take, and visibly demonstrate new behaviours. This section explores five aspects of the coaching conversation, and defines the business coaching conversation as an alliance between coach, client and organisation which is designed to maximise and transform thinking, behaviour and performance:

- achieving desired outcomes;
- the psychology of goals and motivation;
- learning from experience and client stories;
- listening, equality and the genuine encounter; and
- measuring results.

The critical value of business coaching is in helping the individual executive to think clearly about the core issues which present challenges to them in their career, their organisation, their job, and their daily working life. It has been challenging to find one authoritative definition of coaching in the marketplace, not just because every professional body has its own slant on the coaching process, but because there is as yet no agreed global definition. Through my research, I have defined coaching as "a process that creates sustained shifts in thinking, feeling and behaviour – and ultimately in performance. By asking the right questions, coaches help clients find their own solutions".

The focus of a coaching conversation is then to help the client work towards achieving their desired outcomes. It is in this process of reflection, where coach and client reflect on the client's experience, that potential for learning and action emerges. The coach primarily explores with each client what it is that is holding back or preventing the client from achieving their goals, for example by identifying and replacing disempowering assumptions and paradigms with empowering ones.

The psychology of goals and motivation

Business coaching is essentially a one-on-one collaborative partnership to develop the client's performance and potential, personally and professionally, in alignment with the goals and values of the organisation. Business coaching should be aligned strategically with the overall values and objectives of an organisation.

However, an important question is raised for executives: if goals are to be motivationally achieved, are they also aligned with the individual's values, beliefs and feelings? Often organisations merely pay lip service to organisational values, and don't necessarily create them as a synthesis of the core individual values which make up the culture of the organisation. Ethical dilemmas can arise during the coaching process if the executive needs to make difficult choices which are incompatible with their own value system.

Goals and motivation

If you wish to help your clients to improve their behaviour and performance, it is useful to understand the psychology behind adult behaviour, goals and motivation. Alfred Adler, who worked with Freud for ten years, reasoned that adult behaviour is purposeful and goal-directed, and that life goals provide individual motivation. He focused on personal values, beliefs, attitudes, goals and interests, and recommended that adults engage in the therapeutic process using goal setting and reinventing their future, using techniques such as "acting as if", role-playing and goal setting (Stout-Rostron, 2012:26). All these tools are utilised and recognised by well-qualified business coaches worldwide.

Motivational theories primarily focus on the individual's needs and motivations. I have typically worked with coaching clients to help them understand more fully their intrinsic motivators (internal drivers such as values, beliefs, and feelings), and how to use extrinsic motivators (external drivers such as relationships, bonuses, the environment, and titles) to motivate their teams. If an individual's goals are not in alignment with their own internal, intrinsic drivers, there will be difficulties for them in achieving those goals.

A study by Griffiths and Campbell (2008) confirms that coaches often assume clients are aware of their values, but within the confines of the study this assumption appeared to be incorrect. The coaching clients interviewed indicated that they were not aware of their own values, and that acquiring a process of awareness and reflection led them to become more aware of their emotions and values, and of the need to clarify their goals and align these with their values, beliefs and feelings. Whitmore (2002) supports this, and states that the goal of the coach is to build awareness, responsibility and self-belief.

The coach's intervention and questions help the client to discover their own intrinsic drivers or motivators, and help both coach and client to identify whether the client's personal, professional and organisational goals are in alignment.

Ryan (2013) talks about how a coach can support motivation for change. He asks, "What do people really need to flourish?" and explains that, "Not unlike a plant that needs water and sunlight to thrive, the human psyche has some nutrients that it needs to survive. It's in our nature to flourish – to flourish is to develop, to become both more differentiated and integrated, and to become fully functioning; but it is by no means automatic. It requires nutrients. And those nutrients are the three conditions that facilitate intrinsic motivation:

- *Autonomy*: which means absence of pressure, goal choice, strategy choice, task involvement, and promotion of task interest.
- *Competence*: which indicates optimal challenge, positive feedback, and informational rewards.
- *Relatedness*: which includes empathy, warmth, and acknowledgement of emotions".

He explains that "outcomes associated with high *autonomous* motivation are: greater persistence, more flexibility and creativity, better heuristic performance, more interest and enjoyment, better mental health and wellbeing, better physical health, and a higher quality of close personal relationships. These functional effects are apparent across the life span, across genders, and across cultures" (Ryan, 2013).

However, relationships which are universally rated as the most important value are often neglected in school, medical clinics and work climates. Ryan (2013) explains that "relationships are enhanced by supporting another's autonomy, and competence. When in good relationships you want to do well. It's so important to motivation".

For coaches and leaders wondering why they feel great when motivating, helping and encouraging their clients or direct reports, Ryan explains that "receiving autonomy support improves your wellbeing, but if you are the one giving the support then all three of these basic needs (autonomy, relatedness and competence) are met. Helping studies also indicate that the helper feels more positive, more vitality and more self-esteem. And the recipient of help somehow picks up on that willingness to help and feel more vitality. If someone resentfully helps you then you don't feel good about yourself" (Ryan, 2013). These three basic psychological goals are crucial to intrinsic motivation whether you are coaching or mentoring.

Types of goal

The coach is responsible for ensuring that goal-setting conversations get the best results. O'Neill (2000) differentiates between two kinds of client goals, *business and personal*, and links the coaching effort to a business result, highlighting and prioritising the business areas that need attention. According to O'Neill, business goals are about achieving external results; personal goals are what the leader has to do differently in the way they conduct themselves in order to get the business results they envision. This indicates the importance of developing self-awareness in the coaching conversation, as well as developing an understanding of how others actually experience being and working with the executive – two foundation stones of emotional intelligence, self-awareness and self-management.

Yalom talks about two types of goals: *content* (what is to be accomplished), and *process* goals (how the coach wants to be in a session). He describes the importance of setting concrete attainable goals – goals that the client has personally defined, and which increase their sense of responsibility for their own individual change (Yalom, 1980).

Developmental goal setting

If the client is to learn how to learn, they need to cultivate self-awareness through reflection on their experience, values, intrinsic drivers, the impact of these on others, the environment, and on their own future goals. This process is often implicit in the coaching relationship through the process of questions that develop critical reflection, and subsequent actions that develop practice. As a coach, or leader working with a coaching approach, you will be asking questions to help clients or direct reports to reflect, review and gain useable knowledge from their experience. A useful structure for your work with business executives is along the continuum of a development pipeline (Hicks and Peterson, 1999). Your questions and challenges in your coaching sessions can help your clients or direct reports reflect in each of these five areas:

- *Insight*: How are you continually developing insight into areas where you need to develop?
- *Motivation*: What are your levels of motivation based on the time and energy you're willing to invest in yourself?
- *Capabilities*: What are your leadership capabilities; what skills, knowledge and competence do you still need to develop?
- *Real-world practice*: How are you continually applying your new skills at work?
- *Accountability*: How are you creating, defining and taking accountability?

Often within the complexity of the organisational environment, the client's overarching goals may be set by a more senior power, and that senior individual may have different worldviews and paradigms, and differing limiting and empowering assumptions. It is crucial that the client has a "living sense" of what their goal may be (Spinelli, 1989). In other words, goals must be aligned with the values of the individual, as much as with the values of the organisation, if they are to be achieved.

Learning from experience and client stories

Learning, and particularly learning from experience, seems to be one of the major components of the coaching conversation. Learning from experience implies an understanding of the language and content of the client's story, with the coach helping the client to reconstruct their own reality by searching for meaning through dialogue.

There is so much power in the client's language and the content of their stories, that the significance of the client's story comes from both the structure of their telling it, as well as the interpretation and significance given. In some cultures, for example in Latin America, Africa and India, oral history and storytelling remain very important methods of passing on ritual, tradition and customs. The coaching conversation can literally be seen as an extension of "telling one's story" and looking for meaning and significance in the telling.

With this as a precedent, we can look at the "coaching conversation" not just as experiential learning, but as experiential education: learning from one's own life experiences. These definitions suggest that *learning* is the key. This indicates that helping your clients grow, develop and become who they want to be, requires asking for their best thinking, rather than sharing yours. The four levels of coaching intervention with which we are working as coaches are interconnected:

- Doing: *What* tasks and goals need to be accomplished?
- Learning: *How* will you develop the competences needed?
- Way of Being: *Who* are you as you grow and develop; how do you do you? (Weiss, 2004).
- Transforming Self: *Who* are you stepping into becoming as you grow and develop? (Stout-Rostron, 2013).

Listening, equality and the genuine encounter

The structure of the coaching intervention needs to be framed by the coach's ability to listen, and to actively intervene only when needed. *Listening*, *asking questions* and *silence* are core skills for the business coach – as they help to create safety for clients within the external physical environment, as well as enhancing the client's internal thinking environment.

It is also important that the coach–client relationship be based on an assumption of equality. In a coaching relationship, neither coach nor client is superior to the other; both are professionals who bring their experience and expertise together to travel on the client's journey. A "safe thinking environment" is built through the development of this coach–client relationship, and research shows that the relationship is what can help with the onset of change (Stout-Rostron, 2006:80). This is more difficult for a leader developing a coaching approach, who will be working with subordinates. A way to view the coaching conversation then is that both superior and subordinate come into the conversation as professional equals. This has been shown to be of the utmost importance when developing rapport between coach and client, or leader and direct report.

However, in either situation, if coach and client, or leader and direct report is incapable of forming a more meaningful relationship than mere social interaction, then the coaching conversation is bound to fail. I recently experienced such an interaction with a client who was unable to access or to share more than his superficial thoughts and feelings; for this reason it was impossible to continue the interaction as the deeper work of change could not take place. Thoughts and feelings impact behaviour, and visible behaviour change is required within the corporate environment as a result of the overall coaching intervention. Visible behaviour change is impacted from a deeper level of growing self-awareness and mindful reflection within the coachee.

This is the level of conversation where the process of change ultimately becomes possible; it is what Yalom (2001:92) describes as the "genuine encounter". Based on my doctoral research (Stout-Rostron, 2006) the coach's interventions help to build the relationship which then lead to shifts in thinking and feeling – and, ultimately, in behaviour and performance. One of the results of my research is the conclusion that what happens is predominantly a result of the continually developing relationship between client and coach.

Measuring results

In working with an individual client, there is no point in simply developing a leadership plan in isolation from the rest of the business processes. If the coaching intervention is to be successful in organisations, it is critical to develop a systemic, fully integrated coaching strategy that is in alignment with both the business and the talent strategies for the organisation. Moreover, in the business context, results are often measured in three specific areas: behavioural change, improved performance, and the individual's personal and professional development (Ting and Scisco, 2006:58–59).

Any leadership or management development strategy which includes individual and/or team coaching needs to be aligned with the client organisation's performance and business strategy. This includes the required behaviours, values, capabilities and competences which have been identified for a wide range of leadership and management roles. Often an organisation will be redefining their leadership brand through a comprehensive range of leadership development programmes implemented and measured over a one- to three-year period, complemented by an executive coaching intervention.

One of the main reasons for this is that leaders and managers need to be enabled to better facilitate quality conversations one-on-one with their direct reports, in team meetings, and with stakeholders and customers. Often, prior to implementing a *leadership development programme*, a client organisation will already have identified the sets of behaviours which will help to create a results focus and performance orientation. The *individual coaching interventions* can be introduced with a range of *assessment profiles* to help with goal setting and leadership development planning, followed by a *team coaching intervention* to include those executives not taking part in the individual interventions. This three-tier approach can address the emergent needs of management within an organisation, but at every stage visible behaviour change and performance need to be measured.

The business coach's job continues to be one of facilitating insight, which leads to observable behavioural change impacting on performance. This is because organisations expect to see clear, effective deliverables. What is most important is that business coaches understand the imperative on behalf of the organisation, to see *clear behaviour change* and *performance improvement*. What has yet to be identified is the third factor, which is the impact of these two elements on successful *relationship building* within the workplace.

Can coaching produce sustainable behavioural change?

Until we have reliable research from a wide variety of organisations, no one can guarantee that behaviour change is truly sustainable as a result of coaching. However, based on research currently available, there are certainly guidelines for coaching that can help ensure that behaviour change is indeed sustainable.

To address this question, I have spent the last ten years researching how the coaching conversation helps the client to make breakthrough shifts in thinking, feeling and behaviour that significantly impact their performance at work. An equally important question is: how can we actually measure the effectiveness of the coaching intervention – is it just through sustained behavioural change and improved performance? Influencing factors are the client's cultural worldview and the individual assumptions that drive their behaviour.

OUR OWN CULTURAL FRAMEWORK

Our understanding and relationship with the world takes place within our own cultural framework. Because our relation to things is determined by our own individual experiences, intentions and assumptions, our worldview does not necessarily align with those of our peers. This is one of the primary motivations for coaching as clients try to align their own cultural worldview with that of the organisation within which they work.

Coaching practitioners either work with an existing coaching model, or develop their own individual model to look at their individual client's concerns in a structural way. Instead of seeing everything as the client's personal, emotional or internal issue, problems can be seen as part of an overall situation or worldview. It is important that coaches adopt a structural approach that is flexible and suitable to the client and the context. In Chapters 6 and 7 we discuss specific models which can be successfully adapted to the coaching conversation and the overall coaching intervention.

Assumptions and existential issues

Because coaching is a relationship-based process, the coach must be as aware of their own potential assumptions as well as those of the client. Ideally, coaches must divest themselves of their own limiting paradigms, so that they can more effectively question and probe the client's articulated reality and assumptions. This is one of the key purposes of coach supervision, to ensure that the coach has developed a large degree of self-awareness and emotional intelligence, and is not triggered in any way by the issues that beset the individual client with whom they are working.

In existential philosophy, all human beings must create meaning for their own lives. Existentialism stresses freedom of choice and taking responsibility for one's actions. Existential issues that arise in the coaching conversation, such as "freedom", "meaning and purpose" and "choice", are aligned to anxiety. From an existential standpoint, clients can find themselves in a crisis when decisions have to be made that may fundamentally impact their lives. This requires the coach to be conscious of their own fallibility as they probe the client's articulated reality or interpretation of their own experience. Empowering and disempowering assumptions underlie what people say and do, and the coach's fallibility is part of that process.

An existential goal is that of living a "whole life": this is to approach the client as a whole, professionally and personally, working with emotional, rational and spiritual intelligence to understand how they impact self-awareness, self-management, cultural competence and social awareness. Zohar and Marshall (2001), authors of *Spiritual Intelligence*, define spiritual intelligence (SQ) as the intelligence we use to imagine how things could be better. SQ is what we use to transform situations, to look for meaning in our lives, to find a sense of purpose.

Working with the client in the coaching conversation, from this point of view, is about helping clients come to a new way of understanding themselves and their interaction with the world and all the systems of which they are a part.

Guidelines for sustainable behavioural change

Based on my own doctoral research, here is a brief description of ten key coaching guidelines for achieving sustainable behavioural change which impact performance. In the next section I will explore these ten guidelines further:

- *Build the relationship.* A relationship develops as a result of the "coaching conversation", with client issues and concerns teased out by the skill of the coach's interventions.
- *Learn from experience.* Working with our own individual experience is a key to learning. In actively reflecting on experience, coach and client draw meaning from experience, literally entering into a dialogue with "experience", turning it into useable knowledge (Boud and Miller, 1996).
- *Understand the role of others.* Coach and client need to be aware of the powerful role of others in the work they do together. A danger of not understanding the "system" in which the client operates is that the coach risks becoming another part of that system.
- *Develop EQ.* The importance of developing emotional intelligence cannot be underestimated in the business coaching environment.
- *Be flexible.* Spontaneity is important, so beware of using a formulaic approach in your coaching.
- *Make your ethical code explicit.* Part of a coach's code of ethics is to honour confidentiality in the coaching conversation; the client entrusts the coach with confidences, and must feel safe to do so.
- *Be coached yourself.* Create a plan for your own development, no matter how qualified you are.
- *Create a development plan with goals.* The coach is responsible for ensuring that goal-setting conversations get the best results.
- *Measure coaching results.* Take measures of the outcomes of coaching from different perspectives, from the beginning to the end of the coaching intervention.

- *Evaluating and reviewing.* Identify for each individual client and the client organisation overall what has shifted during the coaching intervention, and determine what new behaviours are visible and how performance has improved. Also identify what has shifted in the client that will help to create a shift in individual team members and in the environment.

HOW CAN COACHING SUSTAIN BEHAVIOUR CHANGE?

Clients often ask their coaches, what happens when the coaching contract ends and you disappear? How will they sustain their own internal process and continue to create visible behaviour change impacting positively on performance? Below I consider the ten ways that client behavioural change can be sustained as a result of your business coaching interventions.

Building the relationship

Most research into the "encounter" between client and practitioner has been in the field of psychotherapy, yet it is in the early stages of research in the field of coaching (Stout-Rostron, 2006). A relationship develops as a result of the "coaching conversation", with client issues skilfully teased out by the coach's interventions. These interventions should be part of a structure such as a coaching model, with the coach operating flexibly to cater for the concerns of the client.

The developing relationship creates a safe "thinking environment", and it is the relationship that helps with the onset of change. The coach must be conscious of staying outside the "system" – particularly not being drawn into the client's narrative or "story". In this way, the coach works with the client to assume responsibility for change. Nancy Kline refers to the coach keeping "attention simultaneously in three streams". In the first stream the coach focuses on the content of the client's narrative; in the second, the coach becomes aware of their own thoughts as a response to the client's narrative; in the third, his or her attention creates a thinking environment conducive for the client (Kline, 2012).

Learning from experience

You may be familiar with David Kolb's (1984) Experiential Learning Model (discussed in Chapter 6). Working with our own individual experience is a key to learning. In actively reflecting on experience, coach and client draw meaning from experience, literally entering "into a dialogue with ... experience" turning it into useable knowledge (Boud and Miller, 1996).

The coach's interventions help to build rapport between the client and the coach, with the client's experience being the foundation and source of learning for the coaching conversation. Experiential learning can be viewed as an active process in which the client works with his or her experience to understand meanings they have associated with it.

But learning does not occur in isolation from our social and cultural norms and values.

While clients reconstruct their own experience, they do so within the context of their own unique social setting and cultural values. Other considerations are language, social class, gender, ethnic background and how clients have learned from an early age. In the context of the coaching conversation, when clients talk about their experiences, they create a story. It is critical that coaches develop the skill of hearing and identifying patterns in the language used by the client, to both understand the limiting and liberating assumptions that drive their thinking and behaviour, and to challenge the impact their language may have on how people experience them in the workplace.

If clients do not see themselves as learners or as learning from experience, or even see their stories as "reconstructions" and "re-interpretations" of their reality, how can we then use the coaching conversation to help clients learn, change and achieve their outcomes?

Exercise

Can you think of a time when you were (and were not) living life to the fullest? Describe what you were thinking, feeling, experiencing and assuming when you were, and when you weren't. What can you learn from reflecting on this experience?

Understanding the roles of others in the system

Coach and client need to be aware of the powerful roles of others in the work they do together. A danger of not understanding the "system" in which the client operates is that the coach risks becoming a part of that system. Set up regular meetings with the client's line manager to align the client's values and goals with those of the organisation. In terms of performance, it is critical that changes of thinking, feeling and behaviour show up "visibly" in the workplace. Visible behaviour is what people say and do – as well as what they do not say or do!

If the client has grown in terms of self-awareness, the organisation will want to see this "demonstrated" at work: in relationships, management competence, leadership behaviours and in the application of emotional competence (EQ). Regular meetings with the client's line manager give feedback that the coaching is on track. It may be useful for the coach to shadow the client, observing the client's interactions with others, honestly reflecting back observations. Often, change is embedded physiologically – clients demonstrate a visible change in attitude, in feeling and in how they "be who they are" as they interact with others.

Exercise

When recently have you seen a client "physiologically" demonstrate an insight or understanding into how his or her behaviour impacted on performance, and what reflection did they have that indicated a willingness to change?

Developing EQ

Prior to Daniel Goleman (1996; 1998) popularising emotional intelligence (EQ), previous research in the realm of experiential learning explored putting the heart back into learning, emphasising the "capacity to learn" at an emotional level. It is an area where executive coaches work, particularly in Western cultures where "emotion" is considered to be an inhibitor of clear, rational thinking.

Working to develop EQ helps the client to understand the importance of feelings in generating powerful thinking patterns and helps the client to understand the importance of emotional literacy in the workplace. Denial of emotions can lead to a denial of learning (Kline, 2012). Two influential sources of learning are past experience and our engagement with others. Different kinds of learning emerge depending on whether we view the learning as positive or negative. The way we interpret experience is connected to our view of ourselves and determines how we develop confidence and self-esteem.

Exercise

Jot down what's important to you about both your professional and your personal life. As you answer the question, look for the "intangibles", the "unmeasurables" such as: making a difference, collaboration, integrity, leadership, balance between work and personal life, family, friends, health. These reflect your core values, beliefs and feelings to which we cannot put a quantifiable measure. Create a full list of those intangibles, and then rank them in terms of importance. In order to achieve our goals, they must be in alignment with these intrinsic drivers.

Being flexible

Spontaneity is important, so beware of using a formulaic approach in your coaching. If the coach adheres too rigidly to a coaching model, it can get in the way of the coaching relationship – and the personal and professional growth of the client. It is important that both coach and client learn and change as the relationship grows.

In coaching, as in therapy, the practitioner is not always right. The practitioner is human and makes mistakes; it shows flexibility to admit those mistakes. This enhances trust and safety in the relationship and adds to the practitioner's authenticity. One of the things that I have learned over the years is how much clients appreciate hearing that you have fallen short or failed at something during your working or even personal life; it makes you human and fallible. This is true for both the leader-as-coach and the practitioner coach. As coaches we are not meant to be perfect, nor are we meant to have all of the answers. Our relationship with our individual client is one of learning and discovery at all times – for both coach and client.

Making your ethical code explicit

When client and coach work together, they enter into a verbal and/or written contract that specifies the parameters and boundaries of their work together. Part of a coach's code of ethics is to honour confidentiality in the coaching conversation; the client entrusts the coach with confidences, and must feel safe to do so. In an organisational setting, the coach contracts what will and will not be communicated to superiors, and this confidentiality must be honoured at all times.

Most members of the professional association Coaches and Mentors of South Africa (COMENSA) share the COMENSA ethical code with their clients, as part of their contracting and setting of boundaries for the coaching process. Other professional bodies available to coaches are the International Coach Federation (ICF), the Worldwide Association of Business Coaches (WABC), the European Mentoring and Coaching Council (EMCC), the Association for Professional Executive Coaching and Supervision (APECS) and the Association for Coaching (AC), all having ethical codes with which members are required to comply. With which organisation's ethical code do you align your practice?

Being coached yourself

The importance of being coached or "in supervision" cannot be over-emphasised. Both ensure that the coach understands what the client experiences, and both encourage the coach to work on his or her own issues so that they do not become entangled with those of the client. With the emerging professionalisation of coaching, clients are now asking: "What are your coaching qualifications and experience, and how do you continually develop your competence?" Create your own professional development plan, no matter how experienced you are. Although not yet a given in coaching, supervision is a fundamental underpinning of psychological therapeutic practice, and it is similarly recommended by coaching bodies worldwide.

Take part in the variety of professional organisations available to you. Join a portfolio committee in your country's relevant professional association as a way to develop yourself and the coaching profession. It will help you to understand the developing field of coaching, and specifically to contribute to your own learning, and to that of the profession as your professional body evolves.

Creating a development plan with goals

To ensure that coaching achieves the intended results, it is critical to create a development plan with the client's overall purpose, strategy, developmental objectives, developmental actions, strengths, areas for improvement and obstacles to achievement. The coach is responsible for ensuring that goal-setting conversations get the best results. Mary Beth O'Neill (2000:104) differentiates between business goals and personal goals, and links the coaching effort to a business result by highlighting and prioritising the business areas that need attention. Business goals are about achieving visible external results in the work place; personal goals are less visible and reflect growing self-awareness and an understanding of what the client has to do differently in how they conduct themselves to get business results.

According to Irvin Yalom (1980) there are two types of goals: content goals (what is to be accomplished) and process goals (how the coach wants to be in a session). If you as a coach are aware of your goal, you will stay in response rather than automatic mode when your stress is high. The next step is to ensure that your goal is related to your client's goal (Stout-Rostron, 2006:98). Most executive coaches would first identify the client's goals and guide the client accordingly. O'Neill (2000) says be very clear about your goal throughout the session so that you lose neither signature presence nor "backbone and heart". This however, does not mean that your goal takes precedence; your goal will relate to the achievement of your client's over-arching and specific goals for the session and the overall coaching intervention.

Measuring coaching results

It is important to take measures of the outcomes of coaching from different perspectives. This could be from the client, their line manager, senior management, the client's peers and subordinates. For myself and my business partners, we always ask our coaching clients to complete a questionnaire at the end of the coaching contract, providing a quantitative summary that indicates the impact of coaching on performance. It is useful for coach, client and sponsor to meet in the early months of the coaching intervention to identify organisational and individual client goals, and towards the end of the intervention to discuss what has been achieved and improved.

Despite being more than 50 years old, Donald Kirkpatrick's (1994) four levels of evaluation (*reaction, learning, behaviour* and *results*) are relevant, not just to training and capacity building, but also to coaching and leadership development. The levels can help determine whether the coaching intervention (a) should continue, (b) helps improve performance, (c) demonstrates the value of the coaching, and (d) gives a deliberate process to evaluate performance. In measuring results, coaches need to identify how factors such as leadership and management competence, interpersonal skills, decision making, conflict management, alliance building, teamwork, diversity management, collaboration, empathy and compassion show up in performance.

Evaluating and reviewing

At the end of the coaching contract, there are six factors to consider:

1. Celebrate achievements and plan for the road ahead.
2. Highlight the client's recurring patterns that continue to sabotage his or her success.
3. To ensure long-term sustainability of the coaching intervention, finalise the development plan and who will be supporting the client in this work.
4. You may want to schedule a follow-up session for feedback in four to six months' time. In this way, you gauge the sustainability of the coaching work.

5. To determine the sustainability of behaviour change and performance, ask the client to keep a journal of reflections and learning during the coaching process. At the end of the contract: *ask the client for their reflections on the entire coaching period, and where they see that insights and changes have occurred and impacted on their overall performance.*

6. One of the most helpful post-coaching tools is a reflective, quantitative or qualitative questionnaire. Analyse these for each client to determine what shifted for the client during coaching, and what new behaviours they continue to use. If possible, collate the information for all clients and produce an analysis of the coaching within that organisation.

LIBERATING YOUR CLIENTS' STORIES

Have any of your clients ever come to a session, only to say, "I don't know what to talk about today", or "I haven't thought about it"? Often executives work to such gruelling time schedules, and have so little time to prepare for other important or crucial meetings with stakeholders, that they don't put importance on preparing for their own coaching session.

One of the things that I do for my clients is to send an email or text message the day before, with one or two questions, to get them thinking about their session for the next day. These questions emerge from previous sessions between coach and client, or mention an issue you know is looming large for them that they indicated a need to talk about during your last session. There may also be generic questions such as asking them what issues they wish to raise, or what thinking they wish to generate, in your session together.

What is critically important, is that you as the coach take the time to think about the client prior to your session. Review your notes, note down any questions you may have – and be prepared to sit in a thinking space with them from the moment you both walk in through the door. They may be unprepared; nevertheless, you should *always* be prepared to create a thinking environment for them.

I once had a client come to his fourth coaching session (out of 12 sessions), who said, "I am bored with my coaching sessions!" I looked at him quietly, smiled mischievously, and simply said, "Then bring something for us to work on." There can be a misunderstanding on the part of the client who thinks you are possibly there to tell them what to think, to entertain them, or to do their work for them.

So what to do? All clients are busy, many are stressed, and some may not understand or appreciate the gift they are being handed – i.e. being offered the chance to reflect for several hours on what they never have time for during the complex business of their day-to-day work. It is also important to clarify, in your first few sessions with your client, the difference between the coaching conversation and that of a mentoring or therapy session. Although you bring your professionalism and expertise with you, it is not your job to fix them, to tell them what to think about, make decisions for them, or tell them how to do something. The space in which they work with you is to think, to dream, to argue, to debate, to decide, to rage against the world – this time is a gift, and quite possibly the most important piece of time that they should never lose!

How much are you in the way?

When working with students on one of my Masters programmes, I am always thrilled by their discovery that, although they work hard during a coaching conversation, the real work is done by the client. Trainee or student coaches, and even highly experienced coaches, sometimes think they must ask the brilliant question, parry the eye-opening challenge, lead with their questions and generally be the "brilliant" one. On the contrary – you may have agreed with your client to give an opinion or your advice during the conversation, but the real thinking rests with them. Your job is to be a coach – to create an environment where it is safe for them to think, for you to challenge their thinking and to create a space for them – whether it be to think through decisions, how to manage difficult people, understand complex situations, or create over-arching goals for themselves, their team and the business.

Most experienced coaches, with their 10 000 hours of coaching, will laugh when they say they aren't directive with their clients. They are directive, often. The simple question to ask yourself is, "What is the best way for me to help the client to think individually and independently for themselves without needing my patterns of thinking?" They certainly require your expertise, wisdom and experience *as a coach* – but they don't need you to tell them what to do. What if you aren't right? Just because you have your own body of knowledge and experience doesn't mean that your thinking is superior to theirs. Their thinking is what counts. After all, who is going to think for them when you are no longer in the room, or have moved on to work with another client?

So think carefully about how you listen, how you interrupt, how you intervene and distract them from their thoughts. Silence is powerful in the coaching conversation and can be used to great advantage. One of my mentors and colleagues, Nancy Kline, always says that the "silent thinker is busy thinking". No need to interrupt or intervene until needed. Also, if your eyes are on the eyes and face of the client, you will know whether their thought is complete or not. Your job is to help them think, not to think for them.

Does that render you useless baggage in the conversation? No, it means that you are a crucial component – the catalyst that gives them the space, the time, the ease, the lack of judgement and the challenges where necessary to push them to the edge of their thinking.

New leadership requires new thinking. Together, with the client, with your ability to create a space of ease and freedom to think – who knows where they will get to in that ninety minutes or more that you are together. It is important to remember – although in the coaching conversation, coach and client are equal as professionals – their thinking is what your job is to emerge. How you ask those questions, how you reframe their thinking, how you reflect back to them – that is your skill. And the way you structure the conversation according to your very flexible coaching model will afford you both the freedom to take flight, to dream and to land safely back down again before the session has ended.

Working with tacit qualities to build the supportive relationship

We need to remind ourselves that, at the heart of coaching is the relationship between the coach and the client or coachee. In order to create the conditions that allow for high-quality coaching conversations, the coach needs to think about the interpersonal skills that are required to build the relationship. This refers to the tacit dimension, with a focus on how to *be* in the relationship rather than referring to the skills and competences of the coach, or what they *do* to facilitate the conversation. It is important for the coach to consider their expertise from the point of view of *being* rather than *knowing and doing*.

Burger and Parry (2012) discuss the qualities needed for academic supervisors to support the doctoral supervisory relationship. In other words, what is needed to develop the tacit dimension. These tacit qualities are just as important for the coach–client relationship, as they are for the supervisor–coach relationship. In addition, the ten components of the Thinking Environment® developed by Nancy Kline emphasise the importance of how we give catalytic *attention*, create internal *ease* in ourselves in order to create ease in the other, and create an environment where *diversity* of thinking and feeling is *encouraged* and understood, and where the way we ask incisive questions does not distract the coach or supervisee but enables them to think independently and individually for themselves. These are the tacit qualities needed for the coach to communicate their inner attitudes to the coachee. They are embodied and expressed through their "way of being" with the client (Burger and Parry, 2012).

Burger and Parry (2012) refer to the literature on "way of being", and most particularly the influence of Carl Rogers, psychologist and founder of the client-focused approach to therapy. Rogers refers to the internal attitudes of the facilitator in the relationship that creates an internal climate that is externally (and tacitly) perceived by the candidate. He identified three essential characteristics for an effective therapist–patient relationship that are useful to us in a business coaching environment: *unconditional positive regard*, *genuine-ness* and *accurate empathy* (Rogers, 1961:47–49).

As Burger and Parry point out:

> Rogers (1961) describes four core conditions that need to be internally in place in the facilitator if an effective facilitating relationship is to develop: congruence is the ability to be ... real, transparent and free of defences, present and without roles, posturing or facades; unconditional positive regard is to be non-judgmental and experience a warm, positive and accepting attitude towards what is in the client and regardless of what they think or feel about the client's behaviour, they never implicitly or explicitly threaten to take this attitude away; accurate empathy means to understand the client's world as seen from the inside, grasping the client's frame of reference, experience and feeling, what they mean, so that their remarks fit in with the client's mood and content, the tone of voice conveys the complete ability to share the client's feelings in order to develop the required relationship; finally, it is not enough that the above conditions exist in the facilitator, they must to some degree be successfully communicated to the client, they must be perceived by the client (Burger and Parry, 2012:176).

What about listening?

How well do you actually really listen to your clients? You might be brilliant at the exquisite question, and the parry and strike against the client's answers. But do you really listen? How quickly are you ducking and diving into their story to be sure that the conversation moves in the direction that you assume that it is going? And where do you actually stop, be silent, give the client a chance to download how they are, where they are, what they would like to consider working on – rather than making assumptions or judgments? In most of my client sessions, the client usually talks for a good half an hour, if not more, before we even begin to sift through where we might be headed, or what might be on the menu for our conversation. This isn't because we are good at wasting time, it is because the client needs to download whatever is on their mind, clear the decks, and think through their emotions.

I have heard it said that we haven't arrived in a group space until our voice is heard. I often work with this concept in groups, as once everyone has spoken they are present for everyone else in the room. In a coaching session, a client often doesn't know what they want to think about, or know what they think until they voice it. Once they have cleared the decks of their thinking, we can work out what is on the agenda or up for discussion that day.

CONCLUSION

In this chapter we have discussed the components of the business coaching process and how coaching can produce sustainable behaviour change. We've talked about the importance of building an alliance between coach, client and organisation, and have explored five aspects of the coaching conversation designed to maximise and transform thinking, behaviour and performance:

- the business coaching process;
- the psychology of goals and motivation;
- learning from experience and client stories;
- listening, equality and the genuine encounter; and
- measuring results.

We have considered ten ways that client behavioural change can be sustained as a result of your business coaching interventions: building the relationship; learning from experience; understanding the role of others in the system; developing EQ; being flexible; making your ethical code explicit; being coached yourself; creating a development plan with goals; measuring coaching results; and evaluating and reviewing.

The coach's interventions help to build rapport between the client and the coach, with the client's experience being the foundation and source of learning for the coaching conversation. Finally, working to develop EQ helps the client to understand the importance of feelings in generating powerful thinking patterns, and supports the client in understanding how others are experiencing them in the workplace.

FURTHER READING

Boud, D., and Miller, N. (eds) (1996). *Working with Experience: Animating learning*. London: Routledge.

Burger, N., and Parry, S. (2012). Supervisor qualities in the doctoral supervisory relationship: The tacit dimension. In Kiley, M. (ed.), *Proceedings of the 2012 Quality in Postgraduate Research Conference* (pp. 175–176). Canberra, ACT: Centre for Higher Education, Learning and Teaching, Australian National University.

Griffiths, K.E., and Campbell, M.A. (2008). Regulating the regulators: paving the way for international, evidence-based coaching standards. *International Journal of Evidence-Based Coaching and Mentoring*, 6(1):19–31.

Kirkpatrick, D.L. (1994). *Evaluating Training Programmes: The four levels*. San Francisco, CA: Berrett-Koehler.

Kline, N. (1999). *Time to Think: Listening to ignite the human mind*. London: Ward Lock.

Kline, N. (2012). *The Thinking Partnership® Programme: Consultant's guide*. Wallingford, UK: Time to Think.

Kline, N. (2009). *More Time to Think: A way of being in the world*. Pool-in-Wharfedale: Fisher King.

O'Neill, M.B. (2000). *Coaching with Backbone and Heart: A systems approach to engaging leaders with their challenges*. San Francisco, CA: Jossey-Bass.

Peterson, D.B. (2009). Executive coaching: A critical review and recommendation for advancing the practice. In Zedeck, S. (ed.), *APA Handbook of Industrial and Organisational Psychology: Volume 2: Selecting and developing members for the organisation* (pp. 527–566). Washington, DC: American Psychological Association.

Spinelli, E. (1989). *The Interpreted World: An introduction to phenomenological psychology*. London: Sage.

Stout-Rostron, S. (2012b). *Business Coaching Wisdom and Practice: Unlocking the secrets of business coaching*. Second edition. Randburg: Knowres.

Stout-Rostron, S. (2014). *Business Coaching International: Transforming individuals and organisations*. Second edition. London: Karnac.

Weiss, P. (2004). *The Three Levels of Coaching*. San Francisco, CA: An Appropriate Response.

Yalom, I.D. (1980). *Existential Psychotherapy*. New York, NY: Basic.

Yalom, I.D. (2001). *The gift of therapy: Reflections on being a therapist*. London: Piatkus.

6

The power of coaching models

WORKING WITH METAPHOR AND ANALOGY

Working with metaphors is like working with a picture word. It opens up new perspectives on the client's approach to a subject or a topic. Sometimes, in our first few sessions together, I will ask a client to put together a collage with pictures, objects, colour etc. – almost like a scrap book, or even on a flip chart – and to take me through the story of their life. I ask them to think of an overall metaphor to describe their journey so far. Or even to think of a metaphor to describe themselves on the journey to date.

Within the coaching conversation, analogy or metaphor help you to create a wider perspective, or to vary the approach in how you ask questions, or to retell their story differently – simply to open up a discussion for deeper thinking. Never underestimate the power of metaphors and analogies to illustrate a point or to open up a new perspective.

With one client, I once retold her story back to her in the guise of a metaphor. She had described a very difficult relationship with her superior in the workplace, and needed a moment to catch up with her emotions. By choosing to work with the metaphor of an eagle learning to fly, leaving the nest, she was able to begin to think of herself as an emergent leader taking uncertain steps into a new role. It gave her the space to think about how to work with her line manager during this transition.

With another client, I used the analogy of living in two houses: one house where everything was in black and white, and where there were locks on all the doors and little light could get in; in a second house light could get in, and there was colour, music, singing and dancing. It was an analogy to show him how he had locked himself into a kind of straight jacket in the workplace – the black and white house where he felt all of the life had drained out of him. Instead he escaped to the second house, his home in the evening full of chattering kids, family and life. The black and white context embodied the rules and regulations at work that he was using to protect himself from new learning, from moving forward and from taking edgy steps into the unknown due to the changes within his firm.

We looked at his strategy – the thoughts and feelings that gave him the freedom to be himself in the colourful home space, and identified how he could apply the same strategy to the work place. It helped him to realise that his fear of tackling the new in the workplace was because he was afraid he would fail. And yet he was constantly tackling the new in the home space with children and family. Once we were able to put colour, music and song into the workplace, we identified what steps needed to be taken for him to let go of his fear and tackle the merging of two different cultures at work.

WORKING WITH COACHING MODELS

What coaching models have you learned, and what is the coaching model you have begun to develop and embody as your own? What flexibility does it give you throughout the entire coaching intervention, and yet how does it help you to structure the coaching conversation? In this chapter I will introduce a few of the most effective coaching models that I have used, taught and written about. My intention is to help you think about how the model with which you work gives you and the client freedom to soar.

Models offer structure and flexibility

Coaching models help us to understand the coaching intervention from a systems perspective and to appreciate the need for "structure" in the interaction between coach and client. They offer flexibility and a structure for both the coaching conversation and the overall coaching journey.

There is some confusion in coach education programmes today between the term "model" and "framework". Basically, a model hangs on a frame: triangular, circular, four-quadrant, spiral or even a mnemonic sequence like GROW or CLEAR. Models can seemingly look like a "framework" and in itself look static. But what makes it a model is the third dimension, the process – and in our case it is the coaching conversation between coach and client that brings the model alive. Every model has essentially three aspects: a *structure*, a *process* and an underlying *philosophy or rationale* (e.g. philosophical, psychological, experiential learning, existential, scientific, medical, legal, etc.).

Whichever model you choose to develop or work with, a model simply represents a system with an implied process. It is a metaphor or analogy used to help you and the client to visualise and describe their journey. Models systemically visualise or represent a process that is not directly observable which is why they look static on the page. A coaching model essentially represents what happens, or will happen, in the coaching conversation (micro) and in the overall coaching intervention or journey (macro). I recommend working with simple models that represent both the micro- and macro coaching interventions for greater ease. A model is a simple representation of the coaching journey; its process embodies all of your tools and techniques, including your question frameworks. You bring the skills, experience and expertise to ensure that the model's process works.

It is essential to adopt a structured approach to your coaching conversation. This does not mean that you cannot let the conversation grow and be explorative – I mean structure in a big-picture way. That is the beauty of any model: having the freedom to explore within each part of the model. The importance of your model is its ability to let you and the client be both innovative and flexible.

There are varying degrees of thought in educating and developing coaches. Some schools train their coach practitioners to use only one coaching model. Other coach training schools teach a variety of models and advocate choosing one of them, or learning how to flexibly integrate a few models to develop your own. If you prefer one particular model, it is essential to go through the training or certification to ensure you have a depth of understanding in its use. Eventually, you may want to choose whether to work with one model, or with an integration of several models, or to develop your own. That is not for anyone else to prescribe for you. Whatever you decide, I believe that knowledge is power, and the more understanding of available models you have, the more intelligent your choice will be.

One of the least explored areas of innovation for coaches is in the development of your own coaching model. As it is not possible to work with every coaching model available in the marketplace, it is important for you to gain a sense of the flexibility models can offer you as a coach practitioner. Remember that the coaching conversation is about the client, not about you. If the model is too prescriptive, it means the coach is attempting to fulfil their own agenda, rather than attempting to understand the client's issues. Part of your own continuing professional development (CPD) is to grow and stretch your skills and expertise, and to do this I recommend that you work with new models as they emerge within the field of coaching.

The Scientist-Practitioner Model

Although it is essential to adopt a structured approach to your coaching conversation, the brilliance of any model is having the freedom to develop new thoughts and feelings with your clients throughout the journey no matter where you are in the process. For this reason, I prefer to begin with an over-arching model, the Scientist-Practitioner Model. Adapted from the world of clinical psychology, it has proven to be extremely valuable to the business coach.

The Scientist-Practitioner Model was developed in 1956, following the seminal conference in Boulder, Colorado in 1949 on the training of clinical psychologists. The Model emphasises the need for practitioners to base their work on scientifically valid evidence, and to use scientific methods in assessing their work.

Lane and Corrie (2006) revised the Scientist-Practitioner Model to focus on three key concepts: purpose, perspectives, and process (see Figure 2). The Purpose, Perspectives and Process approach had been developed in 2000 by David Lane of the Professional Development Foundation (PDF). The approach is a way of seeking to be rigorous in the application of theory and scientific evidence by practitioners, and in understanding the limits of scientific evidence in practice.

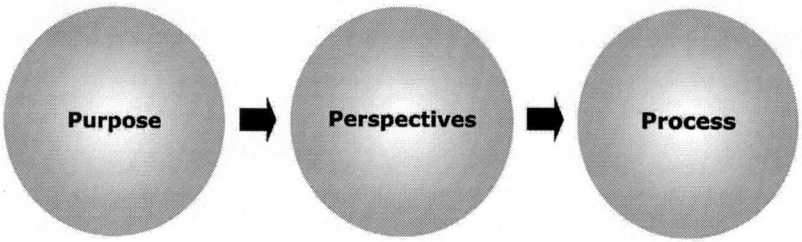

Figure 2: The Scientist-Practitioner Model: purpose, perspectives, process

Source: Lane and Corrie (2006)

Purpose (where are we going and why?)

What is your purpose in working with the client? Where are you going with this client? What does the client want to achieve? Where do they want to go in their overall journey with you as their coach?

For example, one client working in the media said in our first session together, "I need your help because many people in the organisation seem wary of me because of my seniority. What, if anything, can I do about it? I know that I have good credibility with those who are superior or equal to me, but I am disliked and mistrusted by those subordinate to me in position."

As a coach, your questions will relate to the client's purpose, i.e. "Where are we going on our journey together, and what's our reason for going there together?" "What" questions help to create a bigger picture of the journey and create perspective. This client's purpose was to "build bridges and trust with those subordinate to him throughout the organisation, and to maintain and build relationships with those on a par or superior to him".

Perspectives (what will inform our journey?)

What are the perspectives that inform the journey for both coach and client? You both come in with individual backgrounds, experience, expertise, culture, values, motivations and assumptions that drive behaviour.

For the above example, we discussed the perspectives of all of those in the organisation at the varying levels in the hierarchy. We discussed the client's perspective about his experience on every level within the organisation, and explored in great detail how people would "experience" him in the work place – at each level: subordinate, equal and superior. We also discussed what were his assumptions at each level, and what assumptions might be influencing those working above, alongside and below him in the hierarchy.

He also wanted to learn from our work together in order to develop more of a "coaching approach" when working with his direct reports. In this first session together we spent quite a bit of time beginning to identify his overall coaching purpose, exploring the perspectives that were impacting how he accomplished his job, and thinking about how people might be experiencing him.

Process (how will we get there?)

In the early stage of working together with this client, we contracted, set boundaries, agreed confidentiality matters, outlining the fee paying process and the development of a leadership development plan. We also agreed on timing (how often we would see each other and also work with the individual client's line manager). What assessments would be useful for the individual client to complete? How would we debrief those profiles? We discussed potential coaching assignments and timing for the overall contract (including termination and exit possibilities if either party was unhappy) and worked out how to obtain line manager approval.

We set up a separate meeting to agree the process with the line manager and the Group HR Director. And finally, when we began to work together in each individual coaching session, we briefly discussed the process we would use in each coaching conversation.

How can this model help you?

This model can help you in three ways: to contract with the client, to structure the entire coaching journey, and to facilitate each individual coaching conversation. Out of this specific initial conversation emerged the client's purpose, clarification about how our perspectives fit together to help him to achieve his purpose, as well as the perspectives of those at varying levels in the organisation that he needed to understand in order to achieve his purpose, and the process within which we would work to achieve the desired outcomes.

This model can be used for the regular coaching conversations you have with your individual clients. The client brings to the conversation a possible "menu" of topics to be discussed, or even just one particular topic. One of my clients in the field of engineering came to me one day saying, "My purpose today is to understand why I am sabotaging my best efforts to delegate to my senior managers" (purpose). As the coach, I wanted to understand all of the perceptions underlying the client's aim for this conversation (perspectives), as well as identifying the various tools or techniques that we agreed we would use in this particular (process).

Encompassing the coaching conversation and the coaching journey

The Scientist-Practitioner Model can represent the process for just one coaching conversation, but it can also represent the overall journey. For example, the client comes in with the purpose, "I would like to work with you; no one else will work with me as they find me too difficult." This client's purpose became to find a coach who would work with her, to help her to identify how she could not only develop the interpersonal skills to work successfully with others, but to demonstrate her new learning through visible behaviour change at work.

The coach's and the client's perspectives will be unique and different. In working with the client, you bring not just an outside perspective, but also your observations as to how this client seems to be working within the organisational system. In terms of process, you may ask the client to do a range of assessment profiles, or you may shadow the client at work to experience how he or she facilitates meetings or interacts with customers, subordinates, superiors and colleagues. Some coaches begin with a 360° assessment from the beginning of the coaching intervention to bring in the perspectives of those working with or alongside the individual executive. This is a particularly valid and useful exercise as it prevents you as coach from over-identifying with the client's perspective.

Coaching is always an experiential learning conversation

The conversation with your client centres on what is meaningful to them. If significance and relevance are to emerge from the coaching conversation, it doesn't matter what is relevant to you; it matters what is relevant to them. It is therefore important to be aware of your own assumptions about what the client needs. If you are guiding, directing, and giving your clients all the information they need, it will be difficult for them to ever be free of you.

In helping your client to discover what is meaningful to them, one of the core areas in which you work as a coach is that of learning. It is helpful if the client embodies new learning personally and physiologically; you can't do their learning for them. What you do as a coach is to help them reconstruct their own thoughts and feelings to gain perspective and become self-directed learners. In this way, the coaching process becomes a "learning conversation", a term developed in research into self-organised learning by Harri-Augstein and Thomas (1991:24).

At the end of each coaching session with my clients, we integrate their learning with the goals they have set, confirming what action, if any, they are committed to:

- *Vision* – Refine their vision: where is the client going?
- *Strategy* – Outline the strategy: how is the client going to achieve their vision?
- *Outcomes* – What are the specific outcomes that need to be accomplished in the next few weeks in order to work toward achieving the vision, putting the strategy into action?
- *Learning* – Help the client summarise what was gained from the session in order to help underline self-reflection, continuing to help the client understand that they are responsible for their own thinking, their own doing, and their own being.

THE NESTED-LEVELS MODEL

Although models create a system within which coach and client learn, it is essential that models are not experienced as either prescriptive or rigid. If the model is inflexible, or if the client continually needs to "sell" their model to their client, it means it is fulfilling the coach's agenda, rather than attempting to understand the client's issues.

This Nested-Levels Model was developed by New Ventures West (Weiss, 2004), and introduces the concept of horizontal and vertical levels in coaching models. The Nested-Levels Model works first at the horizontal level of "doing", eventually moving into deeper "learning" one level down; reflecting about self, others, and experience at a third "ontological" level where new knowledge emerges about oneself and the world (Figure 3).

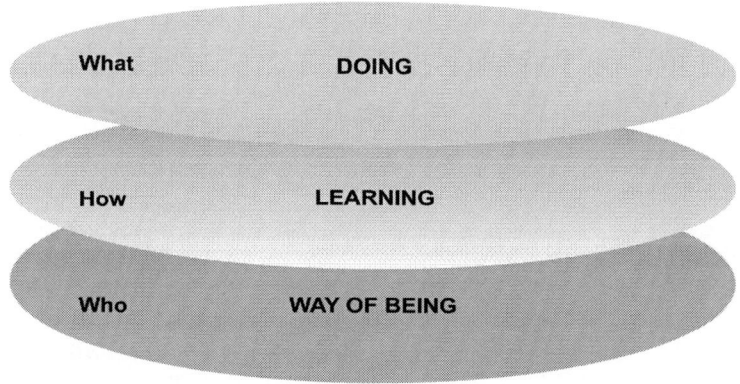

Figure 3: Nested-Levels Model

Source: Adapted from Weiss (2004)

Weiss (2004) talks about two different "camps" of coaches. In jest, I call them the New York versus the Los Angeles (LA) camp. The New York camp says, "I'm the expert, let me fix you", while the LA camp says, "You are perfect and whole and have all of your own answers." Teasing aside, each of these camps comes up short, even though coaches often fall into one or the other. The role of coaching is actually about developing human beings. It is not really about "I have the expertise" versus "you already have all your own answers" (Stout-Rostron, 2012b:93).

Two approaches

The "expert" approach

Contrary to what experts might think, clients are not broken and are not in need of fixing. Clients may be anxious, stressed, nervous, overworked, and even narcissistic – but they don't need fixing. They are mostly healthy human beings going about their jobs and lives, experiencing their own human difficulties. Your job as coach is to help the clients learn for themselves, so that when you are no longer walking alongside them, they have become "self-directed" learners (Harri-Augstein and Thomas, 1991) and do not need you anymore. The second view about "expertise" also has limitations. The role of expertise is that, as a coach, you are an expert; but coaching is not about the coach giving all the answers; that tends to be the role of the consultant, i.e. to find and offer solutions for the client.

The "you-have-all-the-answers" approach

The "you have all the answers" assumption is partially true, but there are several limitations. The first one is that we all have blind spots, and it is your job as coach to help the client to identify their blind spots. Secondly, it's perhaps a bit of "fairytale" thinking that the client has all of the answers already; the flip side of this argument is that, if it does not work out, the client assumes blame and fault. In other words, "If I have all the answers, I should be able to do it myself without help." If that is not the case, they could feel, "If I am not able to do it myself, then perhaps I'm a failure."

Both of these approaches are "horizontal", i.e. they skim the surface of the work you can do with the client. Both help people to maintain the lives they currently have. The expert "New York" approach helps the client to do it better, faster, and more efficiently, and the easygoing "LA" approach may withhold key insights and observations from the coach that could help build the client's awareness of their blind spots. What is important, rather than "fixing" the client, is the skill of "observation" on the part of the coach. There is no problem in helping the client to do it better, faster, or more efficiently – that is often what the organisation hopes for in terms of performance improvement. However, it is important for the client to gain the learning they need to be able to address blind spots and build their own internal capacity and competence.

At the level of learning

If you continue to help people accomplish tasks, achieve goals, and keep on "doing", they risk falling into the trap of being "busy" and possibly overwhelmed. They may not, however, necessarily get the "learning" they need to develop self-awareness and self-management. I know all too well about this trap of being excessively busy; I am quite good at it! If we keep "doing" without reflection, we eventually burn out. To keep individual executives performing better and better, they need to work at one level lower – at the level of learning. They need to learn how to "do the doing" better. As soon as an executive begins to work with a coach, they begin the possibility of working at one or two levels deeper.

As coach, you will be asking questions to help clients reflect, review, and gain useable knowledge from their experience. In the Nested-Levels Model, the higher levels don't include the lower ones, but the lower levels include the higher ones. So we need to help clients address their purpose one level down, at the level of learning. At this level we are addressing competence – how will they learn what they need to – to do the "doing" better. You may ask questions such as, "How are you doing? What are you doing? What are you feeling? How are your peers or colleagues experiencing you / this? What is and what isn't working? What is useful learning for you here? What needs to change and how will you go about changing?" What do you need to learn to do differently in order to make the change?"

Ontological levels: being and becoming

The third and fourth levels of the coaching intervention, using this model, probe who the client is and who the client wishes to become. Your questions move from "What do they need to do?" and "How do they need to do it?" (doing), to "How does their style of learning impact on how they do what they do?" (learning). You might ask at the level of learning, "What do they need to learn in order to improve thinking, behaviour, feeling, performance, or leadership?" to questions such as "What do they need to understand and acknowledge about themselves; who are they; how do they be who they are; and what needs to change to step into that person they wish to become?" (being and becoming).

So what assists people in getting things done? Above all, it is about clarifying goals, creating action steps, taking responsibility, and being accountable. In order to perform more effectively, we need to help clients shift down a gear from doing (performance), to learn how to work with competence (sets of skills), and to understand how that will impact on how they "be who they are".

Open to possibilities

Your job as coach is to help the client be open to the possibility of learning something new, and to help them relate to themselves and others at a deeper level. To use the Nested-Levels Model, you could ask questions such as:

- What is it that your client(s) want to do? What is their aim or purpose in working with you?
- What do they need to learn in order to make the change? What in their thinking, feeling, and behaviour needs to change in order to do the doing better? How can they use their own experience to learn what is needed?
- How do, and how will, their thoughts, feelings, and behaviour impact on how they "be who they are" and "who it is they want to become"? In this way, we work at horizontal and vertical levels. At the end of the day, the client's new attitudes, behaviours, motivations, and assumptions begin to impact positively on their own performance and their relationships with others.

Our aim with this model is to shift any limiting sense of who the client is so that they can interact and engage with the world in new ways. As clients begin to shift, it has an impact on others with whom they interact in the workplace. It also means addressing issues systemically, from a holistic perspective, whether those issues revolve around health, stress, anxiety, performance, or relationships with others. Our task as coaches is to widen the circle, to enlarge the perspective of the client, and help them to learn from their own experience in order to reach their potential.

As I mentioned earlier, a great way to start any coaching intervention is to ask your clients to tell their life story. The coach begins to understand some of the client's current issues and presenting challenges, and begins to observe patterns of thinking, feeling, and visible behaviour. Because we work with Kolb's theory of "understanding experience in order to transform it into useable knowledge", this model helps us to determine the context in which the client operates, where individual and systemic problems may be occurring, and how organisational values and culture impact on individuals and teams. It is at this level that the coach's ability to observe, challenge, and ask appropriate questions can be most transformational.

Nested-levels story

Doing

One client, with whom I have worked for a number of years, came to the session saying that she wanted to design a workshop for all three managerial boards in the company, for all of the line managers, and the thousands of staff. In other words, the workshop had to be designed in such a way as to accommodate the learning needs of all three levels in the organisational hierarchy. Her goal for the session was to design the workshop, and work out who was to facilitate it. At the beginning of the session she felt she was not suitable to facilitate the programme. So we had identified what we needed to *do*.

Learning

Once the workshop was written up in outline form, the target audiences identified, as well as how they would each be catered for – we had a discussion about who would be the facilitator. This was beginning to work at the level of *learning*. We spent quite a deal of time talking about what criteria were needed for the facilitator, who would actually facilitate the workshop, and what was crucial in terms of content knowledge. We identified a variety of people who might be appropriate, none of whom she was happy with. It took quite a while to identify and work through her competences and capabilities which helped her to think about the possibility of facilitating the workshop herself; something she was not originally confident to do. The greatest *learning* came when she realised she had more than the required competence to do the job herself, but also a stream of ideas emerged as she thought about how to train up a team of facilitators (from within the company) to manage and facilitate the programme with her across the country. Her own competences and that of her team grew as their road show began to inspire the company.

Being and becoming

Over the next year, stepping into more and more roles which required public speaking, workshop facilitation and spontaneously inspiring audiences with her company stories of people development – she began to step into the role she had always envisaged for herself – that of a leader. This took time, and in fact, has taken a few years. This is working at the level of *being and becoming*. It doesn't happen overnight, and sometimes carries on long after the coach has completed their engagement with the client.

In working with the model, working at the level of *doing* means clarifying goals, action steps and accountability, and creating a development plan. In working at the level of *learning*, it means shifting down to work with competence, helping coaching clients to learn something new, coaching them into the "how". In working at the level of changing their *being* means shifting from addressing the *issue* to developing the *person*, working on meaning and purpose, choice and freedom. We will pick this up again when we look at an existential approach to coaching at the end of this chapter.

THE COACHING CONVERSATION: AN EXPERIENTIAL ROAD MAP

As mentioned in the previous chapter, the knowledge gained from reflecting on one's own experience, exploring what is working, what needs work, and what one can think, feel or do differently – is one of the roads leading to personal mastery. How coaching clients take responsibility for change can emerge from this experiential learning process.

In business, the coaching conversation provides a thinking environment where executives are able to develop self-awareness and a depth of understanding of themselves and others – embedding newly-acquired skills, competences and attitudes which subsequently *impact* the actions they take, visibly *demonstrating* new behaviours and ultimately *leading* to mastery of self.

Kolb's Experiential Learning Model

Learning, change and growth are the key principles of a coaching environment which considers the coaching conversation as a learning experience. In this environment, the focus of the coaching conversation is to help the client work towards achieving desired outcomes. Coach and client reflect the client's experience and behaviours, devising new thinking, feeling, behaviours and actions. Kolb says that learning is not just an active, self-directed process, but also a process where knowledge is created through the transformation of experience (Kolb, 1984:42).

Sometimes you just cannot get the learning on your own, which is where the role of a coach or mentor comes in. The coaching conversation helps to transform their experience into workable knowledge; learning then becomes an "emergent experience" within a cycle of continuous learning. Kolb (1984) describes this as "insight experience". *Apprehension* or insight leads to *comprehension* or understanding and this is gained from *experience*.

Figure 4 is Kolb's original model. Figure 5 shows my adapted version of Kolb's model to be used in the coaching process, indicating Kolb's learning modes and integrated learning styles. In Figure 5 I have positioned "thinking" in the top right and left quadrants; "feeling" in the bottom two quadrants; "interior / intrinsic" on the left, and "exterior / extrinsic" on the right.

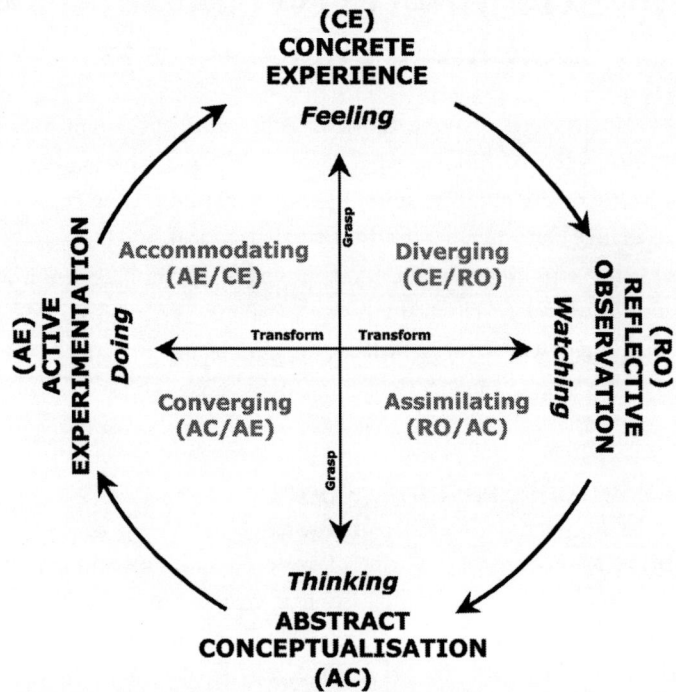

Figure 4: Kolb's original Experiential Learning Model

Source: Adapted from Figure 3.1 in Kolb (1984:42)

Using Kolb's four modes of learning

This is a very useful coaching model, as all clients come into the coaching conversation with their concrete experiences. Coach and client reflect and observe, think and theorise based on the client's observations, and agree what new thinking, feeling and behaviour needs to take place back in the working environment (Figure 6). If the client stays in doing, action and concrete experience (e.g. if we coach continuously without reflection, observation and evaluation) it would not be possible to gain new learning (for both coach and client). Many businesses get stuck because they create business plans, put them into action and complete them but do not take enough time out to review and evaluate.

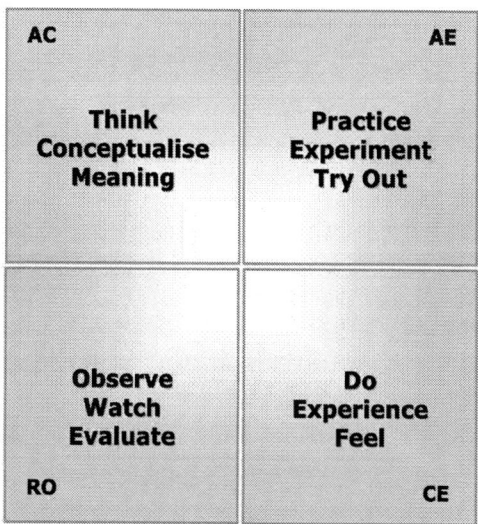

AC	**AE**
Think **Conceptualise** **Meaning**	**Practice** **Experiment** **Try Out**
Observe **Watch** **Evaluate**	**Do** **Experience** **Feel**
RO	**CE**

Figure 5: Coaching with Kolb's Experiential Learning Model

Source: Adapted from Stout-Rostron (2006:331)

The purpose of using the above learning process in coaching is to integrate the four adaptive modes of Kolb's learning model (concrete, abstract, reflective and conceptual). Kolb (1984:41) insists that knowledge is the result of "grasping experience and transforming it into divergent, assimilative, convergent and accommodative knowledge". A further definition of the coaching conversation could be "an integration of reflection and thinking on action and experience". Kolb's definition of each of his experiential learning quadrants is particularly helpful:

- CE (concrete experience) is about feeling and experiencing;
- RO (reflective observation) is about observing and watching;
- AC (abstract conceptualisation) is about thinking and conceptualising; and
- AE (active experimentation) is about doing and being in action.

Kolb's model can be used to structure the coaching conversation and the coaching journey overall. We gain knowledge through our own experience; each individual filters their worldview through their own experience. In reflecting on our concrete experiences, we can transform experience into some kind of useable knowledge. Some people prefer to step into the experience itself; others prefer to watch, reflect and review; some like to conceptualise, hypothesise and theorise; others like to experiment with doing something new. All four work in conjunction with each other. Essentially, each one of us integrates all four learning modes, but we tend to have a preference for one or two.

What Kolb's four learning modes indicate

- *Concrete experiencers*: Adopt a receptive, experience-based approach to learning that relies heavily on feeling-based judgments. CE individuals tend to be empathetic and "people-oriented". They generally find theoretical approaches to be unhelpful and prefer to treat each situation as a unique case. They learn best from specific examples in which they can become involved. Individuals who emphasise concrete experience tend to be oriented more toward peers and less toward authority in their approach to learning. They benefit most from feedback and discussion with their coach and peers.

- *Reflective observers*: Adopt a tentative, impartial and reflective approach to learning. RO individuals rely heavily on careful observation in making judgments and prefer learning situations such as lectures that allow them to take the role of impartial objective observers. These individuals tend to be introverts and require a typically greater reflective approach to the coaching session. Coaching needs to be very reflective for them to access the learning needed to move forward.

- *Abstract conceptualisers*: Adopt an analytical, conceptual approach to learning that relies heavily on logical thinking and rational evaluation. AC individuals tend to be oriented more toward things and symbols and less toward other people. They learn in impersonal, authority-directed learning situations that emphasise theory and systematic analysis. They are often frustrated by, and benefit little from, unstructured "discovery" learning approaches, such as activities and role-plays. The coach needs to be able to provide a structured thinking approach to the session, and could use the Kolb model to help the client to access the other learning modes.

- *Active experimenters*: Adopt an active, "doing" orientation to learning that relies heavily on experimentation. AE individuals learn best when they can engage in such things as projects, homework, developing new techniques inside the coaching conversation that they can take back out to the workplace, and in group discussions. They dislike passive learning situations such as lectures, and tend to be extraverts. AE clients can be active and noisy and may require focused energy in the coaching environment.

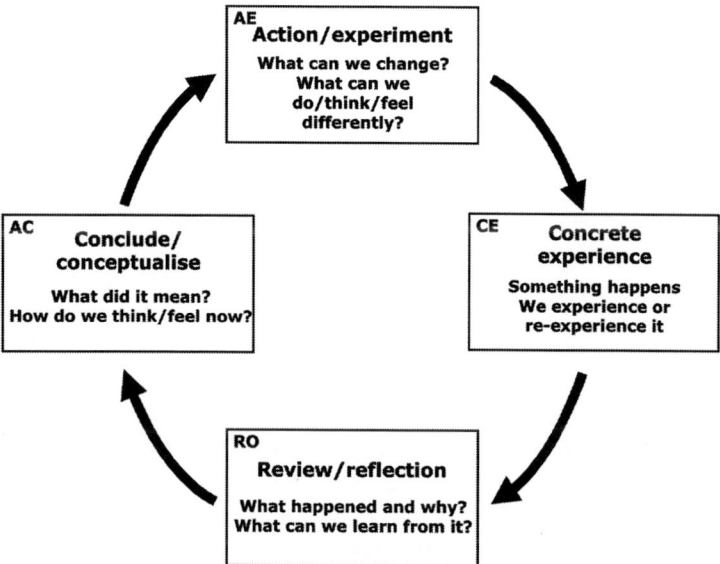

Figure 6: Kolb's adult learning cycle

Source: Adapted from Kolb (1984:42)

Explanation: using Kolb's model as a coaching process

Having read the definitions of each learning mode and the following case study, think about how you can use this model in certain of your coaching situations.

In the coaching conversation, the more time spent in "concrete experience" will guarantee the success of working with this model. When can you use it? Whenever someone has a specific series of events that continue to happen with similar circumstances and outcomes, or when there is something coming up in the future that is similar to something that has happened in the past. First of all, set up the contracting: how much time do you have to spend on this particular coaching session, including an explanation of how the four stages of the process will be experienced. Also agree if you, as coach, will or will not be taking notes. I tend not to take notes and to stay mindfully aware during each stage of the process.

Concrete experience (CE)

Have the client begin by explaining their goal for the session and talking about the specific past experience as if they are actually in it, using present tense language as much as they possibly can. If it is for a future event, have the client describe the future event, and link it to something they have successfully done in the past that is similar. Spend at least 20 or 30 minutes here to understand the point of view of the client, then have them step into the shoes of everyone else involved in the event, and have them speak from the point of view of each person. In this way, the client really begins to understand the thoughts, feelings and point of view of each person involved in the situation. What you will find is that in this first part, the client will actually move through all four stages of the learning cycle – do not be daunted – this is very important for the learning that is to take place. In fact, during each stage of the process you will find the client seemingly going through the entire experiential learning circle; in this way the client begins to find solutions at a very early stage in the process. What is important is that you know where you are throughout the process (in concrete experience in this instance) and don't move too quickly into the next stage of the cycle.

Reflective observation (RO)

In terms of moving on to reflective observation, ensure you help the client to transition with a phrase such as, we are now moving from *being in the experience* to *reflecting on the experience* as if we are looking through a lens – just like in those old fashioned cinemas up in the projection room. Looking through the window onto the audience and the screen in front of us. In this way you move the client into a "third person" lens so that they begin to reflect on what they have been thinking, feeling and exploring in the first part of the session. In reflective observation, ask the client what learning they have experienced as they have talked about and relived the experience. What second-hand learning (i.e. after the experience) is now available to them? Again, you will find the client moving in and out of the "concrete experience", then forward into "new thinking", and finally what they might do differently (active experimentation) in a new situation if they encounter it. This is all important for their own learning, but you are continuing to ask questions that help you to continue working in reflective observation.

Abstract conceptualisation (AC)

When you feel ready, after about fifteen or twenty minutes, you can move into the third phase – what new thoughts or new meanings have emerged from your conversation so far? They will find that they now regard the situation from a new perspective – with some thoughts or feelings on the parts of all the parties that had not occurred to them previously – or had possibly occurred to them but they had not articulated or emerged them into conscious thought. This is quite an important part of the process: they are distilling new thoughts and perspectives and letting go of previous assumptions that may have been limiting their thinking or feeling.

Active experimentation (AE)

And finally – what new thinking, action or feelings may emerge when encountering a similar situation or the same people once again? What are the possibilities for them to deal with a similar situation in a new or different way – and what might that look, sound or feel like?

You might have them future pace a scenario coming up in the near future to identify how they will handle a similar situation, event or persons in the future.

Reflecting on the case study

To conclude this session, ask the client, what have they learned from this session – and how it has helped them to see things from a new perspective or in a new light. Appreciate and acknowledge the individual at the end of the session as it is often quite a deep and sensitive learning experience for them. Ask if there is anything they would like to write down. In your next session you can follow up with them what has happened subsequently.

COACHING IN COMPLEX ENVIRONMENTS

According to Professor Michael Cavanagh at the University of Sydney's Coaching Psychology Unit, there will probably be two changes in coaching over the next five years. Coaching will remain linear and goal-driven on the one hand, and on the other hand, coaches will increase their capacity to deal with complex, non-linear systems, building relationships and resilience within individuals and organisations (Cavanagh, 2013a).

In order to do that, Cavanagh says we need coaches who are able to think in systemic ways and thereby get "ahead of the curve". As coaches we need (a) a bigger perspective; (b) to see the world as a complex adaptive system; and (c) a model of leadership and coaching which is consistent with adaptive complex systems. He asks, "To what degree does our coaching and supervision challenge people's perspectives of the world?", and suggests that we need to engage with tensions that we often ignore and asked if coaches are actually making it worse. We need to:

- take a wider systemic view (who in the system is of interest, and ask about externalities);
- take a broader temporal horizon, i.e. past, present and future; and
- focus on connectedness and process – i.e. performance as a function of the system (Cavanagh, 2013a).

Cavanagh advocates the following behaviours as ways to develop systemic change:

- Listening for meaning, displaying empathy.
- Mindfulness – helping people create a "self-organised" shift.
- Asking different questions.
- Identifying assumptions and rules.
- Identifying either/or's and seeking seek both/and's.
- Extending the system.
- Extending the frames.
- Turning toward tensions.
- Seeking different voices.
- Identifying purposes, keeping goals flexible.
- Noticing emergence, becoming pattern recognition experts.
- Building genuine dialogue (Cavanagh, 2013a).

Cynefin: the decision-making framework

Models are useful to us in managing and dealing with complexity in the coaching conversation. Snowden and Boone (2007) outline the different contexts in which managers operate as simple, complicated, complex and chaotic. The Cynefin decision-making framework identifies the different ways of thinking about our working environment, and helps leaders determine the prevailing context within which they are operating and explores how they can make the appropriate choices and decisions to intervene (Figure 7). "Cynefin, pronounced 'ku-nev-in', is a Welsh word that signifies the multiple factors in our environment and our experience that influence us in ways we can never understand" (Snowden and Boone, 2007:70).

David Snowden has described Cynefin as a perspective on the evolutionary nature of complex systems, including their inherent uncertainty, which explores the relationship between man, experience, and context (O'Neill, 2004). As coaches we need to help leaders learn to shift their decision-making styles according to the type of environment or context in which they are operating. The Cynefin framework can help to correctly identify the governing context, stay aware of danger signals, and avoid inappropriate actions, thereby helping managers to lead effectively in a variety of situations (Snowden and Boone, 2007:75).

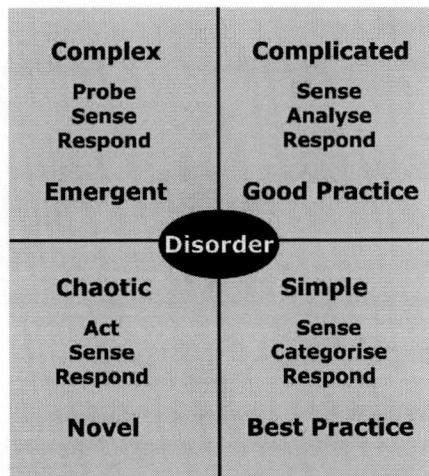

Figure 7: The Cynefin decision-making framework

Source: Snowden and Boone (2007:72)

The Cynefin framework has five domains:

- *Simple*, in which the relationship between cause and effect is obvious to all, the approach is to Sense – Categorise – Respond and we can apply best practice.
- *Complicated*, in which the relationship between cause and effect requires analysis or some other form of investigation and/or the application of expert knowledge, the approach is to Sense – Analyse – Respond and we can apply good practice.

Leadership Coaching for Results: Cutting-edge practices for coach and client

- *Complex*, in which the relationship between cause and effect can only be perceived in retrospect, but not in advance, the approach is to Probe – Sense – Respond and we can sense emergent practice.
- *Chaotic*, in which there is no relationship between cause and effect at a systems level, the approach is to Act – Sense – Respond and we can discover novel practice.
- *Disorder* is the fifth domain, which is the state of not knowing what type of causality exists, in which state people will revert to their own comfort zone in making a decision. In full use, the Cynefin framework has sub-domains, and the boundary between simple and chaotic is seen as a catastrophic one: complacency leads to failure (Snowden and Boone, 2007:72;75).

So how is this model useful to us in our coaching working with leaders? This framework is a tool for managing in a variety of contexts, and particularly useful for working in the complex environment of large corporations today. Also different styles of leadership and management are required dependent on the context. For example, Snowden and Boone (2007:75) recommend a particular way of working within each context as below. What is key is that good leadership requires the ability to be open to change at many levels – individual, team and organisational. Also, there may be a required change in the leaders' behaviour, and decisions to match the context rather than the leader's individual leadership style.

Four practices: best, good, emergent and novel

Best practice (simple environment)

When working with a client in a simple environment where patterns are repeated and events are consistent, and we are dealing with fact-based management, the leader's job would be to use best practice, communicating clearly and delegating – but with an understanding of the need for extensive, interactive communication.

In working with one client in this context, in the domain of best practice, it was simply necessary to assess the facts, evaluate them and help them to base their response on established practice. It was a matter of assessing within a banking institution, how and why a series of ATM robberies had been able to happen. In this instance, the leader and the team shared an understanding of how the technology operated, and the command-and-control style was adopted to move in and identify which automated functions were not working properly. This meant assessing the facts of the situation, categorising them, and then basing their response on established practice to deal with high security issues due to technology breakdowns.

The role of the coach was to work with the leader and the team helping them to think together, enabling a plan of investigation, and to establish a confidential communication network as they delegated the appropriate technological changes. What was important for the team was to be sure not to assume the problem was simple, and to create communication channels along already established lines (Snowden and Boone, 2007:75).

Good practice (complicated environment)

In a more complicated environment which is the domain of experts, the leader would need to diagnose the problems in consultation with a series of experts, trying to discover the cause-and-effect of the problem, identifying the one or more answers that might resolve the issue. In this instance it is important for the leader to create panels of experts and listen to conflicting advice.

Working with one client in a more complicated scenario, meant that there were a possible range of right answers. Snowden and Boone (2007) call this the realm of "known unknowns". Where leaders in a simple context must sense, *categorise* and respond – those in a complicated context must sense, *analyse* and respond. Here good practice is needed.

One client in a retail environment needed to investigate several options when considering a joint venture with another large retailer. This required several teams of experts to evaluate the consequences at multiple levels of the business. It also meant seeking out innovative suggestions by non-experts who had been part of strategically building the business over the years.

The role of the coach was to enable the leader to listen to the experts while considering out-of-the box thinking from others within his team, as well as helping the leader to avoid "analysis paralysis". The leader had never been involved in either a joint venture or acquisition, and found himself needing to approach his decision making more creatively than his normal default way of thinking. This is where the coach was able to play a role shadowing the leader in his various meetings as he dealt with unfamiliar and challenging relationships and data. The coach was able to help the leader think through the problem creatively, often working with metaphor, and to understand the time needed to make what would be a possible right way forward (Snowden and Boone, 2007:75).

Emergent practice (complex environment)

In a complex environment, there would be a great deal of flux and unpredictability with no right answers. There would be competing ideas, emergent rather than predictable patterns, and a need for creative and innovative problem-solving approaches. The leader would need to create an environment that would allow patterns to emerge, and to increase levels of interaction and communication. More importantly would be the need to open up discussion, allowing large group methods and an encouragement of dissent and diversity.

Another situation was working with the possibility that at least one right answer exists. This meant working in the realm of "unknown unknowns" and it is where the business has shifted to today. Unpredictability was introduced into the environment simply due to a bad set of quarterly and annual results, as well a loss of key senior executives who represented years of historical memory inside the organisation. The leader in this instance recognised emergent patterns that were instructive in understanding the bad sets of market results. A solution had to be found otherwise the company would have moved into freefall. The coach's role was to work with the leader and her team to stay away from traditional command-and-control style of management, and to understand their feelings of panic and fear of failure. Instead of trying to impose order they began to identify opportunities for innovation and a new business model, and beginning to understand the need to bring in expertise from outside to go forward (Snowden and Boone, 2007:75).

Novel practice (chaotic environment)

In a chaotic environment, there will be high turbulence with no clear cut cause-and-effect, many unknowables, and many decisions to make with possibly no time to think. Tension will be high. The leaders' job will be to look for what works instead of seeking the "right" answer, and to take immediate action to re-establish order. This may require a "command and control" type of leadership to begin with, moving into another style of leadership as the context changes. Clear and direct communication will be essential.

In this instance, the coach needed to work with the leader to decide on the right style of communication and how to establish order, at the same time creating a sense of stability in the environment. Many employees had left this small organisation unhappy with the previous style of management, and with disappointed expectations in what they saw as a high-tech, innovative and pioneering environment in which they were neither learning, growing nor contributing to innovation. The leader had to prevent the loss of any more highly valuable employees, and to quickly move from chaos to complexity in order to identify emergent patterns that would help prevent a recurrence.

Communication from the leader from top to bottom of the hierarchy was the first step in such a crisis to create a sense of stability and stem the flow of staff. It was also a way to bring in ideas for a way forward in an inclusive process, and to dissipate the turbulence caused by the loss of over 50 per cent of the staff. The leader had to "act", and to create stability, working collaboratively with the staff to discern new ways of working (Snowden and Boone, 2007:75).

CONCLUSION

In the previous chapter we began to explore how to liberate the client's story in the coaching conversation, working with the coach's tacit qualities. In this chapter we have been working with specific coaching models and their underlying philosophies, exploring how to work with analogy and metaphor to create a wider perspective, and to use structure to open up deeper discussion and deeper thinking.

I tend to explore models from an experiential learning premise as the client always brings their experience into the coaching conversation. You, however, will have your own approach with your own underpinning philosophy, experience and expertise.

At the end of this chapter we explored working in more complex environments where adaptability and systemic thinking are needed to help leaders to make decisions within contexts and systems which are continually changing. In the next chapter we look at Daniel Goleman's EQ Model, Ken Wilber's Integral Model, Ernesto Spinelli's Existential Model, and the six-stage coaching process of Nancy Kline's Thinking Environment®.

FURTHER READING

Goleman, D. (1996). *Emotional Intelligence: Why it can matter more than IQ*. London: Bloomsbury.

Hargrove, R.A. (2003). *Masterful Coaching: Inspire an "impossible future" while producing extraordinary leaders and extraordinary results*. San Francisco, CA: Jossey-Bass/Pfeiffer.

Harri-Augstein, S., and Thomas, L.F. (1991). *Learning Conversations, Self-Organised Learning: The way to personal and organisational growth*. London: Routledge.

Kolb, D.A. (1984). *Experiential Learning: Experience as the source of learning and development*. Upper Saddle River, NJ: Prentice Hall.

O'Neill, L.J. (2004). Faith and decision making in the Bush presidency: The God elephant in the middle of America's living room. *Emergence: Complexity and Organisations*, 6(1/2):149–156.

Snowden, D.J., and Boone, M.E. (2007). A leader's framework for decision making. *Harvard Business Review*, 85(11):69–76.

Stout-Rostron, S. (2012b). *Business Coaching Wisdom and Practice: Unlocking the Secrets of Business Coaching*. Second edition. Randburg: Knowres.

Stout-Rostron, S. (2014). *Business Coaching International: Transforming individuals and organisations*. Second edition. London: Karnac.

Weiss, P. (2004). *The Three Levels of Coaching*. San Francisco, CA: An Appropriate Response.

Whitmore, J. (2002). *Coaching for Performance: Growing people, performance and purpose*. London: Nicholas Brealey.

7

Facilitating the coaching conversation

This chapter explores a range of models that influence the work of business and executive coaches worldwide. I highlight the work of Daniel Goleman, Jürgen Habermas and James Flaherty, Ken Wilber, Ernesto Spinelli, and Nancy Kline.

As explained in Chapter 6, coaching models help us to understand the coaching intervention from a systems perspective, and to understand the need for "structure" in the interaction between coach and client. Models help us to develop flexibility as coach practitioners. They offer structure and an outline for both the coaching conversation and the overall coaching journey. However, although models create a system within which coach and client work, it is important that models are not experienced as either prescriptive or rigid.

THE EQ MODEL

The EQ (Emotional Intelligence) Model developed by Daniel Goleman (1996) provides fuel for investigation inside the coaching conversation, usually starting with questions about self-awareness and self-management, moving at a later stage to develop relationship awareness and relationship skills (such as interpersonal communication, managing people, and handling conflict). This EQ Model can represent the journey you and the client engage in together. The coach uses the EQ Model to help the client learn how to manage themselves and relationships. The coaching journey begins with developing the self.

We can relate this model to our use of four quadrants: left side for intrinsic and invisible; right side for extrinsic and visible; individual perspectives in the north, collective perspectives in the south (Figure 8). In the upper left is *developing self-awareness*, which people do not see; it is internal work for the client. That self-awareness shows up in their behaviour (upper right). In the upper right are their interactions with other individuals (*self-management*). In the lower left is their developing awareness of values, beliefs, feelings and organisational culture (*relationship awareness*), and in the lower right, managing relationships at a systemic level (*relationship management*), i.e. how teams, units and all stakeholders interact within an organisation and how they all interact with the society or community at large (or how families work together in a family system).

As clients develop *self-awareness*, they become more aware of what they say and do, and how they engage with others (*self-management*). As they begin to engage differently with others they gain an understanding and awareness of the culture, values and beliefs that exist within that organisation, and the diverse relationships operating concurrently in teams (*relationship awareness*). As their awareness grows, they also become more aware of how the system operates, how teams co-operate with each other or not, and how units, divisions, staff, customers and stakeholders interact with each other (*relationship management*) (Table 3).

EQ Model case study

With one executive with whom I worked with for two years, we focused in our first year on his growing self-awareness. Through our work together he began to think about his own limiting messages that derailed him at important moments in meetings, or stopped him from stepping into situations that would create more professional visibility for himself. We began to transform those limiting personal messages into more liberating ways of looking at his substantial contribution to the organisation (self-awareness).

At the same time, we explored how he communicated with his direct reports, one-on-one, and in the team; as well as how he actually *spoke* to them and with them (self-management). Insights were gained about his tendency to speak too fast, mumble and keep his teeth clenched together as if getting every word out was difficult. It meant that clarity was limited in his communications with his team, and similarly with superiors, colleagues and other important stakeholders in this complex international organisation. As his communication skills improved, I asked him to work with an actress on voice, body and speech to improve how he put his presentations together, how he engaged with both large and small audiences, and how he incorporated stories to create a more dynamic presence (self-management).

We also began to think about the values of his particular business, and where those values were and were not in alignment with the organisation overall (relationship awareness). We began to identify the culture of *encouragement* and *learning* that began to be more present within his business; this was in tandem with his growing self-awareness and different ways of engaging with others. The changes in his behaviour were subtle, but an awareness of more openness in the culture began to be acknowledged (relationship awareness).

As we continued our work together, dealing with the various constraints in the system that he had to contend with, and the resistances he felt towards the matrix system within which he was working, we identified the systemic issues and dynamics that created anxiety in his ability to move his division forward (relationship management). We began to look at the dynamics between the international head office and the regional head office, and both offices' relationship with him as the leader of his business (relationship management). As we began to work with his resistance to the system and its complex rules and complexity, he began to be more aware of the trust put into him and his division for the projects and disciplined work successfully completed in the last two years. This client is now ready to transition into a new role having greater awareness of how he thinks, feels and behaves, as well as how he engages with others and how they experience him in the workplace. He developed a much greater awareness of his own power and reputation and an understanding of his impact and influence on the culture and system overall.

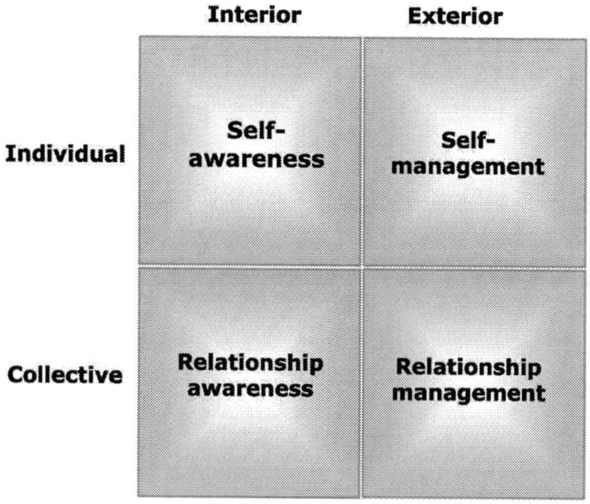

Figure 8: *A four-quadrant adaptation of the EQ Model*

Source: Adapted from Goleman (1996) and Wilber (2006)

Table 3: *Emotional intelligence: competences and associated skill*

Self-awareness ➜	Self-management ➜	Relationship awareness ➜ (Team / system awareness)	Relationship management ➜ (Team / system management)
Knowing self	Interpersonal behaviour	Organisational culture (values, beliefs, feelings)	Team behaviour; Client management
Resistances	Communication skills	Environment	Conflict management
Purpose	Management skills	Politics	Systems integration

Source: Stout-Rostron (2006)

DOMAINS OF COMPETENCE MODEL (HABERMAS/FLAHERTY)

Part of a coach's discipline is to be able to use and understand models to structure the coaching intervention, helping the client to develop self-awareness and change behaviour. The Domains of Competence Model (Figure 9), based by Flaherty (1999) on Jürgen Habermas's concept of domains of reality, is a pre-cursor to understanding Wilber's four-quadrant Integral Model. The Integral Model defines the "general structures of communication" that enable clients to engage in successful interaction (Wilber, 2000:82–83). Habermas defined three domains of reality in the world that exist concurrently: I, We, It. The right-hand drawing below is the original example in James Flaherty's book *Coaching: Evoking excellence in others* (Flaherty, 1999:83). We have adapted it to a holistic framework for our use.

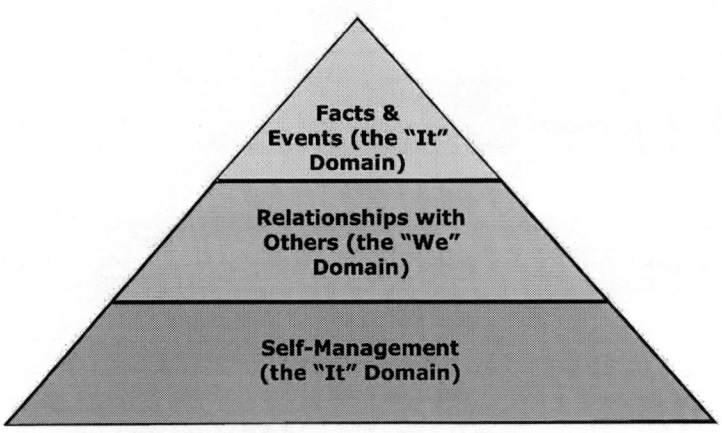

Figure 9: Domains of Competence Model

Source: Adapted from Flaherty (1999) and Weiss (2004)

I: the domain of the individual

The subjective world of the individual who sees the world through his or her own eyes. Access to this domain is through self-observation and developing self-knowledge. The skills required are those of self-observation, self-knowledge, self-management, self-remembering, self-consistency and daring. The competences are purpose, self-knowledge, self correction and persistence. The basis of this domain is "subjective" and the qualities are that of vision, passion, integrity, trust and curiosity.

We: the domain of the collective or the community

This is the collective view of how "we" see the world. This view is embodied in social practices, roles, rituals, meaning, narrative and values that determine what's possible. Access to this domain is through dialogue, conversation and relationships. The skills required to access this domain are listening, speaking, setting standards, learning and innovating (Braaten, 1991). The competences are relationship, communication, leadership and inspiration. The basis of this domain's reality is "subjective". The qualities of this reality are empathy, reliability, openness, and faith.

It: the domain of the external or objective world

This domain is that of science and technology, objective nature, empirical forms, and processes. It deals with objects, and access to this domain is by becoming observant, analysing, predicting and building models. The competences of this objective domain are processes, technology, measurement and statistics, and the qualities of this domain are rigour, objectivity, persistence, creativity and focus (Wilber, 1996).

Leadership Coaching for Results: Cutting-edge practices for coach and client

Practical exercise

Our clients operate in all three of these domains, and we can devise questions in each to further client development. As an exercise devise questions that you could ask, relevant to each domain. These questions are to help your client understand the lens through which they see the world, and to help them begin to think about, experience and see the world through other's eyes. James Flaherty says this model represents the essential domains of life in which a "leader must be competent". Examples of possible questions:

I Domain: How can you continue your own self-development? What are your short-term and long-term goals? How can you balance both work and personal life? What are your blind spots and how can you work with them?

We Domain: How can you use your skills of communication and persuasion to inspire people to action? What is your value to the team? How can you build competence in the team having lost a valued member? What are the values and goals of your team?

It Domain: What are the processes that are working in the organisation? What technical processes need to be written up for your training manuals? What processes are not being strictly adhered to and how can you best apply them?

KEN WILBER'S FOUR-QUADRANT INTEGRAL MODEL

Ken Wilber has written prodigiously about the evolution of his model, and various adaptations of his Integral Model are taught in global coach training institutions. Wilber's Integral Model is an elegant way to map the essentials of human growth and development – socially, psychologically and spiritually. Wilber integrates five factors essential to facilitating human growth which he calls *quadrants, levels, lines, states and types*. However, in this book, we are to work only with his four quadrants, which refer to the subjective and objective realities within each of us (Figure 10).

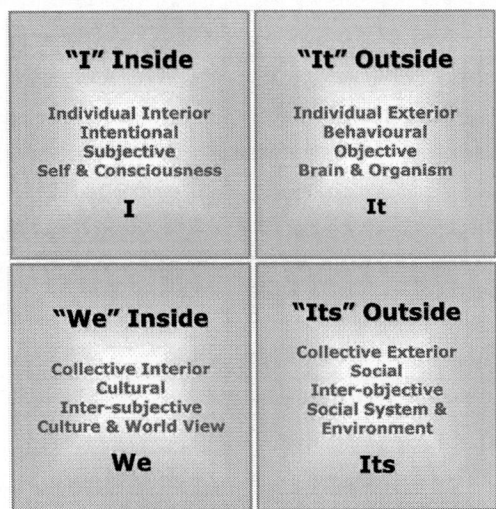

Figure 10: Ken Wilber's four-quadrant Integral Model

Source: Wilber (2006:36–39)

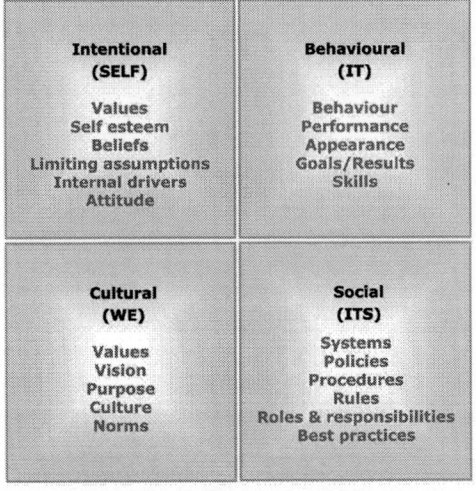

Figure 11: An adaptation of Wilber's four-quadrant Integral Model

Source: Adapted from Pampallis Paisley (2006)

Wilber's (2006:17) philosophy is that "every level of interior consciousness is accompanied by a level of exterior physical complexity". In other words, the more consciousness we have in the interior, the greater our corresponding understanding of the complexities of the exterior world. If as coaches we are helping clients to learn from experience, then it is important that we understand the I (inside the individual), the we (inside the collective), the it (outside the individual), and the its (outside the collective) (Wilber, 2006:20–21).

Leadership Coaching for Results: Cutting-edge practices for coach and client

My purpose is to help you design coaching questions that emerge within each of the quadrants, to develop a growing consciousness in your client's interaction with "self" and the "world". All four quadrants can show growth and development. Wilber explains that the unfolding four quadrants can "include expanding spheres of consciousness ... Self and culture and nature can all develop and evolve" (Wilber, 2006:25). All four quadrants need to be taken into account if we want to work as integrally as possible with our clients, helping them integrate perspectives and awareness (Figure 11).

Upper left (UL)

I (UL) is inside the individual, i.e. self and consciousness; the individual's values, vision, their purpose, their culture, their norm. In this model, the upper left (UL) is *interior*, *individual and intentional*. The internal you is represented by your values, your beliefs, your morals, your feelings, your emotions, your self confidence and self assurance. The UL represents what goes on inside of you and is not visible to the external world.

Upper right (UR)

It, the UR quadrant is described as *exterior*, *individual and behavioural*. The UR shows how your values, beliefs, feelings and emotions show up through your behaviour and interaction with others in the external world. It is outside the individual, i.e. to do with the body, brain and behaviour. This is how the individual shows up in their behaviour with another individual out in the world; it is their interpersonal skills, competences, what they say and do; what they don't say and do. Once this behaviour is visible, i.e. what you say and do, and what you don't say and do, this behaviour is represented in the upper right quadrant (UR).

Lower left (LL)

We, the lower left, is *interior*, *collective and cultural*. We is inside the collective, i.e. culture and worldview of the organisation or the society; what are the values, culture and beliefs of the team, organisation, society, nation that the individual is a part of. This is represented by an awareness of your relationships with others, with the values and beliefs of the collectives in which you operate.

For example: your organisation (superiors, subordinates, peers) or family; or within the communities of your spiritual life. These collectives share similar values. For example, your organisation may be underpinned by family values, health or capitalising on consumer needs with which you are in alignment.

Lower right (LR)

Its (LR) is outside the collective, i.e. the social system and its environment. This is represented by the systems, rules, regulations and procedures within the corporate environment and society in which the client works. The lower right quadrant (LR) is represented by the *exterior collective and the systems* in which you live and work; i.e. the rules, regulations, processes and procedures that operate within your family, society, work place, region, nation and the world. The shared values and the shared relationships meet each other in harmony or conflict in this quadrant.

For example, teams or companies within the system who are able to work collaboratively; or, on the other hand, due to gender inequalities, an organisation who only pays lip service to the development of women in leadership and pulls candidates from training and development programmes without understanding the negative impact it might have on women wishing to move into management roles within that organisation.

According to Wilber (2006), these four quadrants enable us to map every phenomenon, every interest, every area and every process in life according to internal and external processes. We can use this model as coaches to help clients to understand themselves, developing self awareness and a conscious awareness of their interior life. Coaches can also use this model to help clients understand the impact of their interactions with others in the external world, and how they manage themselves and their relationships within the cultures and systems (family, community, organisation, society and nation) in which they live and work.

We can relate this model to the four quadrants of the EQ Model. On the upper left is a developing *self-awareness* which people do not see; that self-awareness shows up in your behaviour; upper right in your interactions with other individuals (*self-management*); in the lower left is your developing awareness of values, beliefs, feelings and culture (*relationship awareness*); and lower right, managing relationships at a systemic level (*relationship management*), i.e. how teams or companies interact within an organisation, and how families work together in a family system.

How the quadrants are represented – in society

In May 2008, in South Africa we experienced a flood of violent, xenophobic behaviour. It had been brewing on the individual interior level (UL) for many years with individuals who feel discriminated against in society. As Jonathan Faull wrote in the *Cape Times*: "Many poor, urban citizens of South Africa's cities feel under- or unrepresented, buffeted by the tides of poverty, subsistence, criminality and the desperate competition for resources and opportunity ..." (Faull, 2008). In poorer areas, foreign nationals have grouped together by nationality to protect themselves and to continue to live within a semblance of a culture that they understand (LL). Locals, nationals and foreign nationals have managed to coexist with each other with the odd external flare-up or demonstration of conflict at an individual level (UR) and between cultures (LR).

The recent xenophobic attacks have been at a systemic level (LR): mob violence and criminal gangs have instituted an array of violent attacks against poorer, isolated foreign nationals. The attackers sense of frustration and discrimination shows up in the attacks on individuals (UR) and on groups of foreign nationals (LR). The sense of despair is due to the lack of enough jobs, housing and the continuing poverty within which many continue to live.

Case study: in the workplace

Recently, I have been working with an executive, Ben, in a retail manufacturing industry who has a history of success. His divisional performance (LR) and his individual performance (UR) have always been rated as excellent. However, in the last two years, Ben has suffered an extreme loss of self-confidence and worrying health problems. This was due to working with a destructive line manager whose behaviour was extremely negative over a two-year period. This line manager undermined Ben constantly, shouting and humiliating Ben in meetings (LR), as well as displaying constant aggressive behaviour one-on-one (UR).

Eventually the constant undermining of Ben began to impact negatively on his performance (UR). The work between coach and client (UR) has been to rebuild the confidence and self-esteem of this individual by increasing his levels of self-awareness (UL). The coach instituted a 360° feedback (LL) and discovered that Ben was highly thought of throughout the organisation (LL). However, the organisation was very concerned for Ben's mental and physical health (UL). Gradually, through a combination of one-on-one coaching conversations between coach and client, with Ben and various senior executives to whom he reports (UR), and coaching conversations in the collective team (LR), Ben has begun the process of working on his confidence and his health by learning new interpersonal skills and competences (UR), developing greater self-awareness of his own and other's assumptions (UL).

Questions in the four quadrants

To use the Integral Model as a coaching process, we can look at the types of questions you might ask the client within each quadrant to build perspective on themselves and their own issues:

- Upper Left (UL): What's going on for you; how are you thinking and feeling?
- Upper Right (UR): Where are you in relation to the other?
- Lower Left (LL): How would you describe the culture, values and relationships in your organisation?
- Lower Right (LR): Where are you in relation to the system or world in which you live and work?

We can devise questions from a macro and a micro perspective, whether for contracting, for the overall coaching journey, or the individual coaching conversation. It should be remembered that this is a very complex model, and we are working with it in its formative stages. Try to devise your own questions before looking at the examples listed in Figure 12.

INDIVIDUAL

What's going on for you?

What's important to you
personally/professionally?
What is motivating you?
What is working for you?
What's not working for you?
How does this make you feel?
What are your goals?
What would that goal feel like?
What do you think about that goal?
What is your feeling about that?
What is your understanding?

**Where are you in relation to
the other?
(actions and behaviours)**

What are you doing and saying?
What are you not doing or saying?
What could you say or do differently?
What would it look like?
What would it feel like?
How are you perceived?
How would you see the other behave if you
changed your behaviour?
How can you consistently work with your new
behaviour?
What will get in your way?

Interior ⟵⟶ **Exterior**

**How would you describe the
culture and values in your
organisation?**

What are the team's values?
What are your team goals?
How do your values and goals fit in with those
of the team?
What is the impact of these values on the
team, organisation and society?
How do others interact with you?
How are you feeling in relation to others?
What makes you comfortable/uncomfortable
in the work environment?
What impact have the company changes had
on people's morale?

**Where are you in relation to
the system/world in which you
live and work?**

What needs to change?
How would your team function if your goals
and that of the team were congruent?
What systems block communication?
How does the performance evaluation system
work?
How can your team impact the organisational
system?
If your team did x...what would the impact be
on ...?
What else goes on in the system?
What has changed in your environment?
How is the economic downturn affecting your
customers and company overall?

COLLECTIVE

Figure 12: Questions in Wilber's quadrants

Source: Stout-Rostron (2012b:115)

EXISTENTIAL ISSUES AND
EXPERIENTIAL LEARNING

All of the underpinnings from the models in this chapter are useful for us to understand when working with an existential coaching philosophy. The coach's intent is not always outcomes-based; it can also focus on *learning*, *development*, *meaning* and *transformation*. The complexity of these issues is often influenced by the three-way intervention between the organisation, the client and the coach.

Leadership Coaching for Results: Cutting-edge practices for coach and client

Within the business coaching context, the coach helps the client to articulate his or her existential concerns such as freedom, purpose, choice and anxiety, and to identify and replace limiting paradigms with empowering paradigms, thus leading to positive change. Existential philosophy regards human existence as unexplainable, and emphasises freedom of choice and taking responsibility for one's acts.

These existential issues are relevant to the coach too. For example, if you look at purpose, the coach might be tempted to confuse their own individual purpose with that of the client, and in the process be seduced to use their position or power to influence the client. The coach often holds "guru" status, especially in the beginning of the relationship, and it is therefore important for the business coach to be aware of their own existential issues as well as those of the client.

Existential issues and experiential learning are strongly linked. In existentialism, the "relationship" comes up as an important factor in being able to learn from experience. According to Boud, Cohen and Walker (1993:11), experience is created in the "transaction" between the individual and the environment in which they operate – in other words, it is relational. More is often lost than gained by ignoring the uniqueness of each person's history and ways of experiencing the world.

In existential terms, the meaning of individual experience is not a given; in coaching, it is subject to interpretation by the individual client in conjunction with their work with their coach. In the coaching conversation, the coaching client learns to actively reconstruct their own experience, attaching their own meaning to events, and yet understanding commonly accepted interpretations of their world.

This concern with change and the client's journey through life is a core component of the coaching process, and combined with the question of "who am I", can present various dilemmas for coach and client within an organisational system. We explore several of these dilemmas as we look at what existentialism means in a coaching context.

What is existentialism?

Existential concerns have been discussed from the beginning of philosophical debate about the human condition, encompassing thinkers such as Socrates and his dialogues. The literary, philosophical and artistic response to modern cultural crises has also massively influenced existentialism. Existentialism displays a concern with individuals in crisis. The term "existence" refers to coming into being or becoming. It derives from the Latin root *ex-sistere* which means to "stand out or emerge". Existential psychology has grown out of the awareness that serious gaps exist in our way of understanding human beings. It sought to analyse the structure of human existence to "understand the reality underlying all situations of human beings in crisis" (May, 1983:44).

Basically concerned with ontology, or the science of being, existentialism is based on the underlying fact that "you and I alone must face the fact that at some unknown moment in the future we shall die" (May, 1983:51). Existential vocabulary includes terms such as *being, choice, responsibility, freedom, death, isolation, mortality, absurdity, purpose in life, limitations* and *willing*.

Being versus doing

Ernesto Spinelli, previously existential professor of psychology at Regent's College London, and now with Ernesto Spinelli Associates, noted in a lecture in Cape Town in February 2005 that:

> At the moment, we inhabit a culture which places tremendous importance on expectations. A group is growing in numbers, who are seen as 'experts-in-living' and who are working with clients. We need our clients to see us as experts, but if someone asks 'What is your expertise?', our tendency is to translate expertise in terms of skills, competences, specialist knowledge, certain forms of personality tests. Our primary focus is 'doing' – experts do.
>
> Existentialism challenges the notion of expertise as 'doing' and reconsiders expertise from the point of view of 'being'. The question then becomes, 'How is it that I am with other human beings, with other living beings, with living and non-living objects?'
>
> The basic idea is this, that the way I reveal myself with other beings or the world in general exposes not only that moment of being, but gives a sense of totality – that individual's general stance towards reality. How I am with you reveals how I am, not only to you, but to myself, to others and to the world in general (Spinelli, 2005).

Being emphasises the activity rather than the goal. *Being in becoming* emphasises *who* the person is rather than *what* the person can accomplish. But it still emphasises the concept of development. The *doing* orientation emphasises accomplishments that are measurable by standards outside of the acting individual (Yalom, 1980:121). If we are to transform organisations – culturally, socially, emotionally and cognitively – then the ultimate goal of coaching is seeking the transformation of self.

Culture plays an important role in the shaping of individual values. Florence Kluckhohn, who pursued research in cultural value orientations, suggested three anthropological value orientations for the individual human: *being, being in becoming,* and *doing* (Kluckhohn and Strodtbeck, 1961:15). There is constant discussion in contemporary coaching circles about which comes first, being or doing; but little mention is made about "being in becoming". This may, in fact, be the existential category where coaches most often work with their clients (McWhinney *et al.*, 1993:28).

Existential dilemma: meaning and purpose

Often in the business coaching environment, the client will state that one of their objectives is to determine meaning in their personal and professional life. The client may be questioning why they do what they do. The start of this personal philosophical thinking tends to originate from questions such as, "What motivates you?" and "What is important to you?" One well-known example concerns two stone masons who were asked what they were doing. One answered, "I am cutting a stone"; the other said, "I am building a cathedral". To ask your client, "What is the meaning and purpose of your work?" can be the beginning of a quest of self-discovery. A surgeon in India wanted to make cataract operations very inexpensive for the poor. Rather than tell his team that this was the ultimate aim, he explained that their real vision was to "cure blindness".

Faith or spirituality speaks to our underlying values and drivers, often being a search for something greater than we are. "Who am I and why am I here?" is ultimately a search for meaning and purpose in life. Often, individuals turn to faith or a spiritual journey with these questions. From a coaching perspective, a client may ask questions about a possible change of career, or even start to think about unfulfilled challenges. Typically, these questions evolve to "Who are they?" and "How do they be who they are?"

Although coaches love to work with existential questions, such questions present a dilemma. If the organisation pays the coach's fees, and the aim of coaching is performance-related, yet the client focuses on an inner search for meaning and purpose, this may present an ethical challenge for the coach. Some clients are lucky and the organisation contracts the coach to pave the individual's road to self-discovery. This, however, is not the norm! It is useful to build this possibility into the contracting process. Often when you begin the coaching process, the client is already in transition, whether to a new position or on their way out of the organisation. It is important to emphasise to the client organisation that change is a normal part of the coaching process.

A framework for coaching (in Yalom's view) may be a synthesis of the business belief system, the coach's model with its theoretical and philosophical underpinnings, plus the development of the relationship. Spinelli (2005) indicated that the "relationship" is the core factor in any therapeutic, coaching, supervisory or counselling session and perhaps even for research. My work and research have examined this and underlined, time and time again, that no matter what level the coaching intervention, it seems that the fundamental work of the coaching intervention establishes the importance of the relationship.

As Yalom puts it (in the context of psychotherapy):

> I am convinced that the surreptitious 'throw-ins' made all the difference ... I believe that, when no one is looking, the therapist throws in the 'real thing'. But what are these 'throw-ins', these elusive, 'off-the-record' extras? They exist outside of formal theory, they are not written about, they are not explicitly taught ... Indeed, is it possible to define and teach such qualities as compassion, 'presence', caring, extending oneself, touching the patient at a profound level, or – that most elusive of all – wisdom? (Yalom, 1980:3–4).

> Existential psychotherapy is a dynamic approach to therapy which focuses on concerns that are rooted in the individual existence ... it is the relationship that heals (Yalom, 1980:5).

According to May (1983), in the Western world, we have managed to dominate nature, but in the process we have repressed the sense of being – the ontological being. Robert Hargrove (2003) says a coach is something that you "be". He asks whether the coach is "being" or "doing" when helping clients inside the coaching conversation. Hargrove promotes the idea of "Kokoro", i.e. perfecting one's inner nature. "One must not only master the technique but also perfect the way of being consistent with the discipline, having a calm and centred inner spirit; to be able to teach people; one must perfect his or her own nature" (Hargrove, 2003:44).

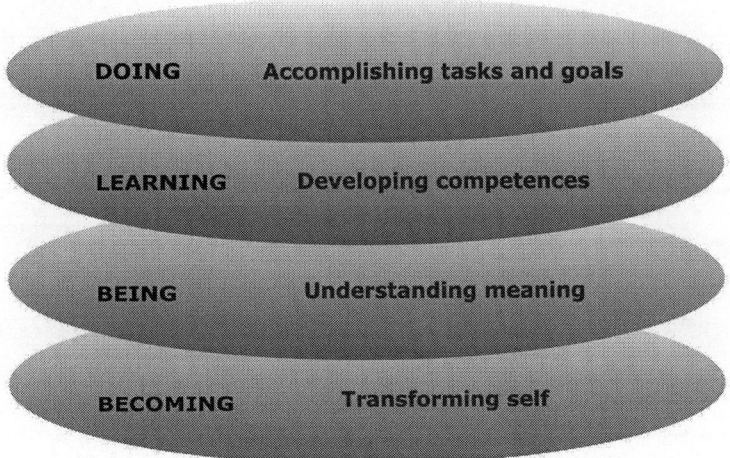

Figure 13: Becoming – transforming self

Source: Adapted from Weiss (2004)

Choice is one of the existential concerns in the coaching process and is related to the process of setting goals and taking action. Hargrove (2003) says the coach can help the client declare new possibilities for themselves through the power of language, and that the power to choose who you need to be exists in your conversations, in your speaking and listening, and not in grappling with your history. This emphasises the performance model versus a psychological model.

Within the coaching conversation, the coach is not necessarily looking for the psychological paradigm, but listening more to what underpins language and linguistic patterns. This resonates with my linguistic background, which predisposes the coach to analyse the context, content, structure and meaning of language when working with clients, either when observing and shadowing them at work or when working inside the coaching conversation.

The rabbit hole story

One of my clients wanted help to structure the way she approached her daily life and business. I helped the client to translate her actions and her way of thinking into meaningful experience. The client discovered that she thinks linguistically and kinaesthetically, but it did not help her to structure her day using words and feelings. She decided that she needed to interpret her world differently, i.e. visually, in order to have more meaningful experiences and make life work better for her.

When the coach and client constructed a learning contract at the end of a first session, the client had as her *purpose*: to learn to structure her thinking differently; as her *strategy*: to use the new way of thinking to manage her life and her business more effectively; and as *specific outcomes*: (1) to work daily with visual thinking and visual language, and (2) to journal daily from words into pictures into visual language.

Previously, the client had constructed a kinaesthetic view of the world and had ascribed meaning to it kinaesthetically and linguistically. She needed to bring in visual thinking to make more sense of her world and to be able to "see her day". The coach and client focused on her limiting assumption that she could not think visually. That changed on the day when client and coach "went down a rabbit hole" in the coaching conversation. The client discovered herself visually by describing her journey down the "rabbit hole"; she came out into the light of the natural world with a visual rather than a kinaesthetic reconstruction of her experience.

In the light of these coaching conversations, the coach was helping the client to interpret her own reality and to see how she constructed meaning within that reality. The client achieved her goal at the end of the "rabbit hole" session – i.e. to identify her avoiding behaviours when trying to think visually (Stout-Rostron, 2006:167).

Personal responsibility and awareness

One of our first areas of focus is awareness: helping the client to grow in awareness and to accept personal responsibility to create change for themselves. How the client takes up responsibility for change emerges from the coaching conversation.

Existentially, choice and change offer a way of taking responsibility and defining one's own self. Sartre also wrote, "authenticity versus self-deception is the absolute personal responsibility" (Peltier, 2001:157). "We cannot make life deliver what we want, but we can control what we think and desire; rigorous self-disciplined thought is the key" (Olson, 1962:11, quoted in Peltier, 2001:158). Not specifically an intervention, but ten existential guidelines are offered for the executive coach by Peltier (2001:164–167):

- anticipate anxiety and defensiveness;
- clients must figure things out in their own way;
- commit to something;
- create and sustain authentic relationships;
- encourage choice;

- get going;
- honour individuality;
- manage conflict and confrontation;
- value responsibility taking;
- welcome and appreciate the absurd.

Coaching guidelines could advocate: reflection, developing insight and awareness, setting goals, using language appropriately, making choices and taking action. Peltier (2001:168) says, "authentic individualism requires extensive self-examination and the willingness to live with the decisions one makes as a result". This may be in contrast with other belief systems or cultural values, such as the principle of *ubuntu* in African cultures, where it is not so much individualism that is important, but relationships within the community.

Ubuntu

The African notion of *ubuntu* can be defined as "morality, humaneness, compassion, care, understanding and empathy. It is about shared values and humanity" (Boon, 1996:31). In *ubuntu* terms, you are only who you are in relation to others. In other words, *ubuntu* is about interaction within the community. *Ubuntu* sends you as an individual on a journey where you will find out who you are when you meet the people in your life. It is about life, relationships and values, and in many ways, this is a very existentialist philosophy. Northern European individualism is a very different philosophy from *ubuntu*, which experiences existence in relation to others, and within a sense of community.

The term *ubuntu* is important in the South African context where I live as it refers to an African view of life and worldview. *Ubuntu* powerfully suggests that man is essentially a social being and that "a person is a person through other persons" (Devenish, 2005). *Ubuntu* is more aligned with the second of the two famously assumed existential states of being: being-for-itself and being-for-others. *Ubuntu* requires the "right balance between individualism and collectivism and is made possible by taking seriously people's need for dignity, self-respect and regard for others. Its emphasis is not on differences, but on accommodating these" (Devenish, 2005).

If we are to work with an existential approach we need to understand underpinning existential themes, knowing that "at all times we have the power to choose who we are being" (Hargrove, 2003):

- Recognising that life is at times unfair and unjust.
- Recognising that ultimately there is no escape from some of life's pain and death.
- Recognising that no matter how close I get to other people, I must still face life alone.
- Facing the basic issues of my life and death and thus living my life more honestly and being less caught up in trivialities.
- Learning that I must take ultimate responsibility for the way I live my life – no matter how much guidance and support I get from others (Yalom, 1980:265)

Ernesto Spinelli's Existential Model

Spinelli's existential approach is that:

- The coach's intention is an attitude of openness to allow the client's experiences to unfold in their own right.
- Observation rather than interpretation lets themes and patterns emerge. However, the coach needs to remain as free as possible from personal assumptions, bias and pre-judgement about the significance and meaning of the client's experience.
- Clients put their own meaning and interpretation onto their own experience, their thinking and the events that happen to them.
- Clients speak their own language relevant to their own background, experience and expertise (Spinelli, 2005).

To work with Spinelli's Model we need to understand his three existential rules for the practitioner conversation. Remember, that in coaching we are not diagnosing or interpreting as in therapy, we are observing and challenging. This is why we "describe" rather than interpret the client's world back to them.

- As the coach, set aside your biases and prejudices of things – in other words, suspend your expectations and assumptions.
- Describe, don't explain or interpret the client's world back to them – remain focused on immediate and concrete descriptions, rather than theoretical explanations.
- Avoid making misleading, highly-based judgements – "they have to choose what is most important to talk about".

NANCY KLINE'S THINKING PARTNERSHIP® MODEL

As I work from an existential point of view in my coaching practice, I find the underlying premise of Nancy Kline's thinking skills to be in alignment, i.e. the individual thinker is best able to do their own thinking, and all clients have the internal mental resources they need to learn or think for themselves. The basis of the Nancy Kline thinking process is that of uncovering limiting assumptions and creating positive liberating alternatives.

In this particular model, the key obstacles to fluid or clear thinking, and the setting and achievement of goals, are usually limiting assumptions (true, possibly true or even untrue). In fact, the obstacles that emerge in life are often from the obstacles in an individual's thinking. When appropriate, working with the six stages of this model – we identify, remove and replace disempowering assumptions with more empowering and liberating ones.

This Thinking Partnership® process developed by Nancy Kline is a six-stage process underpinned by ten components or behaviours, positive philosophical choice, and incisive questions. One of the key theories which determines how we work with clients in the Thinking Environment® "coaching conversation" is that of "positive philosophical choice". Kline's Thinking Partnership® is based on the "chosen philosophical view that human beings are by nature good: intelligent, loving, powerful, multi-talented, emotional, assertive, able to think through anything, imaginative and logical". Kline says that "behaviour to the contrary is seen as the result of assumptions generated over a lifetime by events, conditions and attitudes in a person's environment" (Kline, 2012:4).

Apart from positive philosophical choice and limiting assumptions, Nancy Kline's Thinking Partnership® model is based on one other key factor, that of the ten thinking components or behaviours that are essential to create the external and internal space for the client:

1. *attention* (listening with interest and without interruption);
2. *equality* (treating the other as a thinking peer; keeping agreements and boundaries);
3. *ease* (offering freedom from internal rush or urgency);
4. *appreciation* (a 5:1 ratio of appreciation to criticism);
5. *encouragement* (moving beyond internal competition);
6. *feelings* (allowing sufficient emotional release to restore thinking);
7. *information* (supplying facts; managing organisational denial);
8. *diversity* (welcoming divergent thinking and diverse group identities);
9. *incisive questions* (removing assumptions that limit ideas); and
10. *place* (creating a physical environment that says to the other, "You matter") (Kline, 1999).

The Thinking Environment® coaching process

In Kline's Thinking Environment® process, the crucial work is to identify and replace limiting assumptions with a more powerful worldview by choosing one core limiting assumption at a time to overturn that is relevant to the presenting issue. Kline's framework is based on six stages of questioning (Kline, 2012):

1. *Exploration* (What do you want to think about and what are your thoughts?)
2. *Further goal* (What more would you like to achieve from this session?)
3. *Assumptions* (What are you assuming that is stopping you from / making you [insert goal]?)
    *   Which is the assumption most stopping / making you?
    *   Do you think this assumption is true?
    *   What are your reasons for thinking so? (Look for alignment with the three criteria of positive philosophical choice, logic and information).
        Transition question:
        -   (If it is true or possibly true): That is true or possible, but what are you assuming that causes that to stop you / make you [insert goal]?
        Limiting Alternative Question:
        -   (If it is not true): As [insert untrue assumption] is not true, what are your words for what is true and liberating?
        Invitation question (if there is not complete alignment with the three criteria):
        -   Given that the assumption that [insert assumption] is stopping you from [insert goal], what could you credibly assume instead in order to [insert goal]?

4. *Incisive question* (if you knew that [insert true liberating assumption] how would you [insert goal]?)
5. *Recording* (client records incisive question and action to be taken).
6. *Appreciation* (key component: what quality do you respect / admire in each other?)

Although this process looks to be prescriptive and linear it is far from it. In each of the six stages the thinker dips and soars through emergent thoughts and feelings. What is important, however, is that if you are to work with this process, I highly recommend you find one of the Thinking Environment® Faculty programmes to attend in your area. It is a complex and highly skilled process to work with.

According to Nancy Kline (1999:100–101), team effectiveness depends on the calibre of thinking the team can do. Yet most teams do not operate within a thinking environment with the ten components necessary to enhance quality thinking and decision making. Teams are the most strategic place to begin organisational change, but the limiting assumptions of each team member and the limiting assumptions of the group as a whole need to be identified and replaced with empowering assumptions.

Although this is one of the purest coaching question frameworks I have encountered, its ultimate success in the coaching context is in the client and the team's implementing the goals that are set as a result. These six stages help us to understand the process of identifying limiting assumptions and replacing them with more empowering assumptions. This is a transformative process for the individual client or thinker.

In this process, awareness and insight is the context within which the coach works with the client to identify, understand and change those limiting assumptions that are most getting in the way of the client's taking responsibility, setting goals, taking action, growing and learning.

Existentialism and the Thinking Environment®

My approach is from an existential as well as a phenomenological viewpoint. My clients ultimately wish to talk about their "purpose in life" and the anxiety they experience in trying to "be" who they are and "do" what they need to do within the complexity of the systems within which they work.

Existentialism says there is no subjective or objective frame of reference; there is only the process of thinking about it. From my own work with clients, I have found that coaching helps them to interpret their own reality and understand how they construct meaning from their reality. In other words, we share a lot of experiences as human beings, but ultimately each individual's experience of the world is unique. Each client is unique in the way they think, in the way they see the world, in the way they interpret events. Here existentialism is related to phenomenology, where openness and an attitude of wonder will "allow the specific circumstances and experiences to unfold in their own right" (Spinelli, 1989).

The Thinking Environment® and existential phenomenology

I believe that Kline's work is aligned with existential phenomenology in the sense that it is important for the coach to "bracket" his or her own assumptions, listen intently and approach the coaching conversation with openness and no judgement (Stout-Rostron, 2006). The assumptions the coach helps the client to identify, remove and replace by working through the above stages are at three levels: *true, possibly true,* and *untrue limiting assumptions*. In this process the thinker and coach speak in a ratio of 7:1.

There are two kinds of bedrock assumption in the Thinking Environment®: subjective perceptions of self and subjective perceptions of how life works (Kline, 2012:2). In the Thinking Environment®, accurate *incisive questions* can remove limiting assumptions and create a resurgence of creativity, clarity and courage. And in the Kline diversity process, thinking partners explore the roots of discriminatory attitudes and behaviours by examining the untrue limiting assumptions society and organisations make about people on the basis of their group identities and place in the hierarchy. Participants learn how to remove those limiting assumptions and replace them with true liberating assumptions that free people and groups to reclaim their self-esteem and influence (Kline, 2012:3).

There are two kinds of Thinking Environment®: one provided externally by the coach or person giving attention to the thinker; the other provided internally, residing in the mind of the thinker, provided by positive assumptions about the self as a thinker. Both kinds of environments are affected by society's limiting assumptions about people's group identities (Kline, 2012:30). Kline talks about group identities as they link to worldviews. She reaffirms that prejudice against people is driven by untrue limiting assumptions about their group identities. The core limiting assumption is that you, inherently, cannot think as well as the people outside your group. When this assumption (and the assumption that the dominant group will have to think for you) becomes internalised by members of the group, the group agrees to stay disempowered (Kline, 2012:30).

DESIGNING YOUR OWN MODEL

The purpose in trying to design your coaching model, is to understand the coaching intervention from a systems perspective. If we look at a model as representing a "system" with an implied process – a coaching model can encompass the process and the journey that the coach and client embark on together. Models systemically visualise or represent a process that cannot be directly observed as it is simply two-dimensional on paper. A model therefore represents more than what you see, so we need to best express how the model is lived out in the coaching conversation. In order to do so we need a *structure, a process* and an *underpinning philosophy or rationale.*

Structure

For the *structure* we need to hang our model on a frame of some kind (circular, triangular, quadrant, spiral, ladder) which gives us our *structure*.

Philosophy or worldview

Also, models are underpinned by or resonate with a particular worldview or philosophy: psychological, scientific, legal, medical / health, organisational, systemic, financial / economic, political, ethical or existential. Here we are defining world view as a "framework of ideas, beliefs, or philosophy through which an individual or group interpret the world and interact with it".

Process

And we need to define the *process* that makes the structure work, as described in all of the models above. The Kolb model is a good model with which to think about how to describe your coaching process. It has the *structure* of working with the four specific modes of Kolb's experiential learning cycle (concrete experience, reflective observation, abstract conceptualisation, and active experimentation); the coaching conversation *process* of working with the client through each of these stages; and working with an underlying *philosophy* of experiential learning.

How to design your own model

1. Design the frame your model hangs on (triangle, circles, rectangle, spiral, quadrant or a combination).
2. What is the underlying philosophy or worldview?
3. How do you describe the structure?
4. What is the process you take the client through?
5. Where are the "coach" and the "client" throughout the process?
6. How are you liberating the client's stories?
7. Where is there complete flexibility within the conversation?
8. What are the stages of movement for both coach and client in the conversation?

CONCLUSION

A model represents a system with an implied process. It is a metaphor or analogy used to help visualise and describe the coaching journey. In this and the previous chapter we have begun to explore how to liberate the client's story in the coaching conversation, working first with the coach's tacit qualities, then with specific coaching models and their underlying philosophies. Here we have explored the four-quadrant models of Emotional Intelligence, the

Domains of Competence Model from Habermas and Flaherty which helps us to understand Wilber's Integral Model, existentialism and Spinelli's Existential Model, and Kline's Thinking Partnership® model.

Working with an underpinning of experiential learning helps us understand the client more deeply because the client can only bring their own experience into the coaching conversation. The client's experience is underpinned by a range of factors, including gender, race, culture, education, life experience and personality. I also use an existential approach, working from the premise that the client is always at choice in terms of their own thinking, feeling, and decision making.

You, however, will have your own methodology bringing in your underpinning philosophy, experience and expertise. My suggestion is that you continually to learn to work with new models, bringing them into your repertoire and expanding your skills and competence as a coach. In this way you will not only broaden your experience and expertise, you will begin to create and evolve your own coaching model opening up new perspectives for yourself, your client and your client organisation.

FURTHER READING

Kline, N. (2009). *More Time to Think: A way of being in the world.* Pool-in-Wharfedale: Fisher King.

Spinelli, E. (1989). *The Interpreted World: An introduction to phenomenological psychology.* London: Sage.

Stout-Rostron, S. (2012b). *Business Coaching Wisdom and Practice: Unlocking the Secrets of Business Coaching.* Second edition. Randburg: Knowres.

Strasser, F., and Strasser, A. (1997). *Existential Time-Limited therapy: The wheel of existence.* Chichester: Wiley.

Weiss, P. (2004). *The Three Levels of Coaching.* San Francisco, CA: An Appropriate Response.

Whitmore, J. (2002). *Coaching for Performance: Growing people, performance and purpose.* London: Nicholas Brealey.

Yalom, I.D. (1980). *Existential Psychotherapy.* New York, NY: Basic.

Yalom, I.D. (2001). *The gift of therapy: Reflections on being a therapist.* London: Piatkus.

8

Bringing neuroscience to leadership coaching practice

LEARNING FROM EXPERIENCE

Today we know more about learning than ever before, and learning is the focus of coaching. As we discover more about how to enhance individual differences in learning, research into the fields of neuroscience and neuro-education afford opportunities to advance the disciplines of education and training, human resources, organisational development, coaching and mentoring.

Cognitive neuroscience looks at how the brain learns, stores, and uses the information it acquires, and it is through learning that the brain enables us to adapt to our ever-changing environment. A trans-disciplinary field of study is neuro-education, which explores "learning to learn, cognitive control, flexibility and motivation as well as social and emotional experiences" (Van Dam, 2013:32). Understanding the impact of individual experience on the mind helps us to deepen our grasp of "how the past continues to shape present experience and influence future actions" (Siegel, 1999:2). This is crucial for coach practitioners, as insights into the mind, brain and experience can help us to understand human development.

Neuroscience is the study of the human nervous system, the brain and the biological basis of consciousness, perception, memory and learning. The nervous system and the brain are the physical foundations of the learning process. Neuroscience was traditionally a branch of biology; today it is an interdisciplinary science. Why it is important to us as coaches, HR or OD practitioners and leaders is because the "structure of the brain can be changed by experience" (Siegel, 2011:84). Learning from experience in the workplace is one key to success.

The 1990s was declared to be the "Decade of the Brain" by the US Library of Congress and the US National Institute of Mental Health to enhance public awareness of the benefits to be derived from brain research. We discovered the importance of left and right brains, and the integration of the limbic brain and the higher-thinking cortex. This is particularly important because, due to the way the brain is hardwired, we can't think without feeling, or feel without thinking. Often, in the corporate world, the importance of feelings can be sidelined due to the tendency to assume rational thinking is superior. We need both – rational cognitive decision making complemented by intuitive "gut feel" which is influenced by our experience and expertise.

The first 12 years of the 2000s have become known as the decades of "neuroscience" and "neuroleadership". One of neuroscience's exciting discoveries is that the brain never stops growing in response to experience (Siegel, 2011:xv). "Neuroplasticity" is the term used to describe the brain's capacity for creating these new neural connections and growing new neurons in response to experience. Even after injury, the brain can regain some of its previous functions, even growing new neurons and creating new "neural connections" (Siegel, 2011:5).

Not only are adult brains much more plastic and capable of changing as a result of experience (Rock and Page, 2009:19), new technology has revealed that the "structures" of our brain can be modified by experience. Neuroplasticity is therefore the "term used to describe this capacity for creating new neural connections and growing new neurons in response to experience" throughout life (Siegel, 2011:5). Neuroplasticity is "activated by attention itself" and as "mindfulness requires paying attention to the present moment from a stance that is non-judgemental and non-reactive, it is a form of internal "tuning in" to oneself; this promotes a "foundation for resilience and flexibility" (Siegel, 2011:85–86).

How we focus our attention shapes the structure of our brain, and developing reflective skills activates the very circuits that create resilience and wellbeing – which trigger empathy and compassion. Wellbeing also emerges when we create connections in our lives (Siegel, 2011:xii, 41–42).

THE BRAIN AS A SOCIAL SYSTEM

Siegel describes the brain as a social organ (Siegel, 2011:vi). Due to the discovery of the "relationship" between our subjective experiences (the mind) and our physical bodies (our brains), neuroscientists have begun new ways to "think about thinking". With an emphasis on this social aspect of the brain, we can train our minds to change our brains (Begley, 2007). Coaching has emerged during the last two decades as the change practice that embodies this new paradigm.

Significantly, Siegel's research has identified the core difference between the brain and the mind: "the human mind is a relational and embodied process that regulates the flow of energy and information" (Siegel, 2011:52). Meaning is created by your mind – energy and information go hand-in-hand with the movement of your mind (Siegel, 2011:53). Where the brain is a measurable entity with weight and volume, physical properties and a location, the subjective world of the mind is primarily observed in qualitative terms: "The mind is broader than the brain, revels in relationships and is pregnant with possibilities" (Siegel, 2011:56–57). What is important to us as practitioners is that the brain is measurable and quantitative; the mind is intangible and qualitative. As coaches we are working with the subjective and the qualitative. In the coaching conversation, clients begin to reconstruct their experience, reframing their stories to learn from their own experience, to generate new learning, new thinking and new behaviours to take back into the workplace.

Modern science is based on measurement – which is how the brain works. The brain, according to Siegel, is a system of inter-connected parts – better known as the triune brain. This is represented in the reptilian complex or *old brain*; the cerebrum, i.e. the *neo-cortex* or new brain; and the *limbic* system, otherwise known as the mammalian or mid-brain. Siegel describes a one-hand model of the brain:

You can put your thumb in the middle of your palm, curl your fingers over the top and you have a 'handy' model of the brain (Siegel, 1999:11–12).

Your face would rest in front of the knuckles – the back of the head is toward the back of your hand, and your wrists symbolise the spinal cord (rising from your backbone upon which your brain sits). If you lift up your fingers, and raise your thumb, you'll see the inner brainstem represented in the palm of your hand. Place your thumb back down, and you'll see the approximate location of the limbic system. We have two thumbs, left and right, to make this a symmetrical model. Now curl your fingers back over the top and your cortex is in place (Siegel, 2011:14–16).

These three regions, the brainstem, the limbic system and the neo-cortex, comprise the "triune brain" which has developed over the course of human evolution. At the very minimum, "integrating" the brain involves linking the activity of these three regions; this is known as "vertical integration" which is fundamental to self-organisation (Siegel, 1999:302). The brain is also divided in half, and neural integration involves linking the right and left functions of the brain. This is known as horizontal or bilateral integration.

Knowing about the functions of the brain helps you to "focus your attention" to create the desired linkage. First, the brainstem directly controls states of arousal, the fight / flight / freeze responses, and motivational systems (food, shelter, reproduction and safety). Why this is important is because of the complexity of our emotional responses. Integration is the linking of differentiated elements, in this case the whole system of brain, mind and relationship, with the emotions as the "great summarisers" (Rock and Page, 2009:348).

The limbic area lies deep within the brain; this old mammalian brain works with the brainstem and the body to create our basic drives and emotions. This limbic area is crucial in the way we form relationships. We are, in fact, hardwired to connect with one another! The limbic area regulates the hypothalamus, a master endocrine control centre. And via the pituitary gland the hypothalamus sends and receives hormones for the sexual organs, the thyroid and the adrenals.

Useful for busy managers and executives is to find a way to soothe "limbic firing"; this is crucial to rebalance emotions and diminish the harmful effects of stress. The limbic area creates memory; the amygdala prompts the survival response (fear or flight); and the hippocampus is the master "puzzle-piece" assembler converting moments and experiences to memories (Siegel, 2011:154). In coaching, a connection is often referred to as an "insight or moment of clarity when everything makes sense" (Rock and Page, 2009:264). The hippocampus grows new neurons throughout our lives, weaving emotional and perceptual memory into our autobiographical recollections. The cortex, or "bark" of the brain, is the new mammalian or neo-cortex. It represents our three-dimensional world beyond bodily functions and survival reactions.

The neo-cortex allows us to create ideas and concepts and to develop "mindsight maps" that give us insight into our inner world. Siegel has identified "me-maps" which give us insight into ourselves; "you-maps" which give us insight into others; and "we-maps" which give us insight into our relationships. In this way, we are able to perceive the mind within ourselves or others (Siegel, 2011:8). The neo-cortex actually differentiates us from all other creatures as it allows us to "think about thinking": to imagine, to recombine facts and experiences, and to tell stories. This is why we are so adaptive – our brain relates to our experience.

David Kolb (1984) in *Experiential Learning* explains that learning shapes our course of development, and that this can be described by the level of integrative complexity in his four learning modes: concrete experience, reflective observation, abstract conceptualisation, and active experimentation. He says that development in each dimension proceeds from a state of "embeddedness, defensiveness, dependence and reaction to a state of self-actualisation, independence, pro-action and self-direction", clarifying that this process is marked by "increasing complexity in dealing with the world and one's experience" (Kolb, 1984:140).

Kolb teaches us that knowledge can be acquired only through an interaction between *experience, comprehension* (i.e. understanding) and *apprehension* (i.e. insight). He argues that apprehensions are the source of validation for comprehension And, in Kolb's terms, apprehension is an "intermediate grasping of experience" which we could call "insight experience". He points out Carl Jung's suggestion that "to achieve integrative consciousness, one must first free oneself from the domination of specialised interpretative consciousness, calling this transition to integrative consciousness the process of individuation" (Jung, 1923:28; quoted in Kolb, 1984:157).

MIND AND BRAIN: MINDFULNESS PRACTICE TO DEVELOP AWARENESS

Mindfulness is a crucial capacity for practitioners, being able to direct their attention to the here and now, being present for clients: "mindfulness is the state of awareness in which we are conscious of our feelings, thoughts and habits of mind, and able to let unhelpful ones go so that they no longer limit us" (Rock and Page, 2009:108).

Daniel Siegel talks about "mindsight" as a kind of focused attention that allows us to see the "inner workings" of our own minds (Siegel, 2011). Mindsight helps us to be aware of our mental processes without being swept away by them. Mindsight enables us to get off the autopilot of our own ingrained behaviours and habitual responses, and to move beyond our own habitual and reactive "emotional loops". Mindfulness is a form of mental activity that trains the mind to become aware of awareness itself, and to pay attention to one's own "intention"; as researchers have defined it, mindfulness requires paying attention to the present moment from a stance that is non-judgemental and non-reactive (Siegel, 2011:85–86). A state that is very difficult for many coaches to cultivate is actually that of being "non-judgemental" toward their clients.

Here is a simple exercise to develop mindfulness, which is very useful to reduce stress and induce sleep. Simply breathe in slowly counting 1 ... 2 ... 3 ... 4; pause momentarily on 4 and breathe out slowly to the count of 5 ... 6 ... 7 ... 8 ... 9 ... 10. Relax your breathing and do it again at least ten times. It helps to slow down your heart beat and is useful to calm your nerves prior to giving a speech or presentation, or when negotiating your way through a conflict situation.

Examples show that mindfulness practices are crucial for us to be able to make changes in our lives. According to Rock and Page (2009:108–109), the formation of mental maps enables us to live in a "narrative" rather than to be present in the immediate flow of sensory experiences. This is also what coaching addresses to help clients develop self-awareness, transforming thoughts and feelings to positively change behaviour (Stout-Rostron, 2006:41–44). At the heart of this process is an "internal tuning-in" to oneself that enables you to become cognisant of your own behaviour, understanding how others may experience you in the workplace.

This *attunement* promotes resilience and flexibility and overlaps with the functions of the pre-frontal brain. It leads to a healthy growth of the pre-frontal fibres which regulate mood, stabilise the mind and achieve emotional equilibrium and resilience (Siegel, 2011:27). Focusing on the breath is always a calming and meditative mindfulness–awareness exercise. From East to West, all cultures have developed some form of mindfulness to cultivate wellbeing (Siegel, 2011:89). Try the above breathing exercise, and if it doesn't work for you, find another mindfulness activity which involves breathing such as swimming, a walking meditation, running, yoga, tai chi or a martial art dance.

The Institute of HeartMath® has an array of techniques that can guide you to a state of ease within a few minutes, or simply help you to relax or even generate more energy. These are two examples:

1. *Heart Breathing*: Focus your attention on your heart area, and breathe a little deeper than normal, in for five or six seconds and out for five or six seconds. Breathe deeply but normally, and feel as if your breath is coming in and going out through your heart area. Continue breathing with ease until you find a natural inner rhythm that feels comfortable.

2. *Heart Focus*: Imagine breathing through your heart. Picture yourself slowly breathing in and out through your heart area. Focus your attention on the area around your heart, the area in the centre of your chest. If you prefer, the first couple of times you try it, place your hand over the centre of your chest to help keep your attention in the heart area (Institute of HeartMath®, 2013:2–3).

The concept of mindfulness is a key concept in coaching, as well as an important element in neuroscience research. In the *Mindful Coach*, Silsbee (2004:27) defines mindfulness as the "stage of awareness in which we are conscious of our feelings, thoughts and habits of the mind, and able to let unhelpful ones go so that they no longer limit us". Mindfulness practice is simply focusing our attention on a particular thing or thought. Because of the interdependency of the mind, brain and body, mindfulness practice has an impact on decreasing stress levels and increasing resiliency. A crucial capacity for coaches and leaders is to direct our attention to the "here and now". As a coach we become present for our clients (Rock and Page, 2009:108). This helps us to contribute to our own health and wellbeing, as well as that of the client, enabling them to make changes in their lives. However, in order to be present for our clients, we need to regularly practise focused attention and mindfulness.

CHANGING HABITS USING THE BRAIN'S "WORKING MEMORY"

Brain physiology is a key to why *change* is hard. Trying to change habits requires energy and attention (Rock and Page, 2009:185). The basal ganglia embody one of the brain's core functions, i.e. operating without conscious thought, as long as what we are doing is routine and habitual. "Working memory" on the other hand, in the prefrontal cortex, is used for learning but it has limited resources (Rock and Page, 2009:154). It requires more energy and fatigues more easily than the automatic pilot (Rock and Page, 2009:185). Practice and repeated activities can be taken on by the deeper structures, leaving our "working memory" free to deal with new happenings (for example, when on holiday overseas, driving on the opposite side of the road from what is conventional in your own country). Changing old habits to new ones is very difficult, and many training courses have been run over the years claiming, for example, that "it takes practising at least 21 times to change a habit" (Price, 2011).

The brain is "relational" and makes connections based on use (Rock and Page, 2009:185). When we repeat a behaviour often enough it becomes automatic; in other words, a potential new behaviour can become a habit. However, why forming a habit backfires is because our "working memory", which turns on and focuses our attention, is limited and vulnerable to both internal and external distractions. Trying to change habits requires energy and attention (Rock and Page, 2009:185).

Over time the connections we make, because we are paying attention, become "hardwired" (Rock and Page, 2009:178–179). This is enormously important in organisational cultural transformation, and is critical coaches. If you intervene inappropriately with your questions, and distract the client from their thinking, you actually get in their way of new learning. As the coach you need to become "attuned" to your client. The brain changes physically in response to experience with new mental skills being acquired with our efforts to focus our awareness and concentration (Siegel, 2011:84).

How we focus our attention not only shapes the structure of our brain, but working with attention helps the client to *reflect*. Reflection leads to being *open, observant* and *objective* about what's going on inside of us and inside of others; objectivity helps us to have a thought or feeling without becoming swept away by it, and therefore with reflection we gain the capacity to deal with an intense emotion without becoming lost in it (Siegel, 2011:41–42). If, according to Siegel, the "mind" is a relational process – with energy and information flowing – then both client and coach will be modified in their shared exchange. Working within the complexity and pace of organisational environments today, reflection becomes a critical skill to develop. This is a key role of the coach when working with clients – to help them develop ease within chaotic environments, reflecting and thinking through what seem to be insurmountable problems and difficult decisions. But it needs to be done in a way that does not distract the client but, instead, enhances their thinking and learning from experience. Many coaches believe they need to be "directive", without understanding the depth of "reflection" needed for clients to understand their own thoughts and feelings.

WORKING WITH ATTENTION AND SUSTAINED POSITIVE EMOTIONS

One way to create attention is through telling and hearing people's stories – exactly what happens inside the coaching conversation. Here is one of the most wonderful stories I have heard shared by a colleague about a client. This client was having trouble focusing and connecting to his own emotions and sensibility. The coach blindfolded his client, and walked him around a very lively, city-block-wide garden market in a large city for several hours. The client was asked to describe the colours he imagined, the smells and sounds penetrating his senses, and to get in touch with all of his senses except sight, by touching, tasting, smelling, hearing and describing his experience. This was transformational for the client in developing mindful presence and awareness, helping him to get in touch with both himself and the environment he was in.

Brown (2011) tells a story about the Thinking Environment® as its relates to the brain's management of relationship, energy and information:

> Yesterday I made the most exciting discovery. Have been teaching neuro-behavioural modelling for three days in Hanoi – a group of psychiatrists, psychologists and mental health nurses. Was talking about calming the amygdala, and explaining the processes of the Thinking Environment® and what generative attention and uncorrupted silence were about. I had left on the screen the triangular picture of the mind that I use so much from Dan Siegel's work - defining the mind as the brain's management of *relationship, energy* and *information*.
>
> And what I suddenly realised was that the Thinking Environment® is a method not just for calming the amygdala, but also for accessing the *mind*. What happens is that the Thinking Session process creates *relationship*, mobilises the brain's *energy* and makes it possible for the person to access all kinds of *information* that have been below the threshold of working consciousness. In doing so, the Thinking Environment® accesses the mind and starts to make the mind work more effectively (Brown, 2011:1).

From what we've learned so far, the ability to focus the mind, to focus attention internally, and towards another, is a core skill. Not just for practitioners but also for leaders. Nancy Kline's research reminds us that transformative listening is nearly a work of art. It comes from genuine interest in where your partner will go in their thinking, and from your courage to trust their intelligence. Kline says that to develop this attitude and general behaviour you need to (Kline, 2011:9):

- Settle back.
- Keep your eyes on the eyes of your partner as they speak.
- Cultivate fascination with what your partner will say next.
- Achieve a composure that is wildly dynamic (in your eyes).

- Do not interrupt.
- Trust that not uttering a word is one of the most effective things you can do.
- Know that your job is to help your partner think for themselves, not to think for them.
- Remember that the expression of feelings is often part of the thinking process.
- Be aware that much of what they say will be the result of your effect on them.

Kline explains that "in the quiet presence of your attention, respect, and ease important things can happen for the partner. Fresh ideas can emerge; confusion can dissipate; painful feelings can subside; creativity can explode. It does not matter if you already know what your partner is about to say before they have said it – do not interrupt them or stop them. What matters is what happens for them because they say it" (Kline, 2011:9).

Giving attention is aligned with giving appreciation or acknowledgement, whether from coach to client, or manager to direct report. Several research studies have demonstrated the importance of attention and appreciation, providing scientific evidence that a specific mode of functioning described as "physiological coherence", associated with highly ordered or coherent patterns in heart rhythms, is generated during sustained positive emotions (McCraty and Childre, 2002:3–7).

The work of the Gottman Institute in Seattle, Washington has uncovered the effect of a 5:1 ratio of appreciation to criticism on the satisfaction and longevity of relationships:

> Dr John Gottman charted the amount of time couples spent arguing versus interacting positively – touching, smiling, paying compliments, laughing, etc. – and found there is a very specific ratio that exists between the amount of positivity and negativity in stable relationships. *The magic ratio is 5:1.* In other words, as long as there are five times as many positive interactions between partners as there are negative, the relationship is likely to be stable. It is based on this ratio that Dr Gottman is able to predict divorce! Very unhappy couples tend to have more negative than positive interactions (Lisitsa, 2012:2).

This finding has many implications for leaders and coaches in the workplace. It doesn't mean saying, "I love your work" five times and then launching into a criticism. It actually means treating people well and acknowledging their work on a regular basis, so that when you do have to give constructive criticism it is damaging neither to self-esteem nor performance.

This 5:1 ratio has many implications to building *attuned relationships*. Conversations involve sharing energy and information. Certain types of conversations require a mutual resonance that provides for the "flow of energy and information (Siegel, 1999:3). The process that regulates that flow is our minds (Rock and Page, 2009:422). Over time, such conversations result in *attuned* relationships that stimulate brain integration and the capacity for the mind to reflect on itself (Siegel, 2011).

THE ROLE OF THE BODY AND EMOTIONS IN DECISION MAKING

> Damasio argues in his well-known book [*Descartes' Error*, 1994], that it is wrong to think that only minds think. The body and emotions have a key role to play in the way we think and in rational decision making (Lagerlund, 2010:15).

Damasio's theory stresses "the crucial role of feeling in navigating the endless stream of life's personal decisions ... The intuitive signals that guide us in these moments come in the form of limbic-driven surges from the viscera that Damasio calls 'somatic markers' – literally, gut feelings" (Goleman, 1996:53). Although Damasio's work is widely acknowledged to be "A work with far-reaching implications for understanding mental life" (Goleman, 1996:27), our emotions have an effect on others in our environment – remembering that the human brain is designed to share information and energy with others (Rock and Page, 2009:421).

A human being who is continually "potentiating" works with all three elements required for health and wellness: an integrated brain, a reflective mind, and attuned relationships (Rock and Page, 2009:422). To help with this, practitioners need to work with clients to ensure they incorporate three things into their work–life balance: appropriate diet, sleep and exercise. We know from neuroscience that growth factors, the formation of new connections in the brain, can be enhanced through exercise, sleep and quieting the mind (Van Dam, 2013:32).

Case study

The impact of diet, sleep and exercise is critical to pay attention to when working with clients. One of my clients, Adam, slumped into a chair exhausted when arriving at his third coaching session. He explained that his wife, he and his children had no energy and that they were all exhausted. We began to explore what was actually happening for him and why. Adam explained that he drove to and from work for three hours, five days a week. On top of that, he worked a ten-hour day and returned home to two small children and a newborn baby. Each weekend he spent Saturday mornings coaching a local children's football team, and studied for his MBA in the afternoon. On Sunday mornings the family attended church, and he studied in the afternoon. And so it went on week after week – barring one important point that we uncovered. Neither Adam nor his wife could cook, and they were living primarily on fast food with little in the way of healthy balanced protein, fruit, vegetables and carbohydrates.

A new plan emerged out of this conversation to help Adam and his family to begin a more balanced and healthy regime. He hired a local lad who was learning to drive; this lad became Adam's driver from Monday to Friday. This gave Adam 15 hours each week in the car to sleep, meditate, manage his emails or study because he was no longer driving. He and his wife both attended a local cookery and nutrition course which he organised through his community with several other couples facing similar struggles. Sleep was the toughest issue to manage with a newborn baby – but Adam and his wife created a time schedule in which they shared walking the floor nights to soothe the baby.

If it is true that experience continuously shapes our brain structure and modifies behaviour, the positive change in Adam and his wife's daily life is a powerful example. One year later, Adam was promoted into a more senior position within the engineering environment in which he worked, and his wife managed to restart her studies whilst juggling their family of five. This case illustrates how the brain performs and learns. In this instance, beginning to think differently and creatively helped Adam to positively value and contribute not only to his own and his family's life, but also to his business environment. Our brains continuously draw on our knowledge base – coaching creates the environment to develop wisdom from our own knowledge and to help clients create innovative solutions to complex problems.

Motivation in the brain is driven by emotion, and research now indicates that there is a link between emotion and cognition (Van Dam, 2013:33). Neuroscientists believe that emotions are fundamental to learning, and that an emotionally positive experience motivates us to engage in situations. One of the reasons that coaching is inspirational to many clients is that it is a positive reinforcement of who they are, and who they can step into being.

THE FOUR WORLDS IN EXISTENTIAL PHILOSOPHY

What we have learned is that the way the brain is hardwired, human beings cannot survive without relating to other people. This is akin to existential philosophy, which says that although there is a fundamental unbridgeable isolation from others, existential conflict is the tension between "our awareness of our absolute isolation and our wish for contact – for protection, and our wish to be part of a larger whole" (Yalom, 1980:9).

Alison and Freddie Strasser in *Time Limited Existential Therapy* talk about the four worlds in which we live: physical, public, private and spiritual. The *physical world* is the inherent physical and biological dimensions – and we have flexibility in how we relate to it and to our environment. The *public world* encompasses our relationship to others. This is about our attitudes to social class, race, gender, culture, and general rules of society such as not driving through a red light at an intersection. It is about how we relate to others (Strasser and Strasser, 1997:75;78).

The *private world* is the private, intimate world of the client. This is the space between the intimate relationship we have with ourselves and with our significant others, and with the ontological givens in existential philosophy: anxiety, isolation, loneliness and meaninglessness. The *ideal or spiritual world* is concerned with a person's connection with what may be called spiritual values. This is the dimension where people have their own beliefs about life and death and what gives them personal meaning, i.e. what am I going to do before I die? These are four interconnected parts of each one of us.

The self is not fixed, but is seen as a process which we continually reinterpret and reshape. And although we have been thrown into the world as temporal beings, we express ourselves through all the facets of our world and our relationships. In existential philosophy, a universal given imposed on us by the world is that it is impossible to avoid being with others; we are always with people authentically or inauthentically, either *relating*, *disclosing* or *manifesting ourselves* (Strasser and Strasser, 1997:75).

We are a physical species, a conscious and self-conscious species, and a social species (Rock and Page, 2009:422). Siegel talks about "collaborative, contingent conversations" where both parties contribute and there is no script – where what each person says is dependent and responsive to the other (Siegel, 1999). Are coaching conversations contingent and collaborative? The competences promoted by coaching bodies suggest so. According to Rock and Page (2009:423–426):

- Coaches are trained to be present, putting full attention on client and interaction.
- They are taught to elicit the client's agenda, not their own.
- They are not to be judgemental or give advice.
- The ideal coaching conversation is contingent and collaborative.

Here collaborative and contingent conversations are when "our minds and bodies are in constant nonverbal conversations, stimulating many associations of which we are unaware" (Rock and Page, 2009:424). Coaching focuses on enhancing an individual's ability to engage with, interact with and influence others. Our state of mind can be influenced by engaging and interacting with others. In the organisational context, a leader's frame of mind can easily influence the thoughts, feelings and behaviours of their direct reports, their team and the entire organisation. Emotions are contagious, and when we relate to people we can "catch" emotions that are beneficial or non-beneficial to us. Neuroscience research shows that the brain actively seeks out "an affectionately attuned other" (Siegel, 1999:60–63) if it is to learn, hence the importance of the rapport and relationship developed between coach and client.

Siegel describes mindsight as a combination of insight and empathy, and reminds us that mindsight takes away the superficial boundaries that separate us, one from another, enabling us to see that we are each part of an "interconnected flow, a wider whole" (Siegel, 1999:58).

CONNECTION BETWEEN COACH AND CLIENT – RAPPORT

We could call this connection between coach and client "rapport". However, rapport can be seen as a function rather than a characteristic of the relationship between coach and client. Beliefs, values and culture create the filters through which we see the world. Social neuroscience shows that how we understand, empathise and socialise with others is filtered through our mental processes. Therefore, coach and client both need to be mindful of their own beliefs and values and how they interpret the beliefs and values of others in the environment.

Some interesting research has been done by Boyatzis and McKee (2005), which explores the importance of emotionally intelligent leadership. Boyatzis and McKee show how leaders can recognise the cycles of stress and rejuvenation inherent in their jobs – and actively utilise the qualities of mindfulness and compassion to renew their passion and effectiveness. Although compassionate behaviour is more often experienced by peers than superiors at work, compassion leads to increased positive emotions and strengthens wellbeing (Boyatzis and McKee, 2005).

In the Thinking Environment® we work with ten very specific behaviours which create an environment where people can think easefully, compassionately and creatively together: attention, equality, ease, appreciation, encouragement, feelings, information, diversity, incisive questions, and place.

Wider research shows that compassion reduces stress and frustration, increases a sense of humanity at work, improves performance, commitment and employee engagement, and buffers workers' immune systems (Horne, 2008:3–4). Further, it has been found that "Leading with compassion can favourably impact the bottom line while enabling leaders to sustain their effectiveness for longer periods of time" (Boyatzis and McKee, 2005:185), while "Feeling cared for frees us to care for others" (Goleman, 1998:214).

One of the core aspects of coaching is that of compassion towards the client. What is important, however, is that the coach's compassion is not at the expense of seeing the bigger picture and becoming one with the client against the system. Although the coach definitely becomes part of the system when they begin coaching within an organisation, they need to be cognisant of not perpetuating the dynamics of that system. The coach's job is to be mindfully aware and attentive to the needs of the individual client and the organisation.

Positivity and relationships promote performance and are the glue for any organisation. Companies which focus on promoting positive attributes (such as loyalty, resilience, trustworthiness, humility, and compassion), rather than simply combating negative attributes, perform better, both financially and qualitatively (Horne, 2008:4). And organisations with high-quality connections between people will encourage compassion (Horne, 2008:4). A leader in an organisation can support high-quality connections and the expression of compassion by:

- being available, sensitive and responsive to others' needs and issues;
- making time;
- listening empathically;
- being emotionally present, being in tune and engaging mindfully with others;
- building a team environment which supports compassionate behaviour;
- encouraging compassion from all levels, not just from the top; and
- being curious and having respect (Horne, 2008:4).

Our learning from neuroscience shows that *sustained focus* enables new learning and creative thinking. This means actively silencing the mind through focused attention, i.e. focusing on the major senses while breathing deeply (Van Dam, 2013:33). Or even meditating for 20 minutes a day to improve your ability to stay focused and attentive. Not only does focusing our attention shape the structure of our brain, developing reflective skills activates the very circuits that create resilience and wellbeing, that underlie empathy, and compassion (Siegel, 2011:xii-xiii). Wellbeing emerges when we develop mindfulness and mindfulness practices, as well as providing fertile ground for creative thinking and new learning.

CONCLUSION

Working with sustained attention on another, as in coaching, helps to develop the potential of those engaged in it – developing self-awareness and transforming thoughts and feelings into new behaviours. The good news is that there is no age of finality for any new learning. The brain continues to learn and consolidate new knowledge unconsciously throughout life, although the changes in the brain reverse when we do not apply any new skills that we have developed. For us as practitioners, it is useful to understand the cognitive neuroscience of learning. However, we need to be aware of oversimplified versions of research and questionable claims about brain-based learning.

To emerge our potential means learning how to make connections, with ourselves and others – in other words, learning how to change our mind and our brain.

FURTHER READING

Boyatzis, R.E., and McKee, A. (2005). *Resonant Leadership: Renewing yourself and connecting with others through mindfulness, hope and compassion.* Boston, MA: Harvard Business School.

Immordino-Yang, M.H., and Damasio, A. (2007). We feel, therefore we learn: The relevance of affective and social neuroscience to education. *Mind, Brain, and Education.* 1(1):3–10.

McCraty, R., and Childre, D. (2002). *The Appreciative Heart: The psychophysiology of positive emotions and optimal functioning.* Boulder Creek, CA: Institute of HeartMath®.

Rock, D., and Page, L.J. (2009). *Coaching with the Brain in Mind: Foundations for practice.* Hoboken, NJ: Wiley.

Siegel, D.J. (1999). *The Developing Mind: How relationships and the brain interact to shape who we are.* New York, NY: Guilford.

Siegel, D.J. (2011). *Mindsight: The new science of personal transformation.* New York, NY: Bantam.

Silsbee, D. (2004). *The Mindful Coach: Seven roles for helping people grow.* Marshall, NC: Ivey River.

Van Dam, N. (2013). Inside the learning brain. *T+D*, 8 April, 30–35.

9

Gender diversity – coaching
men and women to lead

INTRODUCTION

In today's workplace we lead and manage in environments with multicultural, power and diversity complexities. Diversity is a critically important issue for everyone connected with coaching, from practitioners and psychologists to academics and researchers as well as organisational and institutional leaders.

Gender diversity encompasses a wide range of organisational theory and research. This includes gender organisation studies which have given voice to women's experiences and made visible the complex, gendered nature of organisational practice. The majority of previous research has approached gender through observed differences and inequalities between men and women, but here we also explore new studies that identify men as the invisible gender representing a privileged base norm. For the growing discipline of executive and business coaching, organisational research into gender diversity is relatively new, yet it is critical for coach education and development, and for practitioners and academics working with diversity in the field.

This chapter focuses on gender diversity in coaching across six contemporary areas:

- understanding gender diversity, power and culture;
- contemporary psychological research;
- gender management and organisational culture;
- diversity and identity within a Thinking Environment®;
- cultural contexts on gender issues in business; and
- academic research in coaching women leaders and managers.

The text of this chapter was originally an unpublished initial study in preparation for a chapter titled "Gender issues in coaching" published in *The Wiley-Blackwell Handbook of the Psychology of Coaching and Mentoring* (Stout-Rostron, 2012a). That chapter is more of a classical literature review, whereas this text is meant to be a practical overview of contemporary issues useful to practitioners and leaders when helping their clients or direct reports to manage complex gender diversity issues.

UNDERSTANDING GENDER DIVERSITY, POWER AND CULTURE

As practitioners we need to analyse and challenge our own assumptions and cultural understanding based on power relations and gender. Society in the twenty-first century is both increasingly diverse and increasingly inter-related. Many strides have been made towards understanding those with cultures different to us, and all practitioners in coaching, psychology, counselling, HR and OD need to become advocates for "self-knowledge, empowerment and multicultural education" (Sue, 1993:48–50) as a means to understand and manage diverse populations.

Our clients operate in disparate environments around the globe, and often people assume that diversity is only about race and gender. But diversity also encompasses assumptions that limit people based on their group identities and their place in their own social and workplace hierarchies. This can be based on race, gender, language, faith, education, class, nationality and tribe (Stout-Rostron, 2012b:148). Ultimately, diversity is about who has power and who doesn't. But it is also about what assumptions drive the behaviour of those who are powerful and those who are powerless. Any form of power exacerbates difference and influences how we perceive and react to another's behaviour. Culture is our shared way of doing things, our shared way of making sense of the world – and power relations have deep roots in our own cultural matrix which informs our personal views, choices and actions (Stout-Rostron, 2014:179–181, 200).

The importance of acknowledging and understanding diversity, power and gender issues is due to the increasing complexity of the world within which we work. This is particularly true in hierarchical systems such as the family, business, organisational, educational and government institutions. Today, more than ever, it is vital that the business coach is able to raise the leader's awareness of crucial diversity issues, both within themselves, their teams, and the culture of their organisation. In order to do so, the coach needs to have a grounding in, and a strong understanding of, the core issues that impact all forms of diversity – and in this particular instance: gender. For example, when working with a client in a coaching conversation, it is useful to help them learn to remove limiting assumptions they hold about themselves, others and the systems in which they live and work.

However, the professional practitioner (whether coach, psychologist, coaching psychologist, counsellor, HR or OD practitioner) needs to become aware of and manage their own responses to questions of diversity before they can help their clients to manage similar issues; this is the same for leaders working with their direct reports and teams. This requires us as practitioners to develop an awareness of our own prejudices, biases, limiting thinking and life conditioning. It means being able to "see" through a multiplicity of lenses, not just our own individual perspective, but the worldviews of our clients whose experience, education, background, hopes and fears may be very different from our own.

I approach this chapter from a variety of perspectives in terms of the contemporary literature available to us. Gender, of course, refers to both men and women, and we will examine the current thinking on how men and women are socialised, the impact of organisational culture, and in what ways the dominant white male organisational culture has affected the development of women in the workplace.

CONTEMPORARY PSYCHOLOGICAL RESEARCH

In grappling with the development of managerial leaders, it is critical that business coaches understand the intrapersonal and interpersonal realms. Psychology has well-established traditions in specialised fields of study such as ethics and supervision, including published research that is highly relevant to our fast-changing, complex organisational and societal systems. I am not saying that business coaches need to be psychologists, but rather they need a practical grounding or "literacy" in psychological research and theory to understand an executive's behaviour and performance.

Coach practitioners need an awareness of current theories of gender and diversity. Bruce Peltier, in *The Psychology of Executive Coaching* (2001:190) rightly says that "Women have arrived in all arenas of the workplace and they are not going back home". Peltier's view is that coaches need to understand how women function within an organisation – the reverse of the standard approach to coaching women, which suggests that they need help in finding a way to fit into organisational culture. Peltier insists that contemporary psychotherapy literature is relevant and invaluable for executive coaches because it is systems-oriented, drawing from models of humanistic, existential, behavioural and psychodynamic psychology (Peltier, 2001:ix–xx).

Although written in 2001, Peltier's book is a welcome addition to the contemporary literature on coaching women in the workplace. He mentions the "glass ceiling" that still prevents women from progressing too high in the organisation; and the "glass walls" that keep women in the new "pink collar" jobs (Peltier, 2001:193) such as human resources, organisational development and marketing. Although Peltier acknowledges that women are socialised differently today, his research was carried out prior to the so-called Generation Y, whose members have a very different outlook on work and career from the previous generation of "Baby Boomers". What Peltier calls "erroneous assumptions" about women in the workplace, e.g. that most leaders assume a woman's highest priority is the family, we now identify as "limiting assumptions" which deliberately exclude women from long-term career development.

In her book, *The Argument Culture* (1999), Deborah Tannen picks up on the never-ending appetite in our contemporary world for conflict, debate and argument – rather than dialogue. Corporations also often operate on an adversarial approach to business, "settling disputes in litigation" (Tannen, 1999:4). The tendency to polarise and win the argument is essentially the nature of business. Tannen, whose earlier work explored the differences in communication styles between men and women (Tannen, 1995), has helped practitioners to understand how the "argument culture" impacts the workplace. She draws attention to military and war metaphors which pervade managerial and boardroom language, affecting behaviour and thinking. Tannen's research has shown how deeply entrenched is the language divide between two polarised ways of thinking and speaking. Her work provides useful thinking for coaches and leaders helping men and women to resolve the differences in their approach to both professional and personal life.

Corporate conflict is where the role of the "alpha male", the dominant white male executive, plays a strong part; Peltier calls it the "Testosterone Culture". Business organisations are typically male-led, dominated by male culture and male assumptions (Peltier, 2001:192). He also mentions that metaphors of war and sport are typical in the standard business environment – almost as if men are continuing to play children's fighting games, keeping score with "clear winners and losers" (Peltier, 2001:192).

For the professional practitioner, an excellent, non-mainstream and comprehensive text on race, gender and culture is *Diversity in Psychotherapy: The politics of race, ethnicity and gender* (Chin, De La Cancela and Jenkins, 1993). They offer a refreshing view which identifies the need for diversity and difference to be respected and valued as an asset instead of a liability. In his foreword, Stanley Sue describes this as a "vivid account of how ethnic and racial issues, as well as other diversity issues such as gender and sexual orientation, are embedded in society in general and psychotherapy in particular" (Sue, 1993:ix).

The book focuses on "diversity involving the issues of race, ethnicity, and gender as it influences the theory and practice of psychotherapy" (De La Cancela, Jenkins and Chin, 1993:9). It expresses concern about the "western ideology of psychotherapy" which "minimises social inequities such as sexism, ethnocentrism, and classism", and that "denial of socio-political factors in therapy is harmful to clients" (De La Cancela, Jenkins and Chin, 1993:9). The authors, whose research derives from their own clinical practice, are suggesting for psychotherapists what is also critical for coach practitioners – "to begin to challenge their own assumptions about diversity, in all its forms of race, gender, ethnicity, culture and empathy" (Brome, 1993:1).

The text is intended as a re-examination of factors which influence the practice of psychotherapy. But it also demonstrates that a paradigmatic shift is needed on the part of coach practitioners who need to work within the complexity of diversity in the workplace. Their examples show how racial, ethnic and economic power differences have affected social esteem and gender role expectations within the groups they discuss.

The authors define diversity as "an openness to new experiences and progressive ideas among practitioners, and a more flexible and socially contextualised view of personal histories among clients". They claim that "diversity is the valorisation of alternate lifestyles, biculturality, human differences, and uniqueness in individual and group life. Diversity promotes an informed connectedness to one's reference group, self-knowledge, empowering contact with those different from oneself, and an appreciation for the commonalities of our human condition. Diversity also requires an authentic exploration of the client's and practitioner's personal and reference group history" (De La Cancela, Jenkins and Chin, 1993:6).

Where does gender fit in – men

How can we learn to address men and women in a "non-sexist and non-homophobic manner", "mindful of avoiding sexist language and inappropriate designations of people" (De La Cancela, Jenkins and Chin, 1993:8)? Research shows that "men and masculinity are located with the norm, while women and femininity are devalued as Other" (Simpson and Lewis, 2007:71).

However, it is important not to assume that women represent the only gender concerns, but to broaden the discussion to include men. Men also suffer from negative self-images on an individual and collective level – depending on the culture and country within which they live and work. Generally, as Simpson and Lewis (2007:69) explain, masculinity is associated with the "world of work and with power", although "working class men" often have little power and may "adopt a macho identity to counterbalance the powerlessness in their jobs". This is worth considering, depending on the culture within which you are coaching.

Also forgotten are the *differences* within the gender construction that is masculinity. What gets forgotten are issues such as the emasculation of Asian males and the "crisis of extinction" that African-American and Latino males are experiencing in the USA (De La Cancela, Jenkins and Chin, 1993:8). Too often, the extent of understanding regarding men of "colour is limited to negative stereotypes related to sexist behaviour" (De La Cancela, Jenkins and Chin, 1993:9). Other stereotypical behaviours are considered to be those of macho, traditional chauvinism. These patriarchal customs are also strong stereotypes in African culture, and influence how both men and women treat each other in the workplace.

The issues of racism, discrimination and prejudice are often denied in the corporate workplace. Yet these factors present massive challenges in the socio-political sphere, and can have a huge impact on confidence and self-esteem. This is present in the issues which present themselves when coaching men of African-American, Puerto Rican, Chinese-American and Hispanic descent in the USA. Men from Asian, Eastern European and African descent also face similar problems in emigrating to other first-world nations where immigrants are defined against the "white majority according to their race rather than their culture" (Jenkins, De La Cancela and Chin, 1993:31).

For example, one of the key issues in coaching African-American men in the USA is to understand that "white supremacy impaired the self- and group-concepts of many African slaves and their descendants for generations" (Jenkins, De La Cancela and Chin, 1993:19). Similarly, South Africans have experienced the destructive impact of apartheid's philosophy of white supremacy, and continue to see how the resulting lack of skills and education is undermining the running of the country today.

Practitioners need to understand the socio-political factors of all their clients, understanding their cultural, educational, ethnic and racial backgrounds. Each practitioner has a responsibility to integrate cultural knowledge into their own education and practice – and most importantly culturally evaluating themselves to understand their own worldview. It is only in this way that practitioners can increase their competence and empower their clients with their interventions. Questions that arise are those of the differences between the practitioner and the client's ethnicity and culture – the practitioner must develop an awareness of their own assumptions that may limit or empower both practitioner and client. Later in this chapter I refer to the subject of limiting assumptions when examining the Thinking Environment® approach developed by Nancy Kline.

Alpha male and alpha female

In 2004, Kate Ludeman and Eddie Erlandson dazzled leaders and academics with their article "Coaching the alpha male" in the *Harvard Business Review*. Defining the alpha male as "highly intelligent, confident, and successful", and claiming that they represent "about 70 per cent of all senior executives", Ludeman and Erlandson depicted alpha males as "people who aren't happy unless they're the top dogs". In their research, they claimed to have rarely found successful female leaders with equally strong personalities, or to find women who matched the "complete alpha profile". Alpha males are described as natural leaders who get stressed only "when tough decisions don't rest in their capable hands" (Ludeman and Erlandson, 2004:58).

When asked why so many of them need executive coaches, the authors explained that the "quintessential strengths are also what make them so challenging, and often frustrating, to work with; independent and action-oriented, alphas take extraordinarily high levels of performance for granted, both in themselves and in others". The flip side, according to Ludeman and Erlandson, is that alpha males have "little or no natural curiosity about people or feelings". Alphas "rely on exhaustive data to reach business conclusions but often make snap judgments about other people, which they hold on to tenaciously. Because they believe that paying attention to feelings, even their own, detracts from getting the job done, they're surprisingly oblivious to the effect they have on others. They're judgmental of colleagues who can't control emotions yet often fail to notice how they vent their own anger and frustration" (Ludeman and Erlandson, 2004:58–59).

The authors claim that alphas make perfect mid-level managers whose primary role is to oversee processes. Unfortunately, in the CEO role they don't necessarily become inspirational people managers. If the organisation can't help their alphas to make the required transition, this is where the role of a skilled and competent coach is needed. Alphas aren't necessarily good at asking for help, and can be "typically stubborn and resistant to feedback". According to the authors, coaches shouldn't undermine the alpha's focus on results, but should improve the process for achieving them (Ludeman and Erlandson, 2004:59).

In *Diversity in Coaching* (Passmore, 2009), two chapters tackle this tricky subject of alpha male and alpha female. Erlandson's chapter on "Coaching with men: Alpha males" suggests that gender is approached as a key to working with men and women senior executives. Erlandson amusingly explains that when dealing with a dominant, confident, results-driven male individual, the coach may uncover evidence of "wreckage caused by boys behaving badly" (Erlandson, 2009:219). He defines four male alpha types, and suggests a coaching approach that is ultimately shared with the leader's team. In "Coaching with women", Kate Ludeman refreshingly details the "micro-inequities" faced by women leaders in the workplace, explaining the characteristics of alpha and beta women (Ludeman, 2009:243). Ludeman suggests a need to understand that different approaches to women leaders are crucial. Difference is celebrated as potential in these two chapters.

Where does gender fit in – women

It is sometimes hard to separate gender issues from racial and cultural issues. For women, access to power and social approval has often been tied to European or American standards of beauty. And, in the USA, the "brown paper" bag test was the classic way to be less black, more white, more acceptable. To survive discrimination, racism and prejudice, women of colour have often been socialised to be twice as competent as their white counterparts simply to receive equal recognition (Jenkins, 1993:51). In South Africa, both men and women have been made "invisible" by being given "European"-sounding names which are easily pronounced by white society. That is now beginning to change as African men and women use their African names in the workplace and in government-held positions.

Yvonne Jenkins suggests that Maslow's hierarchy fails to recognise that, "for collective societies, group esteem is practically synonymous with the Anglocentric conceptualisation of self-esteem". Social esteem is a preferable concept to reflect the "interdependence between value of self and reference group identity that are central to the world view of most pluralistic populations" (Jenkins, 1993:55).

Although *Celebrating Women Coaches* (Hawkes and Seggar, 2000) is dedicated to a small number of well-known women sports coaches in North America, it is a recognition of the changing role of women in society and professional life. This book is well worth reading for its accounts of successful women athletic coaches who share their life stories and experiences – and are outstanding role models for women in the workplace. The authors have presented the personal perspectives and experience of 42 exceptional women who have leapt over social conventions with the implicit message "that women should not aspire to become athletic coaches" (Hawkes and Seggar, 2000:xiii). These 42 women sports coaches have challenged their male counterparts by stepping into positions previously occupied by "high-calibre male coaches. Those males, and other males associated with athletics, started a chain of events that led to hiring selected women" (Hawkes and Seggar, 2000:xiii).

These women developed "national champions, conference champions, All Americans, Olympians, Pan American Games champions, World University champions, and World Cup champions" by:

- rising above obstacles;
- seizing opportunities and translating dreams into realities;
- planting new ideas even in rigid systems in order to cultivate new programmes;
- harvesting respect in a tradition-dominated profession without undermining celebrated programs or personalities;
- superseding limited budgets, spaces and attitudes; and
- excelling at every level of coaching including the Olympic Games (Hawkes and Seggar, 2000:xxi;xiv).

What is interesting is that the women who stepped into these new roles were able to draw on male role models, with only a few female sports coaches then practising – and in so doing began to create their own professional paradigms. Hawkes and Seggar (2000) show that it wasn't an easy process.

GENDER MANAGEMENT AND ORGANISATIONAL CULTURE

Gender, Power and Organisations (Halford and Leonard, 2001) is one of the most comprehensive texts to emerge from organisational gender and management research. The authors tackle the issue of organisational culture as one of male power, and define the "gendered organisation" as all-encompassing. The authors show how power is gained. Through a variety of organisational processes and practices, with power in tiers and levels, each level gains "progressively more power as it nears the top" (Halford and Leonard, 2001:216). Organisational culture is shown to be one of male power – and the question of difference, between women's style of management and male power, tackles the pervasiveness of the "gendered organisation".

In *Voice, Visibility and the Gendering of Organisations*, Simpson and Lewis (2007:69) explore the concept that "capitalism draws men into a network of social relations that encourage sets of behaviours which we would recognise as typically male". They describe men's pervasive dominance of both public and private worlds due to having universalised their experiences. In other words, men are constructed to be representative of the norm and to represent humanity. Men are viewed as "genderless" in organisations, whereas women are seen to be the "other" or "what men are not" (Simpson and Lewis, 2007:53). This concept of men as "gender-free" has been increasingly questioned since the early 1990s, with gender difference being viewed today as an active social construction, "rather than a natural biological category" (Simpson and Lewis, 2007:54). Privilege is generally attached to male *invisibility*; yet men have constructed a visible gender identity by calling attention to being "disadvantaged" by the worldwide implementation of equal opportunities legislation.

In *Coaching Women to Lead*, the authors reviewed a McKinsey survey which looked at the direct and indirect financial performance of gender-rich organisations (Desvaux, Devillard-Hoellinger and Meaney, 2008, cited in Leimon, Moscovici and Goodier, 2011). In studying over 230 organisations which represented 115 000 staff, they concluded that:

- companies with three women or more in their top management teams scored systematically higher in nine organisational dimensions; and
- companies which did score higher in all nine dimensions had a systematically higher financial performance than their peers; an operational profitability that was 68 per cent above the group average; and a market value 62 per cent above the group average (Leimon, Moscovici and Goodier, 2011:20).

Of the many conclusions of the McKinsey survey, the key argument for gender diversity is that high female participation in the management team impacts financial performance strongly and positively (Desvaux, Devillard-Hoellinger and Meaney, 2008, cited in Leimon, Moscovici and Goodier, 2011).

Gender management research in organisations

Coaching Women to Lead describes the research that Leimon, Moscovici and Goodier (2011) carried out in collaboration with an MSc post-graduate student at the London School of Economics and Political Science. They interviewed 125 successful women leaders, of which 107 were working in a corporate environment. The majority worked full-time, and six women were working part-time.

An extensive literature review identified the main barriers to women's advancement in organisations, and the following eight coping strategies thought to be commonly used to overcome these barriers:

- family and career balance;
- understanding corporate culture;
- systematic investment in career and development;
- confidence;
- knowledge of own strengths;
- networking;
- role models; and
- career planning (Leimon, Moscovici and Goodier, 2011:40–41).

A questionnaire survey was then carried out to test the effectiveness of these coping strategies among women in corporate roles. It was found that the women were particularly challenged in five of the eight coping strategies, in the following ways (Leimon, Moscovici and Goodier, 2011:47–49):

- *Career progression* emphasised the need for career planning; being provided with and developing career direction; gaining skills and education to progress career.
- *Confidence* examined the major area for coaching, which is women's lack of self-belief. The interviews demonstrated the need to overcome personal insecurities and inadequacies. Alongside this was knowing when to say no to other's expectations, particularly the cultural understanding in organisations of the need to "be always available".
- *Organisational dynamics* means developing a sufficient understanding of organisational culture, and more importantly, finding out the rules of the game. What shows up is that most women leaders have a deficit in terms of understanding the culture of the organisation in which they work.
- *Relational support*, the fourth area of challenge, made it clear that women lack an understanding of the critical need for networking to progress their careers. Men network to manage their careers, and women are often at a disadvantage as they start to network at a later age than men to progress their careers. Due to the shortage of women in senior and executive management positions, women seriously lack female role models who

have "leveraged their strengths as a female rather than diminished them to get on", and with whom they can work to support their career development (Leimon, Moscovici and Goodier, 2011:48). Women can also be excluded from a variety of informal "one-to-one relationship building sessions in male-dominated environments" such as the locker room and the golf course (Leimon, Moscovici and Goodier, 2011:48).

- *Work–life balance* is not a factor that either men or women often get right. Out of this research women seemed to be at a serious disadvantage in terms of "balancing personal life and career" and "attempting to be all things to all people, i.e. running a home and a career" (Leimon, Moscovici and Goodier, 2011:49).

The authors' research extends beyond the business issues and the coaching relationship by identifying the most significant area for coaching women leaders. Justifying why women professionals need coaching at various stages in their careers, the authors also identify the most important factors needed to reach a board position and advice for younger women starting out in their careers, and for those women struggling to move out of middle management. More importantly, the research has begun to identify what is needed to ensure more women become leaders in the future.

An important aspect of this research has been why there is a need to differentiate in coaching for men and women, identifying what makes a strong woman leader, and developing a model for women's leadership development. Of the eight strategies, those relevant both for coaching and to the organisational employer were family and career balance, systematic investment in career and development, networking, and career planning. Those identified as relevant only for coaching were developing confidence and building knowledge of one's own strengths. Two that seemed more relevant to the organisation were developing an understanding of corporate culture and becoming role models. According to the authors, each of the eight strategies is useful for coaching and important for the organisation. The importance of this type of research cannot be underestimated, and what would be useful would be to conduct similar surveys in organisations in other cultures than the UK.

Interestingly, Rosner (1990, cited in Simpson and Lewis, 2007:12) points to women having adopted a "transformational" leadership style, encouraging "participation, power sharing and information exchange" and a team-based approach. This is in opposition to the more "transactional" style of leadership preferred by men, which focuses on "autonomy, independence and instrumentality, in which leadership is seen as a series of transactions" and where "power is drawn from formal status and authority" (Rosner, 1990, cited in Simpson and Lewis, 2007:12).

The gendering of organisations

Simpson and Lewis (2007) offer insight into how gender is linked to organisations and accounts for differences in the experiences of men and women in the world of work. Research has historically focused on the differences between men and women – and this dense academic text explores the process where some voices are privileged over others and how masculine voices silence and suppress other discourses (e.g. femininity) in order to maintain their dominant position (Simpson and Lewis, 2007:81). The work reviews gender and organisational literature through the parallel concepts of voice and visibility.

Structured around the concepts of "voice and visibility", the authors explore the increasingly diverse field of gender and organisational studies. The authors identify gender as being "discursively produced" and consider whether the factors of voice and visibility are "acquired inherently or through processes of socialisation" (Simpson and Lewis, 2007:26). The authors' approach to gender and organisations integrating the two concepts of voice and visibility is skilful and refreshing, and they have produced a model which identifies both surface and deep conceptualisations of voice and visibility. Also, identifying the fragmented ways in which voice and visibility have been used in the literature, the authors draw on and move outside of three broad feminist perspectives (liberal, radical and post-structuralist) (Simpson and Lewis, 2007:1).

They discuss "how men and women construct each other through the two-sided dynamic of gendering practices and the practising of gender. In this construction ... women's sense of self and confidence are impaired" (Simpson and Lewis, 2007:27). The authors look at the dominant discourses of managerialism and masculinity within organisations, which are hierarchical in relation to each other. Of huge interest for coaches is the exploration of men as the invisible gender(less) subject, embodying the invisible privileges and resources of masculinity.

What is helpful is exposing the backlash from men who do not identify with the oppressive, dominating, uncaring, socially and economically privileged "stereotypical" representation of themselves. Simpson and Lewis (207:57) explore the differentiation between two types of men, based on their orientation to the principle of equality – some who support equality, and others who oppose equality, believing instead in the "rightness" of traditional roles for women. They explore the *victim visibility* which is a means of maintaining *victor invisibility*. In other words, men seek through the backlash struggle to be visible as *victim* and yet keep the material advantages of masculinity hidden from view (Simpson and Lewis, 2007:88). Arguing that the concepts of voice and visibility have not been fully explored in terms of application, the authors have developed a practical framework for the development of female entrepreneurship.

Gatrell and Swan (2008) give an overview in *Gender and Diversity in Management* of the core issues of gender, race, sexuality, disability and diversity in management in the UK. The book is actually intended for students studying management, gender in management, equal opportunities and diversity, and human resource management. There is often conflicting scholarship in this area, and this very focused introduction acknowledges what are the key contemporary issues and presents them concisely for researchers and practitioners. According to Gatrell and Swan, the literature has expanded on men and women in management, particularly due to changes in legislation and policy which have focused on equality of opportunity and diversity. Although the authors refer to the UK marketplace, it is relevant to other cultures where "discrimination within the workplace remains widespread and persistent and leads to further inequalities" (Gatrell and Swan, 2008:1).

The authors refer to the "glass ceiling", a term coined in the 1960s to describe the "barrier which is transparent but impassable, so that women can see the top of the management hierarchy, but may not reach it" (Gatrell and Swan, 2008:12). They also refer to the "concrete wall" which is faced by black and minority ethnic women, meaning that "wherever they turn their career progress is limited, and they are prevented by organisational practices and processes from even seeing the top of the career ladder, never mind climbing it" (Gatrell and Swan, 2008:12). Hamilton observes how women play a "fundamental part both in the establishment and the running of family businesses, but are often excluded from the social and economic rewards" (Hamilton, 2006; quoted in Gatrell and Swan 2008:13).

The authors agree with organisational theorist Joan Acker on the definition of gender: "Although the term gender is widely used, there is no common understanding of its meaning, even amongst feminist scholars" (Acker, 1992:565; cited in Gatrell and Swan, 2008:4). They agree that for most social theorists, gender is a social construction which means that "as for other social categories such as race, sexuality and disability – gender is the result of human social processes, actions, language, thought and practices" (Gatrell and Swan, 2008:4). Gender is seen here as a process, rather than as given traits or essences, with "gender actively produced in and through the workplace" (Gatrell and Swan, 2008:4).

This leads to a debate on the different views of gender in the workplace, and particularly on the topic of gender management versus women in management. "The idea of 'gender and gendering', as opposed to 'women' in management as an analytic lens, means that the relationality between men and women, masculinity and femininity – the way that they cannot be thought apart from each other – can be emphasised. The notion of gender and gendering also draws attention to the social construction of masculinity and femininity" (Gatrell and Swan, 2008:5). The authors examine the notion of diversity in relationship to management and the workplace. Again, "diversity" is an ill-defined and slippery term; the authors consider "diversity in relation to management practices", and survey in some detail "the disadvantaged and oppressive treatment faced by a range of social groups" (Gatrell and Swan, 2008:6).

Gatrell and Swan suggest there is little sign or promise of change, citing evidence that boardrooms in Britain continue to be afflicted by the "pale male" syndrome. Women are still segregated vertically in terms of the career ladder, and horizontally into a "velvet ghetto" of particular jobs seen as less valued and are considered "gendered", such as in human resources, public relations and marketing (Gatrell and Swan, 2008:11–12). The book takes a deep dive into the historical position of women in the UK labour market, looking at liberal feminism and the origins of equal opportunities for women. Feminist thinking is explored, such as the influential examples of Betty Friedan's *The Feminine Mystique* published in 1963, and Germaine Greer's *The Female Eunuch* published in 1970, both seminal works which gave voice to feminist thinking on gender, work and inequality (Gatrell and Swan, 2008:22).

Workplace activism started in the 1960s and 1970s, and the authors acknowledge that "women have always found ways to fight and resist discriminatory practices, individually and collectively" (Gatrell and Swan, 2008:21). The authors also examine social and cultural perspectives on how traditional stereotypes of masculinity and femininity have created the gendered division of labour at work, with particular emphasis on the discrimination of women with and without children (Gatrell and Swan, 2008:36–37). Examining the business case for managing diversity, the authors emphasise that the "business case for diversity presumes that a diverse workforce brings material benefits to an organisation in the form of increased profits, more creativity or more representative customer care" (Gatrell and Swan, 2008:53).

The conclusion is that, despite legislation and campaign organisations such as the Equal Opportunities Commission, and the lobbying group, Fawcett, there is nonetheless a continuing debate on gender and diversity in management. One argument is that not only are there differences between women, we also need to understand the complex ways in which gender operates and the ways that inequality is differentially formed and experienced (Gatrell and Swan, 2008:88).

Gender and the boardroom

It would be remiss of me not to include Thomson and Graham's (2005) findings on the value that women bring to the boardroom. This book is the result of extensive research, identifying critical issues of business cultures and systems which inhibit the progress of women who aspire to executive positions. Emerging from an academic interest in equality and women's rights, the authors take an in-depth look into the barriers, assumptions and habits that are deeply embedded in business and organisational systems. In comparing the gender imbalance of boards and "the gender balance of the marketplace and new graduates" (Thomson and Graham, 2005:57) the authors address the "corporate kings", i.e. current and former chairmen and CEOs of large USA and UK companies, versus the layer of "marzipan" women, or senior women executives who work closely to the board but are not on the board (Thomson and Graham, 2005:57–58).

In articulating the scarcity of women in building the pipeline to the board, culture emerged as a prime culprit. Some of the initiatives proposed to develop a pipeline of women moving through the system and into senior positions are well known: "coaching, mentoring, development, women's networks and recruitment criteria reviews" (Thomson and Graham, 2005:175). However, their summary findings about culture are useful, suggesting that a culture can only become genuinely inclusive when those working within it begin to look "deep inside themselves, at their assumptions and beliefs, and identify, understand and, if necessary, modify or abandon the attitudes and stereotypes guiding their behaviour" (Thomson and Graham, 2005:189).

Previous research shows that women and men think differently, and solve problems differently. However, the crucial question that they pose, which goes to the heart of all diversity, is simply: "Why would you not want people on your board who think differently" (Thomson and Graham, 2005:205)?

DIVERSITY AND IDENTITY WITHIN
A THINKING ENVIRONMENT®

Stout-Rostron, Janse van Rensburg and Marques Sampaio (2014) explain that accepting diversity and equality is about probing many things, including the way we think about identity – especially our own. It is about examining models of identity based on a defensive, even reactionary, antagonism towards what lies "outside" – models such as certain types of nationalism, or forms of identification based on a rejection of "the other", with all the negative connotations that term carries. It is about questioning our perception of what is foreign: of what originates elsewhere, or of those who view the world differently (Stout-Rostron, Janse van Rensburg and Marques Sampaio, 2014:191). This need to re-evaluate our limiting worldviews is an important one for coach practitioners.

Before people can operate as HR or OD practitioners, or as coach or coaching psychology practitioners within an organisational context, they must first work on themselves – learning from their own experience, developing self-awareness, and understanding the impact of their own limiting assumptions. If practitioners are to work with their clients to help them learn from their own experience, it requires honouring genuinely diverse thinking, including an appreciation for difference and an elimination of punishment for being different (Kline, 1999:87).

Thinking Environment® philosophy

It is the everyday, commonplace unconscious assumptions about each other that undermine others (Kline, 1999). Nancy Kline's research, referenced in *Time to Think* (1999) and *More Time to Think* (2009) emphasises the importance of developing diverse Thinking Environments® within organisations. However, diversity must mean an absolute assumption of equality in the face of difference. Kline's development of the Thinking Environment® comes from her and her global faculty's organisational and institutional observation of practice in the USA, UK and Europe, Australia and South Africa. Her work takes an innovative and unique look at how men are socialised to be "thinkers" and women to be "thinking partners".

Having worked for many years with the philosophy of the Thinking Environment®, I have come to understand how important it is for coaches, managers and leaders to first develop themselves – by exploring the roots of their own discriminatory attitudes and behaviours. We do this by starting to examine untrue limiting assumptions which society and organisations make about people based on their group identities, in this case gender. And about their place in their social and workplace hierarchies – based on race, gender, language, faith, education, class, nationality and tribe.

Unconscious attitudes towards others are often the privilege of power. I coached in a major educational institution in South Africa, where all the senior women managers, lecturers and administrators were about to quit their jobs. All these women were of different ethnic backgrounds, languages and ages. Their only common factor was gender. The male culture, comprising men both previously disadvantaged and advantaged under apartheid, tolerated an aggressive and even open disrespect for women. This was just an "unthinking exercise of power"; they were unconscious until the impact of their behaviour was brought to their attention.

It is important in any working environment that the leader or manager becomes aware of and manages their own responses to questions of diversity, before they can begin to lead, manage or coach a direct report on similar issues. In the creation of a Thinking Environment®, Kline has developed a variety of coaching diversity exercises. This is done by exploring the roots of discriminatory attitudes and behaviour, examining untrue limiting assumptions society and organisations make about people on the basis of their individual and group identities. As practitioner, researcher or leader, these exercises help both client, practitioner and executive to remove limiting assumptions, replacing them with true liberating assumptions that free individuals and groups to reclaim their self-esteem and influence.

Assumptions in diversity work

To work with assumptions, it is important to first identify our three levels of thought. Your ongoing narrative is organised by three general levels of thought: automatic thoughts, assumptions and core beliefs. This helps us to understand the reason for transforming limiting assumptions into liberating alternative assumptions.

Assumptions aren't as fundamental as core beliefs, yet they aren't as superficial as automatic thoughts. Assumptions are one of the primary targets of cognitive behavioural therapy (CBT) which aims to restructure a person's thoughts, to reflect adaptable and constructive thinking in working with a practitioner. It is at this level of assumptions where practitioners can work with behaviour change – not just in the coaching conversation but also in diversity work. Assumptions lie midway between automatic thoughts and core beliefs.

Core beliefs develop over time, usually from childhood and through the experience of significant life events or particular life circumstances Core beliefs are strongly held, rigid and inflexible beliefs, that are maintained by the tendency to focus on information that supports the belief while ignoring evidence that contradicts it. These types of belief are the hardest to shake. Core beliefs are the essence of how we see ourselves, other people, the world, and the future. Sometimes certain situations activate these core beliefs – they can be related to an individual's self-concept, or their family or any part of their lives that is important to them (Nathan, Lim and Correia, 2004:2).

Kline explains the power of assumptions and their impact on our behaviour:

> Our thinking (and feeling) is driven by assumptions. Everything we do comes from the assumption we make just before we do it. As dry as this can sound on paper, the discovery of the assumptions that are busy shaping our ideas, our work, our relationships and our feelings is an intensely alive experience. Replacing the assumptions that are stagnating or damaging our lives with liberating assumptions that lift our lives into new levels of joy and meaning is an experience worth the expertise (Kline, 2012).

Here is an example of a Thinking Environment® coaching exercise to transform a limiting to a liberating assumption:

1. What are you assuming about yourself that is holding you back or stopping you from developing or progressing your career?
2. What might be a more liberating assumption?
3. If you knew that [liberating assumption] what would change for you? (Kline, 2012).

Self-evaluation is a key part of being able to coach or counsel around gender diversity issues. In order to understand your own limiting assumptions about gender identity, here is a useful exercise in which you can identify those assumptions that we aren't always consciously able to articulate.

1. What are your limiting assumptions about men, and what are your limiting assumptions about women?
2. Which of these is the most limiting?
3. Are these inherently true (always true) – and what might be a more liberating view for each?

From her work and research in organisations round the globe, Nancy Kline has developed an interesting approach to male and female conditioning. Although it looks like the "extreme" of male and female stereotypes it is useful to discuss and debate and understand how as a coach practitioner you can help your clients to develop more self-awareness of their biases and limiting assumptions about their own identity. The following two examples from Kline's work in diversity identify, in her definition, the socialisation of men as thinkers, and women as thinking partners.

Men are socialised to be thinkers

According to Nancy Kline (1999:87–96):

- Men are trained to play the role of Thinker but not that of Thinking Partner, and to assume that the best way to help is to give others their ideas – and to do their thinking for them.
- Limiting messages in men's culture discourage them from creating a thinking environment for others and dictate against the ten components (these are ten specific behaviours).
- Limiting messages are that "real men don't do feelings; asking questions erodes your power base; criticism is the road to real improvement, and success is defined as winning".
- Liberating messages in men's culture encourage them to create an internal thinking environment for themselves (men's liberating thinking is that they are more intelligent and logical than women; their thinking matters; men should be listened to).
  These suggestions are summarised in Table 4.

Table 4: Comparison between Thinking Environment® values and stereotypical male conditioning

Thinking Environment®	Male conditioning
Listen	Take over and talk
Ask incisive questions	Know everything
Establish equality	Assume superiority
Appreciate	Criticise
Be at ease	Control
Encourage	Compete
Feel	Toughen
Supply accurate information	Lie
Humanise the place	Conquer the place
Create diversity	Deride difference

Source: Kline (1999:87–96)

Women are socialised to be thinking partners

According to Nancy Kline (1999:87–96):

- Women are primarily socialised to play the role of the Thinking Partner but not that of the Thinker.
- Limiting messages in women's culture are to defer to others; keep quiet; women are too emotional; and men are more important than women – all of which discourage women from playing the Thinker role and from creating an internal thinking environment for themselves.
- Liberating messages in women's culture encourage women to develop an external thinking environment for others.
- The liberating messages in women's culture prepare them to support all ten components of the Thinking Environment®.

These suggestions are summarised in Table 5.

Table 5: Comparison between Thinking Environment® values and stereotypical female conditioning

Thinking Environment®	Female conditioning
Voice your ideas	Keep quiet, defer
Remove limits with incisive questions	Accept your limits
See yourself as equal	Assume inferiority
Welcome appreciation	Doubt yourself
Relax, enjoy your turn	Rush, give time to others
Focus on what you really think	Strive to be accepted
Feel feelings to think clearly	You feel feelings because you are weak
Seek accurate information	Soften the truth for others
Let the place say people matter	Defer to men's idea of place
Claim your own diverse identities	Blend in

Source: Kline (1999:87–96).

Working with group identity and limiting assumptions

"Groups With Whom You Identify" is a diversity exercise designed by Nancy Kline (2012) which helps individuals to understand the groups with whom they identify, and about whom society holds many limiting assumptions. It is a useful coaching exercise to engage our thinking around all of the identity groups with whom we identify. Kline hopes this exercise can help women in particular to understand the limiting views they hold of themselves that might be sabotaging their own success. The exercise requires participants to answer the following questions (Kline, 2012):

1. What are the groups with whom you identify and about whom society makes assumptions that can limit those groups' power, dignity and confidence?
2. Of those which are the three group identities that today, for whatever reason, most stand out for you?
3. What is the key group identity for you among those three?
4. What limiting assumptions does the world make about that group?
5. Of those assumptions which one do you think is the most limiting?
6. Do you think that assumption is, in fact, inherently true of that group? What are your reasons for thinking that?
7. What would be your words for a liberating true alternative to that assumption?
8. If you and the world knew that (true liberating assumption), what would change for you and the world?

CULTURAL CONTEXTS ON GENDER ISSUES IN BUSINESS

This section is an overview of the influence of ethnic and/or cultural contexts on how gender issues in business are manifested and responded to by men and women, and how these contexts need to be taken into account in business coaching.

Shaping culture

Part of understanding organisational culture is to clarify the cultural knowledge and social processes that operate within an organisation on a daily basis. There are belief systems in operation about the rights and wrongs of how to do things, and it is through these belief systems that power operates within a company. These power structures create worldviews about hierarchy, identity, performance, relationships, diversity, gender and ethnicity. Also, the position that an individual holds within an organisation shapes their attitudes, their values and their behaviour (Halford and Leonard, 2001:65).

All organisations create their own values, language, rituals and ways of seeing the world as a by- product of what they produce and sell. These are all essentially practices by management to create or build a certain spirit or ethos within the organisation (Peters and Waterman, 1982). Research shows that companies who have strong cultures tend to be highly performance-oriented, with an organisational hierarchy that creates both a structure of power and a way for management to achieve consensus and performance delivery. Organisational culture helps to give employees a sense of identity and direction, but it also includes a way of "creating meaning" within the organisational system. What is important to remember is that organisational culture is a "subjective" experience for each individual working in the system. What is crucial is to discover the shared beliefs, attitudes and assumptions that create the process of working, harnessing performance and ensuring delivery. Also, it is important to understand the hierarchy of power within the organisation.

Culture can actually be seen as a metaphor for an organisation, as organisations operate almost as if they are mini-societies, with culture emerging through the social interactions and negotiations of the members of the organisation (Czarniawska-Joerges, 1992). Although organisational culture can be defined in many ways, it is articulated through some of the less tangible aspects of organisational life, such as the attitudes, beliefs and values – as well as the symbols, languages and practices of an organisation.

Leading in a multicultural and diverse environment

Defining culture within an organisational and an institutional context is a very complex subject, and if a key driver of culture is the "informal channels that communicate it", then Leimon, Moscovici and Goodier are right in suggesting that "women are also the culture and should take ownership of culture change"; however, as we have seen elsewhere, women do not yet represent a "critical mass of women at the relevant level of management" (Leimon, Moscovici and Goodier, 2011:53).

In *Coaching Women to Lead*, Leimon, Moscovici and Goodier (2011) emphasised how essential it is for women to understand corporate culture if they are to progress in their careers. They define corporate culture simply as "a set of understandings or meaning shared by a group of people", or "the rules for behaviour in the organisation". The authors suggest that "in many organisations, the culture is still based on a set of values and norms around the 'white male heritage'. If women can learn about the social conventions associated with these cultures, they have a much better chance of knowing what to do and when to get on in their careers" (Leimon, Moscovici and Goodier, 2011:53). This is where coaching and well-trained coach practitioners have a key role to play.

Binary opposites

Stout-Rostron, Janse van Rensburg and Marques Sampaio (2014) note that in Western cultures one of the key ways of making sense of the world is through binary oppositions. People construct meaning through the recognition of "opposites", defining what something is by knowing what it isn't. "Binary oppositions put the world into clearly defined categories ... between white and black, between masculine and feminine" (Stout-Rostron, Janse van Rensburg and Marques Sampaio, 2014:197–198). These "opposites" usually turn out to be based on unexamined assumptions about socially constructed categories, and that human reality is much more complex than this kind of expedient simplification. Further,

> This division of experience into binary oppositions also reflects a particular structure of power: one side of the opposition has traditionally been privileged (and often exercised that privilege) over the other: men (and masculinity) have traditionally been privileged over women (and femininity); whites over blacks; rich over poor (Stout-Rostron, Janse van Rensburg and Marques Sampaio, 2014:198).

Primarily based on the differences between men and women, the binary view of gender sees masculinity as an invisible set of power relations which avoids scrutiny and hides behind its cloak of essential difference (Simpson and Lewis, 2007:68). In this way, gender is perceived to be associated with women, while men remain invisible as a gender. Simpson and Lewis explore four different types of masculinity identified in a study by Boyle (2000, cited in Simpson and Lewis, 2007:74). These are characterised as (1) *militarised masculinity*, which is inflexible, rigid and hierarchical; (2) *managerial and techno masculinity*, identified with bureaucratic control and growing technology; (3) *heroic*, reflecting deference and admiration; and (4) *nurturing*, associated with caring for emotional needs within the job.

Most gender organisation research reflects the differences between men and women. Although there is a continuous struggle for women to be assimilated equally into the workplace, men continue to maintain their power through their invisible, genderless occupation of the normative position through which power is managed.

It would be an interesting piece of research in South Africa to determine the power differences between the diverse identities of white, black African and mixed-race male leaders – particularly as South African business was historically dominated by white males. Today, due to Black Economic Empowerment (BEE) and a democracy led politically by black males, the power balance is far more complex. However, gender still plays a very strong role with many men uncomfortable or even, as I have experienced when coaching executive women, passively aggressively refusing to report to a woman manager.

ACADEMIC RESEARCH ON COACHING AND GENDER

Over recent decades there has been a plethora of academic research into diversity, gender and culture. However, as new disciplines, coaching and coaching psychology are in the early stages of generating academic research through coach education programmes worldwide and coaching bodies (e.g. the Institute of Coaching at Harvard; the Worldwide Association of Business Coaches; the Institute of Applied Psychology). There is a huge response to this need for research into coaching through the professional coaching and coaching psychology bodies – and a renewed interest in gender diversity research.

Due to the development of certification programmes through the Worldwide Association of Business Coaches (WABC), the founding of the Institute of Coaching at Harvard / McLean Medical School (IOC) with its annual US$100 000 grant for coaching research, and the plethora of academic coach education programmes in graduate schools of business, there is now beginning to be interest in research into gender diversity coaching. But this is only the beginning, and more interest is required if we are to discover what is the impact of coaching for both women and men on core diversity issues.

One excellent study is the unpublished doctoral research by Dr Dorrian Aiken Hodge (2006) which can be located at the Work-Based Learning Centre, Middlesex University London. Her study is entitled *Towards Coaching Across Divides to Create Alliances: An* Integral Approach. Her project objectives were to:

1. Coach managerial leaders in teams and organisations to develop alliances across divides towards shared objectives.
2. Frame an Integral multi-dimensional meta-model and develop an Integral coaching process.
3. Test a core hypothesis on a critical coaching focus in working with clients to build alliances across divides.

Aiken Hodge's Integral coaching approach has proved effective in navigating multi-dimensional complexity within corporate environments in South Africa, and has received positive feedback on its contribution to building alliances at individual, team and organisational levels in those settings. The Integral Model has seemingly also proved highly efficient at mapping congruence and "disconnects" at individual, team and organisational level. However, Aiken Hodge suggests that the "limitations of this coaching framework and model are that the theoretical underpinning is complex and layered, requiring that the coach be competent at managing this complexity, both theoretically and practically. Unless the coach is committed to absorbing and feeling at ease with the elements of the Integral approach, the danger is reductionism to a systems approach. This impacts on the viability of this model for training in-house coaches" (Aiken Hodge, 2006).

In my interview with Suzi Skinner, who recently completed a post-masters research study through the University of Sydney's Coaching Psychology Unit (Skinner, 2012), her gender research findings show that Australia is continuing to grapple with a declining representation of females in decision-making positions. This declining representation means a continued disparity in gender pay and a lack of paid maternity leave sanctioned by the government – all central issues in women's lives. Of particular concern is the trend over recent years – particularly in the private sector – where despite increased dialogue in mainstream media, community and government advocacy groups (concerning gender equality), Australia is actually falling behind its OECD contemporaries in key measures such as the number of women corporate directors. In 2008 only 49 per cent of the top 200 Australia companies had at least one woman on their board – significantly behind the UK (77 per cent of FTSE200 companies), Canada (52.8 per cent of FP500 companies), and the US (91 per cent of S&P500 companies) (Thomas, 2008:4).

Skinner's research study was provisionally titled *Women in Leadership: Understanding how executive coaching can help women leaders thrive in corporate Australia*. She investigated the experiences of women in leadership positions in corporate Australia and the role that executive coaching can take in helping them to be more successful in their positions. This research seeks to increase our understanding of the nature of the perceived challenges women face in leadership roles (specifically senior management) and how executive coaching can be tailored in a more gender sensitive way to assist women to excel in these environments (Skinner, 2012).

Skinner's research sought to understand what these women perceive as barriers in their roles; in which ways their executive coaching was useful (or otherwise) in addressing these barriers and in what ways executive coaching could be tailored to more directly assist women leaders to be successful in their leadership positions. In order to gain insight into the Australian context for women leaders, these interviews are complemented by perspectives gained from stakeholders in government, education and relevant not-for-profit bodies who have an interest in advancing women leaders in Australia (Skinner, 2012).

In South Africa, there is new gender diversity research emerging. Alison Reid completed a Masters research study on *The impact of group coaching on leadership effectiveness for South African women managers* in 2012 at the University of the Witwatersrand's Graduate School of Business. She defines the purpose of her study as "to assess the impact of group coaching on leadership effectiveness in South African women managers" (Reid, 2012:7).

The study's findings indicated that

> leadership effectiveness did change significantly over a six-month leadership development programme, most notably in the areas of enabling self and others, and that

Leadership Coaching for Results: Cutting-edge practices for coach and client

group coaching specifically impacted leadership effectiveness ... This study ... showed that women may benefit particularly from contexts that support traditionally 'feminine' relationship leadership skills, and provide alternative reference groups outside of their male-dominated work environments where safe feedback and appropriate role models are not much in evidence (Reid, 2012:76–77).

The purpose of this study was to assess the impact of group coaching on leadership effectiveness in South African women managers. It aimed to investigate changes in women's leadership effectiveness after attending a business school leadership development programme, which included a group coaching component. It subsequently aimed to explore what impact the group coaching process had on changes in the women's leadership effectiveness. The findings indicate that leadership effectiveness did change significantly over a six month leadership development programme, most notably in the areas of enabling self and others, and that group coaching specifically impacted leadership effectiveness. The described benefits of group coaching are particularly appropriate for modern social and collective relational leadership contexts and especially beneficial to women leaders.

The importance of gender diversity research cannot be underestimated. There is a huge need for gender diversity research globally into the impact of coaching for both women and men on core diversity issues, and particularly on how business and executive coaching can be tailored in a more gender sensitive way to assist women to excel.

CONCLUSION

I have approached this chapter from a variety of perspectives in terms of the contemporary literature available to us. Gender refers to both men and women, and it is important not to assume that women represent the only gender concerns, but to broaden the discussion to include men. If you wish to understand the history of gender activism and the published literature from the 1960s to the present, see Stout-Rostron (2012a).

There is a continuing debate on gender and diversity in management and how the notion of gender and gendering draws attention to the social construction of masculinity and femininity. I have examined current thinking on how men and women are socialised, the impact of organisational culture – and in what ways the dominant white male organisational culture has affected the development of women in the workplace. This chapter is also an overview of the influence of ethnic and/or cultural contexts on how gender issues in business are manifested and responded to by men and women, and how these contexts need to be taken into account by practitioners in coaching, coaching psychology, counselling, human resources and organisational development – and by leaders adopting a coaching approach within their talent development programmes.

Practitioners need to understand the socio-political factors of all their clients, understanding their cultural, educational, ethnic and racial backgrounds. Each practitioner has a responsibility to integrate cultural knowledge into their own education and practice – and most importantly culturally evaluating themselves to understand their own worldview.

It is only in this way that practitioners and leaders can increase their competence, empower their clients or direct reports with their interventions, and value diversity as an asset instead of a liability.

FURTHER READING

Aiken Hodge, D.E. (2006). *Towards Coaching Across Divides to Create Alliances: An integral approach*. Unpublished DProf dissertation. London: Middlesex University.

Bell, E.L.J., and Nkomo, S.M. (2001). *Our Separate Ways: Black and white women and the struggle for identity*. Boston, MA: Harvard Business School.

Eagly, A.H., and Carli, L.L. (2007). Women and the labyrinth of leadership. *Harvard Business Review*, 85(9):63–71.

Chin, J.L., De La Cancela, V., and Jenkins, Y.M. (eds) (1993). *Diversity in Psychotherapy: The politics of race, ethnicity, and gender*. Westport, CT: Praeger.

Connerley, M.L., and Pedersen, P.B. (2005). *Leadership in a Diverse and Multicultural Environment: Developing awareness, knowledge, and skills*. Thousand Oaks, CA: Sage.

Czarniawska-Joerges, B. (1992). *Exploring Complex Organisations: A cultural perspective*. Newbury Park, CA: Sage.

Erlandson, E. (2009). Coaching with men: Alpha males. In Passmore, J. (ed.), *Diversity in Coaching: Working with gender, culture, race and age* (pp. 216–236). London: Association for Coaching and Philadelphia, PA: Kogan Page.

Gatrell, C., and Swan, E. (2008). *Gender and Diversity in Management: A concise introduction*. London: Sage.

Hamilton, E. (2006). Whose story is it anyway? Narrative accounts of the role of women in founding and establishing family businesses. *International Small Business Journal*, 24(3):253–271.

Hofstede, G. (2005). Foreword. In: Connerley, M.L., and Pedersen, P.B., *Leadership in a Diverse and Multicultural Environment: Developing awareness, knowledge, and skills* (pp. ix–x). Thousand Oaks, CA: Sage.

Janse van Rensburg, M. (2012). Diversity, personality and culture. In Stout-Rostron, S. (2012b), *Business Coaching Wisdom and Practice: Unlocking the secrets of business coaching (Second edition)* (pp. 145–195). Randburg: Knowres.

Kline, N. (1999). *Time to Think: Listening to ignite the human mind*. London: Ward Lock.

Leimon, A., Moscovici, F., and Goodier, H. (2011). *Coaching Women to Lead*. New York, NY: Routledge.

Ludeman, K. (2009). Coaching with women. In Passmore, J. (ed.), *Diversity in Coaching: Working with gender, culture, race and age* (pp. 237–254). London: Association for Coaching and Philadelphia, PA: Kogan Page.

Ludeman, K., and Erlandson, E. (2004). Coaching the alpha male. *Harvard Business Review*, 82(5):58–67.

Moir, A., and Jessel, D. (1992). *Brain Sex: The real difference between men and women*. New York, NY: Delta.

Leadership Coaching for Results: Cutting-edge practices for coach and client

Niederle, M., and Vesterlund, L. (2005). *Do Women Shy Away From Competition? Do men compete too much?* NBER Working Paper No. 11474, July. Washington, DC: National Bureau of Economic Research.

Pinker, S. (2008). *The Sexual Paradox: Men, women and the real gender gap.* New York, NY: Scribner.

Prime, J. (2005). *Women "take care", men "take charge": Stereotyping of US business leaders exposed.* New York, NY: Catalyst.

Ramphele, M. (2008). *Laying Ghosts to Rest: Dilemmas of the transformation in South Africa.* Cape Town: Tafelberg.

Simpson, R., and Lewis, P. (2007). *Voice, Visibility and the Gendering of Organisations.* Basingstoke: Palgrave Macmillan.

Stout-Rostron, S. (2012a). Gender issues in business coaching. In Passmore, J., Peterson, D.B., and Freire, T. (eds), *The Wiley-Blackwell Handbook of the Psychology of Coaching and Mentoring* (pp. 155–174). London: Wiley-Blackwell.

Stout-Rostron, S. (2012b). *Business Coaching Wisdom and Practice: Unlocking the Secrets of Business Coaching.* Second edition. Randburg: Knowres.

Stout-Rostron, S., Janse van Rensburg, M., and Marques Sampaio, D. (2014). Diversity, culture and gender. In Stout-Rostron, S., *Business Coaching International: Transforming individuals and organisations (Second edition)* (pp. 173–232). London: Karnac.

Tannen, D. (1995). The power of talk: Who gets heard and why. *Harvard Business Review,* 73(5):138–148.

Tannen, D. (1999). *The Argument Culture: Stopping America's war of words.* New York, NY: Ballantine.

Thomas, A., and Bendixen, M. (2000). The management implications of ethnicity in South Africa. *Journal of International Business Studies,* 31(3):507–519.

Wirth, L. (2001). *Breaking Through the Glass Ceiling: Women in management.* Geneva: International Labour Office.

Wirth, L. (2004). *Breaking Through the Glass Ceiling: Women in management: Update 2004.* Geneva: International Labour Office.

10

Coaching in organisations

BALANCING INTERESTS IN BUSINESS COACHING

by Nick Wilkins and Dr Sunny Stout-Rostron

Business coaching often involves a three-cornered relationship between the *coach* (or team of coaches), the client *organisation* paying for the coaching, and the *individual* executives, managers or other staff members being coached. It is neither easy nor straightforward for the coach to balance the interests of the client firm and the individuals actually being coached, yet failing to get this balance right can land a coach in trouble. To tackle this critical issue, important actions need to be taken well before the coaching process starts.

Business coaching typically aims to improve an organisation's results through enhancing performance, and the client firm will expect the coach, as a contracted service provider, to help the organisation achieve its objectives. Complications may arise if an inexperienced business coach forgets to consider who the actual client is. Is it the organisation that hires and pays the coach's fees to help with a business need? Or is it the individual who is seeking to grow, develop and move forward in their career? The question is essentially answered when an executive personally pays the coach's fee. But to whom does the coach owe loyalty when the company pays the bill? In fact, it is to both the client firm and the individual coachees, which can sometimes create an ethical dilemma (Stout-Rostron, 2012b:286–287).

Understanding, agreement and commitment

A critical first step for the business coach, in balancing the interests of client firm and individual participants, is to ensure that everyone involved understands and explicitly agrees on:

- what business coaching is, and
- how the coaching project can improve the firm's results, through
- using coaching conversations with individual participants to improve their performance.

Negotiations and contracting between all three parties involved in the coaching intervention should produce a *prior* and *explicit understanding, consensus,* and *acceptance* of the coaching project which ensures *support for* and *commitment to* the project by both senior management and all other participants. It is useful to include a definition of coaching within the project contract, specifying how coaching differs from the other helping disciplines such as psychotherapy, counselling, consulting, mentoring and training. For example, coaching can be defined as "a process that creates sustained shifts in thinking, feeling and behaviour – and ultimately in performance (Stout-Rostron, 2012b:40). It is crucial, for instance, that coaching is not viewed as a remedial process inflicted by management on underperforming staff members to "fix" their "problems".

It would help if the coach can provide the firm and its prospective coaching participants with a set of their own standard coaching guidelines, terms and conditions, based on best-practice principles and codes of professional practice, to serve as a basis for negotiation and contracting. The coach can seek help with this from their professional coaching body.

The coaching contract and aligning goals

In essence, the contract sets out ground rules for the coaching relationship, so that all parties are aware of their obligations. The contract describes the relationship between the coach and multiple parties, such as the individual participant, the client organisation, the HR unit, and line management. This helps prevent future misunderstandings, and provides a firm basis to deal with disagreements.

Since the relationship between coach and individual client is set within the context of the team and the organisation, and is part of the overall system, this "bigger picture" needs to be part of the contracting process. The coach should therefore ask the following types of questions during contracting with the client firm and individual coaching participants (Stout-Rostron, 2012b:264–265):

* What are the needs of the individual executive client versus those of the organisation?
* What performance improvements are desired?
* What are the organisational goals for the coaching programme?
* What are the organisational conditions, and are they conducive to coaching?
* Are the line manager and senior management supportive of the process?
* Is the individual ready for coaching, and is coaching appropriate for them?

Aligning values and goals

It is important for the coach to ensure that the coaching intervention is aligned strategically with the overall values and objectives of an organisation, and aligned with other leadership development initiatives being undertaken within the firm. Often within the complexity of the organisational environment, the individual coaching participant's overarching goals may be set by a more senior power; where that senior person may have different worldviews, different paradigms, and differing limiting and empowering assumptions. But if organisational goals are to be motivationally achieved, are they also aligned with the individual coaching participant's intrinsic motivators? It is important to ensure that the values and goals of the individual coachees are aligned with the values and goals of the client firm. Ethical dilemmas can arise during the coaching process if the executive needs to make difficult choices which are incompatible with their own value system.

Professional development plans

The job of the business coach is to develop the core competences of the managerial leader. The development of those competences needs to show up visibly in work-related and behavioural changes. The client's work often starts with growing self-awareness, increased emotional maturity and improved interpersonal skills and competence. Performance improvement should have a direct effect on business results. This may require a systemic and developmental approach on the part of coach and client, integrated with an understanding of the complexities of the client's working context, market environment and level of competence. Within this systemic context, a useful way of defining and structuring coaching objectives for individual coaching participants is to formulate a professional development plan with them which contains:

- *Purpose*: a clear definition of the overall aims of the coaching journey.
- *Developmental objectives*: developmental objectives for the executive, their team and the organisation that is in alignment with business strategy.
- *Strategy*: an outline of how to achieve the purpose and developmental objectives.
- *Monthly actions*: core tasks enabling the coachee to achieve and implement their plan.
- *Obstacles to achievement*: an outline of challenges and constraints envisaged and encountered.
- *Results achieved*: a summary of progress each month.
- *Overall learning from the coaching journey*: regularly updated summary of learning to date.

The Professional Development Plan (PDP) or Leadership Development Plan (LDP) is an organic, evolving document that is shared with the coaching participant's line manager or sponsor. Rather than sharing the content of the coaching conversation, client and coach can share the development plan, over-arching goals and results achieved, protecting the confidentiality of coaching conversations. Ultimately, however, it ensures that the coaching objectives of the individual participant are aligned with organisational objectives. It's a balancing act.

CONTRACTING

Contracting is critical

The contract between coach and client sets out which services have been agreed and details fees, outcomes and deliverables to be expected. The contract sets out ground rules for the coaching relationship so that both parties are aware of their obligations. The coach and client agree to conditions of time, space, fees, confidentiality, cancellation and termination. Very importantly, the contract defines objectives for the individual executive and the organisation, and describes the relationship between the coach and multiple parties, such as the individual client, the client organisation, the HR unit, and line management. It is also important for coach and client to contract how communication is to take place. Covering all these issues clearly and explicitly in the contract helps prevent future misunderstandings, and provides a firm basis to deal with disagreements.

Because contracting is complex, it determines what areas, and how deeply, the coach can work with the organisation at an individual, team and systemic level. Developing the habit of both formal and informal contracting is one of the first steps in beginning to understand the dynamics of formulating a coaching relationship and setting boundaries. The purpose of the contract is to open up the potential for trust between coach and client. This is essential if the client is to trust their own self-exploration. As the agreement lays the foundation for the relationship, it must be adhered to in action for trust to develop.

Overall aim for the coaching

Essentially, to contract the overall journey, coach and client discuss what each brings to the relationship, and the overall aim of coaching for the client (*input*). Coach and client then discuss how the coaching will take place: timing, boundaries, fees, the tools and techniques to be used by the coach, and the way the client would prefer to work (*throughput*). They also discuss the overall results and outcomes the client hopes to achieve from the coaching intervention, results that need to be visible to the organisation, and thinking, feeling and behaviour that the client would like to change (*output*).

As a rule, I start the coaching conversation with *input*: "Where are you now?" "Where do you want to get to by the end of this conversation?" "What do you want to talk about?" "What's on the menu for today?" Once we have identified what needs to be worked on, I move into *throughput*: using whichever question frameworks, tools or techniques are relevant to the process. For *output*, we summarise actions, learning and outcomes from the conversation (Cummings and Worley, 2004).

Define coaching in your contract

It is useful to include a definition of coaching within your contract, specifying how coaching differs from the other helping professions. For example, "The services to be provided by coach to client are coaching as designed jointly with the client. Coaching, which is not advice, therapy, or counselling, may address specific personal or professional projects, business issues, or general conditions in the client's life or profession".

In my organisation I use the following clause in my coaching contracts:

> Throughout the working relationship, the coach will engage with the client in direct conversation. The client can count on the coach to be honest and straightforward in asking questions, making interventions, and facilitating the setting of goals. The client understands that the power of coaching is in the relationship between client and coach. If the client or the coach believes the coaching is not working as desired, either client or coach will communicate this.

Other concerns centre on malpractice for coach practitioners, where "malpractice" is defined as "failure of a professional person to render proper services through reprehensible ignorance of negligence or through criminal intent, especially when injury or loss follows; or any improper negligent practice; misconduct or misuse" (Yerkes, 1989). For example, what if a client organisation sues you for failure on your part as a coaching practitioner to render services as contracted? How important is it to have professional liability insurance, in a similar manner to clinical psychologists? Do you have an arbitration clause in your contract about what the procedures are if conflict or misunderstandings arise?

These may seem like abstract issues that need not concern you at present. But, as coaching continues to grow as a discipline, there will be claims against practitioners who do not provide services as promised. Because there is currently no legislated protection for practitioners, professional bodies such as the EMCC, ICF, WABC and COMENSA may not necessarily provide indemnity insurance, but they can help practitioners to think about contracts, and about which types of protection are needed for coaches to practice and offer high-quality service with confidence and security.

Objectives and review

Objectives for the individual executive and for the organisation need to be clarified, with boundaries made explicit in terms of confidentiality, cancellation and termination of the contract. In coaching the contracting process is often linked to the generation and fulfilment of outcomes. Contracting usually deals with the management of the process, roles played, evaluation of the process, learning and outcomes, and exit clauses.

Another important aspect of contracting is the review of the contract when necessary, including termination or renewal. In any business contracting process, it is important to draw up the "marriage" and the "divorce" papers at the beginning: a bit like a prenuptial contract. It is important to specify the boundaries and parameters of the entire coaching intervention, i.e. how the process will proceed from beginning to end and how to terminate the process, whether at the contracted termination point or sooner if required by either party.

For example, last year one of my clients terminated the contract prior to the agreed upon period for the coaching intervention suggested by her organisation. She and I verbally re-contracted together how she could manage her exit from the coaching process, how she would defend this position to her line manager and sponsor, and how she could negotiate re-entering the coaching process in the future when she felt more ready. This was made very transparent to the sponsoring organisation. It is important that your contracting allows for this type of flexibility, yet keeps you within the bounds of your agreement with the third party or sponsor.

Your model as a contracting structure

A model is a metaphor for the entire coaching journey, yet embodies a structured process. The Purpose, Perspectives, Process approach of the Scientist-Practitioner Model (Lane and Corrie, 2006) can help you in three ways: to contract with the client, to structure the entire coaching journey, and to guide your coaching conversation. Out of the specific conversation about process can emerge the client's purpose; the way your perspectives fit together can help clients to achieve their purpose; and the process within which you will work helps you both to achieve the outcomes desired.

Essentially, to contract the overall journey, coach and client discuss the overall aim of coaching for the client (purpose) and what each brings to the relationship (perspectives). Coach and client then discuss and contract how the coaching will take place: timing, boundaries, fees, the tools and techniques to be used by the coach, and the way the client would prefer to work (process). They also discuss the overall results and outcomes the client hopes to achieve from the coaching intervention, results that need to be visible to the organisation, including thinking, feeling, and behaviour that the client would like to change (outcomes as a result of process).

As a rule, I start the coaching conversation with perspectives: starting from, "Tell me your life story" to "Where are you now?" "What's happening with you?" "What's informing your thinking?" "What are your reflections on your current (or specific) concrete experience?" We move on to identify purpose: what they want to talk about, what their needs are for today, and what key outcomes they want to achieve. Once we have identified what needs to be worked on, we agree on the process we will work with using whichever question frameworks, tools, or techniques are relevant to that process. At the end of the session we summarise actions, learning, and outcomes that have resulted from the coaching conversation.

It's important to note that you may not necessarily inform your client about the model or techniques with which you are working. However, some leaders wish to understand what they are so that they can begin to use them with their direct reports. Any model that you use for your regular coaching conversations can help you to define a structure and process and set boundaries for working with your client. However, the name of the game is flexibility and working to the client's needs, so anything prescriptive would only be representative of your needs. Remember, the conversation is about them.

Often when things go wrong it is due to poor practice on the part of the coach, perhaps from not setting proper boundaries (Ting and Scisco, 2006:19). Contracting and relationship building are crucial to the outcomes of any coaching intervention. Contracting is complex as it determines in what areas, and how deeply, the coach can work with the individual client, the team, and the organisation in a holistic, integrated, and systemic way.

TEAM COACHING IN ORGANISATIONS

Team coaching is crucial for organisational transformation

Once you begin to work with an individual executive, their team often comes to the fore within a few months. Gaps are identified in terms of decision making, communication skills and facilitating meetings. Team coaching is becoming more affordable than individual executive coaching, and ensures that the team is working together in alignment with organisational values and goals.

As a business coach, whether working with individuals or teams, you are helping your clients to learn from and interpret their own experiences, and to understand the complexity of the environment in which they work. Team coaching is essentially about the results experienced through the relationship between the coach, the individuals in the team, and the resulting team dynamic.

Within most organisations there is some confusion between "team coaching" and "group facilitation". It is important for anyone coaching teams or groups to be skilled not just in facilitating group-learning processes, but also in teaching coaching skills and competences for individual team members who need to develop their own direct reports in a coaching manner. Globally, we are still in the beginning stages of researching exactly what "team coaching" comprises.

Team learning enhances performance in the workplace

Business coaches encourage their clients to think for themselves and to develop an awareness of their own conscious and unconscious behaviours, which may influence performance in the workplace. Business coaching focuses on an effective, sustainable and measurable way of developing managerial leaders and their teams. I view "managerial leadership" similarly to the way Jaques and Clement (1991:4–6) describe it in their book *Effective Leadership*; I see leadership as a process and an accountable function of management, rather than as a role in itself.

Traditionally, the development of organisations and corporations supported business and performance development models, but ignored the importance of values to individuals and teams. This crucial lack therefore laid the foundation for the development of individual and team coaching – not just for leaders and senior executives, but for individuals at all levels in the workforce looking to enhance their personal and professional lives.

Measuring results

In working with an individual client, there is no point in simply developing a leadership plan in isolation from the rest of the business and team processes. If the coaching intervention is to be successful in organisations, it is critical to develop a systemic, fully integrated coaching strategy that is in alignment with both the business and the talent strategies for the organisation. Two key factors will be to identify the efficacy of internal and external coaching interventions at an individual level, and the use of group or team coaching to develop key leadership competences that are aligned with business and organisational strategy. Team coaching can also be a way to develop talent at subordinate levels.

Team coaching can help new leaders and their teams manage all aspects of transition, transformation and change. There is a strong link between business results and emotional intelligence (defined as self-awareness, self-management, social awareness, and social skill). Team coaching will need to ensure that both the leader and members of the team improve their emotional intelligence skills, which will lead to better organisational performance. This will move the team to balance the needs of the individuals, the team and the organisation. If the team members have grown in term of self-awareness, the organisation will want to see this "demonstrated" at work – in relationships, management competence, leadership behaviours and EQ.

But, in order to do so, the coach needs to have an in-depth understanding of organisational systems – seeing the coaching intervention from a systems perspective, and understanding the need for "structure" in the interaction between coach, individual client, team and the organisational system. A danger of not understanding the "system" in which the client operates is that the coach risks becoming another part of that system.

RETURN ON INVESTMENT

by Nick Wilkins and Dr Sunny Stout-Rostron

Naturally business coaches want to market their services. And what more tempting way to sell business coaching than to quote nice big numbers about the return on investment (ROI) the client firm can reap? Like this, for example: "The latest study on executive coaching ROI is the International Coach Federation's Global Coaching Client Study of 2009. It found that coaching racks up a whopping 700 per cent ROI for organisations. That means that an $18 000 investment in a coach returns over $110 000 to the bottom line" (Banis, 2010:1). Trouble is, that's not quite what the ICF study actually said. And even if it were, would it be a valid and useful claim to make for coaching?

How hard can it be?

The seminal *ICF Global Coaching Client Study* was carried out for the International Coach Federation (ICF) by the Association Resource Centre Inc. and PricewaterhouseCoopers. They were careful to point out that:

- While ROI is a "hot topic" in the coaching world, there are many debates about how it should be calculated.
- While the formula to work out ROI is straightforward ((*Gain from investment - Cost of investment*) ÷ *Cost of investment*), defining and measuring the costs of and gains from the investment is not. Costs of coaching (which include opportunity cost and logistical cost) are not always obvious or easy to estimate, while the financial benefits of coaching are difficult to isolate and to measure.
- Most of the 2 165 individual clients surveyed around the world for the study either had not experienced a financial gain (or loss!) from coaching, were not sure whether a loss or gain had been experienced, or were unable to quantify the benefits and costs of the coaching they had experienced. Consequently, "*the results of the ROI should be interpreted with caution due to small sample sizes*" (emphasis in the original) (ICF *et al.*, 2009:viii–ix;76–79).

Corporate ROI estimates in the ICF study are summarised in Table 6. This shows that the return on investment in coaching for their companies could be estimated by only 4 per cent of the study respondents. In addition, it is not possible to assess how accurate these estimates of ROI were.

Table 6: Estimates of corporate ROI to coaching in ICF Study

Did your company experience a financial gain or loss due to coaching?	Can you estimate the company's gain or loss and the cost of coaching?	Estimated ROI to the company?	% of survey respondents
No	–	–	41
Unsure	–	–	19
Yes	No	–	36
	Yes	< 100%	1
		≥ 100%, < 1000%	1
		≥ 1000%	2
Total			100

Source: Adapted from ICF et al. (2009), Exhibits 8–5 and 8–6.

Put another way, what the ICF study actually said was that (ICF et al., 2009:78):

1. Among the small minority of survey respondents (169 people or 7.8 per cent) who reported achieving a *personal* monetary gain (or loss!) from coaching *and* were able to estimate the gain or loss and the cost of the coaching, the *median* ROI on coaching was estimated to be 344 per cent (i.e. half this segment of respondents estimated a lower ROI figure than 344 per cent, the other half estimated a higher ROI figure).

2. Among the even less statistically significant minority of survey respondents (83 people or 3.8 per cent) who reported achieving a monetary gain (or loss!) to their *company* from coaching *and* were able to estimate the gain or loss and the cost of the coaching, the *median* ROI on coaching was estimated to be 700 per cent.

So, it is clearly not valid to infer (or to imply to prospective clients) that all business coaching generates an average ROI to companies of 700 per cent.

Credit or blame?

But there is another, fundamental conceptual difficulty involved in estimating the ROI for business coaching. Let's assume that you, as a business coach, deliver a programme of individual and team coaching to senior executives of a large company, assisting them in formulating a medium-term strategic plan. The coaching, which costs the company $250 000, helps the executives clarify their thinking on key issues, so that they can draw up a robust strategic plan. The plan focuses on eliminating unnecessary expenditure, more effective product design, further staff development, and better marketing. It certainly seems plausible that the company should achieve an increase in net profit, due to this coaching intervention, of many times the $250 000 investment. But any of the following scenarios might then happen:

- *Scenario A*: The cost-cutting works, and corporate net profit before tax improves by $10 million over the next three years. You, as the business coach involved, are happy to claim an ROI on coaching of 3 900 per cent.
- *Scenario B*: Due to adverse exchange rate movements and stronger overseas competition, the company loses a major export market and net profits decrease by $120 million over the next three years. Are you happy to claim a negative ROI on coaching of -48 100 per cent?
- *Scenario C*: Some of the "unnecessary" expenditure eliminated by the strategic plan relates to safety measures. As a result, a serious accident causes an environmental disaster which lands the company with a clean-up bill, fines and penalties of $600 million. As the business coach, are you happy to claim a negative ROI on coaching of -240 100 per cent?

The point is that effective business coaching will deliver an immediate improvement in the quality of executive and managerial thought within the firm (an *output*, or an *intermediate outcome*). What the firm's management does with that enhanced thinking is up to them – and whether those managerial actions in turn actually result in improved financial and other corporate results (an eventual *outcome*) is also up to a range of other factors.

The business coach is not going to be able to ensure (a) that the actions steps formulated during the coaching are the best options for the company, or (b) that those action steps are actually (and effectively) carried out by the individuals concerned. And there is a wide range of external economic, political, social, institutional and other factors impacting the company's results, which may counteract the beneficial outputs and outcomes of the coaching process.

So it will not always be valid – or helpful – for business coaching to be viewed in terms of the logical fallacy *post hoc, ergo propter hoc* ("after this, therefore because of this", i.e. the change in corporate results happened after the coaching, hence must have been caused by the coaching).

Better measures for business coaching

The *ICF Global Coaching Client Study* includes a much more useful "metric" on the potential impact of coaching – an index of "return on expectations", which measures the impact of coaching on aspects of key importance to the client. This provides authoritative evidence, from a majority of the surveyed respondents, of very significant positive impacts on the areas of concern which had motivated clients to seek coaching in the first place (ICF *et al.*, 2009:79–81).

The study also cites invaluable qualitative evidence, including direct quotes of feedback from coaching clients, of the positive impact of coaching on these key areas – which include self-esteem or self-confidence, communication skills, interpersonal skills, work performance, work–life balance, wellness, personal organisation, business management, time management, team effectiveness, corporate culture, and financial organisation (ICF *et al.*, 2009:67–75).

Grant (2012) is highly critical of the use of ROI to assess the results of coaching. In an article titled "ROI is a poor measure of coaching success", he argues that

> ... although financial ROI is an accepted metric, flaws and weaknesses in the overly simplistic way that it is calculated mean that financial ROI is an unreliable and insufficient measure of coaching outcomes. Organisational coaching initiatives should of course be evaluated, but we need far more comprehensive measures for this task than financial ROI (Grant, 2012:75).

He goes on to point out that

> It is often extremely difficult to delineate specific causal relationships between a coaching intervention and improvements in organisational metrics. In addition, ROI calculations tend to ignore the impact of other variables such as market context and team input. Moreover, while there can be reasonable certainty about the direct costs of coaching, indirect costs (e.g. opportunity costs) tend not to be included (Grant, 2012:77).

Grant suggests that coaching results should be evaluated using a "wellbeing and engagement framework" (WBEF), which measures two dimensions: the wellbeing of employees, and their workplace engagement. "These humanistic metrics are able to give a far more meaningful and holistic view of the impact of a coaching intervention than a single monetary figure" (Grant, 2012:78). Measurement of coaching participants along these two dimensions, both before and after a coaching intervention, would show the extent to which the coaching has moved the individuals concerned towards a position of high wellbeing and high engagement.

Grant (2012:81) acknowledges that the WBEF is at present a conceptual model, and specific WBEF measures have not yet been developed. However, there are several already existing quantitative measures that could be used to operationalise the wellbeing dimension of the WBEF, such as the Positive and Negative Affect Scale (PANAS). Existing quantitative measures of workplace engagement that could be used include the Gallup A12 questionnaire (Grant, 2012:81–82).

Grant's concluding broadside on this topic is worth noting:

> Although a monetary appraisal of the financial viability of coaching engagements is an essential part of the natural due diligence that organisations should conduct, a myopic focus on financial issues runs the risk of client organisations being blinded to the very real potential of coaching to create a broad range of positive humanistic outcomes. With coaching being able to deliver such a rich array of potential human benefits, financial ROI is indeed a poor and impoverished measure of coaching success (Grant, 2012:82).

Treat ROI figures with caution

The message is clear – ROI figures in general should be treated with a great deal of caution, and will not often be valid for business coaching. It is therefore risky to cite astronomical numbers on the alleged ROI of business coaching. Over-hyping potential benefits may well lead to disappointed and disillusioned clients, and a serious discrediting of business coaching in general. Business coaches should rather emphasise the very real and direct improvements in the quality of executive and managerial thinking that coaching can deliver to corporate clients – which is likely to translate ultimately into significant, but hard-to-quantify, financial and other results.

CONCLUSION

In this chapter we identified that business coaching typically aims to improve an organisation's results through enhancing performance, and the client firm will expect the coach, as a contracted service provider, to help the organisation achieve its objectives.

As a business coach, whether you are working with individuals or teams, it is critical to help your clients to learn from and interpret their own experiences, and to understand the complexity of the environment in which they work. In choosing the most suitable and effective approaches to evaluating a coaching intervention, several key considerations need to be kept in mind, including the difficulty in attempting to calculate a return on investment (ROI).

Developing the habit of both formal and informal contracting is one of the first steps in beginning to understand the dynamics of forming a coaching relationship and setting boundaries, with both the client organisation and the individual executives being coached. Agreement needs to be made about the conditions of time, space, fees, confidentiality, and how goals will be set and communicated. It is also useful to include a definition of coaching within your contract, specifying how coaching differs from the other helping professions. In essence, the contract sets out ground rules for the coaching relationship so that all parties are aware of their obligations.

Team coaching is useful to help new leaders and their teams manage all aspects of transition, transformation and change. It is considered to be more affordable than individual executive coaching, but it is also seen as a useful complement to individual executive coaching. Team coaching has been identified as essentially about the results experienced through the relationship between the coach, the individuals in the team and the resulting team dynamic which ultimately can impact on the culture and performance of the organisation.

Effective business coaching can deliver improvement in the quality of executive and managerial thinking within the firm which will have a positive impact on communication skills, decision making, team building, and enhancing the culture of the organisation.

FURTHER READING

Chapman, L. (2010). *Integrated Experiential Coaching: Becoming an executive coach.* London: Karnac.

Grant, A.M. (2012). ROI is a poor measure of coaching success: towards a more holistic approach to using a wellbeing and engagement framework. *Coaching: An international journal of theory, research and practice,* 5(2):74–85.

International Coach Federation (ICF). Association Resource Centre Inc. and PricewaterhouseCoopers LLP (2009). *ICF Global Coaching Client Study: Final Report June 2009.* Lexington, KY: ICF.

Jaques, E., and Clement, S.D. (1991). *Effective Leadership: A practical guide to managing complexity.* Oxford: Blackwell.

Stout-Rostron, S. (2012b). *Business Coaching Wisdom and Practice: Unlocking the secrets of business coaching.* Second edition. Randburg: Knowres.

Stout-Rostron, S. (2014). *Business Coaching International: Transforming individuals and organisations.* Second edition. London: Karnac.

Ting, S., and Scisco, P. (2006). *The CCL Handbook of Coaching: A guide for the leader coach.* San Francisco, CA: Jossey-Bass.

11

Safe and ethical practice

PROTECTING YOUR PRACTICE

by Nick Wilkins and Dr Sunny Stout-Rostron

Coaches need to protect themselves from a range of professional risks, such as accusations of malpractice due to ineffective or damaging interventions, being caught in a conflict of interest, or divulging confidential information.

Protecting oneself against professional risk has much in common with protecting yourself against road accidents, crime or infectious disease: it is unglamorous, unexciting and tedious but critically important, and it involves some effort and foresight in (a) learning what fundamental actions are needed, and (b) carrying them out unfailingly from day to day as a matter of routine. In coaching, the fundamentals of safe practice are focused in five key areas: competence, supervision, ethics, contracting, and credentialing.

Competence

"Competence" can be defined as knowing and effectively applying the skills and expertise necessary to practise coaching at or above the required standard. Specified and benchmarked competences provide clarity on how coaches might be selected, what is expected from them, and how the emerging coaching discipline could develop and improve greater professionalism (Stout-Rostron, 2012b:198). In the meantime, various national and international coaching associations have drawn up competence frameworks in an attempt to self-regulate and professionalise the industry as far as possible, including:

- The International Coach Federation (ICF, 2008a), which groups its defined competences into four clusters (Setting the foundation; Co-creating the relationship; Communicating effectively; Facilitating learning and results).
- The Worldwide Association of Business Coaches (WABC, 2008b), which focuses on competences in three areas (Self-management; Core coaching skill-base; and Business and leadership coaching capabilities).
- The European Mentoring and Coaching Council (EMCC, 2010), which defines core competences in four categories (who we are; our skills and knowledge; how we coach and mentor; and how we manage the process).
- COMENSA (2009b), which adapted its *Membership Criteria and Standards of Competence (MCSC) Framework* from the EMCC competence framework. The MCSC *Framework*

focuses on four categories (self-awareness / who we are – personal attributes for coaching; managing the process – what we will do as part of our coaching practice to maintain and develop an effective and professional approach; ability to coach – skills we will use during the coaching process; and facilitate learning and development – how we will demonstrate that we are able to apply what we have learned). COMENSA is currently revising its competence framework, with finalisation due in 2014.

- The Standards Australia handbook on *Coaching in Organisations* provides guidelines for the professional practice of coaching in organisations and for the training of professional coaches who work in organisations. Chapter 6 of the handbook outlines the emerging consensus in the coaching industry as to the core areas of knowledge and competency required for executive coaching, and describes generic coaching competences in the following areas: foundation micro-skills; conceptual and technical skills; self-management and development skills; and boundary management skills (Standards Australia, 2011).

From the specific competences outlined in the above competence frameworks, and from global studies of coaching competences which have been undertaken, it is clear that business coaches should focus on developing the following core competences:

- building the coaching relationship;
- listening and questioning;
- developing self-awareness through the process of self-reflection;
- continuous learning and development;
- expanding your knowledge and core coaching skills base;
- business and leadership coaching abilities; and
- upholding ethical guidelines and professional standards.

Developing competence in coaching means undergoing effective education and training at a suitable coach training institution, and then carrying out the necessary level of continuing professional development (CPD) every year after qualifying. It is important to ensure that coach training will qualify one to practise at the standards of professional competence defined by one's coaching association, and that the training institutions have appropriately qualified and experienced staff and facilities to deliver this outcome.

Supervision

Supervision of practitioners has long been a key professional underpinning of psychotherapy, but is not yet a given for the coaching industry. The key roles of coach supervision are to ensure that the coach understands what the client goes through, to support the coach in working through their own issues so that they do not become entangled with client concerns, to support the development of the coach practitioner, and to assess the practitioner's competence. The term "supervision" describes the process by which the work of the practitioner is overseen and guidance is sought.

The benefits of supervision include (Stout-Rostron, 2006:14):

- For the coach to deal with any unresolved issues of their own (an ongoing process for any coach), and specifically to learn not to bring personal concerns to the coaching conversation.
- For the individual's coaching practice to benefit from invaluable and ongoing supervision.
- To provide the coach with a helpful tool to understand the client–practitioner process from another perspective, i.e. from the client's perspective rather than that of the practitioner.
- Practitioners who are coaching specific individuals within a particular organisation have a chance to meet each other. In addition, the supervising coach ensures that all practitioners have a sound understanding of the organisational systems at play.
- Coach supervision in groups can become an important regular meeting where the coaches connect with and learn from each other, beginning to understand the systemic connections between their individual clients.

COMENSA (2010) and Standards Australia (2011) have developed clear, practical guidelines on supervision, and coaches should follow these in their own practices as closely as possible.

Ethics

By virtue of membership in the WABC, all members have a Safe Harbour and Adjudication Process for any ethical claims through its Code of Business Coaching Ethics and Integrity. The WABC Ethics and Integrity Committee oversees the consultation, adjudication, monitoring and review processes. The Code is monitored continuously and reviewed annually to ensure that it stays relevant (WABC, 2008a).

The International Coaching Federation (ICF) *Code of Ethics* covers four key areas for coaches:

- professional conduct at large;
- conflicts of interest;
- professional conduct with clients; and
- confidentiality and privacy (ICF, 2008b).

The EMCC updated their *Code of Ethics* in 2008 to promote best practice and ensure that the highest possible standards are maintained in the coaching relationship. The EMCC *Code of Ethics* covers the following: competence, context, boundary management, integrity and professionalism (EMCC, 2008).

Chapter 10 of the handbook on *Coaching in Organisations* (Standards Australia, 2011) provides guidance for all stakeholders on the issue of ethics in the current environment. The handbook aims to offer practical advice and suggestions, such as a list of professional bodies providing ethical coaching codes for their members which includes (apart from the WABC, ICF and EMCC mentioned above):

- Association for Coaching (AC);
- Australian Human Resources Institute (AHRI);
- Association for Professional Executive Coaching and Supervision (APECS);
- Australian Psychological Society (APS); and
- Society for Coaching Psychologists (SCP) (Standards Australia, 2011:64).

COMENSA's (2009a) *Revised Code of Ethics* serves to set the ethical standards for South Africa in the field of coaching. Considerable progress has been made in the development and implementation of the *Revised Code of Ethics*, with its four core values (autonomy, beneficence, non-maleficence and justice), and its seven guiding principles (inclusivity, dignity, competence, context, boundary management, integrity and professionalism). Apart from informing and educating the coaching industry and its clients on ethical practices, one immediate practical benefit of this policy framework has been the institution of a system for dealing with ethical grievances within the Association. The further strengthening of ethical regulation in coaching will yield even greater benefits, as coaches and their clients realise that membership of COMENSA means adherence to a meaningful and binding code of ethical practice.

You can find most of the professional body ethical codes on the web:

- COMENSA (2009a) *Revised Code of Ethics* (www.comensa.org.za);
- EMCC (2008) *Code of Ethics* (www.emccouncil.org);
- ICF (2008b) *ICF Code of Ethics* (www.coachfederation.org);
- WABC (2008a) *Code of Business Coaching Ethics and Integrity* (www.wabccoaches.com); and
- Standards Australia (2011) *Coaching in Organisations* (www.standards.org.au).

Contracting

As explained in Chapter 10, the process of contracting with a coaching client involves:

- explaining what best-practice coaching is, and how the coach will apply it;
- clearly defining the potential benefits and risks of the coaching intervention;
- outlining what inputs, efforts and commitments will be required from the client organisation and individual clients; and
- negotiating how long the intervention should last, what it should cost, and on what terms the project should be delivered by the coach.

It is essential for the coach to brief the management of the client organisation, and the individual coaching participants, as clearly and effectively as possible, and to explicitly ensure that all three parties have reached the same understanding and consensus on the nature and details of the coaching intervention. This is critically important to minimise the risk of future confusion and non-compliance during the actual coaching process, and to avoid the possibility that the intervention may fail altogether.

It follows that the actual contract between coach, client firm and individual coaching participant(s) must explicitly define the nature and purpose of the coaching intervention, including:

- the nature of the coaching services to be provided;
- objectives and intended outcomes or results for the organisation and for the individual coaching participant(s);
- ethical ground rules and boundaries; and
- confidentiality and reporting requirements and boundaries.

Since the relationship between coach and individual coaching is set within the context of the team and the organisation, and is part of the overall system, this "bigger picture" needs to be part of the contracting process. The coach should therefore ask the following types of questions during contracting with the client firm and individual coaching participant(s) (Stout-Rostron, 2012b:264–265):

- What are the needs of the individual executive client versus those of the organisation?
- What is the organisation looking for?
- What are the goals for the individual client?
- Which performance improvements are desired?
- What are the organisational goals for the coaching programme?
- What are the organisational conditions and are they conducive to coaching?
- Are the line manager and senior management supportive of the process?
- Is the individual ready for coaching and is coaching appropriate?
- How do you know?

The whole process of contracting with clients is probably the most neglected area of coaching practice. This is extremely unfortunate, as much misunderstanding, conflict and mutual disappointment between coach and clients could be avoided by spending a modicum of time and effort on this unglamorous and tedious but potentially invaluable routine. To paraphrase Gypsy Rose Lee, coaching is love – but get it in writing. Or as the old Middle Eastern proverb advises, trust in God, but tether your camel.

Credentialing

Efforts are being made by a range of national and international representative bodies, and within previous forums such as the Global Coaching Community (GCC), the International Coaching Research Forum (ICRF), international conferences, professional bodies, and graduate schools of business to promote the professional development of coaching. What type of professional status these initiatives will eventually achieve for coaching is a wide-open issue, and the possible options range from the continuation of the more or less self-regulated *status quo*, through the evolution of a form of semi-professional specialisation, to the creation of a full profession.

In the meantime, coaching associations such as such as the ICF, EMCC, WABC and COMENSA play a crucial role in providing at least an interim form of credentialing. Credentialing is very important to coaches, because if it is done properly, with effective implementation of standards of competence and codes of ethics (including meaningful sanctions for their contravention), prospective clients will feel confident that accredited coaches will know what they're doing. The development of authoritative credentialing is, however, a two-way street – not only must coaching associations such as COMENSA institute the necessary benchmarks, standards, codes and guidelines, but coaching practitioners must support them in doing so.

Professional liability insurance

In today's world of business coaching it is important to purchase insurance to cover your practice. We have not yet reached the state of litigation in the sense of unhappy clients litigating their dismay at what they achieve in their coaching sessions. However, as business coaching grows more popular every year and in every country, you need to protect yourself as a practitioner, your practice as a business, and your reputation as a coach.

Don't be lulled into complacency by the inherent goodwill of your clients – if they work within a corporate environment, are unhappy with their situation, and for any reason at all are unhappy with your coaching, you need to be sufficiently protected. It is your own "assurance" of a safety net. What is critical, is that you keep up your own continuing professional development, adherence to a rigorous code of ethics, and careful contracting – and you should be fine.

Ensuring professional success

Putting the above fundamentals of coaching practice in place is crucial to ensure the professional success and wellbeing of any practising coach. But it will also inevitably protect the interests of their clients, which is a key reason why prospective clients of coaching need to be informed of the benefits of engaging coaches with the relevant qualifications, experience and professional credentialing.

THE PRACTICE OF ETHICS AND THE ETHICS OF PRACTICE

Ethics and integrity

Ethics are most often recognised as the rules of conduct in respect of a particular group or culture, or the moral principles of an individual. Ethics is known as the branch of philosophy dealing with values which relate to human conduct (Yerkes, 1989).

Ethics is one of the more important domains of knowledge for the coaching practitioner. In the foreseeable future, a key prerequisite will be that business coaches also conform to organisational demands, aligning with the specific ethics, supervisory framework, standards and competences of those organisations. In South Africa we have already seen several examples of corporations who are beginning to define their own standards of assessment to regulate the employment of internal and external coaches.

"Integrity" is an uncompromising adherence to a code of values. So, for a coach to act with integrity, means intentionally acting from a personal vision that is values-based. This includes understanding what you, as a practitioner, want out of your life and work. But it also means adhering to an agreed set of core organisational, or client, values that are aligned with your own personal values, no matter what challenging situations confront you from day to day (Stout-Rostron, 2008).

It often takes immense courage to act from integrity and to be continually aligned with your core values, even more so in times of stress. For the executives you may be coaching, apart from environmental factors such as lack of resources, an important cause of stress is when their individual and organisational goals are not in alignment with their personal and professional values. This can create anxiety, interfere with self-confidence, and prevent a leader from making decisions, managing relationships, or working effectively within the system (Stout-Rostron, 2008).

Ethics is a neglected field

The one competence that continues to be neglected in the coaching field is ethics. One of the reasons that it is crucial for practitioners to belong to a professional body is that this commits them to the ethical code of that body. Psychologists and psychotherapists are bound to their professional ethical code, and can be disciplined or struck off their professional register if they violate the code in any way. Because coaching is not yet a profession, and therefore not yet regulated, it is still up to each individual coach practitioner to uphold their own individual, or their professional body's ethical standards.

The importance of an ethical code is that it identifies the core values, standards and fundamental principles with which coach practitioners align themselves, and to which they agree to adhere. Also, an ethical code provides a benchmark against which individual practitioners agree to be assessed.

Professional ethical codes

However, human behaviour is always complex. A key difficulty with an emerging profession is that there are no precise guidelines for ethical behaviour – which is what the international coaching bodies are gradually trying to build into their ethical codes for members.

The WABC's *Code of Business Coaching Ethics and Integrity* tries to address the diverse range of business interactions faced all over the world by members, and has established a process to handle ethical dilemmas and issues (WABC, 2008a:1–4). The EMCC states in its *Code of Ethics* that "a coach must maintain a relationship with a suitably qualified supervisor, who will regularly assess their competence and support their development" (EMCC, 2008).

The Chartered Institute of Personnel and Development (CIPD) in the UK cites guidelines for buyers of coaching and recommends that practitioners articulate what formal supervision arrangements they currently have in place (Jarvis, 2004).

The purpose of COMENSA's *Code of Ethics* (COMENSA, 2006:1) and *Revised Code of Ethics* (COMENSA, 2009a:1) is to "set the ethical standards for South Africa in the fields of coaching and mentoring". The COMENSA *Revised Code of Ethics* defines its "core values" as autonomy, beneficence, non-maleficence and justice, and its "guiding principles" as inclusivity, dignity, competence, context, boundary management, integrity and professionalism (COMENSA, 2009a:2–5).

Rules of the game: living ethical values with integrity

There are many ways to define the "rules of the game", and in business coaching some rules are implied while others are contracted. For example, if you sign a contract with your organisational client, you usually contract to improve the performance and potential of a specific individual within the organisation, which often includes the development of leadership competence so that the executive concerned lives organisational values with integrity. It is usually implied that you will not coach them into another position in a different company.

NAVIGATING THE LABYRINTH

Which ethical dilemmas have arisen for you in your practice? It is useful in your supervision sessions to discuss, on a regular basis, any ethical issues that arise. For example, it is recognised that there are circumstances where the coach may have two "clients", the individual being coached and the organisation who may have commissioned the coaching. As explained in Chapter 10, coaches often overlook who the actual client is: is it the organisation that hires and pays the coach's fees, or is it the individual being coached? To whom does the coach owe loyalty?

Another dilemma is in the difference between clinical and commercial practice. In clinical practice, clinicians look after their client's interest. These interests are the hub of the contract, and the arrangement is a co-operative one. However, in business there is a proprietary culture based upon a competitive market philosophy. Both providers and buyers of coaching compete for the best deal they can get, and each party expects the other party to behave competitively. One party does not expect the other to look out for them or their interests.

Coaches need to navigate these two cultures. One is a business culture, where profit is the motive, and the other is the ethics of care for individual clients. A coach practitioner needs to understand the point of view of the organisation and find a way to integrate the co-operative and the competitive points of view. This can often present a coach with dilemmas that challenge their ability to be loyal to both the organisation and the individual client (Stout-Rostron, 2012b:286).

Complexity and self-awareness

It is critical that the coach develops self-awareness with the ability to self-regulate. Awareness of the ethical situations that arise is a first step; the second step is to manage them. Without self-awareness, integrity and the ability to manage complexity, ethical decisions may prove difficult or even remain in the unconscious.

Personal lives, careers and organisations are often at stake, and there is a high moral responsibility in this interpersonal journey. Bonds of trust, openness, fragility and honesty are developed at high levels, and these need to remain honoured and deeply respected (Stout-Rostron, 2012b:295). Therein lies the rub.

EXISTENTIAL ETHICAL THEMES TO CONSIDER

A dilemma can potentially develop when the client feels that their underlying value system clashes with that of their organisation. People often have a strong sense of ethical, moral or faith-based values. When they voice their concerns inside a coaching assignment, they are often reflecting on where their value system is in conflict with the values of the organisation. The issues frustrating them may not be clear-cut, and more often than not are complex. The issues raised could be related to performance ratings, recruitment procedures, or even whether the organisation's actions are in alignment with its public claims.

The "rules of the game" imply that business coaching should be aligned strategically with the overall values and objectives of an organisation. Existential dilemmas can arise during the coaching process if the executive needs to make difficult choices which are incompatible with their own value system – and with whose rules are they then in conflict?

Executive dilemma

The story of Jim (Stout-Rostron, 2012b:35–36) illustrates a recognisable scenario. Jim is a senior dispensing pharmacist who manages a major pharmaceutical retail chain in southern California. He grappled with a personal and professional dilemma, having been asked to lay-off highly qualified and experienced staff in order to increase bottom-line profits for shareholders – not an uncommon position for business executives today. His inner turmoil was highlighted by the fact that the families of his pharmacists would be economically affected by the loss of one family member's income with no guarantee of replacing it, plus the loss of quality service to loyal customers. This was balanced against the short-term profits to be made by shareholders, including himself as the owner of a recently inherited share portfolio.

Jim also faced the problem of having to employ less-qualified, less-experienced and therefore less-expensive dispensers, who would be unable to provide the quality service for which the pharmacy was reputed. One of Jim's concerns was that, although larger profits would be made for the retail organisation's shareholders, these would be at the expense of a seriously reduced quality of expertise offered to a trusting public. A second unease was that all of his experienced staff already worked long hours; the enforced cuts to qualified staff would mean even more gruelling working hours for those still gainfully employed, with no seeming concern for the public on the part of shareholders.

"It's a moral dilemma for me, not only because I am faced with laying-off people who are providing an expert quality service, but the staff who remain will be asked to take even greater strain, working longer hours yet providing an inferior service. My heart absolutely goes out to the people who are being sacrificed for short-term profits, as well as those who will step into their shoes.

On the other hand, a couple of years ago my pharmacist father left me a very solid portfolio of shares, on which I need to make good financial returns as part of my retirement planning. In the end, my decision has been to implement what I know to be a fundamentally unfair, un-business-like, yet profit-driven decision. It is not business-driven in the long term, because having built up our customer base on loyalty and good service, we will now sacrifice quality of service and expertise for immediate cash returns – but in the end I fear our customers will drift away to our rivals."

In terms of the "Rules of the Game", Jim took the corporate line and did as requested by his line management; however, it was a tough decision for him, and one that troubled him personally. This is one of the most common dilemmas faced by executives today all over the world, and is a direct result of intense "bottom-line" pressure. Critically important is that coaching helps the client to think through such issues and dilemmas, with the coach asking questions, making observations and challenging the client's thinking – helping them to understand the impact of adhering or not adhering to the "Rules of the Game".

UNDERSTAND WHAT ETHICS MEANS IN PRACTICE

For a business coach to be prepared to deal ethically with potential situations in coaching practice, they need to think through their optimum responses to contingencies which might arise. They need to consider what their policies should be on specific issues and ethical concerns, such as (Stout-Rostron, 2012b:292–295):

- How do you handle the need to report back to the senior manager and the organisation, while maintaining the confidentiality of the coaching conversations?
- What do you do if the coaching conversation leads an individual to decide they want to leave the organisation which contracted you?
- Is it ethically acceptable to coach all the members of one team, including the team leader?
- How do you honour confidentiality when coaching a senior manager as well as their boss?
- What should your policy be about meeting with the individual executive and line manager together? How do you manage the issue of confidentiality if you meet the line manager (a) with, and (b) without the individual client?
- How should you address interference in the coaching intervention from a leading executive?
- Should you disclose knowledge of illegal activity by an individual coaching participant to (a) the management of the client firm, and/or (b) the relevant authorities?

Let's take the first of the above questions as an example. How do you handle the giving of information to the senior manager and the organisation? The business coach should ensure that the written contract specifies the bounds of confidentiality between all parties, with agreed terms for reporting back to the organisation. However, it is also important to verbally contract with the individual coaching participants to ensure agreement about how each of the coaching conversations will be held, and how written reports to the organisation will be handled. In general, any written communication to a third party should be seen and agreed to by the individual coaching participant concerned before it is passed on to senior management.

In addition, a useful way of defining coaching objectives for individual coaching participants is to formulate a "professional development plan" with them. This should specify the purpose, objectives and strategy of the coaching intervention; regularly define actions to be undertaken and potential obstacles; and review results achieved and overall learning. The plan should be shared with the coaching participant's line manager. In this way, rather than sharing the content of the coaching conversation, coach and coaching participant can share the development plan and its results with other stakeholders in the coaching process, without infringing the confidentiality of coaching conversations.

Include ethics in your contracting

The two most critical areas in contracting are defining the scope of the coaching intervention, and defining a framework for handling ethical issues. In general, it would help if the business coach can provide the firm and its prospective coaching participants with a set of their own standard coaching guidelines, terms and conditions, based on best-practice principles and codes of professional practice, to serve as a basis for negotiation and contracting. These should include a clarification of the coach's adherence to the ethical code of their professional body, together with a brief outline of the coach's stance on, and ground rules for, key areas of ethical concern – such as the question of confidentiality discussed above. A business coach's ethical position will be much easier to defend if it has been explicitly defined and demarcated, in advance, within the coaching contract – rather than merely asserted after an ethical conflict has arisen.

BEHAVIOURAL BOUNDARIES IN BUSINESS COACHING

by Nick Wilkins and Dr Sunny Stout-Rostron

Best-practice coaching involves the coach acting as a thinking partner for a client, helping them structure their conscious thinking around a specific practical issue. This process is based on the assumption that the client is willing and able to engage constructively and effectively in the coaching conversation, and benefit from the coaching process. But what happens when the coach realises that a particular individual is not capable of this? How should the coach handle the situation? Clients with behavioural issues that are clearly problematic are unlikely to benefit from coaching, and the coaching process may well make the issue worse – apart from being very dysfunctional and frustrating for both coach and client.

As Kennedy and Charles (2001:255) put it, in the context of counselling: "It is not unusual to discover – although it is difficult to admit – that despite our best efforts there are persons we cannot seem to help. We fail to reach them or they do not seem able to respond".

This can be a particular source of stress for counsellors, especially those motivated by a liking for people and a desire to help them:

> When they meet people who do not like them or with whom they cannot establish a successful relationship, they are frustrated and disappointed. ... These people also frustrate other typical ideals of counsellors, namely, the optimistic Western and democratic notions that, with a little effort, we can stand on common ground with almost anybody; that things can be worked out; and that no matter what the difficulty, some kind of a solution is always possible. It is extremely stressful when non-co-operative individuals challenge such basic personal and professional beliefs (Kennedy and Charles, 2001:255).

The same concerns are relevant in business coaching. Several factors may make coaching a particular individual very difficult or completely infeasible by seriously reducing their motivation or cognitive ability or upsetting their emotional balance. These may include a medical problem (such as kidney disease); grief over the recent death of a parent, partner or child; emotional stress due to divorce or separation; severe depression or anxiety; chronic work-related stress; post-traumatic stress syndrome (e.g. due to recent experience of violent crime or domestic abuse); or substance abuse.

Or the client may be suffering from a personality disorder. The American Psychiatric Association's *Diagnostic and Statistical Manual of Mental Disorders* (Fourth Edition, text revision), known as *DSM-IV-TR*, defines a personality disorder as "an enduring pattern of inner experience and behaviour that deviates markedly from the expectations of the individual's culture, is pervasive and inflexible, has an onset in adolescence or early adulthood, is stable over time, and leads to distress and impairment" (Kennedy and Charles, 2001:256). Personality disorders have been estimated to affect between 10 and 18 per cent of the US population (Kennedy and Charles, 2001:257), and the proportion may well be higher in South Africa due to the impact of long-term social and political repression, pervasive poverty, and high crime rates.

The DSM-IV-TR defines ten personality disorders in three clusters (Kennedy and Charles, 2001:261–310):

- Cluster A personality disorders: *paranoid* (pervasive distrust and suspiciousness of others); *schizoid* (pervasive detachment from social relationships and a restricted range of emotional expression); and *schizotypal* (social deficits characterised by acute discomfort with, and a reduced capacity for, close relationships).
- Cluster B personality disorders: *antisocial* (disregard for and violation of the rights of others); *borderline* (instability in interpersonal relationships, self-image, and emotions); *histrionic* (excessive emotionality and attention-seeking behaviour); and *narcissistic* (grandiosity in fantasy or behaviour, a need for admiration, and a lack of empathy).
- Cluster C personality disorders: *avoidant* (social inhibition, inadequacy and hyper-sensitivity); *obsessive-compulsive* (preoccupation with orderliness, perfectionism, and mental and interpersonal control); and *dependent* (pervasive and excessive need to be taken care of).

It is important for coaches to have the basic psychological literacy to be able to identify such issues and possible pathology in their individual coaching clients, and be able to recommend that the client seek guidance on any such issues from an appropriately trained and qualified professional. In addition, coaches should know where the boundaries are between coaching and psychotherapy, and not try to play psychologist in the coaching process. Coaching is not psychotherapy. Even if the coach happens to be a professionally qualified psychotherapist, they should not undertake psychotherapy with a coaching client. The two disciplines involve very different objectives and methodologies, and practising both with the same client may cause serious confusion within the client – and possibly the coach as well.

This is why the *Code of Ethics* of the European Mentoring and Coaching Council (EMCC) requires coaches to "At all times operate within the limits of their own competence, recognise where that competence has the potential to be exceeded, and where necessary refer the client either to a more experienced coach, or support the client in seeking the help of another professional, such as a counsellor, psychotherapist or business / financial advisor" (EMCC, 2008:3). The same requirement is included in Clause 4.2.5(c) of COMENSA's (2009a:3) *Revised Code of Ethics*.

Similarly, Clause A1 of the *Professional Coaching Core Competencies* of the International Coach Federation (ICF) requires that the coach "Refers client to another support professional as needed, knowing when this is needed and the available resources" (ICF, 2008:1). And the Worldwide Association of Business Coaches (WABC) makes the same point in Clause 1(a) of "Core Coaching Skill-Base" in its *WABC Business Coaching Competencies*: "Recognise the limits of your own competence, and refer to other professionals when appropriate" (WABC, 2007:4).

The coach needs to know what appropriate professional services are available, and be able to provide details of these to the client. The coach's recommendation that the client consult such a professional obviously needs to be handled carefully and tactfully, to avoid placing any further distress on the client. At the same time, the coach needs to bear in mind that their noting the possible presence of a fundamentally adverse issue or pathology in a client does not represent a professional diagnosis. Nor does their recommendation that the client consult a relevant and suitably qualified practitioner constitute a "referral" in the way the term is defined in the medical profession, i.e. transferring the care of a patient from one clinician to another in compliance with a specified protocol – it is simply a recommendation. A carefully worked-out protocol, or at least a set of guidelines, for the referral of coaching clients to other disciplines would certainly be helpful to coaches, and coaching bodies could explore this as part of their definition of professional standards and ethics for coaching practice.

At the very least, the coach should ensure that any such "referrals" of individual clients are covered by appropriate clauses in their coaching contracts, so that:

- the coach retains the right not to have to continue coaching an individual who in their carefully considered judgement is currently unable to benefit from the coaching process, but may (a) terminate the coaching process indefinitely or (b) continue the coaching process on the condition the individual client seeks appropriate professional support;

- the coach does not have to specify the reason for the referral and possible termination of coaching to corporate management, as this may prejudice the interests of the individual client; and
- the termination or suspension of the coaching process by the coach may not be used to prejudice the interests, conditions of service, advancement or development of the individual client in any way.

The last point is likely to be of particular significance in the triangular relationship between coach, individual client and organisational client which characterises much of business coaching. The last thing any coach needs is to be held responsible for having prejudiced an individual client's career prospects by withholding coaching services. As pointed out above, the coach's ethical position will be much easier to defend if it has been defined in advance in the coaching contract.

CONCLUSION

Being an ethical business coach means *being prepared* to coach ethically – which in turns means doing the homework, explaining your position to your client organisation and individual coaching participants, and putting it in writing through a formal coaching proposal that is legally valid. It also requires adherence to the ethical code of the professional coaching body with whom you are a member – and being willing to change your practice if needed according to the professional body code.

In addition, coaches should know where the boundaries are between coaching and psychotherapy, and not try to play the role of psychologist with clients who may require professional psychological or psychiatric support. Instead, coaches should be able to recommend appropriate professional care to clients who may need it.

FURTHER READING

Coaches and Mentors of South Africa (COMENSA). (2009a). *Revised Code of Ethics*. Webpage: www.comensa.org.za/ABOUT_US/What_is_our_Code_of_Ethics_.aspx.

European Mentoring and Coaching Council (EMCC) (2008). *Code of Ethics*. Webpage: www.emccouncil.org/src/ultimo/models/Download/4.pdf.

International Coach Federation (ICF). (2008b). *ICF Code of Ethics*. Webpage: www.coachfederation.org/about%2Dicf/ethics%2D%26%2Dregulation/icf%2Dcode%2Dof%2Dethics/.

Worldwide Association of Business Coaches (WABC) (2008a). *Code of Business Coaching Ethics and Integrity*. Webpage: www.wabccoaches.com/includes/popups/code_of_ethics_2nd_edition_december_17_2007.html.

Standards Australia (2011). *Coaching in Organisations*. Draft handbook produced by Coaching Guideline Working Group HB41 of Standards Australia HR and Employment Committee MB 9. Sydney, NSW: Standards Australia. (Available at www.standards.org.au).

12

Coach supervision

THE CHANGING LANDSCAPE

As the coaching landscape changes, what are the implications for coach supervision? And how can we develop systemic and relevant developmental models for coach supervision going forward? We need to explore the major challenges facing coaching in the next ten years to determine the implications for the subsequent stages of development for coach supervision. As I discussed in earlier chapters, participation in collaborative and international dialogue is growing, and benchmarks are being set to collaborate in developing standards and competences for coaches worldwide. Oxford Brookes University is setting a standard with its annual international Coaching Supervision Conference which shares research, theory and practice in supervision.

According to David Lane, Founder of the Professional Development Foundation (PDF) in the UK, most supervision sits in one of four areas:

- traditional master-to-apprentice;
- peer mentoring (which can be simply the blind leading the blind);
- supervision by non-coach practitioners (particularly those with human resources or organisational development backgrounds); and
- peer-to-peer coach supervision by experienced coaches and coaching psychologists who are trained as coach supervisors (Lane, 2013, pers. com).

This fourth area is what we need to develop skilfully worldwide as our coaching communities continue to develop.

If we are to stay ahead of our game, we will need to begin to share our case studies, and the developmental work we are doing with coach supervision, particularly development of our own coach supervision models. However, as a pioneering industry we need to take a greater part in emergent and collaborative dialogues around coach supervision.

Coach supervision is growing in maturity, and it currently takes three to ten days' training, plus a practicum, to become a coach supervisor. We are just beginning to understand the crucial need for supervision to ensure the coach's and the client's mental, emotional, and physical health. As coach supervision is self-reflexive practice, we need to be developing supervisors who have an understanding of coaching as well as psychology, with organisational and business experience.

KEY QUESTIONS ON COACH SUPERVISION

At the Rainbow Convention of the Global Coaching Community (GCC) in Cape Town in May 2011, I facilitated a dialogue session on coach supervision around the question "Should qualifications or the market place decide on who supervises?" This chapter outlines some answers to the following key questions raised by participants during the session:

- *Definition*: What is supervision, and what is it not? What is its intent and purpose?
- *Benefits*: What are the benefits and outcomes of supervision? How can these be measured?
- *Types*: What are the differing supervision needs of coaches? Should there be different types of supervision for these different needs?
- *Organisational context*: How should the organisational context of business coaching influence the type(s) and content of supervision received by business coaches?
- *Supervisor selection*: What or who should determine who supervises – the coach, or the supervisor's competences?

Why coach supervision?

The term "supervision" describes the process by which the work of the practitioner is overseen and guidance is sought. The importance of the "coach being coached" or in supervision cannot be over-emphasised. While supervision has been a fundamental underpinning of psychotherapy from the beginning, it is not yet a given for the coaching industry worldwide. The purpose of coach supervision is to ensure that the coach understands what the client goes through, and more importantly, to support the coach in working through their own issues so that they do not become entangled with client concerns.

As Yalom (2001:48) says, human problems are "largely relational", and an individual's interpersonal problems will ultimately manifest themselves in the here and now of a clinical encounter. The same is true of the coaching environment. The client's interpersonal issues will soon emerge in the relationship between coach and client. The client can trigger a coach's underlying drivers, even in a small way. For example, if coach and client are both going through similar personal problems such as divorce or parenting a child with substance abuse problems, it is important that the coach is able to maintain a "meta-position" throughout the coaching conversation if these issues come into the conversation. We talk more about this in later sections on parallel processes and working with shadow.

What is the role of the supervisor?

The role of the supervisor is to support the development of the coach practitioner and to assess their competence. What coach supervision refers to is not the inspection of the coach's work within a hierarchical power relationship, as in managerial supervision, but rather consultation arising out of the needs of the coach and their individual and organisational clients (Stout-Rostron, 2012b:275, 277).

A key component of a coach's personal and professional approach to their coaching practice is to work on a regular basis with a supervising coach, counsellor or therapist. COMENSA (2010:1), defines the importance of supervision as follows: "Accountability, effectiveness and professionalism are core values for coaches ... Supervision serves to help the coach ... manage high levels of complexity, have a mechanism for ensuring accountability and ethical practice and maintain continued professional development." Supervision is useful as it ensures that the coach works to the client's agenda, not to the coach's agenda. The need for supervision is something that COMENSA recommends for all coaches in their continuing professional development (CPD), in alignment with other professional associations for coaching internationally.

What are the benefits of individual and group supervision?

The benefits of supervision are threefold: first, and crucially, for the coach to deal with any unresolved issues of their own (an ongoing process for any coach), and specifically to learn not to bring personal concerns to the coaching conversation. Second, for the individual's coaching practice to benefit from invaluable and ongoing supervision. Third, the supervision process provides the coach with an invaluable tool to understand the client–practitioner process from another perspective, i.e. from the client perspective rather than from the perspective of the practitioner It provides an excellent alternate perspective on the coaching intervention (Stout-Rostron, 2006:14).

There are multiple benefits for the individual practitioner in group supervision, as well as for the client organisation. Practitioners coaching specific individuals within a particular organisation have a chance to meet each other, and the supervising coach ensures that all practitioners have a sound understanding of the organisational systems at play. Coach supervision thus becomes an important regular meeting where the coaches can connect with and learn from each other, and can begin to understand the systemic connections between their individual clients without sharing any confidential information about their coachees.

Supervision helps practitioners to grow their skills and competence whether they are supervised individually or in groups. The capacity of the coaches to facilitate learning for their clients is also significantly increased. Other benefits are:

- ensuring that the client organisation is getting significant benefits from the coaching for their business;
- ensuring that a high value is placed on truly understanding their clients;
- ensuring that the coach is as likely to enhance and develop self-awareness as the client; and
- the creation of a safe space to explore the heart of the practitioner's coaching practice (Stout-Rostron, 2012b:281).

Group coach supervision will observe the developmental stages of the practitioners within their group forum. This type of supervision is more collegial and consultative, encouraging the practice of self-supervision. The lead coach or supervisor also needs to take note of their own developmental stages in the profession as they gain in expertise (Stout-Rostron, 2012b:282).

What happens when supervision doesn't work?

There are similarities between poor supervision and poor coaching practice. If conflict arises in supervision sessions, it is often due to the lack of skill on the part of the supervisor. It is important for there to be open, transparent dialogue about what is working, and what is not working, for supervisors and practitioners in any session. For example, I have experienced poor supervision when the supervisor, or one of the practitioners, has been operating from a lack of awareness of their blind spots. Also, if a practitioner begins to "advocate" for the supremacy of their individual "client" versus another "client", it suggests that the practitioner has become part of the systemic dynamics of the organisation.

The parallel processes and complexity of supervision require skill and self-awareness on the part of both the supervisor and the practitioner. These parallel processes are frequently where the greatest learning lies. Supervision ensures that the coach maintains the highest standards of competence, best serves the needs of the client, is professionally trained and skilled in the practice of coaching, and is committed to a programme of continuing professional development throughout their years of their practice.

Supervision exercise

To experience what work with a supervisor entails, think of a recent successful piece of work and describe it by answering the following questions:

- What went well in a recent piece of work you were involved in?
- What skills and strengths have you brought to this piece of work to enable it to go well?
- When did you first become aware of these qualities?
- How will you know these qualities are getting stronger in your work?
- How might your colleagues or clients know these qualities are getting stronger?
- What do you see yourself doing differently having reflected on this piece of work?

What types of supervision are appropriate?

Kadushin (1976) describes the three main functions of supervision as *educative, supportive* and *managerial*. He describes these functions as *formative* (namely educational), *normative* (which focuses on policies, organisation and evaluation), and *restorative* (including a debriefing of both positive and negative feedback on practice).

In organisations and coach training institutions today, there are several ways to access supervision. There is one-on-one supervision, peer supervision, team supervision and group supervision. Many coach training institutes set up a peer supervision process for senior and junior graduates to work together in the supervision process, either individual, peer or group. Following Kadushin (1976), we can define the four specific types of supervision as *educational*, *administrative*, *supportive* and *managerial* (Stout-Rostron, 2012b:283–284).

Typically, *educational* supervision is used to assess the skills and needs and to facilitate the learning for practitioner coaches. *Administrative* supervision is to monitor the workload of the coaches within the group or the organisation, ensuring that the purpose, vision and goals of the organisation are met. *Supportive* supervision is to provide an environment for practitioners where their emotional needs are met, and where they are able to build skills and competence, whether in a one-on-one or group forum. *Managerial* supervision is to ensure that the individual client, coach and line manager meet regularly to ensure that the client is on track to meet the objectives set out for the coaching intervention (Stout-Rostron, 2012b:283–284).

Pampallis Paisley considered the nature of working within different contexts in her supervision research, while working with a group of coaches:

> ... all of whom may be utilising different models and frameworks; who have varying levels of competencies, training and consciousness; impacts on what is brought into the supervisory room. Unlike therapeutic supervision, for example, where an object relations therapist would work with a supervisor who is skilled in object relations theory and practice, this in-depth but narrow band – or what I call *vertical depth of field* – of specialisation may not be the domain of the coaching supervisor. ... with regards the supervision of coaches working with leadership in complex organisations, coaching supervisors would need to have a broader focus, or what I call a *horizontal depth of field*. It follows then that the supervision of coaching is in itself a complex discipline – one that requires levels of understanding, and a comprehensive framework of knowledge and skills, which cover both the horizontal planes and vertical depths that coaching encompasses (Pampallis Paisley 2006:92).

There are multiple benefits for the coach in supervision, as well as for the individual or team being coached, and the client organisation. The coach practitioners have a chance to meet with the supervising coach, ensuring that all practitioners have a sound understanding of the organisational systems at play. Coach supervision is an important regular meeting where the coaches can connect with each other, and can begin to understand the connections between their clients. It is an important meeting where the individuals in the group facilitate learning from each other (Stout-Rostron, 2012b:280;289).

How important is the organisational context of supervision?

Huge investment is often made in executive development programmes, sending executives off to expensive business schools who are often unsure of what they need to develop as leaders. On their return to the organisation, however, the environment is not supportive enough to allow them to nurture any newfound or critical leadership capabilities. In addition, coaches often work in isolation with their executives, not aware of the systemic issues within an organisation, eventually becoming another "cog" in blocking systemic change due to their own lack of systemic knowledge. This is why supervision of coaches is crucial within any systemic change process which involves coaching (Stout-Rostron, 2011d).

Without lead coaches or supervisors overseeing the entire coaching intervention within an organisation, there is no way of harnessing the "systemic" issues or "systemic" trends that are emerging; "silo" coaching can become the norm (Stout-Rostron, 2011d).

Some of the main themes that have arisen from research into executive coach supervision are (Pampallis Paisley, 2006, cited in Stout-Rostron, 2012b:276):

- boundary management;
- whether supervision interventions need to have a client-centred or coach-centred focus, or both;
- how to cope with the complexity of the supervisory system in which client, coach and organisation are represented – the triangulations;
- the depth to which one should go in the coaching relationship; and
- the importance of creating a space to think.

There are some disadvantages to group supervision, and practitioners need to be particularly careful when managing client confidentiality. The advantages are the observations that the group can make when observing each other. The 1:1 supervision encompasses more intimate learning on the part of the individual coach, with the time to go into depth about the client situation and one's own individual issues or concerns as a coach. It is almost inevitable that the coach can become enmeshed in some of the organisation's systemic dynamics. It is helpful to have an observant supervisor who can help the coach to step into a bigger-picture position, looking at the client–coach–system dynamics from a fresh perspective (Stout-Rostron, 2012b:281–282).

THE SUPERVISORY RELATIONSHIP

At the heart of supervision is the supportive relationship between supervisor and coach. It's not about being nice or friendly, but more about setting the conditions that elicit high-quality work. The work of Burger and Parry (2012) on doctoral supervision can be extended to coach supervision.

Research shows that supervision can fail to meet the expectations of and outcomes for doctoral candidates due to the lack of skill, defined purpose and ability on the part of the supervisor to work one-on-one. Grant (2003:175) describes the importance of personal relationship skills when building supervision practice, and describes supervision as differing "from other forms of teaching and learning in higher education in its peculiarly intense and negotiated character, as well as in its requirements for a blend of pedagogical and personal relationship skills".

The implication is the importance of the "tacit dimension" of supervision. "The outcome of supervision is not only to teach the student skills but to teach the student *how to be* ... to avoid the pitfall of according all power to the supervisor ... Supervision comes face to face with this strangeness in an intense way and must somehow, and often does, work in spite of this" (Grant, 2003:180;188).

The term "tacit knowing" or "tacit knowledge" was first introduced into philosophy by Michael Polanyi (1958). He later introduced the idea in *The Tacit Dimension* (1966), asserting that "we can know more than we can tell". According to him, knowledge cannot be adequately articulated by verbal means, and all knowledge is rooted in tacit knowledge.

The focus in supervision is usually on the dimensions of "knowing and doing", rather than on "how to be" in the supervisory relationship. The argument is for supervisors to reconsider their expertise from the point of view of "being" versus "knowing and doing" (Burger and Parry, 2012). The supervisor needs to ask, "How am I being perceived by the coach?", in addition to the necessary knowledge and skills for effective supervisors. This means that we need to identify the "tacit" qualities of effective supervisors, understanding what role "tacit" qualities play in creating an effective and supportive supervisory relationship.

Burger and Parry elicit such qualities as: attentiveness, easefulness, empathy, appreciation, being intellectually challenging, and continuous encouragement employed intentionally or intuitively (Burger and Parry, 2012). Although not necessarily articulated, these qualities can be perceived and felt. The values of the supervisor also underpin their attitude to the coach (in this case their client), producing an "internal climate" that is externally, but tacitly, perceived by the client. If, as suggested by Burger and Parry, tacit qualities are distinct from knowledge and learning, how are they expressed and can supervisors be trained in how to convey them? The study by Burger and Parry (2012) is useful to us in identifying possible first principles for supervisors of "how to be" with coach-clients, and how to give guidance and feedback.

The study argues for recognition of certain attitudes and tacit qualities in supervision relationships which are characterised by some of the Thinking Environment® qualities we encountered earlier in this book, such as ease, encouragement and attention:

> New ways of being for supervisors require changes in values and the development of inner attitudes or qualities that are conducive to effective supervisory relationships and new knowledge outcomes. We argue for recognition of certain attitudes and tacit qualities in effective supervisors, characterised by equality, ease, attention, encouragement, empathy, that are the conditions for mutually respectful relationships to develop. When these attitudes are consistently present then trust, reciprocity, co-creation and a sense of collegiality emerge (Burger and Parry, 2012:176).

Supervision is not only concerned with the outcome of the supervisor–coach process, but also with the transformation of the coach into an independently informed and self-aware coach, aware of parallel process, organisational systemic issues, and able to build rapport with the client. This transformation is effected through the working relationship that "engages the coach and supervisor in productive power relations". According to Grant (2003) this is a view that sees supervision as an ethical practice.

Parallel processes

Another important aspect of coach supervision is identifying parallel processes. If the coach is not aware of what they are feeling, or what is playing out for them in the coaching session with their client, then they are not conscious enough to voice it. One definition of parallel process is "the me in you", i.e. "What's happening in me that is mirroring something in the system that is not spoken?" By naming it, it breaks the unconscious communication between coach and client; this is what the supervisor helps the coach to identify.

As supervisors we work with issues that our coach-clients bring to us. The role of the coach supervisor is to explore what might be happening to the coach, the client and the dynamic between the two of them. Parallel process is an important part of this learning.

Below is a group exercise you might find useful when facilitating one of your own group supervision sessions, to help the group to consider what might be happening within the group that reflects any parallel process. This exercise also helps us to consider what might be operating in the coach–client–organisational system and the insights it gives us.

Exercise

Part 1

Working in the here and now, and experientially – work with parallel process in small groups of four or five. Ask everyone in their small groups to introduce themselves and their learning outcomes for the forum. Ask each one to explain their expectations from the session that you are facilitating – and how it is impacting the way they show up in the room. Then have everyone compare what they've heard from each other, and ask all the groups to come back into the plenary. You, as facilitator, then ask each one:

- What did you notice – in yourself and in the group?
- Did you have a lead supervisor?
- What self-reflecting questions were you asking yourself?

Part 2

Ask everyone to go back into their smaller groups, and to reflect on what they personally noticed in themselves and others.

- What came up for you?
- What story did you tell yourself?
- What assumptions were you making?
- How did this impact on how you showed up?

Ask everyone to rejoin the plenary, then request a sharing of individual reflections and insights to identify the parallel processes in their groups and in the room.

Working with shadow

We develop what Jung termed a "Persona", a social self that we present to the outside world. In reality, the persona is that which we are not, but which we and others think that we are. It is a mask which makes us acceptable, which enables us to fit in and meet the expectations of others. The downside of this is that, in order to meet these external expectations, we have to suppress parts of ourselves – emotions, qualities, character traits, talents, different sides to us, feelings and so on – essential parts of who we are, but that don't fit with the mask (Prentice, 2013).

According to Carl Jung and Sigmund Freud, the "Self" in each individual is made up of the Conscious and the Unconscious. The Conscious is called the "Ego", and is the part of the Conscious in which the individual has identified who he or she is. There is also a "Personal Unconscious" which contains, amongst other things, "repressed" sensations, feelings, thoughts or intuitions which do not conform with the Ego's consciously decided role or identity. Jung calls this rejected alter-ego the Shadow (Prentice, 2013).

Jung identified the Shadow as one of the four principle archetypes of the collective unconscious. It is composed of the dark elements of the personality, having an emotional and primitive nature which resists moral control. Shadow is essentially:

* the part you cannot name;
* the part that is undifferentiated; and
* what we recognise within ourselves that we don't want to own or admit to (Prentice, 2013).

The shadow in coaching

The coach and the client can influence each other in hidden and unexpected ways. According to de Haan (2012:71), this can be brought out with the help of a supervisor acting as a detached but reflective outsider. The supervisor helps the coach to step back and "explore their own assumptions, prejudices, expectations and unconscious signals" (de Haan, 2012:72).

At the Third International Conference on Coaching Supervision in 2013 at Oxford Brookes University, Karyn Prentice shared a range of ways that the shadow can appear in the coaching and the coach supervision setting. Some examples of shadow are shame, envy, anxiety, irritability, creativity and latent talents. These feelings may be there for a range of reasons, and can be a part of our own, or our supervisee's shadow, joining the conversation (Prentice, 2013).

Working with shadow in supervisory relationships, the coach works on understanding their own shadow first – noticing their own physical, mental and emotional reactions in the coach–client relationship. The more awareness the coach can develop of their own hooks or triggers will allow them to work with compassion, and to notice or observe what is emerging in the supervision dialogue. The supervisor might ask questions about the coach–client relationship, such as "Are there any strong emotions emerging?"; "What is happening with the energy between the two of you?"; and "What aspects of yourself are showing up that you may not want to be in the room?" (Prentice, 2013).

Prentice explains that there are a variety of ways in which we can meet our shadow:

- in exaggerated feelings about others;
- in negative feedback from others who serve as our mirrors;
- in repeated interactions in which we have the same troubling effect on several different people;
- in our impulsive and inadvertent acts;
- in situations in which we are humiliated; and
- in our exaggerated anger about other people's faults (Prentice, 2013:12).

> **Exercise with shadow**
>
> Here is a shadow exercise for you to work through:
>
> - What makes you special?
> - What don't you want your clients to know?
> - What comes up for you when you ask those two questions?

So, how can we work with shadow safely and appropriately? I would suggest that two of the best ways are:

- through a case study in a group supervision session, or
- in exploring the coach–client relationship within the safe boundaries of the coach supervision session, examining in what ways shadow may appear between the coach and the client.

According to de Haan (2012:72–73), the supervisor listens carefully to the coach's narratives, not necessarily believing them to be "truth". The supervisor helps the coach to track the narratives which reside just below the surface, helping the coach to reframe these narratives, seeing that they are distortions and emotional patterns from which learning can emerge.

WHO SHOULD SUPERVISE?

The question is far from resolved whether market supply and demand, or qualifications and competence, should determine who acts as a coaching supervisor. In the meantime, professional associations such as COMENSA do not prescribe rigid requirements for practice as a coach supervisor, but simply recommend guidelines that coaches should follow.

When hiring a supervisor, a coach should look for someone who:

- has knowledge of ethical, legal and regulatory aspects of the helping professions;
- is able to form a peer or collegial relationship as a supervising consultant;
- is sensitive to diversity issues of culture, ethnicity, gender, age, socio-economic and educational background;
- has knowledge of current research in the coach supervision field;

- has competence and expertise as a business coach; and
- has training in supervision (Stout-Rostron, 2012b:283).

The supervision process in coaching may differ in significant ways from that in other professions, such as psychotherapy and counselling. However, both coach practitioner and supervisor will be bound by the code of ethics of their professional body (Stout-Rostron, 2012b:275). For the moment, there are no international guidelines to measure the positive impact of supervision for clients and coach practitioners. This is certainly a topic worthy of future practitioner and academic research.

CONCLUSION

The purpose of coach supervision is to ensure that the coach understands what the client goes through. Most importantly, the supervisor supports the coach in working through their own issues so that they do not become entangled with client concerns.

The focus in supervision is usually on the dimensions of "knowing and doing", rather than on "how to be" in the supervisory relationship. The argument is for supervisors to reconsider their expertise from the point of view of "being" versus "knowing and doing" (Burger and Parry, 2012). Also, the role of the coach supervisor is to explore what might be happening to the coach, the client and the dynamic between the two of them – understanding parallel processes is an important part of this learning. Working with shadow in supervisory relationships, the supervisor helps the coach to step back and explore their own assumptions and unexpected reactions.

As coach supervision is self-reflexive practice, we need to be developing supervisors who have an understanding of coaching as well as psychology, plus organisational and business experience. Supervision can be seen as an empowerment tool, with a commitment to best practice. Today we have a critical need to educate coach supervisors, practitioners and managers in understanding the need for supervision (Stout-Rostron, 2012b:304).

FURTHER READING

Burger, N., and Parry, S. (2012). Supervisor qualities in the doctoral supervisory relationship: The tacit dimension. In Kiley, M. (ed.), *Proceedings of the 2012 Quality in Postgraduate Research Conference* (pp. 175–176). Canberra, ACT: Centre for Higher Education, Learning and Teaching, Australian National University.

De Haan, E. (2012). *Supervision in Action: A relational approach to coaching and consulting supervision.* Maidenhead: Open University.

Grant, B. (2003). Mapping the pleasures and risks of supervision. *Discourse: Studies in the cultural politics of education*, 24(2):175–190.

Hawkins, P., and Shohet, R. (2000). *Supervision in the Helping Professions.* Buckingham: Open University.

Jones, R., and Jenkins, F. (eds). (2006). *Developing the Allied Health Professional*. (Allied Health Professions: Essential Guides.) Oxford: Radcliffe.

Kennedy, E., and Charles, S.C. (2001). *On Becoming a Counsellor: The basic guide for non-professional counsellors*. Dublin: Newleaf.

Pampallis Paisley, P. (2006). *Towards a Theory of Supervision for Executive Coaching: An integral vision*. Published DProf dissertation. London: Middlesex University.

Prentice, K. (2013). *Me and My Shadow*. Presentation to the Third International Conference on Coaching Supervision, Oxford Brookes University, 23 June. Webpage: business.brookes.ac.uk/commercial/work/iccld/coaching-supervision-conference/2013.

Stout-Rostron, S. (2006). *Interventions in the Coaching Conversation: Thinking, feeling and behaviour*. Published DProf dissertation. London: Middlesex University.

Stout-Rostron, S. (2011a). How is coaching impacting systemic and cultural change within organisations? *International Journal of Coaching in Organisations*, 8(4):5–27.

Stout-Rostron, S. (2012b). *Business Coaching Wisdom and Practice: Unlocking the Secrets of Business Coaching*. Second edition. Randburg: Knowres.

Stout-Rostron, S. (2014). *Business Coaching International: Transforming individuals and organisations*. Second edition. London: Karnac.

13

The future of business coaching

WHERE WILL COACHING BE IN 2020?

Although we can't say with any certainty, there are some indications of where the discipline is headed. In the last two years I interviewed several eminent thought leaders in coaching to try to answer this question, particularly with regard to the future of business coaching.

As Chapter 3 explained, business coaching is essentially about systemic coaching interventions whose results impact on the overall performance of the organisation. A key component of business coaching is a focus on executive coaching, i.e. developing senior managers and executives to improve their individual and team performance, thereby optimising their organisational results.

A few years ago Nic Bednall, then Managing Director of the international advertising agency BBDO Cape Town, told an audience of coaches that "Coaching is an industry in need of a belief in itself" (Bednall, 2008). That belief may come from two things. First, the need to research and define coaching as a distinct discipline in its own right; and second, the essential "professionalisation" of coaching practice. Although the industry is "professionalising" to an extent, despite current research coaches are themselves not rigorously defining coaching as a distinct discipline. Even those conducting formal research into the discipline often don't define "coaching" in their studies. If business coaching is to make a fundamental difference to the world, what do we, as coach practitioners and leaders-as-coach, need to be thinking about and making happen?

Although multi-disciplinary, coaching is not "disciplinary" enough – in terms of rigour, a universally accepted definition of coaching, and the alignment of required coaching competences with coach education curricula worldwide. The bigger question is: "If business needs to find the will to change, balancing personal ambition with corporate and social responsibility, what is the role we as business coaches need to play – with clients, colleagues, and within our wider society?" Business coaching is often showing up as something potentially profound and radical – but are coaches simply maintaining the *status quo* inside the systems and organisations within which they work? This chapter talks about five areas key to the future of business coaching as we move rapidly toward 2020: *professionalisation; education and development of coaches; mastery of practice; coaching research;* and *coaching and society.*

PROFESSIONALISATION

Coaching in South Africa is currently a service industry. To date, COMENSA's overriding brief has been to develop the credibility of this emerging profession, aligning national standards of professional competence to international standards. A crucial role for COMENSA is to build relationships between buyers and providers of coaching services, building connections with professional bodies such as the Worldwide Association of Business Coaches (WABC), the European Mentoring and Coaching Council (EMCC), and the International Coach Federation (ICF).

In *Coaching and Buying Coaching Services: A guide*, published by the Chartered Institute of Personnel and Development (CIPD) in the UK, Jessica Jarvis (2004:21) states that one of the CIPD's surveys found that "four-fifths of respondents now use coaching in their organisations", but there remains a major concern about the "number of 'cowboy' coaches entering the market who are inexperienced, have little training and lack the appropriate knowledge and skills".

One of the challenges in the UK is a "growing number of business advisers and consultants who have reinvented themselves as coaches and, without any further training, now operate as full-time coaches" (Jarvis, 2004:11–12). This adds to the complexity of a service industry which still lacks legislation and regulation. For the time being, coaching continues to be self-regulated worldwide.

It seems that, as in most other countries, there is not yet consensus on what are the criteria for a good coach, or the best way to assess individual coaches, or how best to evaluate the results produced as a consequence of coaching. As a result, coaching is seen as somewhat fragmented, and that recognition as a distinct discipline (let alone as an emerging profession) remains contentious. Despite different power brokers taking contrary views on the legitimacy of coaching, participation in collaborative and international dialogue on its future is growing. The Global Convention on Coaching (later the Global Coaching Community or GCC) established in 2007, and the International Coaching Research Forum at Harvard (ICRF) launched in 2009, helped put us on the road to defining universal standards and developing a professional body of knowledge for coaching. This was followed by an initiative on coaching standards led by the Worldwide Association of Business Coaches (WABC), and work to define coaching standards in Australia (Standards Australia, 2011).

The WABC is a leading international association dedicated exclusively to business coaches and business coaching. For three years the WABC led an initiative to develop international professional standards for business coaches, whose purpose was to research a relevant set of principles that inform real-world business coaching practice. This research and consultation identified ten standards (or principles) for business coaches:

- *Professionalism and ethics* – applying high standards of honesty and integrity to service provision and behaviour.
- *Client focus* – putting the client first while at the same time respecting the objectives of the client's organisation.
- *Business and organisational context* – operating in the interests of the client's business and organisational contexts.
- *Business coaching process and contracting* – putting into place an appropriate coaching services agreement (oral or written) to work with clients towards agreed-upon objectives.
- *Boundaries* – operating in areas where clear boundaries need to be recognised and drawn.

- *Confidentiality* – practising coaching in a way that promotes confidentiality and respects the client's privacy.
- *Diversity* – respecting cross-cultural diversity and personal uniqueness at all times.
- *Responsibility and respect* – a professional responsibility to act as an effective role model.
- *Professional development* – being committed to professional development and to continuously enhancing own competence.
- *Promotion of the emerging profession* – as a member of the WABC, being committed to the advancement of the Association and the emerging profession of business coaching (WABC, 2013).

Wendy Johnson, President and CEO of the WABC, sees business coaching as a completely separate emerging profession, and views the power broking between all the professional bodies as a positive and natural process. All established professions have gone through decades of competition amongst themselves – with new professional bodies continually merging, dissolving and being recreated. She contends that competition and diversity give rise to creativity (Johnson, 2013, pers. com.).

More importantly, Johnson insists that business coaching is not taken seriously enough, and that most coaching bodies don't differentiate business coaching from other forms of coaching – apart from academic business schools, the Association for Professional Executive Coaching and Supervision (APECS), and the Association of Corporate Executive Coaches (ACEC). Johnson hears three divergent opinions:

- business coaching is merely a skill set (other "tool" in your toolbox);
- business coaching is an established profession (yet we aren't regulated); and
- business coaching is an emerging profession (which signals that we haven't yet met the test for a profession).

Johnson's view is that we are an emerging profession, and since we don't have regulators breathing down our necks we can be self-paced. Time is on our side for the industry to mature, and to complete more extensive research. "Let the evidence guide us", she explains, and "in the meantime let's address the issue of the lack of good research" (Johnson, 2013, pers. com.).

Between 2009 and 2011, 26 professional bodies in Australia participated in the Coaching Guideline Working Group under the aegis of Standards Australia, to produce a handbook on *Coaching in Organisations* (Standards Australia, 2011). Gordon Spence of the Australian Institute of Business Wellbeing (AIBWB) and Sydney Business School, and Ann Whyte, Chair of the Human Resources and Employment Committee of Standards Australia, say the handbook is receiving attention from organisations and coaches alike, and is currently undergoing review and revision (Spence, 2013, pers. com.; Whyte, 2013, pers. com.). Rather than being an attempt by government to impose regulations on the field of coaching, this completely independent initiative has set a benchmark for collaboration in developing coaching standards. *Coaching in Organisations* is one of the most comprehensive guidelines for coaching service provision, competencies and training to date. It is also the first guideline on coaching standards to be created under an ISO-aligned national standards body.

In November 2012 in the UK and Europe, the European Mentoring and Coaching Council (EMCC), International Coach Federation (ICF), Association for Coaching (AC), and the Société Française de Coaching (SFCoach) formed the Global Coaching and Mentoring Alliance (GCMA). The GCMA sees its purpose as professionalising the fields of coaching and mentoring, developing a shared view of the practice of coaching worldwide. It continues to invite other coaching bodies to work with them to collaborate, to facilitate exchange and to distribute information for all industry shareholders, about shared good practice (GCMA, 2011).

Like its precursor the GCC, the GCMA is a working alliance whose main goal is to establish a benchmark for ethics and good practice in coaching and mentoring. Its other main goal is to promote public confidence in coaching and mentoring as a process for professional and personal development. In June 2011 the GCMA published their *Professional Charter for Coaching and Mentoring*, with its stated mission to promote and ensure good practice in coaching and mentoring, forming the basis for self-regulation (GCMA, 2011). The Charter has not yet been adopted by a regulatory authority, nor does it have the force of law, but it has been adopted by the above-mentioned professional bodies to establish a benchmark standard of ethical and professional practice. Lise Lewis, President of the EMCC, says that "We not only need to co-operate and collaborate, but we also need to determine what our future is about – and what we actually are asking coaches to do" (Lewis, 2013, pers. com.). She sees the GCMA as a huge step forward.

What is clear is that if coaching wants to become a "profession" it needs to fulfil certain criteria. According to Gordon Spence (2007:261), these should include:

- some formal academic qualification;
- adherence to an enforceable code of ethics;
- practice licensed only to qualified members;
- compliance with state sanctioned regulation; and
- a common body of knowledge and skills.

Spence (2013, pers. com.) has also indicated that coaching cannot become a profession without state-backed regulation, and that this is unlikely unless clients start becoming damaged. For that scenario, there are no "case precedents".

For the foreseeable future, it looks as if coaching will continue to "professionalise". According to David Lane, Chairman of the UK-based Professional Development Foundation (PDF), the current position and disputes about status in the field of coaching mirror those around parallel fields such as psychotherapy. Lane suggests that unless coaches adapt and maintain a strongly collaborative approach globally, the result will be various schools of coaching each with their own standards body. If, however, practitioners train as coaches first and specialists second, an overall accrediting body could be created, with overarching standards and competencies (Lane, 2013, pers. com.).

Another alternative is that of the European Federation of Psychologists Association. Coaches could determine the guiding principles of practice, rather than treating coaching as a practice of limited modalities (i.e. business coaching, coaching psychology, leadership and executive coaching, and career or life coaching). According to Lane (2013, pers.com.), the ideal would be to create statutory frameworks collaboratively, rather than claiming ownership of the field. In contrast, some influential voices in psychology, which in most countries (including South Africa) is a regulated profession, claim ownership of the field and deny that coaching can be a separate discipline.

History shows us that the coaching industry has emerged because professions have lost their monopoly on knowledge. Knowledge grows in communities of practice, and coaches are a community of practice. Medicine is a superb example, where there is competition from alternative practitioners such as homeopaths, herbalists, acupuncturists and *sangomas*. David Drake, Executive Director of the Centre for Narrative Coaching in Sydney and San Francisco, moves us beyond the traditional notion of "profession" and towards a craftsperson's view of professional practice – blending science and art in what he calls "the pursuit of conscious mastery". He also advocates moving beyond our own biases for specialised, professional knowledge towards a co-creative process (Drake, 2013, pers. com.).

The more we can continue to work towards rigorous multi-disciplinary co-operation and a multi-disciplinary perspective, the more we will enrich the field through collaboration. This will move us away from dividing the coaching community through narrow areas of practice. The *Dublin Declaration on Coaching* signed in July 2008 identified ten core areas of immediate collaboration and consultation including research, ethics, education and development, standards of competence, and supervision (GCC, 2008).

EDUCATION AND DEVELOPMENT

Employees tend to acquire coaching skills through short-term programmes using coaching as a "dialogical" tool for continuing professional development (CPD) rather than as an area of practice. According to Drake, coaching will become integral to every job description, becoming a "verb" rather than a "noun", referring to the way we do something and becoming the dominant model in the way we teach people to do things (Drake, 2013, pers. com.). Ann Whyte in Australia suggests that there are more coaches than ever before. But she is concerned that coaching is becoming "invisible". This, she says, is primarily due to the training of managers as coaches, the development of organisational suites of internal coaches, and the lack of practitioner research on internal coaching. Due to these factors, " ... we're actually losing the sense of a coaching culture inside organisations". She also says that "one of the inherent problems with internal coaches is that they don't necessarily have 'line' and business experience" (Whyte, 2013, pers. com.).

According to David Lane in the UK, internal coaching is growing, but it needs more support. Internal coaches need supervision, better education and training, and to be taken seriously. The overall norm for coach practitioner training has increased versus the thinking up to six years ago (Lane, 2013, pers. com.). Current thinking, with the development of tertiary certificates and diplomas, Masters and Doctoral programmes in coach education, has increased the norm up to 20 days' training, with a practicum of at least six months to a year. Lane also explains that even though team coaching is not yet researched or well-defined enough, it's now seen to be a cheaper option than individual executive coaching. This is despite the fact that most team coaching essentially involves facilitation or group therapy processes, rather than being "pure" team coaching.

As organisations see a growing need to include coaching as part of their culture, a greater number of certificate and degree-granting, postgraduate institutions are offering executive and organisational coaching programmes. Leaders want to develop a coaching approach, yet there are no uniform curriculum standards. This is a particularly important issue as internal coaching becomes more prevalent, and organisations begin to employ internal coaches as an integral and permanent part of an organisation. The ICF has created an Internal Coach Certificate, but many internal coaches don't see the need to be ICF-accredited unless this is required by their organisation. Most recently, coaching is being viewed as a leadership skill within organisations, with executives and other managers expected to coach subordinates, peers and teams as part of a management "coaching culture". So, as coaching becomes integral to organisational management, graduate schools are including executive coaching in their curricula.

As the wider field of coaching studies is not yet a discipline, but draws upon traditional disciplines such as education, management science, adult learning and psychology, the Graduate School Alliance for Executive Coaching (GSAEC) was formed specifically to develop an aligned curriculum for graduate schools. Most academic research into coaching is coming from a business school orientation, which is why GSAEC has collaborated with university business schools worldwide to create coach education curricula. In South Africa, Wits Business School has aligned its Business and Executive Coaching Certificate and Masters in Business Coaching with GSAEC.

Irene Stein, former head of the ICF Research Special Interest Group, and Linda Page, Founder of the Adler Graduate Professional School, point out that if the coaching profession is to remain viable, "schools that institute coaching programmes need to address the question of how to contribute to the body of knowledge related to coaching". They go on to point out that "Teaching coach practitioners at any academic level how to do research in their own practice would serve to add knowledge to a coaching field in its early stages of knowledge creation." Further, Stein and Page ask the following key questions about the role of education programmes in the professional development of executive coaching:

> How can a community of alumni and other stakeholders be built and maintained? How can graduates be encouraged to contribute to the profession? Given that graduates of programs such as these will be the people who will define, shape, and even determine the survival of coaching and executive coaching as fields and as practices, what must educational institutions be aware of and do now? (Stein and Page, 2010:63).

Clearly, collaboration and contribution are what will take business and executive coaching forward.

MASTERY OF PRACTICE

Eric de Haan's recent research indicates that the quality of an experienced coach's work is determined primarily by their ability to tolerate tension, and deliberately enquire into tensions within coaching relationships. Otherwise they are seriously in danger of becoming merely good conversation partners (de Haan *et al.*, 2010). According to Michael Cavanagh, there will probably be two changes in coaching. On the one hand, coaching will remain linear and goal-driven. And on the other hand, coaches will increase their capacity to deal with complex, non-linear systems, building relationships and resilience within individuals and organisations. In order to do that we need coaches who are able to think in systemic ways – and to be part of the overall coaching intervention. This needs to be an important part of coach education and development (Cavanagh, 2013a).

According to Cavanagh, the world is creating more and more complexity, from the need for water to climate change, and leaders today need to move from solving national to international problems. Leaders will look for people to help them, not only to cope with greater complexity and systemic issues – but because leaders today are struggling to cope. How many great leaders do we actually have? Leaders struggle with complexities inside their own organisations and very rapid rates of change (Cavanagh, 2013a).

Lew Stern, Founding President of the International Leadership Foundation in Boston, indicates where coaching helps is by offering "compassionate partnership" which is focused on both individuals and organisations. To achieve specific results, he says what we face in the next ten years is a radically changing global environment with financial challenges; vocational and technological change; more violence and conflict; greater ideological, religious and social differences; and more competition in every industry. Even though we seem to be more global, we are also much more self-protective. He asks "How can coaches help people survive: emotionally, physically and fiscally, yet grow their intellect and deal with changing roles in education, and in family and societal systems – growing all of our intelligences?" At the same time, organisations will need to change their expectations, from the professional external coach to thinking about developing internal or leader-as-coach capabilities as part of the organisation (Stern, 2013, pers. com.).

During 2010 and 2011 I conducted a series of interviews to look at the impact of coaching on leadership that aimed at large-scale systemic change. From my range of interviews emerged the need to develop coaching practice at the highest level, embracing a new perspective on real change in leadership coaching for transformation. This means working collectively where there is energy to stimulate reflection, original thought, and innovative collaboration. What also emerged was the vital need for bold, visionary leadership to shape our future; not just the future of organisations and institutions, but also our increasingly complex and interdependent cultures and societies (Stout-Rostron, 2011a).

In his book *Mindsight: The new science of personal transformation*, Daniel Siegel (2011) explores how we focus our attention, and how that shapes the structure of our brain. As explained in Chapter 8, the mind is a relational process, so energy and information flow between client and coach, and both are modified in the exchange (Siegel, 2011:84). Working with attention helps the client to reflect, but reflection gives way to objectivity and gaining the capacity to deal with intense emotion without becoming lost in it.

As we head towards 2020, although the gap will continue to grow between "commodity coaches" and internal coaches versus master coaches, we're going to need a new model of profession that is not just competency-based. Work is starting this year at Middlesex University to begin to explore this possibility. More and more, international agencies have suites of coaches who will provide the coaching contracts for larger corporates alongside the business schools. And although psychology won't necessarily take over coach education and training, it may become imperative that coach education programmes aim to develop psychological literacy in graduating coaches.

We will never be without emergent leaders in society, government, education and business. Therefore, business and executive coaching will continue to grow, and mastery of practice – as the ability to manage complexity and complex systems – will not only be a prerequisite, but master coaches will need to develop the capacity to work with greater complexity. Buyers of coaching services will continue to become savvier as they educate themselves as coaches, and research will need to be not just evidence-based, but based more on observation of working coaching practice.

COACHING RESEARCH

A growing number of professional bodies and business schools in the field have dedicated themselves to research-led models, including the Coaching Psychology Unit at the University of Sydney; the WABC in North America; the EMCC in Europe; and the Institute of Coaching at Harvard / McLean Medical School (IOC). The concept of primary, evidence-based research into best-practice coaching has been a key feature of the movement for coaching to be an evidence-based discipline. This also raises the question of the role of coaches as "scientist-practitioners". This concept of practitioners as scientists (Lane and Corrie, 2006) has its origins in clinical psychology, and has since been extended into all areas of professional psychological practice.

While the need for evidence-based practice is largely accepted, as is the need for coaching to be a reflective practice, a crucial question emerges: "Is it incumbent on all practitioners to contribute to the emerging profession through research from their practice?" Why do I ask this? Because practitioners contribute very little to published literature, peer-reviewed or not. And case study contributions from coaches, for the development of coaching, can offer a broader and critically informative perspective. I see this as a crucial role for all practitioners. For coaching to move forward towards 2020, we need to promote five cornerstones of professional practice:

- aligned theory in our education and training programmes;
- research – both academic / scholarly and practitioner research;
- self-reflective practice and supervision (a core component being one hour of supervision per 15 hours of coaching; this also means developing coaching supervisors who have an understanding of coaching);

- developing core competence through our own CPD and mastery of practice; and
- membership of a professional body with an enforceable code of ethics.

The International Coaching Research Forum (ICRF) has worked to promote the value of research and critical, self-reflective practice, and the development of a coaching knowledge base. As part of this process, a group of internationally recognised coaching researchers, coach practitioners and other coaching stakeholders gathered in September 2008, and thereafter annually for three years, to foster progress and community in coaching research. After its first Forum in 2008, the ICRF published a set of 100 coaching research proposals on the website of the Institute of Coaching (www.instituteofcoaching.org), with the aim of promoting new coaching research studies (Kauffman, Russell and Bush, 2008).

Lew Stern and I spent most of 2012 trying to answer the question, "What progress has been made in coaching research in relation to the 16 ICRF focus areas from January 2008 to end June 2012?" We explored the extent to which the focus areas of the 100 research proposals generated by the ICRF have been addressed in substantive, primary, evidence-based research. We chose the ICRF focus areas because the Forum's 100 research proposals were generated through an open, multi-disciplinary forum of experts, representing many regions, disciplines and roles in coaching, i.e. they held very diverse perspectives. We identified 16 main focus areas recommended for research, based on a categorical aggregate of themes emerging from the 100 research proposals, and by reviewing the frequency of questions and topics within the proposals (Stern and Stout-Rostron, 2013a:72–73).

We determined to what degree each of these 16 focus areas had been researched, by compiling and reviewing abstracts of peer-reviewed journal articles on research into coaching published during January 2008 to June 2012. Our compilation was based on the available English-language, peer-reviewed articles found on the web, from journals primarily published in the USA, UK, Australia, Canada and South Africa. It became clear that Grant's (2011) bibliography, covering workplace, executive and life coaching research published up to December 2010, was the most comprehensive source of abstracts on coaching research. However, Grant (2011) included non-peer reviewed journal articles and articles which were other than research (e.g. opinion, comment or promotional pieces), which we therefore excluded from our review. We located 130 journal websites for the abstracts we found, but excluded those journals which were not peer-reviewed (Stern and Stout-Rostron, 2013a:73;75).

We subsequently made the following four documents, which compile key research data from our study, available via the website of the Institute of Coaching (www.instituteofcoaching.org):

- a bibliography of coaching research abstracts published from January 2011 to June 2012 (Stern and Stout-Rostron, 2013b);
- a list of peer-reviewed journal articles on coaching research published during January 2008 to June 2012 (Stern and Stout-Rostron, 2013c);
- a list of peer-reviewed journals which published coaching research from January 2008 to June 2012 (Stern and Stout-Rostron, 2013d); and

- a list of scholarly dissertations completed during January 2011 to June 2012 (Stern and Stout-Rostron, 2013e).

Focus areas identified for coaching research from ICRF 100 research proposals

The 16 focus areas of coaching research from the ICRF 100 research proposals are:

1. *Coach education and training*: self-directed, classroom, practice, supervision.
2. *Coaching relationship*: chemistry, matching factors, gender same / different, style, background, etc.
3. *Coaching outcomes*: relationship with satisfaction, emotional, social, functioning, effectiveness, wellbeing, sustainable leadership, self-understanding, lifestyle, outcomes of health coaching (for different diagnoses, age groups, etc.).
4. *Coaching in organisations*: who, why, outcomes, internal systems for support, impact of coaching on organisations (ethics, productivity, etc.).
5. *Coaches*: competencies, characteristics and practices, compassion, good to great, theoretical awareness and application, impact of experience level of coaches on outcomes.
6. *Coaching process*: what is being done, directive versus non-directive, use of questions, assignments, feedback, espoused theories versus coaching practices, and the impact of these practices, coaching approaches and impact (strengths-based, gap-based, etc.), coaching methods and results for different types of coaching (teachers, parents, etc.), coaching failures and related factors (process, coachee, coach, organisation, support, etc.).
7. *Research methods and findings in coaching*: random samples, control groups, outcome measures, goal-attainment measures, measurement instruments, baseline of coaching research findings, what coaches want / need from research.
8. *Supervision practices*: how contracted and conducted, the impact on coach accountability and visible behavioural change, how learning is recognised and coach competence brought into awareness.
9. *The business of coaching*: professionalisation of coaching (policy, ethics, governance), intervention processes in organisations / institutions and their evaluation (business trends, pricing, contractual arrangements).
10. *Coaching versus other helping practices*: When should coaching be used versus something else, what differentiates coaching?
11. *How coaching differs by geographic region internationally*: activities, theories, assumptions, processes, impact of language, contracting, goals, models, approaches, interactive effects – coachee characteristics, readiness, states of mind and emotion, developmental stages, coaching methods, outcomes.
12. *Peer coaching*: in coach education and development programmes, businesses, friends, and elsewhere.
13. *Contracting*: the formal and informal agreements between coaches, coachees, client organisations, guidelines for confidentiality, communication, support, etc.

14. *Coaching readiness by the coachee*: criteria to evaluate, evaluation, decision making, is the coachee encouraged positively or coerced negatively into coaching?
15. *Use of assessment in coaching*: what is done, how does it help, what is the impact (assessment or data gathering about the individual or group being coached, their relationships, their teams or groups, their organisation); forms of data gathering (standardised instruments, observation, 360-degree surveys and interviews, etc.); before, during, and after coaching.
16. *Impact of coaching on society*: how coaching is moving from organisations / institutions out into the broader community, and what is its positive impact (Stern and Stout-Rostron, 2013a:74–75).

What research categories emerged in their own right?

Several new research categories indicating types of coaching emerged in addition to the 16 focus areas defined above:

- existential coaching;
- family business coaching;
- gender coaching;
- stress management coaching;
- team and group coaching; and
- teenage, adolescent and youth coaching (Stern and Stout-Rostron, 2013a:76).

What are the opportunities for coaching research in the next five years?

The following are the major gaps in the research that Lew Stern and I have identified:

- Definition of coaching – development of common definitions.
- Research into certain specialty areas (e.g. health and wellness, team coaching, internal coaching, leadership and executive coaching).
- The need to broaden out into organisational case studies, HR initiatives using coaching for middle management, senior executives, and team coaching, and other areas such as coaching in society, social responsibility, and coaching the underprivileged.
- Gap in the longitudinal studies examining trends and longer-term results of coaching.
- Measurement of independent and dependent variables which to date have focused solely on psychological or physical measures of individual clients rather than on systemic factors associated with the individual within their larger and complex environments.
- We need to study the basic questions: who is being coached, by whom and with what process, practices and results.
- Finally, the professional bodies could strongly promote practitioner research and practitioner case studies – as a way to start to address the gap of coaching research in organisations.

Three focus areas that are particularly critical for the professional development of coaching were found to be very under-served:

- *Coaching versus other helping professions*: It is important for coach and client to recognise when coaching is required versus other forms of support. We need to define coaching more clearly, so both know what's best for clients.
- *Business of coaching*: Which covers the professional development of coaching. This is very understudied and encompasses the work of the coaching bodies worldwide, i.e. the development of ethical codes, standards of competence and equivalent standards for coach education and training.
- *Coach education and training*: This needs more emphasis as it is woefully under-served. How should coaches be trained that will provide the most effective coaching practice, and best promote the professional development of coaching? (Stern and Stout-Rostron, 2013a:76–77).

What did we learn, and what do we recommend as a way forward?

Without a greater number of rigorous research projects, it will be difficult to generalise the results of specific studies, or to develop a clear, evidenced view of what coaching is, how coaching works, and for whom it works in what circumstances. What is clear is that "coaching" needs to be defined. Further, clinical trials are appropriate to test the effectiveness of various forms of coaching process, but are not appropriate to answer some key research questions which need to be addressed to promote the professionalisation of coaching, such as:

- How should best practice be defined in order to have the most impact?
- What are the most effective forms of education and training for coaches?

The following recommendations can be drawn from our study:

- More collaboration is needed amongst professional bodies worldwide to work together and to inspire and promote coaching research, and to share their findings at international conferences.
- For masters programmes worldwide in coaching, coaching psychology, leadership development and organisational development to focus on research into how coaching is being used in organisations and education / government institutions to develop talent.
- More peer-reviewed research to be encouraged through academic coach education programmes. The potential for coaching is wide.
- We need to encourage and study: coaching in society, social responsibility, health and wellness, and challenging situations and environments and geographic regions to empower people to help themselves.

Eric de Haan, Director of Ashridge's Centre for Coaching, and author of Relational Coaching, says that coaching research will only move forward when organisations are ready to pay for it, and when it begins to address how coaching is impacting behaviour change (de Haan *et al.*, 2010). The key question we need to research is: "What visibly is changing as a result of coaching in organisations, and what visibly needs to be addressed for business coaching to evolve?"

Practitioner research and reflective practice

The role of research is to determine the competences necessary to educate and develop coaches worldwide, and most importantly to create a definition of coaching that the global coaching community will accept. The new and innovative context worldwide is not just for academic researchers to contribute to relevant evidence-based practice, but also for coach practitioners to contribute to the development of self-reflective practice and practitioner research. In this way we may begin to move forward to being "professional".

The general characteristics of practitioner research are that:

- The research questions, aims and outcomes are determined by the practitioners themselves.
- The research is usually designed to have a benefit or an impact which is immediate and direct.
- It focuses on the professional's own practice and/or that of their immediate peers.
- It is small-scale and short-term.
- Usually it will be self-contained, and not part of a larger research programme.
- Data collection and management is typically carried out as a lone activity.
- It is one kind of "own-account research".
- The focus is not restricted. While it will commonly be evaluative, it may be descriptive, developmental or analytical (Shaw, 2003; cited in Fillery-Travis, 2009:5).

You can continually research your own practice, ultimately developing your own professional competence. David Peterson (2009), Director: Leadership and Coaching at Google, suggests simple ways to conduct your own practitioner research. For example, try different techniques in your coaching – e.g. with alternate clients, do a background interview that is only one-third of your normal interview; see what happens, and take notes on what you observe.

Secondly, you can generate a list of experimental ideas for your coaching from reading about new techniques, new types of questions or new processes. Try one new thing every coaching session and record your findings. Thirdly, you can ask your coaching participants: what was the most effective thing you (as coach) did in the session, and why was it helpful. Also ask what was the least effective thing, and why was it not helpful. Record your feedback, looking for patterns and substitute new processes for the least effective things. You can also participate in coaching research studies, or help to find participants from your own coaching practice to participate in studies. Most importantly, think critically about and read current coaching research, and try to incorporate findings into your own practice.

For the future, we need to promote our knowledge base through academic and practitioner coaching research. And if possible, collaborate to create a repository for coaching research that can be accessed by all shareholders. Although the Institute of Coaching at Harvard is strongly encouraging and financing coaching research, it is not proactively promoting what research is to be done. But all the professional bodies should reach out to practitioners, academics and cross-disciplinary groups. Secondly, the coaching bodies could strongly promote practitioner research and practitioner case studies as a way to start to address the lack of coaching research in organisations.

COACHING IN SOCIETY

According to both Lane (2013, pers. com.) and Drake (2013, pers. com.), if we are to move from strength to strength, our future lies in our ability to build a new professional model. Secondly, we need to develop mastery of practice within all coaching contexts and situations.

And as coaching becomes more a part of every manager, supervisor and leader's job description, mentoring will offer a complementary and powerful process for learning and development. Lise Lewis, EMCC President, says that the EMCC is looking at how to put the "M" more powerfully into the "EMCC" (Lewis, 2013, pers. com.). The mentoring process is often underestimated, and yet if it is grounded in the principle that people make the most progress when they are self-motivated, *autonomous*, can feel respect from others, and can take charge of their own learning journey – then a mentoring programme can run a twin track in organisations alongside coaching, inspiring opportunity for learning and development.

If we have a conviction as a budding profession that we have something to offer in terms of bringing out the best in people and in organisations, then perhaps our greater challenge is: "Does coaching also have a positive role to play in society as a whole?" Each country has its own challenges, and I don't think we can prescribe what the answer may be in any country. I can really only talk about South Africa, where I live and work. Due to South Africa's very fraught and unjust past, the question many of us are asking is: "Should coaching merely be limited to top executives of large corporations, many of whom are precisely the people who gained the most from an unjust past?"

Fortunately, in many organisations and institutions there is a realisation that the people who might gain the most from coaching are a little lower down the rung in the hierarchy with equal if not greater talents. And although deprived of education and opportunity in the past, with the aid of coaching and mentoring they can catch up on what had been kept from them before. That's a real contribution that coaching can make. In the USA, Lew Stern (2013, pers. com.) has a driving conviction that coaching has a mission to play in creating a just and more meaningful society.

So my last question is more philosophical, "How can we take coaching from inside organisations or institutions out into the wider community – in order to deal with major social concerns?" If coaching is to become part of every job description, keeping coaching limited to business is possibly preserving it in a narrow field – and doesn't fully reflect what this discipline is fully capable of offering society as a whole. If coaching can produce results for business, surely it can produce equally good results for the benefit of society and social wellbeing?

CONCLUSION – TO BE OR NOT TO BE A PROFESSION?

Coaching as a form of practice has been adopted worldwide in business, education and other fields, although recognition as a profession remains contentious, with different authorities taking differing views. Some options in this regard are summarised below.

If coaching is to emerge as a discipline with a professional future, a wide variety of difficult conversations needs to take place in international forums, and events hosted by professional bodies, where practitioners and stakeholders can share their expertise and work collaboratively together.

It has been recommended, as a result of the Global Convention on Coaching (GCC) process and the work done by the International Coaching Research Forum at Harvard (ICRF) and the Advisory Research Board at the Institute of Coaching at Harvard / McLean Medical School, that we need empirical evidence proving that coaching makes a difference for individuals, organisations, and society. Because there still remains a lack of clarity and consensus as to what professional coaching actually is, and what makes for an effective and reputable coach, it has been agreed that research needs to continue to be conducted around the globe.

And although it is an appropriate aim to strive for more "professionalism" in the field of coaching, some argue that it might not be in the best interests for practitioners and clients to follow the traditional route of becoming a "profession". It may be that coach practitioners need to think about different forms of "association"; all alternatives need to be thought about. Some options suggested by Lane, Stelter, and Stout-Rostron (2009) are that:

- Coaching could be an integrated, beneficial and useful enterprise in other professions.
- Because the concept of "profession" has changed, it may not be realistic for coaching to become a traditional profession.
- Using interdisciplinary efforts based on research and evidence-based practice, coaches can be "professionalised".
- Voluntary bodies in collaboration with coaching can begin to define new models of association that sit outside of traditional professions and retain the positives rather than the negatives of other professions.
- The various national and international coaching associations collaboratively pursue full professionalisation along traditional lines.

The role of research is to determine the competences necessary to educate and develop coaches worldwide, and most importantly to create a definition of coaching that the global coaching community will accept. The new and innovative context worldwide is not just for academic researchers to contribute to relevant evidence-based practice, but also for coach practitioners to contribute to the development of self-reflective practice and practitioner research. In this way we may begin to move forward to being "professional".

As you continue your journey through the next and last chapter of this book, I hope this question emerges as one worth pursuing for you as a practitioner, leader and within your professional body, and I hope that this chapter has left you with some fresh thoughts and new perspectives.

FURTHER READING

Standards Australia (2011). *Coaching in Organisations*. Draft handbook produced by Coaching Guideline Working Group HB41 of Standards Australia HR and Employment Committee MB 9. Sydney, NSW: Standards Australia.

De Haan, E., Bertie, C., Day, A., and Sills, C. (2010). Critical moments of clients and coaches: A direct-comparison study. *International Coaching Psychology Review*, 5(2):109–128.

Drake, D.B. (2007). The art of thinking narratively: Implications for coaching psychology and practice. *Australian Psychologist*, 42(4):283–294.

Global Coaching and Mentoring Alliance (GCMA) (2011). *The Professional Charter for Coaching and Mentoring*. Brussels: European Economic and Social Committee.

Lane, D.A., and Corrie, S. (2006). *The Modern Scientist-Practitioner: A guide to practice in psychology*. Hove: Routledge.

Stern, L.R., and Stout-Rostron, S. (2013a). What progress has been made in coaching research in relation to 16 ICRF focus areas from 2008 to 2012? *Coaching: An International Journal of Theory, Research and Practice*, 6(1):72–96.

Stern, L.R., and Stout-Rostron, S. (2013b). *Bibliography of Coaching Research Abstracts January 2011 – June 2012*. Research data compilation. Webpage: www.instituteofcoaching.org/index.cfm?page=resources. Belmont, MA: Institute of Coaching Professional Association.

Stern, L.R., and Stout-Rostron, S. (2013c). *Bibliography of Coaching Research: List of journal articles by focus area, date and author*. Research data compilation. Webpage: www.instituteofcoaching.org/index.cfm?page=resources. Belmont, MA: Institute of Coaching Professional Association.

Stern, L.R., and Stout-Rostron, S. (2013d). *Peer-reviewed journals which have published coaching research from January 2008 – June 2012*. Research data compilation. Webpage: www.instituteofcoaching.org/index.cfm?page=resources. Belmont, MA: Institute of Coaching Professional Association.

Stern, L.R., and Stout-Rostron, S. (2013e). *Bibliography of Coaching Research: List of dissertations by focus area, date and author*. Research data compilation. Webpage: www.instituteofcoaching.org/index.cfm?page=resources. Belmont, MA: Institute of Coaching Professional Association.

Worldwide Association of Business Coaches (WABC) (2013). *WABC Professional Standards for Business Coaches*. Webpage: www.wabccoaches.com/includes/popups/ professional_standards.html#preamble.

14

Epilogue – coaching for new leadership

WHAT ARE THE CHALLENGES FACING LEADERSHIP COACHING GLOBALLY?

To answer that question, we need to look at what impact coaching is having on systemic change within business, education and government. We also need to look at how coaching is being used to develop leaders who can build sustainable policies which can impact change systemically, in organisations, society and government.

Organisations today are challenged by the complexity and swiftness of change within business, social and political environments. Leaders are expected to quickly adapt their skills and competence in volatile and crisis-driven markets and societies. The inherent nature of leadership has changed, and we need altogether different expressions of leadership from those familiar to us. We must find new and novel ways of breaking out from our current mental models to make explicit interpretations of the past if we are to create realistic futures, rethinking, renewing and inspiring new possibilities.

This is why leadership and our role as coaches of leaders must focus more on greater capability and greater responsibility for them and for ourselves within all of our human institutions, organisations, communities and governments. We need to focus on strategic relevance: innovation, speed of learning, systemic viability and wellbeing.

In our increasingly complex, global and highly uncertain and forever changing business and social environments, we need to find new ways of "connecting", inspiring and liberating people, as well as their passions, imagination and intellect. Leadership and management coaching is a vital component of this journey. In the last few years, I completed a number of qualitative research projects using semi-structured interviews, including these three projects, to answer the following questions:

- How is coaching impacting systemic and cultural change within organisations? (Stout-Rostron, 2011a).
- What are the emerging trends in coaching for transformational leadership? (Stout-Rostron, 2011b).
- How does coaching positively impact organisational and societal change? (Stout-Rostron, 2011c).

These research studies included "stories" and "self-reflexive" inquiry from emerging global corporate thinkers, business school leaders, coach practitioners and academics who are using coaching to manage people in new ways, to develop innovative leaders in their business schools, or to introduce systemic coaching interventions within their client organisations.

I interviewed a range of corporate leaders, heads of business schools, coaching psychologists, and management consultants in a variety of regions and countries (USA, UK, Europe, Middle East, Asian Pacific, African continent, Near and Far East) and at various business schools (Bristol, Harvard, Berkeley, Sydney, Osnabrück).

The interview process was designed to find out how coaching is being used to develop leadership competences in the corporate, non-profit, educational and governmental sectors. The responses I received require us to think seriously about how we as practitioners, educationalists, business and political leaders can help develop the leadership needed for "a new emergent global reality". This new reality is not just a globalised workplace, but a newly "diversified" workplace driven by "sustainable values" such as: trust, integrity, bringing heart into relationships, health and work–life balance. There is an emerging consciousness of global issues; there's a need to effectively manage change and complexity and the desire of people to ensure their work makes a positive contribution to their communities (Stout-Rostron, 2011b).

Business drives the modern world, and is motivated by profit. One result is that we live longer, communicate faster, and have a supposed increased quality of life, and yet we are irreparably damaging our planet. Elizabeth Debold (2005) in the "Business of Saving the World" argues that the corporate juggernaut is so powerful, fuelled by survival and status needs, that altering its course seems impossible. However, another force is working within our corporations, not just the "human force" but the promise of "human community". The question is, how are we developing these communities with their potential for innovation and creativity?

- What are their values?
- What difference are they making in organisations?
- What difference are they making in communities and societies as a whole?

This is what our education and development of coaches needs to address, and that is what my various sets of interviews set to find out. The original purpose of my research was to ask how coaching is being used to build sustainable policies and systems, and more specifically how coaching is contributing to change globally within a visionary organisational context (Stout-Rostron, 2011a). As people look to their leaders worldwide for more accountability, integrity and authenticity, I have asked what impact coaching is having on systemic change within business, education and government, and specifically what is emerging in terms of developing sustainable accountable and responsible leadership.

Reflective exercise

- How are you helping your clients to think for themselves – individually and independently?
- In what way do you interfere or intervene or direct their thinking process?
- What needs to shift in you in order to facilitate change in them?

Leadership Coaching for Results: Cutting-edge practices for coach and client

According to Debold (2005), the infrastructure, hierarchical nature and ultimate aims of business, haven't moved away from the social inequalities plaguing societies round the world. Even leaders wanting to make a change at a systemic level in their organisations are fighting a machine that often gets the better of them. But something new is happening – multinationals have tightly globalised the workplace so we are rapidly experiencing a cross-pollination of cultures.

The world becomes more complex at an exponential rate, as new media develop in leaps and bounds and bring almost everything around the world – particularly in business – to our attention. To unravel all this complexity, which sometimes seems beyond our control, to make sense of it all and help us to see a credible, humane way forward, we need leaders that we can trust and follow. Above all, we need leaders with a fresh, new vision, based not on the old hierarchical, top-down authoritarianism, but on collaboration and inclusivity. This is the way to liberate creative individuals to think for themselves and produce new solutions.

HOW IS COACHING MAKING A DIFFERENCE IN ORGANISATIONS AND SOCIETY?

I asked each coaching leader to describe what drew them to their current work, and how they personally experience and use coaching in their work. They shared the differences they have seen as a result of their work, and what they would still like to see in terms of social and organisational change. What comes through clearly is a passionate belief in the potential and power that coaching can unleash. I have let them speak directly for themselves, their freshness, originality and enthusiasm share radical views on the potential of coaching for change.

Reflective exercise

- What are you assuming about yourself as a coach that motivates and inspires you?
- What are you assuming that gets in your way?
- What would be a more credible, liberating alternative that would take you the next step in your practice?

Lee Salmon: the entrepreneurial go-to place for executive coaching

Lee Salmon is recently retired as an executive coach and management consultant with the Federal Consulting Group of the US Department of the Interior in Washington, DC. He currently runs his own private practice, Learning for Living, and was until recently a member of the Board of Directors for the International Consortium for Coaching in Organisations (ICCO), a group of senior-level coaches who are committed to working in public and private organisations to have a positive impact.

"In the last ten years, I have created and built a coaching and consulting practice that serves all government agencies. We provide extraordinary coaches and consultants to help in personal and organisational transformation, having built a reputation as the 'go-to place' for executive coaching. Coaching has helped me to accomplish my particular personal goals – to affect the quality of leadership in the organisation, and be able to create a government that serves the needs of society.

"I have started working with other government agencies to help them develop coaching programmes for future leaders in their organisations. It's only now that we have the capability to provide coaching services from individual assignments, to full organisational and systemic coaching programmes that play an ongoing part of leadership and succession planning.

"We have had phenomenal results in terms of the impact and the way leaders show up, engage others, and have impact in their organisations. For example, in clearer communication, effectiveness in activity, partnering and reaching out to other organisations, and in the leaders' ability and capacity to be adaptable and flexible in times of crisis and change. There's something else. We realised the work we needed to do in changing these leaders and making them more effective was to build their emotional and social skills – with a strong focus on emotional intelligence, working in areas that relate to emotional effectiveness. We administer an EQ 360° Instrument at the very beginning of each coaching programme, using that to help guide the developmental work of our clients.

"What I would like to see, however, is more work with leaders around transition. It seems that not only are leaders willing to get used to change, but they live in a sea of constant change. All of them need to develop flexibility in their leadership style and competence, with the ability to adapt to a rapidly changing world. The big challenge is to get people to actually take part in the coaching intervention, and to integrate their learning into their existing leadership style. That sustainable long-term perspective on leadership is yet to be recognised by most organisations.

"We know change is constant, and that government leaders will continue to move from one crisis to another. This area of crisis leadership is coming to the fore. For social and emotional effectiveness, how can we build practices and capability to help leaders step up to these crises, to survive, thrive and lead organisations and people in times of extraordinary change? I believe that a new consciousness is emerging" (Stout-Rostron, 2011a; 2011c).

Nancy Kline: independent thinking to create societal change

Nancy Kline is President of Time to Think Inc., a leadership development company specialising in the Thinking Environment®. Time to Think is currently developing consultants, facilitators and coaches in the UK, USA, South Africa, Ireland, Sweden and Australia. Author of *Time to Think* (1999) and *More Time Think* (2009), Kline's Thinking Partnership® is based on the "chosen philosophical view that human beings are by nature good: intelligent, loving, powerful, multi-talented, emotional, assertive, able to think through anything, imaginative and logical".

For several years, I have been drawn to the work of Nancy Kline who consistently pursues the question: How can we help each other to think for ourselves? Kline advocates that an increasing awareness of what isn't working in human life and organisations can be traced to the conformity, inaccuracies and inhumanity of people's thinking. Her Thinking Environment® process has created coaching results widely in one-to-one relationships, in groups and in corporate cultures helping to create a world in which every human being knows they matter.

"I teach, coach, write about and research the Thinking Environment® – having been drawn to my work through one observation and one question. The observation, dry but chilling, is that the quality of everything we do depends on the quality of the *thinking* we do first. The question that arises from this observation is: 'How can we help each other to think *for ourselves* with rigour, imagination, courage and grace?' I think I became interested in this question when I was seven years old. My mother, a quiet, understated woman who never shouted at anyone, one day charged through the living room with her fist in the air shouting, 'There is no greater crime than the waste of a single human mind', then disappeared down the hall. I was mystified; but as children do, I stored that memory, filing it under 'I' for incomprehensible but immensely important.

"Ten years later when I was 17, I was sitting with my father going through his old papers. I picked one up, began to read it and then to cry; it was a speech he had delivered when *he* was 17, in which he called for complete equality for African Americans. That was in 1920 in Tennessee when black people were segregated from white people by law. I marvelled at his courage and asked, 'Dad, how did you ever get permission to deliver this speech? Weren't you scared?' He looked it over and said, 'Well, honey, I didn't ask for permission. I just asked myself the question, "What is the most important issue facing my generation?" I immediately knew the answer, so I asked myself another question: "If I weren't afraid, what would I say about that issue in my speech?" As I was delivering it at the graduation ceremony, about halfway through, I looked out at the audience of faculty, student body, parents, board of trustees – and noticed that they had all stood up and were walking out. As I stood there, looking out at the empty auditorium, I decided I needed to do only two things with my life. One: to keep thinking for myself, and two: not get killed.'

"Those are two of the earliest experiences of my being drawn to the importance of independent thinking. Over the years I decided somewhere inside of me that I would pursue the question, 'How can we help each other to think for ourselves?' I was also drawn to this work because of an increasing awareness that most of what wasn't working in human life and in organisations could probably be traced to the conformity, inaccuracies, and inhumanity of people's thinking. I wanted to contribute to a core level of change by seeing if independent thinking could make a difference. I soon found myself growing interested in organisational and societal transformation.

"My coaching sessions each week are vital to the development of my work. My coaching keeps me courageous, and it keeps me from getting lost in my fears or unwarranted reluctance to go to the cutting edge. It helps me to be less concerned about myself, and more focused on generating others' independent thought. It seems to me that at the heart of societal change is the resurgence of pride in our own group identities. As a female, a New Mexican, and a woman over 60, I think my coaching indirectly and sometimes directly helps me to be more of *myself*. This matters because we can think *for* ourselves only if we can think *as* ourselves. Finally, coaching is the key to my work because I think that it is only out of our own breakthroughs that we can offer a breakthrough process to others with confidence.

"From the beginning, my work has been motivated by a passion for a world that works beautifully for everyone. I would like to see a world in which every human being knows that they matter, that their thinking and their contributions are central to our success as a society, and a world in which every human being lives well. I would like to see a world of work in which people come home with a spring in their step because they have spent all day knowing that their thinking was valued. I would also like to see a world in which war is a thing we learn about only through our history books, a thing that seems an outrageous aberration of human activity. Many years ago I began to wonder what might be one change that could change everything else. I reasoned that because everything depends on the quality of the thinking we do first, creating structures in which people could think for themselves might have a chance of helping to bring about some significant, human changes in society.

"Certainly one of my greatest challenges has been sustaining a thinking environment in conflict. A key question is: how can we keep each other thinking well for ourselves when the message we are delivering is hard, and when it is born of anger or fear? How do we express difficult things so that the person can *keep thinking* while we are expressing it?

"I saw this challenge handled beautifully recently. One of the members of a team was feeling discriminated against by his colleagues. It had to do with his not being selected to deliver some of the work others were delivering. He wanted to understand the selection criteria and he was angry. He called together a teleconference of the team. He consciously created a thinking environment. He said, 'I would like to speak and say everything I want to say as if I am handing you the moon. And then I would like everyone to have a chance to speak as if you were handing me the moon.' And he did exactly that. He talked about the things that were upsetting him; his tone was loving, he was not urgent; no one interrupted; and at the end of the turn he felt different and more open to hearing what the others were saying. The others weren't feeling threatened by him, and they spoke calmly and intelligently. As we went round the circle, there was an accumulation of accurate information about how the people had been selected, information that hadn't been communicated during the selection process. He was satisfied with the criteria, and they decided that in the future they would communicate all criteria in particular ways, creating transparency to prevent the perception and the experience of marginalisation. At the end, this man spoke again, generating his freshest thinking which was useful to everyone; then everyone appreciated him, and he appreciated them. In my view, what took place in that 45 minutes probably prevented a year of misunderstanding" (Stout-Rostron, 2011a; 2011c).

Leadership Coaching for Results: Cutting-edge practices for coach and client

Mark Rittenberg: theatre practices to develop holistic, authentic leaders

Dr Mark Rittenberg has worked as an executive coach all over the world for the last 20 years. In addition to coaching leaders from Fortune 500 companies, he acts as Master Coach for consultants from the major US consulting firms, and has been instrumental in instituting organisational coaching programmes to grow emerging and aspiring leaders. An award-winning actor and director, he teaches at a number of business school faculties including the Kellogg School, Olin School of Business, and Haas School of Business of the University of California at Berkeley, where he is the designer and senior consultant for the Executive Coaching Institute. He divides his time between Berkeley and Johannesburg, South Africa, where he is an executive coach and designer of internal coaching programmes working with the new black leadership in several South African institutions.

His programmes coach leaders in the practices of Active Communicating®, which are based on Angeles Arrien's four principles: show up and choose to be present; pay attention to what has heart and meaning; tell the truth without blame or judgement; and be open to outcome, not attached to outcome.

The main challenge Rittenberg has had to overcome in his work is his own fear of being able to really help a leader who desperately wants to commit to personal change. The idea of taking a CEO and turning them into a "storyteller" when giving an annual report is usually taboo!

"I was drawn to my current work after having been an actor and theatre director for many years. In 1984, I won an award at the Jerusalem Festival for a play called *Life or Theatre*, and I was subsequently invited to direct it at Harvard University. I recast the play with a group of Harvard MBA students who shared with me that this was 'the most profound leadership development' they had ever experienced, despite their current MBA classes. Their request was that I facilitate similar theatre-based work with their peers and colleagues at the Harvard Business School – for them this work was about authentic leadership.

"When I asked what they liked about the work, they said that I was coaching them holistically, as an actor, in voice, body, and individual leadership. They said that, 'You're not afraid to go deep, yet somehow you create a safe space for each individual to find their own authentic, true voice. We have all changed as a result of this rehearsal process, and we believe that this work will greatly impact on leaders who want to motivate their work groups and become authentic, inspirational leaders.' From that moment in the mid-1980s, the theatre-based Active Communicating® work began. We coached several teams at Harvard Business School, and those already successful, final-year MBA students invited us into their companies to facilitate theatre-based workshops on the Art of Leadership Presence.

"As a result of the work that I'm doing, I want to see leaders who operate from the head and the heart, becoming more in touch with themselves and others. If more in touch with others, they are more tolerant, understanding that people have different work and learning styles – i.e. one size doesn't fit all. But what does it mean to embrace a variety of learning and leadership styles? One of the stories that springs to mind is an executive I coached for a number of years; he was a command-and-control leader in a large American multinational corporation.

"As a result of the coaching process he became an extraordinary visionary – an exceptional individual who could see and act on the future of his company. Although many people in his workforce were intelligent, diligent and hard-working individuals, they could not meet his high expectations. During the second year of the coaching relationship, he shared his concerns about succession planning, worrying that there was no one to take his place or that of the other vice-presidents.

"As one of his coaching goals was to pay attention to succession planning, we created a leadership institute within the company; he put his most aspiring leaders through an intensive, high-level leadership development programme to give them the skills and competence to become 'leaders of tomorrow'. I made an observation that what was missing was his 'relationship' with those leaders, even though he had created the programme. To open the Institute's first morning, I asked him and the other seven vice-presidents serving as faculty to create their individual leadership story and share it with the audience. The stories were to illustrate how they became the leaders they are today. He exclaimed, 'I don't have a leadership story; I don't even know what I want to say'. I suggested, 'Why don't you speak about the events in your early life that really touched and challenged you? I think that should be the context of your leadership story'.

"He resisted for a long, long time. On the opening day he told his story: 'I am not a storyteller and so will have to share my story with you in three sentences. My father died when I was six, and from that moment my mother had to go out each night, after her day job, to work in the wealthy homes of people who lived in the next neighbourhood. She cleaned their houses every evening to provide school uniforms for myself and my five brothers. My mother will be 89 next month and she remains my greatest hero.' The entire room dissolved in tears. The barrier that had always been between him, his direct reports and the entire workforce disintegrated. From the moment he told his story, the leadership team began to rise to the occasion as he had wanted them to. Somehow previously they had been too intimidated or too frightened to do so. Everything he wanted began to happen. And the reason was because he too had begun to show his vulnerability.

"Leaders move away from traditional corporate stereotypical roles when they get in touch with what people want to hear, and with what really motivates and inspires them. I have seen such miracles happen by not being afraid myself, helping a leader to open their own creative possibilities through storytelling. This means encouraging leaders to talk about their failures and challenges through their own stories" (Stout-Rostron, 2011a; 2011c).

Lew Stern: positively influencing leadership for global sustainability

Dr Lew Stern is President of Stern Consulting and Founding Executive Director of the Foundation for International Leadership Coaching. Lew is a licensed psychologist in Massachusetts, and since 1977 has served as a leader, executive and leadership coach, and consulting psychologist. Lew has coached and consulted to senior leaders of private- and public-sector organisations around the world. He serves as Senior Advisor to the Institute of Coaching at McLean Hospital, Harvard Medical School and has a faculty appointment as Clinical Instructor at Harvard Medical School.

Lew insists that the Foundation's mission is most important right now, to have an impact so that leadership coaching can change the future of our world. "I feel passionately that our world is headed in the wrong direction, and that government and NGO leaders are in control of funds, policies and resources that, if shifted, coaching could positively influence global sustainability, for the environment, international peace, and worldwide quality of life. I believe coaching can positively influence our world leaders and their impact on our future.

"However, most coaches aren't hitting that. Instead, they are helping large corporations make more money to improve the lives of the people working in those organisations, but they are not making a difference to our global society. What's drawing me to it? I'm a grown-up hippie; a pacifist; an environmentalist. What I hope to do now is help bring the world's leading coaches together to build the leadership capacity of international leaders and ultimately to shift the direction of our planet. Coaching has changed my whole outlook on life, on my profession and on my place in the world.

"Almost everyone I speak to, including coaches, teachers, leaders, and individuals from many different perspectives, see the need to build international leadership capability. All view the potential of positive psychology and coaching as having the capacity to build leaders who can build the future of our world. I am told leadership stories from day to day and am asked, 'What can we do?' Many organisations have similar exciting missions in different parts of the world. Some focus on organisation development, another takes coaching to third world villages; others work with leadership development for government leaders; others bring leaders together across international boundaries – e.g. the Centre for Creative Leadership (CCL) and their Leadership Beyond Boundaries Programme. There are many different voices. For example: The Coach Initiative, The Coaches Alliance for Social Action, Coaching in Philanthropy Project, Coaching Beyond Boundaries, Coaching for a Cause, Coaching the Global Village, the Global Coaching Community; there is a separate Group for Societal Change; the Mirus Coaching for Social Change; International Coach Federation who offer *pro bono* grants for coaching and education; Root Cause, the Kennedy School of Leadership; the Clinton Foundation who send coaches to Ethiopia to work on Aids; Mexican ICF: Social Initiative for Social Change.

"There are many organisations trying to build world leaders in their own way. We are collaborating, reaching out to as many organisations as possible to leverage each other's resources" (Stout-Rostron, 2011c).

Marilyn Johnson: coaching for leadership and community awareness

Marilyn Johnson, an African American born in Tennessee, USA has 30 years of corporate experience and recently retired as General Manager for Africa for Cummins Filtration Africa. Her high energy and results-oriented focus has helped her experience and learn how to live and work in a wide range of African cultures. Her strategic and tactical know-how lends itself to the development and implementation of wide-scale organisational change initiatives while successfully managing to achieve business objectives.

"Coaching has helped to keep me grounded; it allows me to step back and think strategically and in a focused manner to accomplish my goals. Specifically coaching has helped me get to the end game by giving me different perspectives on how to manage the business. But for me coaching is not just about work: it's about my overall being and ensuring positive results when making tough decisions. It allows me to look at things from a different viewpoint and stretches me mentally. Coaching is also a good networking opportunity; it broadens my capacity to reach further when making career decisions.

"Before coming to South Africa, my line manager convinced me that she recognised what she thought were natural abilities to become a General Manager. The position has given me an opportunity to experience all facets of the business, from sales to finance, manufacturing, operations and logistics, as well as involvement with the key parameters, particularly human relations, that make Cummins Filtration a successful business.

"The opportunity to work in Africa meant stepping into the role of an expatriate; living and working in a new country, and experiencing and learning a wide range of African cultures. This experience has given me the opportunity to contribute and to make a difference. I want to leave a legacy, so that the generations to come will benefit from some of the work that I and my team have contributed to the continent in my role as General Manager. Some of the key corporate social responsibility initiatives that my team and I have led, and consider rewarding for the organisation and the local communities are:

- Building a Habitat for Humanity home in Pietermaritzburg.
- Building the Masakhane crèche, a crèche for young children born to parents with HIV/AIDS.
- Awarding a significant contribution to the SOS Children's Village in Pietermaritzburg.
- Leading a committee to secure a Cummins Foundation grant of $325 000 for the Ithemba Institute of Technology in Soweto (for high school grades 10–12; learnerships and skills training programmes for unemployed youths and young adults; and trade courses for adults in mechanics, computer science and welding).

"I use coaching and mentoring with my direct reports. When I recognise my managers may be going off track, I step in to coach them back on track. I use different approaches, from one-on-one mentoring-type conversations to offer guidance, or exposing them to different views through team coaching. My intention is always to use coaching to help my staff become better managers and leaders. I also use coaching for goal setting, and to manage my expectations of them, helping them to think through processes through questions and discussion.

"I even coach my customers! I believe the success of my customers depends upon the relationship they have with us at Cummins. In Africa, the business practices are quite different from those used in the United States. I've spent a lot of time transferring processes and skills to my customers, e.g. providing marketing support and participating in joint marketing campaigns, making observations to help their business, engaging them in leadership development opportunities so that they can better develop their staff. We have hosted business / sales conferences that are phenomenal in educating customers, not only on our product line but also on sales techniques. Sharing best practices has helped customers develop their team. The positive results are shown through customer loyalty.

"As a result of my work, the differences that I would like to see are success in managing conflict and diversity issues. For example, because of persisting racial division, difference and conflict within the management team, I brought in a facilitator to work with the managers, and also brought the shop floor employees and the managers together. I used team coaching to help them to understand each other as individuals. The result was to help them to understand each other, because they were simply working in silos. They discovered that 'We've got something in common; I can talk to you, and you aren't going to bite my head off'. It raised self-awareness, and now they are working together more as a team; managers are getting input from shop floor people when decisions are to be made, and shop floor employees are more willing to participate. They built self-esteem and grew their interpersonal skills – so coaching helped both the organisation in terms of performance, and the individual from an interpersonal development point of view".

Johnson says coaching helped her overcome her fear factor, stepping into a General Manager role in Africa. She used a coaching approach to help each of her managers to share experiences, challenges and best practice, stepping into their own ability to think and lead (Stout-Rostron, 2011c).

Nonkqubela Maliza: driving the transformation agenda

Nonkqubela Maliza says that her work as Director for Corporate and Government affairs for Volkswagen South Africa (VWSA) is to advance corporate objectives and priorities while enhancing and promoting relationships at all levels of government and in the community. She drives the transformation agenda, the Black Economic Empowerment (BEE) codes, company strategy and the transformation budget. She champions stakeholder engagement for corporate affairs and social investment.

"VWSA is known to be the best at what it does, and I wanted to work with the best in the big league. It's very meaningful work as it's about transformation, which is of crucial importance to the nation and the company. I'm drawn to the work of corporate social investment as a contribution to development, and the transformation agenda serves national priorities and national objectives. It is about development rather than charity, and is a strong way of contributing to development in communities that are underdeveloped. There is the potential to do meaningful work that can leave a positive change legacy and a development legacy.

"Coaching has helped me to feel more self-confident, and has helped me to be more competent in going about my work. I have tried to use coaching with my stakeholders and my team, as well as in my other roles chairing various boards and steering committees. I am drawn to creating a thinking environment, creating an empowering environment where people's thoughts and problem-solving skills are honoured and encouraged. This makes the teams more effective, and makes the work more joyful and qualitatively better. That people's minds are ignited, that is my goal.

"My story is a mentoring story, and to simply encourage people to think for themselves. We have started a mentoring programme in Midrand, and are about to set one up in the Eastern Cape, in our own plant. This is inspiring, as people feel they are making a personal contribution. I love the flyer which said, 'You give nothing when you give your possessions; when you give of yourself that is when you truly give'. With mentoring you can make a difference to someone's life. There are a couple of challenges in the social development space. I manage VWSA's Community Trust; but you have to walk with the community – they must own the process so that they can drive it. I don't live in their community, they do. We need to get the community to own the projects so that they can drive them and lobby and help them to grow and grow and grow.

"One of the projects in Uitenhage is to build an early childhood centre, a preschool for very young children in that community. Employees have been giving the equivalent of one hour of their monthly wages for the project for the past three years. We are using these people's money for the project, which we call 'One Hour for the Future'. They have a vested interest in the project and are supportive and proud of it. For this project we have partnered with local government, who gave us the land for free. We are setting up a world-class infrastructure, including environmentally-friendly aspects such as solar power for heating and insulation, because in South Africa access to electricity is an issue. My learning is to work alongside the community and have them take an active part in the project" (Stout-Rostron, 2011c).

Reflective exercise

What story can you share with a fellow coach, client, direct report or colleague that would inspire or motivate them to take whatever next step they need to take in their personal, and/or professional development?

Shani Naidoo: coaching and social networking

Shani Naidoo is Managing Director HR and Managing Director At Home for The Foschini Group in South Africa. She has spent the last 20 years in human resources practice. She is known for her well-developed technical expertise in Human Resources, her vision in developing world-class solutions and pursuing a sound understanding of the business she works in to deliver these solutions. As a senior Industrial Psychologist, she mentors psychology internship candidates and continually pushes the boundaries of HR practice in business. Not willing to wait and see what business requires, her motto is to predict and develop solutions before it is needed in business.

"My work is to develop the best people solutions in support of the business achieving its goals. These people solutions involve the entire human value chain in the organisation, and my job is to optimise, research and diagnose the business issues as they relate to people, finding solutions that are business and people appropriate. What drew me to this work is its complexity. There is more than just one business unit, and there are quite distinct cultural attributes, even a different DNA within individual business units. When I arrived, these business units were quite disparate, and one of my roles has been to realign them. Retail is a fast moving, dynamic, people-focused business, and because Human Resources is a critical and strategic function in Foschini, I wanted to work in an organisation where people are important.

"Coaching has helped me as an individual leader to think and diagnose without emotion, to talk something through, to see the wood for the trees, to create space in my mind to see the picture clearly. Through working with a coach, I have been able to develop distance and perspective and improve my decision making as a result.

"In my work, coaching has helped me to improve individual and company acceleration towards a goal. For example, coaching has helped individual executives find solutions quickly, and coaching has helped individual executives when they have been stuck – helping them think something through, finding a solution. Sometimes coaching has resulted in clear change and achievement of an individual's objectives. Coaching has also been used for longer term interventions to grow and develop an individual's certain weaker attributes, as well as to assist them in improving and building new relationships. I think coaching has even helped our leadership to appreciate the value of coaching; it has helped our very senior executives develop a greater awareness of the nexus between individuals and the achievement of business objectives.

"The differences that I would like to see as a result of coaching is collaboration, particularly greater collaboration between silos. There has been social change between business units who previously worked very separately. But now we have chat rooms where individuals in Foschini get together across business functions and units to develop relationships and business solutions. This is due to the need for change processes to be bedded down quickly. We are currently experiencing an economic slowdown, and we need to identify what processes require improvement, which requires people to work across functions and to create new processes. Change in itself is requiring us to change our practices.

"The other area that is still new for me is social networking. Facebook and Twitter have affected how our business operates internally and externally, and is changing the social interaction of our employees and with our customers. If you want to interact with people on Facebook, it can be in real time; people respond and make comments on your wall, and this is definitely starting to filter into our business! We will post a business problem and it can be debated and blogged using social networking technology. We will soon be trialling that technology with my performance management tool. Having developed a paper-based tool in the last few years, we will use some of the aspects of social networking to optimise performance management in our business. Social networking is changing how we engage, communicate and tell stories inside the organisation" (Stout-Rostron, 2011c).

EMERGENT TRANSFORMATIONAL LEADERSHIP

As coaching gains momentum at both practitioner and academic level, two key questions being asked are "Can coaching help; and if so, what are the trends suggesting that it can?" I posed these and related questions to business leaders, coaching consultants, researchers and academics, and coaching, HR and OD practitioners around the world. The interview process was designed to find out how coaching is being used to develop leadership competences in the corporate, non-profit, educational, and governmental sectors (Stout-Rostron, 2011b).

Our new reality is not just a globalised workplace, but a newly diversified workplace driven by sustainable values (such as trust, integrity, bringing heart into relationships, health and work–life balance, and making a difference), an emerging consciousness of global issues, a need to effectively manage change and complexity, and the desire of people to ensure that their work makes a positive contribution to the community. But are we actually consciously developing the talent and potential of our human communities, and creating a new level of consciousness that will help us to work together with less conflict, and develop the ability to care for our fragile planet (Stout-Rostron, 2011b)?

We need a new vision, a new way of working and a new way of thinking, and a new level of trust to run organisations in the private, public and non-profit sectors. Coaching is a critical means of support which can assist leaders to chart the way forward for their organisations, and pioneer a new way of working (Stout-Rostron, 2011b). But it requires a *seismic shift* in how leaders "be" leaders, and how they inspire leadership in others.

The range of leaders interviewed is as broad as the number of countries in which coaching is developing. Common themes have emerged from this study that help us understand what coaching has achieved in developing people, improving performance, managing organisational change, and making a positive impact on local communities. What stands out from these themes are strong reflections on:

- how coaching is currently being used;
- current trends in coaching; and
- the importance of systemic change for transformation to occur (Stout-Rostron, 2011b).

Annette Fillery-Travis: facilitators of learning and the third sector

Dr Annette Fillery-Travis is the Director of Programmes for coaching research at the University of Middlesex London. She looks after the research advisors, and the research done by the masters and the doctoral candidates round the world. Fillery-Travis explains that her perspective is as a coach educator looking at coaching research and identifying what is having impact: "For me, the dilemma inside my own organisation is helping to make our advisors facilitators of learning."

She sees her main job as developing leadership competence and human development. "We have to add more value than a classic academic institution. Our candidates are change agents for any of the professions they find themselves within. I'm talking to one of my candidates at the moment who develops boards for the National Health Service (NHS). Her entire perspective is looking at the development of these boards in terms of governance. But, in her doctoral research, she is looking at how can we go further than that and identify how the good work of the boards impacts on the organisation; what is the consequence for those boards and the health trusts they lead? Her impact is across the entire NHS, which is huge! The NHS is the biggest employer in the country; that is enormous and it impacts on every single one of us." Fillery-Travis has a large role to play; she is developing coaching through research, developing coaches, and developing the practitioner research base (Stout-Rostron, 2011b).

Fillery-Travis also talks about coaching work in the *third sector* that is having impact. "For *pro bono* I'm talking about coaching in schools, and coaching with young offenders. At the Institute for Work-Based Studies at Middlesex University London, we're working extensively in the third sector, i.e. with social entrepreneurs, charities and NGOs; we have a sense that coaching speaks to their values and belief systems. It is obviously useful when working with volunteers, and we are seeing a huge amount of effort in that arena. I'm interested in the research side as it's under-reported. The third sector has changed as a result of coaching because it empowers the volunteers and has brought on social entrepreneurs" (Stout-Rostron, 2011b).

Italia Boninelli: global mining and its impact on communities and society

When I asked Italia Boninelli, then Senior Vice-President: Human Resources of Gold Fields of South Africa Ltd, and the Chairperson of the Gold Fields Leadership and Business Academy, how Gold Fields has used coaching to develop leadership competence and human development, we looked at the layers of leadership development within the organisation. "Executive coaches help people to confront their personal limitations, understand their risk preferences and leadership styles, and enable them to make the transition to being a real leader, and not just a manager. The organisation applies coaching as a structured development intervention on two levels." The first is that coaching is seen as "a key driver of leadership development in a highly structured but progressive programme for high-potential and future leaders of the organisation", and secondly, coaching is seen "as a highly individualised process for senior and executive leaders" (Stout-Rostron, 2011b; 2011c).

Coaching has only been utilised in a formal fashion within the organisation in the last three years. It is predominantly applied in leadership development and in helping senior staff transition to new roles or to adjust their personal styles. Increasingly it is being used to accelerate the development of emerging talent in the senior talent pools. Lower down in the organisation, it is positioned as a premium solution – and is seen as aspirational to candidates (Stout-Rostron, 2011b).

As Boninelli explains it, the "key to the values is not so much the particular choice of words (many organisations share similar values) but in the living of the values. The organisation recognises the importance and role that values should play as a strategic driver and in the day-to-day operations. The values also inform the language used by the company, providing a specific meaning to how each employee thinks and behaves in the organisation." Her final comment is about congruence in terms of living with the values and their relation to coaching to develop people. "As the Head of HR, but also as an executive of the Company, the internal journey around values is as important to my effectiveness as any of the technical skills that I bring to the job. It is only when I am acting in congruence with my personal values and those of the company that difficult decisions will resolve themselves in the best interests of all." When she speaks about coaching and its role in helping the executive with their internal journey, and particularly around values, it is important to recognise "incongruence between personal values and organisational values" and bring them "to the fore and address them constructively" (Stout-Rostron, 2011b).

Daniel Doherty: coaching research to understand organisational and economic shifts

Dr Daniel Doherty is MSc Programme Director in Strategic Management, at the school of Economics, Finance and Management at Bristol University. He is also Chair of the University's Critical Coaching Research Unit, a research network he developed to build an awareness of the need for coaching and practitioner research. "The community we serve is a mixture of coaching practitioners, academics, commissioners of coaching and coaching clients, although increasingly the preponderance of people coming along are practitioners. It's been running for four years and is becoming a practitioner-research community in its own right." When originally set up, the commissioners of research were more involved. These are the HR directors, CEOs or divisional directors inside the organisations who said that they needed "systemic coaching input, or we need to create a coaching culture, or we have senior managers to be coached".

When I asked Doherty about the values this coaching research community is working to, he explained that it is to take a research approach to coaching. "We were noticing a coaching contagion taking off in Europe, and much of it with benefit statements that weren't researched. We noticed that coaching may have been falling into a 'fashion area', and so we asked, 'What is really going on here? What happens when coaching is launched in an organisation?' The other was to take a critical approach to question the extent to which coaching was used as a tool for managerial-ism, as opposed to a means of personal empowerment, career development and life development. We had a hunch that coaching was being appropriated to become another tool of managerial-ism."

According to Doherty, managerialism is the Trojan Horse of personal development, i.e. come and do some coaching, it's good for you. "The managerial-ism is that, 'We will manage your performance through coaching and you will be complicit in setting the standards that you will work towards, and you have little option in that'. So we put in the word 'critical', and called ourselves the 'Critical Coaching Research Unit'. We would take a critical view of what was occurring, not immediately trusting what was said, but sceptical of what was happening, and get others to stand back and take a more critical view of what was occurring. I think those values and beliefs are really important – if anyone comes along to that community with a view to marketing and selling, they are quickly ejected! We are here to examine our own practice, and the values and beliefs that govern our practice. At times it is painful to examine what they do, but it is important to take a good look inside of themselves and at their work" (Stout-Rostron, 2011b).

Nick Craig and Carol Kauffman: heirs apparent taking a deep dive

Two dynamic and pioneering leaders in the field of authentic leadership, whose programmes are strongly integrated with coaching, are Nick Craig, Head of the Authentic Leadership Institute (ALI) based at Harvard, and Carol Kauffman, Assistant Professor of Psychology and Head of the Institute of Coaching based at Harvard / McLean Medical School. The following is a brief extract of a three-way dialogue between myself, Kauffman and Craig.

- *Craig*: "The programmes that we do as leaders, we've gotten them to the place in a couple days where they can go to an extremely deep place, which would take six months to a year coaching. Clarity, transparency, getting the ego out of the room, getting into their deepest voice of wisdom; and it's in the process of doing it that they help each other get there. For each group of six, there is a coach on the journey who is with them for three to four days. They tell stories they have never told anyone in their life ... On the programme with a $40 billion multinational (whose brand name must remain confidential), their 360s helped them to come up with their plan for their career. They have already met with their boss; meeting them as they come into the programme, and getting a sense of where they are leading them through this journey which is as deep as anything they have ever gone on. These are not people who said they wanted coaching; they have been identified as potential 'heirs apparent'; their future within somewhere between two to five years of being the two-to-five top people in a multibillion dollar company. By the time these two days are over, these people are treating us ... as if it is after a year of coaching. So what happens after that? We now know everything about them, and where all the heavy interesting juicy stuff is. And from there, the coaching for those who continue is the *deep dive* into the underlying piece of work to be worked on. We do this within a couple of months, and that normally takes one to two years in coaching. The model dramatically accelerates getting to the really good stuff; as coaches we know that there are layers of what you do, and you know when you get to the powerful transformational conversation.

We will have had that conversation over the two to four days of the programme."

- *Kauffman:* "Before the programme they get a 360 that most people never see. It's incredible feedback; these are the toughest 360s you've ever seen. ... The key thing is that we also read articles about authentic leadership and true north – they share their ·*crucible* stories, i.e. who they really are. And their crucible stories are where they have been in the fire, and learned their most powerful stories in their lives. These people bond when they tell their crucible stories and their *strength's* stories. They know they are handpicked; they have written out two of their crucible stories, and in their first day we do these intense coaching sessions. They have a powerful transformative experience in that first session, and say that, 'It would be worth it if I had to leave now'."

- *Craig:* "That starts it, with this cascade, and it goes further throughout the week. And really important, and all of that deep dive stuff is linked back into their work performance, their development plan, not deep into their personal space. First you figure out your purpose in life, and then link it back up to your goals and performance in the organisation. It's very powerful and intense. You share the best or the worst experiences of your life, and how did you learn, how can you best metabolise those and learn. They dive into purpose and link it back into the organisation. It is a great experience. We spent four years of getting this to the point that this programme just sings; most groups are multinational groups of people, a minority are Americans."

As Craig and Kauffman express the passion and exhilaration of working in a deep-dive, five-week advanced management programme, with large multinationals, Craig explains that this type of intervention really works cross-culturally. This is because it is a well-developed model which dramatically accelerates the journey for groups of executives, while integrating coaching with other learning processes. The programme includes different levels of intervention, such as professors from Harvard Business School coming in and additionally teaching through the case method. "We're doing the first year MBAs at MIT, and the second year MBAs at Harvard, and at Wharton we do the Executive Education programmes. This is the best thing we have ever done; we have pulled together the magic of world-class coaching. I'm talking about world-class delivery that helps people to go really deep" (Stout-Rostron, 2011a; 2011b).

Mark Broadbent: opening up emotional intelligence

From an individual and personal standpoint, in October 2009, Mark Broadbent started an international consulting business with a focus on the USA, South Africa, Abu Dhabi and Saudi Arabia. He says "I am harnessing in my 'university of life' experience because I don't have an MBA. I have spent the last 14 years in business management and business development, running large companies with a lot of time spent in sales and marketing. I am in a very fortunate position and have hands-on experience in multinational companies. That's where the coaching side of it came in, with WACO International; that's where I got exposed to coaching and leadership."

I asked him how he has personally used coaching to develop his own leadership competence and ability to manage change, and how his organisation had used coaching to develop leadership competence and human development. "I'm going to focus on SGB-Cape WACO Africa, the business where I ended up working for five years before leaving to go to the US. This is where I was exposed to coaching, and it changed my whole career outlook and was a turning point for me. The company invested in a 360º evaluation. We did a full 360, and got our subordinates, peers and supervisors to evaluate us to identify areas of strengths, areas lacking, and blind spots. Blind spots I considered very important as they had ceased to be strengths. Then we did some further investment in bringing on board a coach for which the MD took a lot of flak from the WACO International board. Once you've done a 360, you focus on making your strengths stronger, and try to turn weaknesses into strengths. If we knew how to do it we would have done it a long time ago. 70 per cent of what was in there we already knew, but we didn't know how to make strengths stronger. We brought an executive coach on board for 18 months, and it was a very hands-on process. Investment in the 360, a hands-on trained professional coach, and regular one-on-one coaching sessions once a month. If we needed more we could call for more. Lots of it was tailored around our challenges on the job, how to tackle certain situations, almost on-the-job training."

Broadbent insists that "coaching forced me to confront my weaknesses, my blind spots and my strengths. My natural leadership style is participative and visionary, but it can be a weakness depending on the situation at hand. I needed more of an affirmative leadership style which I would unknowingly shy away from. ... Blind spots, they forced me to confront these weaknesses. Now that I understood my weaknesses, I developed self-awareness, and could focus on self-management, and I needed help with that. My coach played a critical part – working on the job with him I learned to manage my strengths and to focus on my weaknesses, and to push them up. In some situations you need to be more visionary and less an affirmative leader, and *vice versa*. It also changed the way I looked at things; I became less reactive and more focused on emotional intelligence. I started listening more, keeping quiet and reflective, and asked value-added questions – and confirming and reassuring people which I never did before. 'So what you are saying is ...' where usually I've already come to the conclusion; it opened up a new aspect to emotional intelligence. I had more compassion and could put myself in a situation with the other person" (Stout-Rostron, 2011b).

Garth Towell: what is required for transformational leaders?

For each of those interviewed in this study, I asked what are the values and beliefs which inform your work, and how do they relate to coaching.

Garth Towell, Managing Director of Kimberly-Clark, South Africa said that his company has embraced a step into executive coaching, but embedded with the values they firmly believe in and try to live. "I am leading a medium-to-large-size organisation with 850 employees, and lead through a combination of values and beliefs. I think KC has always lived certain values, and coupled with certain behaviours, they have served this 137-year-old organisation well throughout the world. When faced with tough decisions and when faced with opportunities, you call upon one of the four values that we profess and that we live to: authenticity, accountability, caring (caring for colleagues and for the community, caring for your work and your company) and innovation. Innovation is not limited to product innovation; it encompasses a set of behaviours and actions we want to encourage. I am viewed, rightly or wrongly, as needing to be the role model in this business. Besides living our values, there are three other behaviours that we want to encourage: diversity and inclusion, passion to win and putting the company and the consumer first. This is what informs me on a day-to-day basis on how to lead this company effectively.

"One of the best decisions I have made was to undergo a coaching intervention myself. The reason was two-fold. First, there is no doubt every leader has areas that need introspection and development. We had these high-potentials on this programme and I heard about some problems; so, I said that I wanted first-hand experience of this. It has been a fascinating learning for the last 18 months; I have had feedback from my team and my wife, and it has had a significant impact on the way I work. I am seeing the needle shift, based on feedback from my executives and deputies, and seeing those behaviours rubbing off on others. The amount of work that I have to do in this (coaching) relationship and the chemistry with the coach cannot be emphasised enough. You cannot leave everything up to the coach, you need to be taking the lead. What you put in, you get out. This is not a mentoring relationship which is win–win. This is a coaching relationship and it is about competency development and your own personal development."

Towell explains that, as MD "your behaviour is impacting others, and therefore the coaching contract started with a very specific brief. But it has transcended that. The coaching relationship is no longer focused on the original brief; things have evolved naturally. And what I am finding now is that, where the coaching was initially looking at personal leadership styles, service, my individual shortcomings and potential pitfalls, we are now starting to talk about business leadership – 'transformational leadership' – and what is required of transformational leaders. It has come about quite naturally and is enriching. That is the kind of space I need to be creating" (Stout-Rostron, 2011a; 2011b).

Siegfried Greif: building a trusting relationship

Siegfried Greif, based at the University of Osnabrück in Germany, talks about trust in the leader based on the findings from their global research study. Greif is one of the mentors of German coaching theory and research. He has supported and developed coaching as a practitioner and a researcher since the 1970s. Professor Greif is currently managing director of a consulting institute and associate of a consulting company, having been a full professor at the Free University of Berlin and the University of Osnabrück. Greif integrates practical knowledge assessed through interviews of practitioners at all organisational levels globally, on their expertise on the success and failure of change management and coaching.

Based on a global research study conducted in seven different countries, the most important finding in all these countries, from all of the questionnaires and interviews conducted, was the crucial importance of being able "to trust in the information of the leader". In other words, do the employees trust or mistrust the leader, and what is the impact?

According to Greif's research, coaching has an important role to play in this field. He says that, if the leader isn't trusted, "change this person, and find someone who is trusted. Build on trust and build a trusting relationship. This is a core variable of transformational and authentic leadership". Greif advocates that coaching is a primary way to analyse trust. "If changes are never completely predictable, and there is always uncertainty, you must trust someone who gives you information" (Stout-Rostron, 2011b).

It is thus clear that moving from a first generation to a second generation of coaches requires tougher supervision, higher expectations of professionalism, an alignment with organisational and individual values, and a broader range of experience and expertise within the field of coaching and research. This means that the practitioners themselves need to devote time to their own professional development, being coached and supervised themselves, but also that practitioners begin to pioneer the way forward, stepping into their own sense of authentic leadership and personal transformation. Only in that way will they be able to impact the development and direction of this emergent and transformational discipline (Stout-Rostron, 2011b).

Mark Rittenberg: coaching civil disobedience

Mark Rittenberg of Corporate Scenes says that for years, "I've had a curious relationship with those in very senior leadership positions; often they insist that the leaders and the teams are not ready to work on building relationships, becoming powerful communicators, or engaging in building trust through partnership and collaboration. Often, building trust is not even on the radar screen of work to be done with leaders.

"Although I haven't committed these acts of 'civil disobedience' deliberately, when I conduct a leadership study I ask the sponsor, 'If you were his coach what would you be working on?' Or, 'What are the three things as a workplace community that you would like to become in the next year?' I hear things like, 'We need to be better communicators and partners in the building process, able to understand what makes each other tick. We've never had time to build relationships with each other. In addition, we'd like our leaders to communicate with us, to let us know what is happening, and what challenges lie ahead that keep the leadership awake at night'. Internal communication between leader and staff continues to rank as the loudest 'positive change' employees want to see in their workplace" (Stout-Rostron, 2011c).

It is still a radical thought to encourage people to think for themselves in organisations and institutions, and it seems that coaching is pioneering this "civil disobedience". The impact of coaching is far wider reaching than any of us have yet to realise. As the fields of coaching, coaching psychology, and internal coaching in organisations grow, we will begin to see the results of these "inspiring conversations" which just may begin to change the way in which we perceive and manage our world (Stout-Rostron, 2011c). But there's more.

Richard Hames: leadership consciousness and domains of learning

Richard Hames of The Constellation believes that leadership can best be explained by taking into account the level of consciousness of the leader. In undertaking research over a period of ten years for his book *The Five Literacies of Global Leadership* (2007), Hames is convinced that our fixation on leadership competences is, at best, a peculiarly occidental distraction and, at worst, confusingly irrelevant.

"While management is clearly about discrete skills, processes, and methods employed consistently within the context of organising, leadership has become more of a collective phenomenon applied within a specific social context. Talking about leadership 'performance' or leadership 'competencies', as if it were merely a discipline that can be learned in a workshop, betrays a shocking naiveté vis-à-vis the dynamically complex nature of leadership today."

Hames argues that most orthodox beliefs about leadership, which assume that "leading" is an advanced or more sophisticated form of management, are flawed, misleading and ultimately nonsensical in terms of contemporary realities and the consequent task of leading. He contends that if leadership competences do exist (and not merely as outworn clichés in lieu of a more precise term), they manifest within shifting domains of learning which comprise yet-to-be-embodied knowledge. He refers to these domains of learning as "literacies".

Quite controversially, Hames maintains that a far more intelligent expression of contemporary leadership is to be had by discarding the entire notion of leadership competencies, viewing leadership instead as an evolving, collaborative, integral praxis, in which "leaders" intimately represent the social identity and overarching purpose of a particular group. They deliberately set about amplifying and accelerating a new consciousness of possibility amongst the group's members (Stout-Rostron, 2011a).

Suzanne Lines: leadership and values-based transformation

Suzanne Lines, Director with Abamentis in the UK, shared her perspective on the increasing importance of living values and authenticity in working with leadership and change.

"I am getting a sense of a change in acceptable behaviour for leaders; more of a values-based approach, a different drive to really live the behaviours of the organisation; to ask and to listen to feedback and then, more importantly, to act on that feedback. I believe that creating a safe environment where one can test thoughts, ideas, be supported and challenged, and as one client described it, 'to be challenged with empathy', enables us to really look at how we are working and the impact we are having. Sustainable change that will harness the potential of what we can offer as individuals, teams, and organisations is a key driver for me. Having a greater awareness enables us to have greater choices and greater flexibility in how we lead both ourselves and others".

Based on feedback from clients, Lines believes their best work is when they work with the values and beliefs of the leaders and teams within the organisation which enable sustainable transformation. She takes a "strengths-based approach to ensure we create a really strong foundation from which to refine the changes a client is looking to achieve." She helps them to "become true to themselves" believing that authenticity provides a strong base from which to listen, offer feedback, and challenge in a way that nurtures and sustains growth both for the individual and the wider organisation and environment (Stout-Rostron, 2011a).

Richard Narva: working with family narrative and entrepreneurship

Richard Narva, a lawyer and head of Narva and Company based in Boston, Massachusetts, works with family entrepreneurship as a profound engineer of change. "Entrepreneurship drives economic growth; it drives values; it drives change. What people don't understand is how integral family systems are to entire ventures. Entrepreneurship is crucial to social development in emerging nations and is often nurtured by the entrepreneur's family, contributing access to financial capital and labour resources" (Stout-Rostron, 2011a).

Narva primarily works with families who control large enterprises. He says that the drive of family shareholders and family control group members is often constrained by deficits in leadership and management skills. These block their relationships, personal development, corporate growth, and enterprise success. He advises his clients around three concurrent issues: sustaining the growth of the enterprise, continuing the family's control of the enterprise, and continuing and enhancing the quality of family relationships within the family control group. He does this in an interdisciplinary team, typically where there is at least one advisor who is experienced and skilled in advising business, and another skilled in counselling families.

Narva starts from several assumptions: (1) the family is the source of strength, and the source of culture in a values-driven organisation, and their performance can be measured and enhanced; (2) great companies are family controlled, and the best companies to work in are family, values-driven companies; and (3) families can be liberated from the myth that they are short-lived, and work instead from the premise that they sustain job growth, sustain coherence in the community, and offer tremendous fulfilment in their jobs.

Narva says that, in terms of values, it is important to understand the family culture so that you can understand these values-driven enterprises. Family systems offer propellants and constraints on the leadership development of family members and non-family executives who lead the enterprise. Narva explains that through individual and team coaching they help the family to construct a new narrative by eliciting from the principals a consciousness of their values and enhancement of their family relationships; in that way the family can articulate corporate strategies. This work requires great respect for the power and complexity of the family system, rigorous ethical standards and helping the clients to develop a narrative of their future (Stout-Rostron, 2011a).

Gordon Spence: research support for systemic change

From 2007 through 2010, Dr Gordon Spence, currently head of the School of Business at the University of Wollongong, and previously of the Coaching Psychology Unit at the University of Sydney, was working on one large leadership research programme testing a new model of leadership. Working with two industry partners, a law firm, and a public health service on the design and importance of leadership development programs, the Unit tested a new model of leadership: perspective-taking capacity, mindfulness, purpose, and positivity – the latter being the interpersonal or socio-cultural dimension of their leadership model. The project was headed up by Dr Michael Cavanagh, with Drs Gordon Spence, Paul Atkins, and Tony Grant as co-investigators. The project team has designed a programme around this model. Spence explains that it has given them the ability to assess how much impact training had on each leader's performance and subjective experience, as well as looking at the incremental additional benefit coaching brought to the development of the leader.

"We have been using developmental coaching to help leaders take a perspective on themselves, others, the environment, and the system, and to do so in a particular way. In approaching developmental coaching on the back of this model, we have supervised our coaches to help their coachees approach tensions wherever they exist, and to explore what bigger perspectives it might be possible to take on their circumstances. The project has taken an approach to developmental coaching which is about supporting people to understand the tensions in their circumstances, and understanding those tensions more fully. It's growing their ability to increase their perspectives, but to deal more effectively with complexity."

Throughout the project, the researchers have been interested in working simultaneously with two dimensions of development – vertical development (related to the mindset and perspectives needed for effective leadership) and horizontal development (related to the skills and techniques needed for leading). Coming from a "research study perspective", the individuals in these cohorts were encouraged to address real issues through cross-functional teams. There has been positive feedback on the systemic impact of the leadership coaching project (Stout-Rostron, 2011a).

I heard during many of my interviews that huge investment is often made in executive development programs, sending executives off to expensive business schools who are often unsure of what they need to develop as leaders. On their return to the organisation, however, the environment is not supportive enough to allow them to nurture any newfound or critical leadership capabilities. In addition, coaches often work in isolation with their executives, not aware of the systemic issues within an organisation. They eventually become another "cog" in blocking systemic change due to their own lack of systemic knowledge. This is why supervision of coaches is crucial within any systemic change process which involves coaching (Stout-Rostron, 2011a).

TIPPING POINTS FOR CHANGE

Collectively, tipping points for change revealed the need to develop coaching practice at the highest level, embracing a new perspective on real change in leadership coaching for transformation. According to Rand Stagen and Brett Thomas (2006), "next-level" leaders see market places in ways that allow them to: change the rules of the game, to outmanoeuvre competitors and to dominate entire industries. They hold a unique perspective that reflects a formula of success. According to Stagen and Thomas (2006), there are six characteristics that define next-level leaders:

- They change the game rather than playing the game to win.
- They go beyond current formulas and establish new practices, rather than following established formulas and just leveraging best practices.
- They move from being transactional leaders to being transformational – connecting and transcending current practices.
- They are big-picture, whole-systems thinkers moving away from narrow linear thinking.
- They see what no-one else can see (e.g. Southwest Airlines designed regional superior service at lower cost; Dell Computers invented the no-inventory business model).
- They are versatile leaders who display versatility across multiple strengths rather than being limited to one or two strengths.

COACHING FOR NEW LEADERSHIP

Thinking about thinking involves reflecting and changing the reasoning behind our behaviours and seeing problems and solutions in new ways – that is where new leadership has a role to play.

Core leadership competencies cover a wide range of business, people and management skills. They range from driving performance and results, to leading high-performing teams, thinking and acting strategically, managing diversity, encouraging creativity and innovation, and leading change. Five critical leadership competencies that have emerged from these interviews are: living organisational values with integrity, intellectual curiosity, big picture orientation with attention to detail, strategic thinking, and self-awareness and adaptability.

Questions for us as leaders

- How are we as coach practitioners and leaders consciously developing the talent and potential of our human communities – specifically within our professional world?

- How are we "pioneering" the way forward to create a new level of consciousness that will help us to work together collaboratively with authenticity, innovation and less conflict?

- How can coaches help leaders to chart a new way forward in their organisations – but with a developing awareness in their need to shift consciousness in themselves as well?

Living organisational values with integrity

"Integrity" is the uncompromising adherence to a code of values. For a leader to act with integrity, it means intentionally acting from a personal vision that is values-based. This includes understanding what you, as a leader, want out of your life and work. It also means adhering to an agreed set of core organisational values aligned with your own personal values – no matter what challenging situations confront you from day to day (Stout-Rostron, 2008).

Values-based actions

What are values-based actions? A "value" is a quality or principle considered desirable, meaningful or significant. Values-based leaders create a shared vision with their teams that provides a sense of meaning and purpose and inspires excellence; they remain open and receptive, encourage honest debate, and are sensitive to issues of diversity, culture and fairness. Values-based leaders are committed to telling the truth and to operating with transparency in thought, feeling and deed (Stout-Rostron, 2008).

Courage

As a leader, it takes courage to act from integrity and to be continually aligned with your core values – even more so in times of stress. Apart from environmental factors such as lack of resources, an important cause of stress is when a leader's individual and organisational goals are not aligned with their personal and professional values. This can create anxiety, interfere with self-confidence, and prevent a leader from making decisions, managing relationships, or working effectively within the "politics" or implied rules of the system (Stout-Rostron, 2008).

Understanding intrinsic drivers

Intrinsic or internal drivers are the core values, beliefs and feelings that motivate us to do a good job and give our best; they are intangible, and are not to be confused with goals which are tangible and quantifiable. They are literally what make us jump out of bed in the morning, or stay late to work on a key job. Some key motivators are: achievement, balanced life, peace of mind, recognition, higher purpose and affiliation. Extrinsic or external motivators used by executives to manage their teams are factors such as the working environment, recognition, titles, bonuses, benefits, and leadership development training (Stout-Rostron, 2008).

Whether you are a coach working with a client, or a leader, working individually with your team members, ask: "What is important to you professionally, and what is important to you personally?" By important I mean those intangible values and beliefs that drive you to do your best, such as integrity, professionalism, making a difference. Your job as coach or leader-as-coach is to write down their answers, but not to interfere with the other's thinking. As a coach, you will be able to align over-arching goals with these intrinsic drivers; as a leader you will be able to ensure that the individual's values are aligned with performance goals that augment your corporate values-based vision (Stout-Rostron, 2008).

The purpose of these interviews has been to hear the voices of those who are working at the cutting edge of coaching for systemic and cultural change in organisations and institutions within a business context. There are rich connections in these stories, as well as a wide range of perspectives, examining what is innovative and collaborative in the coaching community at an organisational and institutional level. If leaders represent the social identity and overarching purpose of a particular group, these stories explain how coaching has the power to transform organisations into human communities united by a common purpose. We have heard about the importance of independent thinking, values-driven leadership, the level of consciousness of the leader, and the significance of storytelling (Stout-Rostron, 2011a).

We are experiencing coaching being used in a variety of ways to develop leaders around the globe, to build sustainable institutional and organisational policies, managing cultural change and societal complexity. In some ways my interviews that I have shared in various chapters in this book illustrate how coaching is influencing the coach's ability to take risks, to develop edgy conversations that get to the heart of issues and concerns that create change at a systemic level. So, what then are the questions we are left with as "reflective" leaders and practitioners if we are to coach effectively (Stout-Rostron, 2011a)?

David Lane: emerging client stories

David Lane, Founder of the Professional Development Foundation, suggests answering three questions if we are to coach effectively:

- What is your purpose as a coach and what is your purpose in engaging with each of your clients?
- What perspectives inform your work as a coach and what are your clients bringing to the conversation?
- What is the process of working with your client like, what do you actually do and how are you drawing out your client's compelling stories? (Stout-Rostron, 2011a).

CONCLUSION

Hopefully this chapter, and the book as a whole, have helped you to think about what story or stories are emerging from your own professional practice, whether you are a coaching practitioner or using a coaching approach as a leader. How is your coaching helping you to move with your clients, direct reports or your organisation through needed systemic and cultural change and transformation? There's more work that needs to be done, and that work actually starts with you – as you continue to develop the future leaders of tomorrow.

Traditional command and control processes in the workplace just don't work anymore. Yet in many global organisations, managers continue to bully rather than lead their people. The question is: how can we motivate, move and grow people inside our organisations, unless we look at changing the way we treat, manage and inspire them? We have, according to a previous Vice Chancellor of a leading South African university, a "managerialism" approach where the manager steps in believing capacity is lacking, versus a more empowering, collaborative and coaching approach. He talks about the importance of people within society becoming "active citizens", taking a more proactive, engaged approach to South Africa as an emerging nation (Private, pers. com., 2011).

Corporations don't nurture the human spirit, yet today people want to have a reason, a purpose and a mission in their working lives. So my research looked at how organisations worldwide are beginning to "humanise" the workplace. What models of success and sustainability are they working to, and how can they plan to inspire new learning and to develop skills and competence, developing ownership and leadership in every single person, from the shop floor to the CEO? *This is new leadership.*

Coaching seems to be one of the ways in which corporations can chart their way forward, "pioneering" a new way of working. But it requires a "shift" in how leaders "be" leaders, and how "coaches" coach leaders, and how both inspire leadership in others. What came across clearly in my interviews, from business leaders, government leaders, educational leaders and coach practitioners, educators, and consultants, is the necessity to stay true to core personal values and always be searching for authenticity and integrity. There was a strong undercurrent that coaching should not be there to make the worst aspects of corporate culture more efficient and cost-effective – and that coaching is not an "art" to be applied merely to knock off the "rough" edges of the worst kinds of "managerial" behaviour. Across the globe, common themes emerged from my range of interviews to help us understand what coaching has achieved in:

- developing people;
- improving performance;
- managing organisational change; and
- and making a positive impact on communities (Stout-Rostron, 2011a).

What emerged was the importance of:

- innovative and authentic leadership; and
- specifically working with personal narrative for deep growth and learning (Stout-Rostron, 2011a).

Those interviewed emphasised the need for values-driven leadership, allowing for individual thinking, personal and professional and spiritual alignment, and an acceleration of "deep-dive" work for personal transformation, as well as the importance of inter-disciplinary teams, action research projects, and a personal commitment to change. Collectively, tipping points for change revealed the need to develop coaching practice at the highest level, embracing a new perspective on "real change" in leadership for transformation. What emerged is that the level of maturity of the leader, and the interdisciplinary and collaborative approach of the team, were critical aspects for leadership success (Stout-Rostron, 2011a).

My questions aimed at evoking how leaders are currently being developed around the globe, and what are the behaviours, consequences and expertise that leaders need to manage organisational and societal complexity. Another purpose of these interviews was to hear the voices of those working at the cutting edge of coaching for systemic and cultural change.

The interviews suggest that coaching is potentially profound and radical and not just a "prop" to sustain the *status quo*. They suggest that we need a new way of thinking and working, a new level of trust to run organisations and institutions in all sectors as a critical means of support. Coaching can assist leaders to chart a new way forward in their organisations However, it requires a shift in consciousness, a shift in how leaders "be leaders" and how they inspire leadership in others (Stout-Rostron, 2011a).

The entire impetus of all the foregoing suggests that, for both coach and leader, everything begins with self-reflection. Like many obvious truths, this is easier said than acted upon, and too often remains at the level of lip service. It's not necessarily an easy thing to do, but if leaders cannot follow through on this, they are almost inevitably condemned to leading in the dark. Self-reflection and self-knowledge is not a one-off process. With self-development there is no endpoint. It is a lifelong practice and commitment. Perhaps what both coach and leader should take away from this knowledge is that, like life, leadership, learning, and self-reflection are all a work in progress. If there is one thing that Nelson Mandela taught us, it is that you should never, ever stop learning, reflecting or developing. That in itself is the beginning of great leadership.

APPENDIX: SAMPLE RESEARCH SURVEY QUESTIONS

1. Can you describe what work you (and your organisation or institution) do – and the values and beliefs which inform your work?
2. How has your organisation or institution used coaching to develop leadership competence and human development?
3. How have you personally used coaching to develop your own leadership competence and ability to manage change?
4. What positive and/or negative changes are a result of systemic coaching interventions, and can you tell me a story that relates to this?
5. What other processes and methodologies does your organisation (or client organisations) use to achieve change?
6. What are the current trends for coaching within your organisation or institution or the organisations you provide service to (e.g. coaching circles, team coaching, or developing your own internal suite of coaches)?
7. What impact has coaching had on large-scale systemic change within your own or your client organisations? Can you give me an example or tell me a story that relates to this?
8. If you could apply your process of change anywhere around the world, and to any system, what would you choose to focus on and why?
9. Where do you see the tipping points occurring in your local or the global community (i.e. the systems or pressure points that may have the most leverage or impact)?
10. Is there anyone else you know that is working in this area of systemic change and transformation as a result of coaching? (Stout-Rostron, 2011b).

INTERVIEWS

Boninelli, Italia. Senior Vice-President: Human Resources, Gold Fields of South Africa Ltd; Chairperson: Gold Fields Leadership and Business Academy, Johannesburg. Interview 29 June 2010.

Broadbent, Mark. General Manager: Brand Energy and Infrastructure Service, Denver, CO; formerly

Director and Business Development Manager, SGB-Cape WACO Africa. Interview 11 June 2010.

Craig, Nick. President, Authentic Leadership Institute. Interview 27 June 2010.

Doherty, Dr Daniel. Chair: Critical Coaching Research Unit, Chair: Faculty of Social Sciences and Law Quality Assurance Team, and Programme Director: MSc in Strategic Management, School of Economics Finance and Management, University of Bristol. Interview 24 June 2010.

Fillery-Travis, Dr Annette. Director of Programmes, Institute of Work-Based Learning, Middlesex University, London. Interview 22 June 2010.

Greif, Professor Dr Siegfried. Director: Change Management and Coaching, Institut für wirtschaftspsychologische Forschung und Beratung GmbH, Osnabrück, Germany. Interview 15 June 2010.

Hames, Richard. Founding member of the Stewardship team, The Constellation; Asian Forsight Institute, Thailand. Interview 12 June 2010.

Johnson, Marilyn. General Manager – Africa, Cummins Filtration, South Africa. Interview 21 February 2010.

Kauffman, Dr Carol. Assistant Professor of Psychology, Co-founder and Director: Coaching and Positive Psychology Initiative, Harvard / McLean Medical School, Belmont, MA; Co-Editor-in-Chief of *Coaching: An International Journal of Theory Research and Practice*. Interview 27 June 2010.

Kline, Nancy. President of Time To Think, Inc.; author of *Time To Think: Listening to ignite the human mind*. Interview 10 February 2010.

Lines, Suzanne. Director, Abamentis, UK. Interviews 30 June and 26 July 2010.

Maliza, Nonkqubela. Director for Corporate and Government Affairs, VWSA. Interview 15 February 2010.

Naidoo, Shani. Managing Director for HR for The Foschini Group (TFG). Interview 23 February 2010.

Narva, Richard. Founder and senior advisor, Narva and Company, Boston, MA; formerly Partner, Roseview Group. Interview 16 June 2010.

Rittenberg, Dr Mark. President of Corporate Scenes Inc., Berkeley, CA; Guest Professor, Executive Education Division, Kellogg School of Management, Northwestern University, IL, Senior Consultant, Executive Coaching Institute, Haas School of Business, University of California at Berkeley. Interview 19 June 2010.

Salmon, Lee. Executive coach; formerly management consultant with Federal Consulting Group, US Department of the Interior, Washington, DC; representative of International Consortium for Coaching in Organisations (ICCO). Interview 2 July 2010.

Spence, Dr Gordon. Leading Australian coaching psychologist; Programme Director of the Master of Business Coaching at Sydney Business School, University of Wollongong. Interview 29 June 2010.

Stern, Dr Lew. President Stern Consulting and Founding Director of Foundation of International Leadership Coaching. Interview 16 February 2010.

Towell, Garth. Managing Director, Kimberly-Clark South Africa, Johannesburg. Interview 15 June 2010.

FURTHER READING

Chapman, L., and Stout-Rostron, S. (2010). The impact of stress on learning. In Chapman, L., *Integrated Experiential Coaching: Becoming an executive coach* (pp. 219–248). London: Karnac.

Chapman, L. (2010). *Integrated experiential coaching: Becoming an executive coach*. London: Karnac.

Corrie, S., and Lane, D.A. (2010). *Constructing Stories, Telling Tales: A guide to formulation in applied psychology*. London: Karnac.

Global Convention on Coaching (GCC) (2008). *Dublin Declaration on Coaching: Including Appendices*. Dublin: Global Convention on Coaching.

Hames, R.D. (2007). *The Five Literacies of Global Leadership: What authentic leaders know and you need to find out*. San Francisco, CA: Jossey-Bass.

Kauffman, C.M., Russell, S.G., and Bush, M.W. (eds) (2008). *100 Coaching Research Proposal Abstracts*. International Coaching Research Forum. Belmont, MA: The Coaching and Positive Psychology Initiative, McLean Hospital, Harvard Medical School and The Foundation of Coaching.

Kilburg, R. (2002). *Executive Coaching: Developing managerial wisdom in a world of chaos*. Washington, DC: American Psychological Association.

Kline, N. (1999). *Time to Think: Listening to ignite the human mind*. London: Ward Lock.

Kline, N. (2009). *More Time to Think: A way of being in the world*. Pool-in-Wharfedale: Fisher King.

Kolb, D.A. (1984). *Experiential Learning: Experience as the source of learning and development*. Upper Saddle River, NJ: Prentice Hall.

Kouzes, J.M., and Posner, B.Z. (2002). *The Leadership Challenge*. Third edition. San Francisco, CA: Jossey-Bass.

Lane, D.A., Stelter, R., and Stout-Rostron, S. (2009). The future of coaching as a profession. In Cox, E., Clutterbuck, D., and Bachkirova, T. (eds), *The Sage Handbook of Coaching* (pp. 337–348). London: Sage.

Raelin, J.A. (2003). *Creating Leaderful Organisations: How to bring out leadership in everyone*. San Francisco, CA: Berrett-Koehler.

Siegel, D.J. (1999). *The Developing Mind: How relationships and the brain interact to shape who we are*. New York, NY: Guilford.

Stagen, R., and Thomas, B. (2006). *Next-Level Leadership*. Dallas, TX: Stagen Leadership Institute, Inc.

Stern, L.R. (2008). *Executive Coaching: Building and managing your professional practice*. Hoboken, NJ: Wiley.

Stout-Rostron, S. (2011a). How is coaching impacting systemic and cultural change within organisations? *International Journal of Coaching in Organisations*, 8(4):5–27.

Stout-Rostron, S. (2011b). Emerging trends in coaching for transformational leadership. In Boninelli, I., and Meyer, T. (eds), *Human Capital Trends: Building a sustainable organisation* (pp. 304–326).

Randburg: Knowres.

Stout-Rostron, S. (2011c). How does coaching positively impact organisational and societal change? In Biswas-Diener, R. (ed.), *Positive Psychology as Social Change* (pp. 237–266). Dordrecht: Springer.

Stout-Rostron, S. (2012b). *Business Coaching Wisdom and Practice: Unlocking the Secrets of Business Coaching*. Second edition. Randburg: Knowres.

Stout-Rostron, S. (2014). *Business Coaching International: Transforming individuals and organisations*. Second edition. London: Karnac.

BIBLIOGRAPHY

Adair, J. (1988). *Effective Leadership: How to be a successful leader*. Second edition. London: Pan.

Aiken Hodge, D.E. (2006). *Towards Coaching Across Divides to Create Alliances: An integral approach*. Unpublished DProf dissertation. London: Middlesex University.

Banis, L. (2010). How can executive coaching impact your bottom line? *EzineArticles.com*, 5 September.

Bar-On, R. (2006). The Bar-On model of emotional-social intelligence (ESI). *Psicothema*, 18(S1):13–25.

Bass, B.M., and Bass, R. (2008). *The Bass Handbook of Leadership: Theory, research and managerial application*. Fourth edition. New York, NY: Free Press.

Bass, B.M., and Riggio, R. (2006). *Transformational Leadership*. Second edition. Mahwah, NJ: Erlbaum.

Bednall, N. (2008). Keynote address. COMENSA *Western Cape Provincial Chapter Annual General Meeting*, Cape Town, 19 June.

Begley, S. (2007). *Train Your Mind, Change Your Brain*. New York, NY: Ballantine.

Bell, E.L.J., and Nkomo, S.M. (2001). *Our Separate Ways: Black and white women and the struggle for identity*. Boston, MA: Harvard Business School.

Bennis, W.G. (2009). *On Becoming a Leader*. Twentieth anniversary edition. Philadelphia, PA: Basic.

Bennis, W.G., and Nanus, B. (2003). *Leaders: Strategies for taking charge*. Third edition. New York, NY: HarperCollins.

Berne, E. (1975). *The Structure and Dynamics of Organisations and Groups*. New York, NY: Ballantine.

Betof, E. (2009). *Leaders as Teachers: Unlock the teaching potential of your company's best and brightest*. San Francisco, CA: Berrett-Koehler and Alexandria, VA: ASTD.

Blake, R.R., and Mouton, J.S. (1964). *The Management Grid: The key to leadership excellence*. Houston, TX: Gulf.

Blanchard, K., and Johnson, S. (1982). *The One Minute Manager*. New York, NY: William Morrow.

Boje, D.M. (2000). *The Isles Leadership: The Voyage of the Behaviourists*. College of Business, New Mexico State University. Webpage: business.nmsu.edu/~dboje/teaching/338/behaviors.htm#katz_michigan.

Boon, M. (1996). *The African Way*. Sandton: Zebra.

Boud, D., Cohen, R., and Walker, D. (eds). (1993). *Using Experience for Learning*. Buckingham: SRHE and Open University.

Boud, D., and Miller, N. (eds) (1996). *Working with Experience: Animating learning*. London: Routledge.

Boyatzis, R.E., and McKee, A. (2005). *Resonant Leadership: Renewing yourself and connecting with others through mindfulness, hope and compassion*. Boston, MA: Harvard Business School.

Braaten, J. (1991). *Habermas's Critical Theory of Society*. New York, NY: State University of New York.

Brome, D.R. (1993). Part one. In Chin, J.L., De La Cancela, V., and Jenkins, Y.M. (eds), *Diversity in Psychotherapy: The politics of race, ethnicity, and gender* (pp. 1–4). Westport, CT: Praeger.

Brown, P. (2011). *Three Features of Mind (Dan Siegel) and the Thinking Environment: Thoughts from Professor Paul Brown*. ME Associates resource upload. Webpage: www.providingthinkingspace. co.uk/links-resources/.

Buckingham, M. (2012). Leadership development in the age of the algorithm. *Harvard Business Review*, 90(6):86–94.

Burger, N., and Parry, S. (2012). Supervisor qualities in the doctoral supervisory relationship: The tacit dimension. In Kiley, M. (ed.), *Proceedings of the 2012 Quality in Postgraduate Research Conference* (pp. 175–176). Canberra, ACT: Centre for Higher Education, Learning and Teaching, Australian National University.

Burns, J.M. (1979). *Leadership*. New York, NY: HarperCollins.

Burns, J.M. (2003). *Transforming Leadership*. New York, NY: Grove.

Cavanagh, M.J. (2013a). *Coach Supervision for the Twenty-First Century: New models for a new era*. Keynote presentation to the Third International Conference on Coaching Supervision, Oxford Brookes University, 23 June.

Cavanagh, M.J. (2013b). The coaching engagement in the twenty-first century: New paradigms for complex times. In Clutterbuck, D., Megginson, D., and David, S. (eds), *Beyond Goals: Effective strategies for coaching and mentoring*. London: Gower.

Chapman, L. (2010). *Integrated Experiential Coaching: Becoming an executive coach*. London: Karnac.

Chapman, L., and Stout-Rostron, S. (2010). The impact of stress on learning. In Chapman, L., *Integrated Experiential Coaching: Becoming an executive coach* (pp. 219–248). London: Karnac.

Chemers, M.M. (1997). *An Integrative Theory of Leadership*. Mahwah, NJ: Erlbaum.

Chemers, M.M. (2001). Leadership effectiveness: An integrative review. In Hogg, M.A., and Tindale, R.S. (eds), *Blackwell Handbook of Social Psychology: Group processes* (pp. 376–399). Oxford: Blackwell.

Cherry, K. (2013a). *Leadership Theories: The 8 major leadership theories*. About.com Psychology. Webpage: psychology.about.com/od/leadership/p/leadtheories.htm.

Cherry, K. (2013b). *What is Transformational Leadership? How transformational leaders inspire*. About.com Psychology. Webpage: psychology.about.com/od/leadership/a/transformational.htm.

Chin, J.L., De La Cancela, V., and Jenkins, Y.M. (eds) (1993). *Diversity in Psychotherapy: The politics of race, ethnicity, and gender*. Westport, CT: Praeger.

Clarke, N. (2013). Model of complexity leadership development. *Human Resource Development International*, 16(2):135–150.

Coaches and Mentors of South Africa (COMENSA) (2006). *Interim Policy on Supervision*. Cape Town: COMENSA.

Coaches and Mentors of South Africa (COMENSA). (2009a). *Revised Code of Ethics*. Cape Town: COMENSA.

Coaches and Mentors of South Africa (COMENSA). (2009b). *Membership Criteria and Standards of Competence Framework*. Cape Town: COMENSA.

Coaches and Mentors of South Africa (COMENSA). (2010). *Coach/Mentor Supervision Policy*. Cape Town: COMENSA.

Cohen, E. (2007). *Leadership Without Borders: Successful strategies from world-class leaders*. Singapore: Wiley.

Cohen, S.L. (2009). *Four Key Leadership Practices for Leading in Tough Times*. Burlington, MA: Right Management.

Connerley, M.L., and Pedersen, P.B. (2005). *Leadership in a Diverse and Multicultural Environment: Developing awareness, knowledge, and skills*. Thousand Oaks, CA: Sage.

Corrie, S., and Lane, D.A. (2010). *Constructing Stories, Telling Tales: A guide to formulation in applied psychology*. London: Karnac.

Covey, S.R. (1991). *Principle-Centred Leadership*. New York, NY: Simon and Schuster.

Cummings, T.G., and Worley, C.G. (2004). *Organisation Development and Change*. Mason, OH: South-Western Cengage Learning.

Čurdová, A. (2005). *Discrimination Against Women in the Workforce and the Workplace*. Report of the Committee on Equal Opportunities for Women and Men, Document 10484. Strasbourg: Parliamentary Assembly of the Council of Europe.

Czarniawska-Joerges, B. (1992). *Exploring Complex Organisations: A cultural perspective*. Newbury Park, CA: Sage.

Deci, E., and Ryan, R. (1990). A motivational approach to self: Integration in personality. *Nebraska Symposium on Motivation*, 38:237–288.

De Haan, E. (2012). *Supervision in Action: A relational approach to coaching and consulting supervision*. Maidenhead: Open University.

De Haan, E., Bertie, C., Day, A., and Sills, C. (2010). Critical moments of clients and coaches: A direct-comparison study. *International Coaching Psychology Review*, 5(2):109–128.

De La Cancela, V., Jenkins, Y.M., and Chin, J.L. (1993). Diversity in psychotherapy: Examination of racial, ethnic, gender, and political issues. In Chin, J.L., De La Cancela, V., and Jenkins, Y.M. (eds), *Diversity in Psychotherapy: The politics of race, ethnicity, and gender* (pp. 5–16). Westport, CT: Praeger.

Debold, E. (2005). The business of saving the world. *EnlightenNext*, 28:60–91.

Derue, D.S., Nahrgang, J.D., Wellman, N., and Humphrey, S.E. (2011). Trait and behavioural theories of leadership: An integration and meta-analytic test of their relative validity. *Personnel Psychology*, 64(1):7–52.

Devenish, G. (2005). Understanding true meaning of *ubuntu* is essential in politics. *Cape Times*, 17 May.

Drake, D.B. (2007). The art of thinking narratively: Implications for coaching psychology and practice. *Australian Psychologist*, 42(4):283–294.

Drake, D.B. (2013). Personal communication, 13 March.

Drucker, P.F. (1996). Foreword: Not enough generals were killed. In Hesselbein, F., Goldsmith, M., and Beckhard, R. (eds), *The Leader of the Future: New visions, strategies and practices for the next era* (pp. xi–xvi) San Francisco, CA: Jossey-Bass.

Duff, T. (1999). *Plutarch's Lives: Exploring virtue and vice*. Oxford: Oxford University.

Eagly, A.H., and Carli, L.L. (2007). Women and the labyrinth of leadership. *Harvard Business Review*, 85(9):63–71.

Einstein, A. (2014). *Quotation: On Defining the Problem*. Gurteen Knowledge. Webpage: www.gurteen.com/gurteen/gurteen.nsf/id/L004680/.

Erlandson, E. (2009). Coaching with men: Alpha males. In Passmore, J. (ed.), *Diversity in Coaching: Working with gender, culture, race and age* (pp. 216–236). London: Association for Coaching and Philadelphia, PA: Kogan Page.

European Mentoring and Coaching Council (EMCC) (2008). *Code of Ethics*. Webpage: www.emccouncil.org/src/ultimo/models/Download/4.pdf.

European Mentoring and Coaching Council (EMCC) (2010). *EMCC Competence Framework*. Webpage: www.emccouncil.org/webimages/EMCC/EMCC_Competence_Framework.pdf.

Faull, J. (2008). We can harness outrage over violence to rejuvenate democracy, bring change. *Cape Times*, 5 June.

Fiedler, F.E. (1967). *A Theory of Leadership Effectiveness*. New York, NY: McGraw-Hill.

Fillery-Travis, A. (2009). *Practitioner Research: Getting started*. Presentations to Practitioner Research Workshops, GCC Rainbow Convention, Johannesburg 7–8 September, Durban 9–10 September, Cape Town 14–15 September.

Flaherty, J. (1999). *Coaching: Evoking excellence in others*. Boston, MA: Butterworth-Heinemann.

Forsyth, D.R. (2010). Leadership. In *Group Dynamics (Fifth Edition)* (pp. 245–280). Belmont, CA: Wadsworth.

Foti, R.J., and Hauenstein, N.M.A. (2007). Pattern and variable approaches in leadership emergence and effectiveness. *Journal of Applied Psychology*, 92(2):347–355.

Frankl, V.E. (1946). *Man's Search for Meaning*. London: Hodder and Stoughton.

Garms, E.T. (2013). Practising mindful leadership. *T+D*, 8 March, 32–35.

Garvin, D.A. (2013). How Google sold its engineers on management. *Harvard Business Review*, 91(12):74–82.

Gatrell, C., and Swan, E. (2008). *Gender and Diversity in Management: A concise introduction*. London: Sage.

George, B., Sims, P., and McLean, A. (2007). Discovering your authentic leadership. *Harvard Business Review*, 85(2):129–138.

Global Coaching and Mentoring Alliance (GCMA) (2011). *The Professional Charter for Coaching and Mentoring*. Brussels: European Economic and Social Committee.

Global Convention on Coaching (GCC). (2008). *Dublin Declaration on Coaching: Including Appendices*. Dublin: Global Convention on Coaching.

Goleman, D. (1996). *Emotional Intelligence: Why it can matter more than IQ*. London: Bloomsbury.

Goleman, D. (1998). *Working with Emotional Intelligence*. New York, NY: Bantam Dell.

Goleman, D. (2000). Leadership that gets results. *Harvard Business Review*, 78(2):78–90.

Goleman, D., Boyatzis, R., and McKee, A. (2002). *Primal Leadership: Learning to lead with emotional intelligence.* Boston, MA: Harvard Business School.

Graen, G.B., and Uhl-Bien, M. (1995). Relationship-based approach to leadership: Development of leader–member exchange (LMX) theory of leadership over 25 years: Applying a multi-level multi-domain perspective. *The Leadership Quarterly,* 6(2):219–247.

Grant, A.M. (2011). *Workplace, Executive and Life Coaching: An annotated bibliography from the behavioural science and business literature.* Sydney, NSW: Coaching Psychology Unit, University of Sydney.

Grant, A.M. (2012). ROI is a poor measure of coaching success: Towards a more holistic approach to using a wellbeing and engagement framework. *Coaching: An international journal of theory, research and practice,* 5(2):74–85.

Grant, B. (2003). Mapping the pleasures and risks of supervision. *Discourse: Studies in the Cultural Politics of Education,* 24(2):175–190.

Griffiths, K.E., and Campbell, M.A. (2008). Regulating the regulators: Paving the way for international, evidence-based coaching standards. *International Journal of Evidence-Based Coaching and Mentoring,* 6(1):19–31.

Grint, K. (2005). *Leadership: Limits and possibilities.* Basingstoke: Palgrave Macmillan.

Halford, S., and Leonard, P. (2001). New identities? Professionalism, managerialism and the construction of self. In Exworthy, M., and Halford, S. (eds), *Professionals and the New Managerialism in the Public Sector* (pp. 102–121). Buckingham: Open University.

Hames, R.D. (2007). *The Five Literacies of Global Leadership: What authentic leaders know and you need to find out.* San Francisco, CA: Jossey-Bass.

Hamilton, E. (2006). Whose story is it anyway? Narrative accounts of the role of women in founding and establishing family businesses. *International Small Business Journal,* 24(3):253–271.

Hargrove, R.A. (2003). *Masterful Coaching: Inspire an "impossible future" while producing extraordinary leaders and extraordinary results.* San Francisco, CA: Jossey-Bass/Pfeiffer.

Harri-Augstein, S., and Thomas, L.F. (1991). *Learning Conversations, Self-Organised Learning: The way to personal and organisational growth.* London: Routledge.

Hawkes, N.R., and Seggar, J.F. (2000). *Celebrating Women Coaches: A biographical dictionary.* Westport, CT: Greenwood.

Hawkins, P., and Shohet, R. (2000). *Supervision in the Helping Professions.* Buckingham: Open University.

Hersey, P. (1984). *The Situational Leader.* Escondido, CA: Centre for Leadership Studies.

Hersey, P., and Blanchard, K.H. (1969). Life cycle theory of leadership. *Training and Development,* 23(5):26–34.

Hersey, P., and Blanchard, K.H. (1988). *Management of Organisational Behaviour: Utilising human resources.* Fifth edition. Englewood Cliffs, NJ: Prentice-Hall.

Hicks, M.D., and Peterson, D.B. (1999). The development pipeline: How people really learn. *Knowledge Management Review,* 9:30–33.

Hofstede, G. (2005). Foreword. In: Connerley, M.L., and Pedersen, P.B., *Leadership in a Diverse and Multicultural Environment: Developing awareness, knowledge, and skills* (pp. ix–x). Thousand Oaks, CA: Sage.

Horne, A. (2008). Compassion: Our hearts at work. *Positive Psychology News Daily*, 22 September.

Howell, J.P. (2013). *Snapshots of Great Leadership*. Hove: Routledge.

Immordino-Yang, M.H., and Damasio, A. (2007). We feel, therefore we learn: The relevance of affective and social neuroscience to education. *Mind, Brain, and Education*. 1(1):3–10.

Institute of HeartMath® (2013). *HeartMath® Appreciation Tool™ and Exercises*. Webpage: www.heartmath.org/free-services/tools-for-well-being/heartmath-appreciation-tool.html.

International Coach Federation (ICF). (2008a). *Core Competencies*. Webpage: www.coachfederation.org/research%2Deducation/icf%2Dcredentials/core%2Dcompetencies/.

International Coach Federation (ICF). (2008b). *ICF Code of Ethics*. Webpage: www.coachfederation.org/about%2Dicf/ethics%2D%26%2Dregulation/icf%2Dcode%2Dof%2Dethics/.

International Coach Federation (ICF), Association Resource Centre Inc., and PricewaterhouseCoopers LLP (2009). *ICF Global Coaching Client Study: Final Report June 2009*. Lexington, KY: ICF.

Janse van Rensburg, M. (2012). Diversity, personality and culture. In Stout-Rostron, S. (2012b), *Business Coaching Wisdom and Practice: Unlocking the secrets of business coaching (Second edition)* (pp. 145–195). Randburg: Knowres.

Jaques, E., and Clement, S.D. (1991). *Effective Leadership: A practical guide to managing complexity*. Oxford: Blackwell.

Jarvis, J. (2004). *Coaching and Buying Coaching Services: A guide*. London: CIPD.

Jenkins, Y.M. (1993). Diversity and social esteem. In Chin, J.L., De La Cancela, V., and Jenkins, Y.M. (eds), *Diversity in Psychotherapy: The politics of race, ethnicity, and gender* (pp. 45–64). Westport, CT: Praeger.

Jenkins, Y.M., De La Cancela, V., and Chin, J.L. (1993). Historical overviews: three sociopolitical perspectives. In Chin, J.L., De La Cancela, V., and Jenkins, Y.M. (eds), *Diversity in Psychotherapy: The politics of race, ethnicity, and gender* (pp. 17–44). Westport, CT: Praeger.

Johnson, W. (2013). Personal communication, 11 February.

Jones, R., and Jenkins, F. (eds). (2006). *Developing the Allied Health Professional*. (Allied Health Professions: Essential Guides.) Oxford: Radcliffe.

Kabat-Zinn, J. (1994). *Wherever You Go There You Are: Mindfulness meditation in everyday life*. New York, NY: Hyperion.

Kadushin, A. (1976). *Supervision in Social Work*. New York, NY: Columbia University.

Karlin, D. (2011). *Leaders: Their stories, their words: Conversations with Human-Based Leaders®*. Ottawa, ON: A Better Perspective.

Kauffman, C.M., Russell, S.G., and Bush, M.W. (eds) (2008). *100 Coaching Research Proposal Abstracts*. International Coaching Research Forum. Belmont, MA: The Coaching and Positive Psychology Initiative, McLean Hospital, Harvard Medical School and The Foundation of Coaching.

Kennedy, E., and Charles, S.C. (2001). *On Becoming a Counsellor: The basic guide for non-professional counsellors*. Dublin: Newleaf.

Kets de Vries, M. (2011). *The Hedgehog Effect*. San Francisco, CA: Josey-Bass.

Ketter, P. (2013). The seven decades of leadership development. *T+D*, 8 March.

Khurana, R. (2007). *From Higher Aims to Hired Hands: The social transformation of American business schools and the unfulfilled promise of management as a profession*. Princeton, NJ: Princeton University.

Kilburg, R.R. (2002). *Executive Coaching: Developing managerial wisdom in a world of chaos*. Washington, DC: American Psychological Association.

King, S.N., Altman, D.G., and Lee, R.J. (2011). *Discovering the Leader in You: How to realise your leadership potential*. San Francisco, CA: Jossey-Bass.

Kirkpatrick, D.L. (1994). *Evaluating Training Programmes: The four levels*. San Francisco, CA: Berrett-Koehler.

Kline, N. (1999). *Time to Think: Listening to ignite the human mind*. London: Ward Lock.

Kline, N. (2004). Keynote address. In *Coaching in a Thinking Environment®*. Wallingford: Time to Think.

Kline, N. (2012). *The Thinking Partnership® Programme: Consultant's guide*. Wallingford, UK: Time to Think.

Kline, N. (2009). *More Time to Think: A way of being in the world*. Pool-in-Wharfedale: Fisher King.

Kline, N. (2010). Personal communication, 10 February.

Kline, N. (2011). *Transforming Meetings*. Wallingford: Time to Think.

Kline, N. (2012). *The Consultant's Course*. Wallingford: Time to Think.

Kluckhohn, F.R., and Strodtbeck, F.L. (1961). *Variations in Value Orientations*. New York, NY: Harper and Row.

Kolb, D.A. (1984). *Experiential Learning: Experience as the source of learning and development*. Upper Saddle River, NJ: Prentice Hall.

Kouzes, J.M., and Posner, B.Z. (2002). *The Leadership Challenge*. Third edition. San Francisco, CA: Jossey-Bass.

Lacida, K. (2012). *Toxic Leadership*. Lead Change Group, 17 August. Webpage: http://leadchangegroup.com/toxic-leadership/.

Lagerlund, H. (2010). *Forming the Mind: Essays on the internal senses and the mind/body problem from Avicenna to the Medical Enlightenment*. Dordrecht: Springer.

Lane, D.A. (2013). Personal communication, 15 January.

Lane, D.A., and Corrie, S. (2006). *The Modern Scientist-Practitioner: A guide to practice in psychology*. Hove: Routledge.

Lane, D.A., Stelter, R., and Stout-Rostron, S. (2009). The future of coaching as a profession. In Cox, E., Clutterbuck, D., and Bachkirova, T. (eds), *The Sage Handbook of Coaching* (pp. 337–348). London: Sage.

Lang, A., and Thomas, B. (2013). Crossing the canyon from technical expert to first-time leader. *T+D*, March, 26–39.

LaPort, K.A. (2012). *A Multistage Model of Leader Effectiveness: Uncovering the relationships between leader traits and leader behaviours*. Unpublished PhD dissertation. Fairfax, VA: George Mason University.

Leimon, A., Moscovici, F., and Goodier, H. (2011). *Coaching Women to Lead*. New York, NY: Routledge.

Lewin, K., Lippitt, R., and White, R.K. (1939). Patterns of aggressive behaviour in experimentally created "social climates". *Journal of Social Psychology*, 10:271–299.

Lewis, L. (2013). Personal communication, 5 March.

Lipkin, N. (2013). *What Keeps Leaders Up At Night? Recognising and resolving your most troubling management issues*. New York, NY: American Management Association.

Lisitsa, E. (2012). The positive perspective: Dr Gottman's magic ratio! *The Gottman Institute Relationship Blog*, 3 December. Webpage: www.gottmanblog.com/2012/12/the-positive-perspective-dr-gottmans.html.

Lothian, A. (2006). *Insights® Discovery*. Dundee: Insights Learning and Development.

Lubar, K., and Halpern, B.L. (2003). *Leadership Presence*. New York, NY: Gotham.

Ludeman, K. (2009). Coaching with women. In Passmore, J. (ed.), *Diversity in Coaching: Working with gender, culture, race and age* (pp. 237–254). London: Association for Coaching and Philadelphia, PA: Kogan Page.

Ludeman, K., and Erlandson, E. (2004). Coaching the alpha male. *Harvard Business Review*, 82(5):58–67.

Mandela, N.R. (1994). *Long Walk to Freedom*. Edinburgh: Little, Brown.

Maslow, A.H. (1966). *The Psychology of Science: A reconnaissance*. New York, NY: Harper and Row.

Maxwell, P. (1998). *The 21 Irrefutable Laws of Leadership: Follow them and people will follow you*. Nashville, TN: Thomas Nelson.

May, R. (1983). *The Discovery of Being*. New York, NY: Norton.

McCraty, R., and Childre, D. (2002). *The Appreciative Heart: The psychophysiology of positive emotions and optimal functioning*. Boulder Creek, CA: Institute of HeartMath®.

McClelland, D.C. (1961). *The Achieving Society*. Princeton, NJ: Van Nostrand.

McClelland, D.C. (1987). *Human Motivation*. New York, NY: Cambridge University.

McGregor, D. (1960). *The Human Side of Enterprise*. New York, NY: McGraw-Hill.

McWhinney, W., Webber, J.B., Smith, D.M., and Novokowsky, B.J. (1993). *Creating Paths of Change: Managing issues and resolving problems in organisations*. Venice, CA: Enthusion.

Meyerson, D., and Fletcher, J.K. (1999). A modest manifesto for shattering the glass ceiling. *Harvard Business Review*, 78(1):127–136.

Miner, J.B. (2002). *Organisational Behaviour: Foundations, theories and analyses*. Oxford: Oxford University.

Moir, A., and Jessel, D. (1992). *Brain Sex: The real difference between men and women.* New York, NY: Delta.

Moss Kanter, R. (1993). *Men and Women of the Corporation.* Philadelphia, PA: Basic.

Mumford, M.D., Zaccaro, S.J., Harding, F.D., Jacobs, T.O., and Fleishman, E.A. (2000). Leadership skills for a changing world: Solving complex social problems. *The Leadership Quarterly,* 11(1):11–35.

Nathan, P., Lim, L., and Correia, H. (2004). Module 8: Core beliefs. In Nathan, P., Correia, H., and Lim, L., *Panic Stations! Coping with Panic Attacks.* Perth, Western Australia: Centre for Clinical Interventions, Department of Health, Government of Western Australia.

Neider, L.L., and Schriesheim, C.A. (eds) (2010). *The "Dark" Side of Management. Research in Management Series.* Miami, FL: University of Miami.

Niederle, M., and Vesterlund, L. (2005). *Do Women Shy Away From Competition? Do men compete too much?* NBER Working Paper No. 11474, July. Washington, DC: National Bureau of Economic Research.

O'Neill, L.J. (2004). Faith and decision making in the Bush presidency: The God elephant in the middle of America's livingroom. *Emergence: Complexity and Organisations,* 6(1/2):149–156.

O'Neill, M.B. (2000). *Coaching with Backbone and Heart: A systems approach to engaging leaders with their challenges.* San Francisco, CA: Jossey-Bass.

Pampallis Paisley, P. (2006). *Towards a Theory of Supervision for Executive Coaching: An integral vision.* Published DProf dissertation. London: Middlesex University.

Passmore, J. (2008). *Psychometrics in Coaching.* London: Kogan Page.

Passmore, J. (ed.) (2009). *Diversity in Coaching: Working with gender, culture, race and age.* London: Association for Coaching and Philadelphia, PA: Kogan Page.

Peltier, B. (2001). *The Psychology of Executive Coaching: Theory and application.* New York, NY: Brunner-Routledge.

Peters, T., and Waterman, R. (1982). *In Search of Excellence: Lessons from America's best-run companies.* New York, NY: HarperCollins.

Peterson, D.B. (2009). Executive coaching: A critical review and recommendations for advancing the practice. In Zedeck, S. (ed.), *APA Handbook of Industrial and Organisational Psychology: Volume 2: Selecting and developing members for the organisation* (pp. 527–566). Washington, DC: American Psychological Association.

Peterson, D.B. (2007). Executive coaching in a cross-cultural context. *Consulting Psychology Journal: Practice and Research,* 59(4):261–271.

Pinker, S. (2008). *The Sexual Paradox: Men, women and the real gender gap.* New York, NY: Scribner.

Polanyi, M. (1958). *Personal Knowledge: Towards a post-critical philosophy.* Chicago, IL: University of Chicago.

Polanyi, M. (1966). *The Tacit Dimension.* London: Routledge.

Prentice, K. (2013). *Me and My Shadow.* Presentation to the Third International Conference on Coaching Supervision, Oxford Brookes University, 23 June.

Price, C. (2011). *21 Days to Self Discovery: Define what you want out of life and discover how to get it!*. Audio seminar. Boulder, CO: CareerTrack .

Prime, J. (2005). *Women "take care", men "take charge": Stereotyping of US business leaders exposed*. New York, NY: Catalyst.

Raelin, J.A. (2003). *Creating Leaderful Organisations: How to bring out leadership in everyone*. San Francisco, CA: Berrett-Koehler.

Ramphele, M. (2008). *Laying Ghosts to Rest: Dilemmas of the transformation in South Africa*. Cape Town: Tafelberg.

Reid, M.A. (2012). *The Impact of Group Coaching on Leadership Effectiveness for South African Women Managers*. Unpublished Master of Management research report. Johannesburg: University of the Witwatersrand.

Rock, D., and Page, L.J. (2009). *Coaching with the Brain in Mind: Foundations for practice*. Hoboken, NJ: Wiley.

Rosenthal, S.A., and Pittinsky, T.L. (2006). Narcissistic leadership. *The Leadership Quarterly*, 17(6):617–633.

Rost, J.C. (1993). *Leadership for the 21st Century*. Westport, CT: Praeger.

Rumsey, M.G. (ed.) (2013). *The Oxford Handbook of Leadership*. Oxford: Oxford University.

Ryan, R.M. (2013). *Self-determination*. Notes compiled by Stout-Rostron, S., from presentation to Coaching in Leadership and Healthcare Conference 2013, Harvard / McLean Medical School, Cambridge, MA, 28 September.

Ryan, R.M., and Deci, E.L. (1985) *Intrinsic Motivation and Self-Determination in Human Behaviour (Perspectives in Social Psychology)*. New York, NY: Plenum.

Salovey, P., and Mayer, J.D. (1990). Emotional intelligence. *Imagination, Cognition and Personality*, 9(3):185–211.

Senge, P.M. (1990). *The Fifth Discipline: The art and practice of the learning organisation*. New York, NY: Doubleday.

Senge, P.M. (1996). Leading learning organisations: The bold, the powerful, and the invisible. In Hesselbein, F., Goldsmith, M., and Beckhard, R. (eds), *The Leader of the Future: new visions, strategies, and practices for the next era* (pp. 41–48). San Francisco, CA: Jossey-Bass.

Senge, P.M. (1999). Leadership in living organisations. In Hesselbein, F., Goldsmith, M., and Somerville, I. (eds), *Leading beyond the walls* (Wisdom to Action series, The Drucker Foundation) (pp. 73–90). San Francisco, CA: Jossey-Bass.

Siegel, D.J. (1999). *The Developing Mind: How relationships and the brain interact to shape who we are*. New York, NY: Guilford.

Siegel, D.J. (2009). Mindful awareness, mindsight, and neural integration. *The Humanistic Psychologist*, 37(2):137–158.

Siegel, D.J. (2011). *Mindsight: The new science of personal transformation*. New York, NY: Bantam.

Silsbee, D.K. (2004). *The Mindful Coach: Seven roles for helping people grow*. Marshall, NC: Ivey River.

Simpson, R., and Lewis, P. (2007). *Voice, Visibility and the Gendering of Organisations*. Basingstoke: Palgrave Macmillan.

Skinner, S. (2012). *Coaching Women in Leadership or Coaching Women Leaders? Understanding the importance of gender and professional identity formation in executive coaching for senior women*. Unpublished report on research project *Women In Leadership: Understanding how executive coaching can help women leaders thrive in corporate Australia*. Sydney, NSW: Coaching Psychology Unit, University of Sydney.

Snowden, D.J., and Boone, M.E. (2007). A leader's framework for decision making. *Harvard Business Review*, 85(11):69–76.

Spence, G.B. (2007). Further development of evidence-based coaching: Lessons from the rise and fall of the human potential movement. *Australian Psychologist*, 42(4):255–265.

Spence, G.B. (2013). Personal communication, 6 March.

Spinelli, E. (1989). *The Interpreted World: An introduction to phenomenological psychology*. London: Sage.

Spinelli, E. (2005). *Existential Phenomenology*. Notes compiled by Dolny, H., from lecture to i-Coach Academy, Cape Town, 8 February.

Stagen, R., and Thomas, B. (2006). *Next-Level Leadership*. Dallas, TX: Stagen Leadership Institute.

Standards Australia (2011). *Coaching in Organisations*. Draft handbook produced by Coaching Guideline Working Group HB41 of Standards Australia HR and Employment Committee MB 9. Sydney, NSW: Standards Australia.

Stein, I.F., and Page, L.J. (2010). Graduate study in executive and organisational coaching: Considerations for programme development. *Journal of Psychological Issues in Organisational Culture*, 1(3):56–64.

Stern, L.R. (2008). *Executive Coaching: Building and managing your professional practice*. Hoboken, NJ: Wiley.

Stern, L.R. (2013). Personal communication, 2 February.

Stern, L.R., and Stout-Rostron, S. (2013a). What progress has been made in coaching research in relation to 16 ICRF focus areas from 2008 to 2012? *Coaching: An International Journal of Theory, Research and Practice*, 6(1):72–96.

Stern, L.R., and Stout-Rostron, S. (2013b). *Bibliography of Coaching Research Abstracts January 2011 – June 2012*. Research data compilation. Belmont, MA: Institute of Coaching Professional Association.

Stern, L.R., and Stout-Rostron, S. (2013c). *Bibliography of Coaching Research: List of journal articles by focus area, date and author*. Research data compilation. Belmont, MA: Institute of Coaching Professional Association.

Stern, L.R., and Stout-Rostron, S. (2013d). *Peer-reviewed journals which have published coaching research from January 2008 – June 2012*. Research data compilation. Belmont, MA: Institute of Coaching Professional Association.

Stern, L.R., and Stout-Rostron, S. (2013e). *Bibliography of Coaching Research: List of dissertations by focus area, date and author*. Research data compilation. Belmont, MA: Institute of Coaching Professional Association.

Stout-Rostron, S. (2002). *Accelerating Performance: Powerful new techniques to develop people*. London: Kogan Page.

Stout-Rostron, S. (2006). *Interventions in the Coaching Conversation: Thinking, feeling and behaviour*. Published DProf dissertation. London: Middlesex University.

Stout-Rostron, S. (2008). Integrity and values-based actions. *Finweek*, February.

Stout-Rostron, S. (2009). The global initiatives in the coaching field. *Coaching: An International Journal of Theory, Research and Practice*, 2(1):76–85.

Stout-Rostron, S. (2011a). How is coaching impacting systemic and cultural change within organisations? *International Journal of Coaching in Organisations*, 8(4):5–27.

Stout-Rostron, S. (2011b). Emerging trends in coaching for transformational leadership. In Boninelli, I., and Meyer, T. (eds), *Human Capital Trends: Building a sustainable organisation* (pp. 304–326). Randburg: Knowres.

Stout-Rostron, S. (2011c). How does coaching positively impact organisational and societal change? In Biswas-Diener, R. (ed.), *Positive Psychology as Social Change* (pp. 237–266). Dordrecht: Springer.

Stout-Rostron, S. (2011d). Key questions on coaching supervision. *COMENSAnews*, June.

Stout-Rostron, S. (2012a). Gender issues in business coaching. In Passmore, J., Peterson, D.B., and Freire, T. (eds), *The Wiley-Blackwell Handbook of the Psychology of Coaching and Mentoring* (pp. 155–174). London: Wiley-Blackwell.

Stout-Rostron, S. (2012b). *Business Coaching Wisdom and Practice: Unlocking the secrets of business coaching*. Second edition. Randburg: Knowres.

Stout-Rostron, S. (2013). *Integrating Business Process and Models*. Unpublished lecturing notes for MPhil programme, University of Stellenbosch. Cape Town: Sunny Stout-Rostron Associates.

Stout-Rostron, S. (2014). *Business Coaching International: Transforming individuals and organisations*. Second edition. London: Karnac.

Stout-Rostron, S., Cunningham, N., and Crous, W. (2013). *Leadership Development Survey Report 2013*. Randburg: Knowres.

Stout-Rostron, S., Janse van Rensburg, M., and Marques Sampaio, D. (2014). Diversity, culture and gender. In Stout-Rostron, S., *Business Coaching International: Transforming individuals and organisations (Second edition)* (pp. 173–232). London: Karnac.

Strasser, F., and Strasser, A. (1997). *Existential Time-Limited therapy: The wheel of existence*. Chichester: Wiley.

Sue, S. (1993). Foreword. In Chin, J.L., De la Cancela, V., and Jenkins, Y.M. (eds), *Diversity in Psychotherapy: The Politics of Race, Ethnicity, and Gender* (pp.ix–x). Westport, CT: Praeger.

Sunday Times (2013). Mandela. *Sunday Times*, 8 December.

Tannen, D. (1995). The power of talk: Who gets heard and why. *Harvard Business Review*, 73(5):138–148.

Tannen, D. (1999). *The Argument Culture: Stopping America's war of words*. New York, NY: Ballantine.

Thomas, A., and Bendixen, M. (2000). The management implications of ethnicity in South Africa. *Journal of International Business Studies*, 31(3):507–519.

Thomas, C. (2008). *(A)Gender in the Boardroom*. Sydney, NSW: Egon Zehnder International and Equal Opportunity for Women in the Workplace Agency.

Thomson, P., and Graham, J. (2005). *A Woman's Place is in the Boardroom*. Basingstoke: Palgrave Macmillan.

Ting, S., and Scisco, P. (2006). *The CCL Handbook of Coaching: A guide for the leader coach*. San Francisco, CA: Jossey-Bass.

Van Dam, N. (2013). Inside the learning brain. *T+D*, 8 April, 30–35.

Weiss, P. (2004). *The Three Levels of Coaching*. San Francisco, CA: An Appropriate Response.

Wheatley, M.J. (2006). *Leadership and the New Science: Discovering order in a chaotic world*. Third edition. San Francisco, CA: Berrett-Koehler.

Whitmore, J. (2002). *Coaching for Performance: Growing people, performance and purpose*. London: Nicholas Brealey.

Whyte, A. (2013). Personal communication, 14 March.

Wikipedia (2013). Leadership. *Wikipedia*. Webpage: en.wikipedia.org/wiki/Leadership.

Wilber, K. (1996). *A Brief History of Everything*. Dublin: Colourbooks.

Wilber, K. (2006). *Integral Spirituality*. Boston, MA: Integral.

Wilson-Starks, K.Y. (2003). Toxic leadership. *Transleadership Inc*. Webpage: www.transleadership.com/ToxicLeadership.pdf.

Wirth, L. (2001). *Breaking Through the Glass Ceiling: Women in management*. Geneva: International Labour Office.

Wirth, L. (2004). *Breaking Through the Glass Ceiling: Women in management: Update 2004*. Geneva: International Labour Office.

Worldwide Association of Business Coaches (WABC) (2008a). *Code of Business Coaching Ethics and Integrity*. Webpage: www.wabccoaches.com/includes/popups/code_of_ethics_2nd_edition_december_17_2007.html.

Worldwide Association of Business Coaches (WABC) (2008b). *Business Coaching Definition and Competences*. Webpage: www.wabccoaches. com/includes/popups/definition_and_competencies.html.

Worldwide Association of Business Coaches (WABC) (2011). *Business Coaching Definition*. Webpage: www.wabccoaches.com/includes/popups/definition.html.

Worldwide Association of Business Coaches (WABC) (2013). *WABC Professional Standards for Business Coaches*. Webpage: www.wabccoaches.com/includes/popups/ professional_standards.html#preamble.

Yalom, I.D. (1980). *Existential Psychotherapy*. New York, NY: Basic.

Yalom, I.D. (2001). *The gift of therapy: Reflections on being a therapist*. London: Piatkus.

Yerkes, D. (ed.) (1989). *Webster's Encyclopedic Unabridged Dictionary of the English Language*. New York, NY: Random House.

Zaccaro, S.J. (2001). *The Nature of Executive Leadership: A conceptual and empirical analysis of success*. Washington, DC: American Psychological Association.

Zaccaro, S.J. (2007). Trait-based perspectives of leadership. *American Psychologist*, 62(1):6–16.

Zaccaro, S.J., Rittman, A.L., and Marks, M.A. (2001). Team leadership. *Leadership Quarterly*, 12(4):451–483.

Zohar, D., and Marshall, I. (2001). *Spiritual Intelligence: The ultimate intelligence*. London: Bloomsbury.

Leadership Coaching for Results: Cutting-edge practices for coach and client

INDEX

effective, 20, 23, 32
emergent, 87, 218
good, 13, 14, 19, 34, 40, 50
government, 230, 235, 254
innovative, 9, 227
inspirational, 25, 233
institutional, 37, 145
managerial, 147, 165, 173, 177
next-level, 250, 251
senior, 39, 40, 235
toxic, 30, 31
transactional, 251
transformational, 24, 25, 27, 245, 246
visionary, 15, 217
women, 7, 145–168
leadership, 4, 11–17, 19–24, 26, 28–34, 36–43,
74, 107, 168, 227, 228, 230, 235, 236, 244,
248–250, 253–255
attributes, characteristics, 4, 13, 21, 31–34
authentic, 13, 27, 41, 233, 234, 243, 244,
247, 254
definition, 4, 11, 14–16, 26
distributed, 4, 12, 26
effective, 15, 21, 23, 27, 30, 250
functional, 4, 12, 23
good, 40, 105
inspire leadership in others, 1, 240, 254
managerial, 24, 177
narcissistic, 29, 30, 93, 196
nature of, 39, 41, 227, 248
new, 1, 9, 83, 227–256
principle-centred, 27, 28
styles, 3, 4, 11, 19–24, 28–30, 36, 37, 105,
107, 154, 230, 234, 241, 246
successful, 12, 15
theories, 4, 12, 19–28, 28
toxic, 29–31
transactional, 14, 21, 24
transformational, 9, 14, 24, 25, 154, 227,
240–250
leadership development, 3, 4, 9, 11, 13, 15, 17, 18,
37, 39, 40, 55, 57, 65, 74, 81, 90, 154, 166,
167, 172, 173, 222, 230, 233–235, 237, 241,
249, 250, 252
leadership development plan (LDP), 57, 65, 74,
90, 173
leadership development programmes, 3, 11, 13,
17, 18, 40, 55, 74, 166, 167, 234
Leadership Development Survey, 15–18

learning, 3, 5–7, 12, 13, 25–27, 37, 38, 41, 46,
50–52, 56, 58–61, 66, 70, 72, 73, 76–82, 85,
87, 88, 91, 92, 94–103, 107, 110, 112, 117–
119, 123, 124, 127, 129–132, 134, 136, 139,
140, 142, 143, 158, 173–177, 185, 186, 195,
201–206, 208, 209, 216, 220, 224, 227, 230,
233, 236, 238, 240, 241, 246, 248, 254, 255
learning journal, journal of reflections, 58, 82
learning modes, 97–101, 134
learning organisation, 26
legislation, 2, 152, 155, 157, 212
Leimon, Averil, 152–154, 163, 164
Lewis, Lise, 214, 224
Lewis, Patricia, 149, 152, 154, 155, 164
limbic system, 49, 131–133, 139
limiting assumptions, 53, 123, 125–128, 146, 147,
150, 158–160, 162
limiting paradigms, 5, 75, 119
Lines, Suzanne, 248, 249, 256
listening, 5, 27, 33, 34, 50, 51, 59, 60, 69, 73, 74,
83, 85, 103, 106, 112, 122, 126, 128, 137,
142, 160, 161, 186, 208, 245, 248, 249
Lubar, Kathy, 14
Ludeman, Kate, 150

M

Maliza, Nonkqubela, 237, 238, 256
malpractice, 175, 185
managerialism, 155, 243, 253
Mandela, Nelson Rolihlahla, 32–34, 255
Marques Sampaio, Daniel, 36, 37, 158, 164
mastery, mastery of practice, 5, 8, 35, 36, 38, 63,
64, 66, 97, 211, 215, 217–219, 224
Maxwell, Peter, 14
May, Rollo, 119, 121
McKee, Annie, 15, 141, 142
meaning and purpose, 56, 66, 75, 96, 120, 121,
252
mentoring, 4, 24, 38, 47, 50, 51, 53, 71, 82, 131,
157, 172, 192, 199, 214, 224, 236, 238, 246
mentors, 19, 50, 51, 58, 63, 83, 97, 185, 239, 246
metaphor, 5, 87, 88, 106, 107, 129, 147, 148, 163,
175
Miller, Nod, 76, 77
mindfulness, 4, 37–39, 103, 132, 134, 135, 141,
142, 250
mindfulness practice, 6, 7, 134, 135, 142
mindsight, 133, 134, 141
mindsight maps, 133

models:
    Cynefin, 6, 104–107
    Domains of Competence, 6, 111–113, 130
    EQ, 6, 61, 107, 109–111, 116
    Existential, 6, 107, 125, 130, 130
    Experiential Learning, 6, 77, 97–99
    Integral, 6, 107, 111, 113–119, 130, 165
    Nested-Levels, 6, 92–96
    Scientist-Practitioner, 6, 89–91, 175
    Thinking Partnership®, 6, 53, 125–128, 130, 230
Moscovici, François, 152–154, 163, 164
Moss Kanter, Rosabeth, 12
motivation, 5, 19, 20–22, 25, 28, 31, 32, 34–36, 69–72, 75, 85, 90, 95, 131, 133, 140, 172, 196

N

Naidoo, Shani, 238–240, 256
narrative, 9, 41, 63, 77, 112, 135, 159, 208, 249, 254
Narva, Richard, 249, 256
neo-cortex, 132–134
Nested-Levels Model. *See* models
neural integration, 133
neurons, 132, 133
neuroscience, 6, 41, 131–143
new behaviours, 7, 69, 77, 82, 97, 132, 136, 143
Northern European, 124

O

O'Neill, Mary Beth, 71, 72, 80, 81
ontological, 6, 92, 94, 95, 121, 140
organisational change, 9, 127, 229, 236, 240, 254
organisational systems, 91, 119, 157, 163, 178, 187, 201, 203, 205, 206
organisational values, 27, 70, 95, 176, 192, 242, 251

P

Page, Linda J., 51, 52, 132–136, 138, 139, 141, 216
Pampallis Paisley, Patricia, 114, 203, 204
parallel processes, 200, 202, 205, 206, 209
Parry, Sharon, 84, 204, 205, 209
Passmore, Jonathan, 150
Peltier, Bruce, 123, 124, 147, 148

performance, 4, 7, 9, 15, 19, 24, 26, 29, 36, 40, 45–49, 52, 53, 55, 56, 60, 69–71, 74–78, 81, 82, 85, 94, 95, 103, 117, 121, 122, 138, 142, 147, 150, 152, 163, 171–173, 177, 181, 182, 189, 192, 193, 211, 237, 240, 243, 244, 248–252, 254
persona, 207
personality disorders, 52, 196
Peterson, David B., 72, 223
phenomenology, 127, 128
philosophers, philosophy, 6, 12, 28, 75, 88, 107, 114, 118–121, 124–126, 128–130, 140, 141, 149, 158, 190, 192, 205, 224, 230
Plato, 12
Plutarch, 12
Polanyi, Michael, 205
power, 7, 12, 13, 21, 28, 30, 31, 33, 34, 37, 72, 89, 110, 119, 122, 124, 145–149, 151, 152, 154, 158–160, 162–165, 172, 205, 212, 213, 229, 249
power relations, power relationship, 146, 164, 200, 205
practitioner, 2, 3, 6–9, 11, 37, 39, 48, 55, 65, 69, 75, 77, 79, 88, 89, 91, 109, 125, 131, 132, 134, 137, 139, 143, 145–150, 155, 158–160, 164, 167, 168, 175, 186, 187, 190–192, 197, 199–204, 209, 211, 214–216, 218, 219, 221, 223–226, 227, 228, 240–242, 246, 247, 251, 253, 254
practitioner research, 9, 215, 218, 221, 223–225, 241, 242
prejudices, 125, 128, 146, 149, 151, 207
Prentice, Karyn, 207, 208
professional bodies, 2, 3, 51, 54, 69, 80, 175, 187–189, 191, 195, 198, 209, 212–214, 218, 219, 221, 222, 224–226
professional development plan (PDP), 80, 173, 195
professional practice, 2, 63, 66, 172, 186, 195, 214, 215, 218, 253
professional risk, 8, 185
psychological literacy, 51, 52, 197, 218
psychological research, 7, 32, 145, 147–152
psychology of goals and motivation, 5, 69–72, 85
psychotherapy, 52, 77, 121, 147, 148, 172, 186, 197, 198, 200, 209, 214
Puerto Rican, 149

systemic issues, 56, 110, 204, 205, 217, 250
systemic thinking, 5, 107
systems perspective, 5, 88, 109, 128, 178

T

tacit dimension, 5, 84, 204
tacit knowing, tacit knowledge, 205
tacit qualities, 84, 107, 129, 205
talent development, 11, 38, 56, 167
Tannen, Deborah, 147
team coaching, 53, 74, 176–179, 182, 215, 216, 221, 236, 237, 249, 255
team learning, 7, 177
therapy, 4, 47, 51, 52, 79, 82, 84, 121, 125, 148, 159, 174, 216
thinking, 1, 2, 6, 33, 34, 49, 78, 82–85, 94, 95, 99, 123, 125–127, 136, 137, 146–148, 157–160, 231, 232, 251, 252
    client's, 194
    creative, 142
    feminist, 156
    independent, 230–232, 253
    managerial, 182
    new, 5, 6, 52, 83, 97, 98, 102, 132
    visual, 123
thinking environment, 5, 46, 53, 69, 73, 77, 82, 97, 127, 160, 161, 232, 238
Thinking Environment®, 7, 38, 53, 84, 107, 125–128, 137, 142, 145, 150, 158–162, 205, 230, 231
thinking partners, 53, 55, 128, 158, 160, 161, 195
thinking partnership, 46
Thinking Partnership® model. *See* models
Thomas, Bradford, 38
Thomas, Brett, 250, 251
Thomas, Laurie F., 92, 93
Ting, Sharon, 74, 176
tipping points for change, 1, 9, 250, 251, 254, 255
Towell, Garth, 245, 246, 256
training, 2–4, 8, 11, 38, 49–51, 53, 57, 81, 116, 131, 136, 172, 236, 245, 250, 252
traits, 4, 12, 17, 19, 21–22, 24, 31, 32, 37, 40, 60, 156, 207
trait theory/theories, 4, 12, 19, 21, 24
transactional theories, 4, 12, 24
transformational theories, 4, 12, 24, 25
transformative listening, 137
transparency, 11, 62, 84, 175, 202, 232, 243, 252
triune brain, 132, 133

trust, 7, 9, 11, 15, 20, 25–27, 30, 31, 33, 41, 51, 60, 66, 76, 79, 80, 90, 110, 112, 137, 138, 142, 174, 189, 193, 205, 228, 229, 240, 243, 246, 247, 254
trusting relationship, 9, 246, 247
tuning-in, 7, 135

U

Ubuntu, 124
unconscious, unconscious behaviours/assumptions/attitudes, 46, 48, 56, 143, 158, 159, 177, 193, 206, 207
United Kingdom (UK), 154–158, 166, 192, 199, 212, 214, 215, 219, 228–230, 233, 245, 248
United States of America (US, USA), 131, 149, 151, 157, 158, 196, 219, 224, 228, 230, 236, 244

V

values, 8, 12, 13, 15, 21, 27, 35, 41, 55, 57, 59, 62, 66, 70–72, 74, 77–79, 90, 95, 109–113, 115–117, 120, 121, 124, 140, 141, 161–164, 172, 176, 177, 188, 190–193, 201, 205, 228, 240–243, 245–249, 251, 252, 254, 255
values-based, 4, 9, 12, 26–28, 191, 248, 249, 251, 252
vision, 11, 13–15, 21, 24–26, 28–30, 33, 34, 50, 57, 92, 112, 115, 121, 238, 240, 251, 252
volitional motivation, 34, 35

W

Walker, David, 119
Weiss, Pam, 73, 92, 93, 112, 122
wellbeing, 33–35, 71, 132, 135, 141, 142, 181, 190, 220, 224, 227
Wheatley, Margaret J., 15
Whitmore, John, 55, 71
Whyte, Ann, 213, 215
Wilber, Ken, 6, 107, 109, 111–118, 130
working memory, 6, 136
Worldwide Association of Business Coaches (WABC), 48, 59, 60, 80, 165, 175, 185, 187, 188, 190, 191, 197, 212, 213, 218

Y

Yalom, Irvin, 72, 74, 81, 120, 121, 124, 140, 200

Z

Zaccaro, Stephen, 12, 21, 23, 39, 40